THE OFFICIAL®

1998 PRICE GUIDE TO WORLD COINS

FIRST EDITION

Marc Hudgeons, N.L.G.
and Tom Hudgeons

HOUSE OF COLLECTIBLES • NEW YORK

Important Notice. All of the information, including valuations, in this book has been compiled from the most reliable sources, and every effort has been made to eliminate errors and questionable data. Nevertheless, the possibility of error, in a work of such immense scope, always exists. The publisher will not be held responsible for losses that may occur in the purchase, sale, or other transaction of items because of information contained herein. Readers who feel they have discovered errors are invited to *write* and inform us, so they may be corrected in subsequent editions. Those seeking further information on the topics covered in this book are advised to refer to the complete line of *Official Price Guides* published by the House of Collectibles.

Published by: House of Collectibles
201 East 50th Street
New York, NY 10022

Distributed by Ballantine Books, a division of Random House, Inc., New York, and simultaneously in Canada by Random House of Canada Limited, Toronto.

http://www.randomhouse.com

Manufactured in the United States of America

ISSN: 1094-1207

ISBN: 0-876-37945-5

Cover design by Kayley LeFaiver
Cover photo © George Kerrigan

First Edition: August 1997

10 9 8 7 6 5 4 3 2 1

CONTENTS

BOARD OF CONTRIBUTORS

Q. David Bowers
Tom Culhane
Bob Leuver
Brad Reed
Michael White
Tom Bilotta
Victor England

The authors would like to express a special thank you to:

- **Q. David Bowers and Chris Karstedt at the Bowers and Merena Galleries, Inc.,** Wolfboro, NH, for the "Introduction," the article on "Coin Auction Sales," and information and photographs from the Norweb Collection auction catalog and sale for the section titled "Canadian Numismatic Chronology,"
- **Tom Culhane of the Elusive Spondulix,** Union, NJ, for his pricing information on Irish coinage,
- **Brad Reed, Product Development at Coin World,** Sidney, OH, for his article "Coins Online,"
- **Michael White at the Department of the Treasury,** United States Mint, Washington, D.C. 20001, for the section "World Coins Minted by U.S. Mints, 1876–1980,"
- **Tanya Sperl at the Gold/Silver Institute,** Washington, D.C., for the information on the International World Mints,
- **Arnoldo Efron at the the Monetary Research Institute,** Houston, TX, for the International Rates of Exchange Table from their "MRI Bankers' Guide to Foreign Currency,"
- **Tom Bilotta of Carlisle Development,** Carlisle, MA, for his coin listing information from his "Collector's Assistant" software,
- **Victor England of Classical Numismatic Group,** Lancaster, PA, for the section on "Ancient Coins."

SHARE YOUR KNOWLEDGE

I would be interested in your questions and comments regarding buying and selling one piece or an entire collection.

OR

You may have information that would be of interest to your fellow collector. In either case please write to:

Marc & Tom Hudgeons, P.O. Box 690312,
Orlando, FL 32869-0312

Please send a SASE for a reply.

Are you interested in becoming a. . . .

CONTRIBUTOR?

If you would like to join our Board of Contributors and have your name printed in the next edition, please let me hear from you.

Please send a SASE for more information to:

Marc & Tom Hudgeons, P.O. Box 690312,
Orlando, FL 32869-0312

INTRODUCTION: THE PLEASURES OF COLLECTING WORLD COINS

by Q. David Bowers

The field of world coins—generally described in the United States as being coins *other than* those issued in America—is as vast as the world itself. Over the years, several hundred countries have been formed and dissolved, some of which are remembered today largely by the things they left behind. As an example, world coin specialists know well the beautiful specimens from German New Guinea minted in 1894 and displaying a bird of paradise, although the country is no longer to be found on a map. Time was when Germany, Austria, and certain other areas of European geography were divided into city-states, under different rulers and often issuing their own coinage.

Among countries still in existence today, many have a rich tradition. Struck pieces of England have been dated since 1551, and were produced for several centuries prior to that time. Kings and queens are depicted in regular order as they ascended and left the throne, punctuated by Oliver Cromwell, who is an exception to the ruler (pun intended). Indeed, a specialized collection of English coins would comprise thousands of pieces.

Our neighbor to the north, Canada, also has a rich coinage history, consisting of decimal issues from 1858 to the present day, plus hundreds of interesting tokens, medals, and other items before and after that time. France, Brazil, Japan, China—the list goes on—each with a rich numismatic history.

Today, the typical collector of world coinage is apt to specialize. Quite popular is the acquisition of dollar-size coins, one each from as many different countries as possible. Or, for those numismatists who like precious yellow metal, collecting pieces of $5 gold size is a pleasant endeavor and dozens of different varieties can be acquired. Coins picturing ships, or cathedrals, or birds offer other possibilities. Of course, the coinage of a particular country can be concentrated upon, such as silver decimal coins of Canada, or trade dollars of Hong Kong, or copper halfpence of England—again the list is virtually endless.

The beauty of coin collecting is that in nearly all instances, great scarcities and rarities can be obtained for small fractions of what their counterparts in the United States series would cost. For certain countries, an incredibly important cabinet can be acquired for just a few thousand dollars, and several tens of thousands of dollars may well yield one of the very finest collections in existence. As you peruse the pages of this book, many possibilities will suggest themselves. Enjoy!

BUYING AND SELLING WORLD COINS

Intelligent coin buying is the key to building a good collection at a reasonable cost. Today, with the added confusion of grading and the questionable practices of some coin sellers, it is more necessary than ever to be a skilled buyer.

In the interest of supplementing the coin pricing and identification in this book with practical advice on astute buying, the editors present the following article. It reviews major pitfalls to which an uninformed buyer might succumb and gives specific suggestions on getting the most for your money when buying coins.

The editors wish to state clearly that the exposure of questionable practices by some coin sellers, as detailed below, is not intended as a general indictment of the coin trade. The vast majority of professional coin dealers are ethical and try to please. Moreover, it can be safely stated that if the hobbyist restricts his buying exclusively to well-established coin dealers, he runs very little risk.

QUESTIONABLE SOURCES FOR BUYING COINS

Unsatisfactory sources of coins—those entailing a higher than necessary degree of risk—include flea markets, antiques shops, garage sales, private parties who are unknown to you, auction sales in which coins are offered along with non-numismatic merchandise, and advertisements in magazines and newspapers published for a general readership rather than for coin collectors. This advice is given to benefit the non-expert buyer and especially the beginner. Advanced collectors with full confidence in their coin buying skills will sometimes shop these sources to find possible bargains.

MAIL-ORDER ADS IN NATIONAL MAGAZINES

The sharp rise in coin values during 1979 and 1980 encouraged many promoters to deal in coins. (Promoters are persons who aren't coin dealers in the accepted sense of the term, but who utilize coins for large-scale mail-order promotions.) The objective, nearly always, is to sell coins to buyers of limited knowledge and thereby succeed in promising more, and charging more, than would a legitimate professional coin dealer. Undoubtedly such promotions are extremely successful, to judge from the number of such ads that appear regularly.

The ads look and sound impressive. They show enlargement of the merchandise. They quote facts and figures, often with historical data. They present a variety of guarantees about the coins, and there is no misrepresentation in those guarantees. But the price you pay is twice to three times as much as it would be if you bought from a *real* coin dealer. In the legitimate coin trade, the coins sold via these ads are looked upon as "junk coins." They command a very small premium over their bullion value. They are not only the most common dates but are usually in undesirable condition.

To lend credibility, the promoters will normally use a company name which gives the appearance of being that of a full-time coin dealer. There is nothing illegal in doing this, but it does contribute to the misleading nature of such ads.

Let's examine some of the specific methods used in today's ever-increasing deceptive coin ads. You will soon see why coins, especially silver coins, have become a favorite of mail-order promoters: they can be "hyped" in a most convincing manner, without making statements that are patently false. Thus, the advertisers skirt around—though narrowly—allegations of mail fraud. (Fraud cannot be alleged on the basis of price, as a merchant is free to charge what he pleases for whatever he sells.)

1. Creating the impression that the coins offered originate from a hidden sequestered cache not previously available to the public. This is accomplished by use of such phrases as "just found 2,367 specimens," "now released to the public. . . ." The assertion that they were "just found" is not wholly inaccurate, however. The advertiser has more than likely located a dealer who could supply wholesale quantities of junk coins. The coins themselves were never lost or hidden. "Now released to the public" has nothing to do with official release. It simply means the advertiser is selling them.

2. Leading the potential customer to believe the coins are scarcer or more valuable than they really are. This is done via numerous techniques. Among the favorites is to compare the advertiser's selling price against prices for other coins of the same series. They are rare, desirable dates in UNC condition, not the common, circulated coins you receive from the advertiser.

When coins are offered, it will be said that "you just can't find them in circulation any longer." It's entirely true that they cannot be found in day-to-day circulation. But coin dealers have them and sell them for less than you will pay through such an ad. The fact that these coins are not found in circulation is not an indication of rarity.

Many coins carrying very little premium value over their face value cannot be found in day-to-day circulation.

3. Emphatic guarantee that the coins are genuine. On this point the advertiser can speak with no fear of legal repercussion. His coins are genuine and nobody can say otherwise. But, even where absolute truth is involved, it can be—and is—presented in such a manner as to give a false impression. By strongly stressing the coins' authenticity, the message is conveyed that many non-authentic specimens exist and that you run a risk in buying from someone else. Such is far from the case. Any large coin dealer can sell you quantities of perfectly genuine coins.

4. Implication that the coins offered are "special," as opposed to specimens of the same coins available at coin shops. This presents an obvious difficulty for the advertiser, as his coins are just the opposite of special; usually heavily circulated, often with actual damage such as nicks, gouges, etc. This problem is not, however, insurmountable. The advertiser can keep silent about the condition of his coins and present them as some sort of special government issue. Usually this is done by selling them in quantities of four or five and referring to them as "Sets," "Government Mint Sets," or something similar. The uninformed reader believes he is ordering a set assembled and packaged by various mints. Mints do assemble and package sets, as everyone knows. But they had no part in these! Assembling and packaging was done by the advertiser. Regardless of how attractive the box or case may be, it is not of official nature and lends absolutely nothing to the value.

5. Failure to state actual silver content. This falls under the heading of deception by silence. The potential customer is left to draw his own conclusions and the advertiser knows full well that those conclusions will be wrong; provided, of course, the ad is worded in such a way that it lends itself to incorrect conclusions. When silver coins are advertised collectors automatically think in terms of 90% silver. Yet the advertiser is legally within his rights in referring to 40% silver coins as silver. As the 40% silver coins look just like their 90% silver predecessors, few purchasers will suspect they've overpaid. Until they have them appraised.

6. Creation of gimmicked names for coins. By calling a coin something different than its traditional numismatic name, it is made to seem more unusual or special.

7. False references. Advertisements of this type are sometimes accompanied by doubtful or fairly obvious fake references on the advertiser's behalf. Taking his cue from legitimate coin dealers, whose ads nearly always refer to their membership in coin organizations and often carry other easily verifiable references as well, he feels he must present similar assurances of his background and reliability. Since he has nothing too convincing to offer in the way of genuine references, he manufactures them. He invents the name of a mythical coin organization, of which he is either a member in good standing, an officer, or perhaps even president. If he chooses not to go quite that far, since he might be caught in the deception, he can take a less volatile course and claim membership in "leading coin collector and dealer organizations" without, of course, naming them.

RECOMMENDED SOURCES FOR BUYING COINS

As a general rule, coin purchasing should be confined to the following sources:

1. Professional coin dealers who sell coins at a shop and/or by mail order.
2. Auction sales conducted by professional coin dealers or auction houses making a specialty of coins.
3. Shows and conventions for coin collectors.

Another acceptable source, though unavailable to many coin hobbyists, is the fellow collector with duplicate or surplus specimens to sell or trade. This source is acceptable only if the individual is known to you, as transactions with strangers can result in problems.

If a coin shop is located in your area, this is the best place to begin buying. By examining the many coins offered in a shop you will become familiar with grading standards. Later you may wish to try buying at auction. When buying from dealers, be sure to do business only with reputable parties. Be wary of rare coins offered at bargain prices, as they could be counterfeit or improperly graded. Some bargain coins are specimens that have been amateurishly cleaned and are not considered desirable by collectors. The best "bargains" are popular coins in good condition, offered at fair prices.

The dangers of buying from sources other than these are overgraded and consequently overpriced coins; non-graded and likewise overpriced coins; and coins that have been doctored, "whizzed," chemically treated, artificially toned, or otherwise altered. Buying from legitimate, recommended sources greatly reduces but does not absolutely eliminate these risks. The buyer himself is the ultimate safeguard, if he has a reasonably thorough working knowledge of coins and the coin market. In this respect experience is the best teacher, but it can sometimes be costly to learn from bad coin buying experiences.

COIN BUYING GUIDELINES

Smart coin buyers follow certain basic strategies or rules. They will not buy a rare coin that they know little or nothing about. They will do some checking first. Has the coin been frequently counterfeited? Are counterfeits recorded of that particular date and mint mark? What are the specific grading standards? What key portions of the design should be examined under magnification to detect evidence of circulation wear?

The smart coin buyer may be either a hobbyist collecting mainly for the sport of it or an investor. In either case he learns not just about coins but the workings of the coin trade: its dealers and auctioneers and their methods of doing business. It's essential to always keep up to date, as the coin market is a continual hotbed of activity.

When buying from the recommended sources there is relatively little danger of fakes, doctored coins, or other obviously unwanted material. If such a coin does slip through and escape the vigilance of an ethical professional dealer, you are protected by his guarantee of authenticity. It is highly unlikely that you will ever be "stuck" with a counterfeit, doctored, or otherwise misrepresented coin bought from a well-established professional.

Merely avoiding fakes is, however, not the sole object of intelligent coin buying. It is, in fact, a rather minor element in the overall picture. Getting the absolute most for your money in terms of properly graded coins at fair prices is the prime consideration. Here the responsibility shifts from seller to buyer. It is the dealer's responsibility not to sell fakes or mis-identified coins. But it is the buyer's responsibility to make certain of getting the best deal by comparing prices and condition grades of coins offered by different dealers. Quite often you can save by comparison shopping, even after your incidental expenses are tabulated. The very unique nature of the coin market makes this possible.

Prices do vary from one dealer to another on many coins. That is precisely the reason—or at least one of the primary reasons—for the *Blackbook*. If you could determine a coin's value merely by checking one dealer's price, or even a few dealers' prices, there would be minimal need for a published price guide. The editors review prices charged by hundreds of dealers to arrive at the median or average market prices that are listed in the *Blackbook*. Prices are matched condition grade by condition grade, from UNC down the line. The results are often little short of astounding. One dealer may be asking $50 for a coin priced at $30 by another. And there are sure to be numerous other offerings of the coin at $35, $40, $45, and various midpoint sums.

It is important to understand why prices vary and how you can utilize this situation to your advantage.

Some readers will remark, at this juncture, that prices vary because of inaccurate grading.

It is unquestionably true that personal applications of the grading standards do contribute to price differences. It is one reason for non-uniform prices. *It is not the only one.*

Obviously the lower-priced specimens are not always those to buy. Smart numismatic buying calls for knowing when to take a bargain and when to pass. A low price could result from something directly concerning the coins. Or it may be tied to matters having nothing to do with the coin or coins. A dealer could be oversupplied, or he may be offering coins in which he does not normally deal and wants to move them quickly. He may have a cash flow imbalance and need to raise funds, in which case he has probably reduced most of his prices. He may be pricing a coin low because he made a fortunate purchase in which the coin cost him very little. In all of these cases—and examples of all can be found regularly in the coin trade—the lower than normal price is not a reflection upon the coin's quality or desirability. These coins, if properly graded, are well worth buying. They do save you some money and cause no problems.

Personal circumstances of the dealer are, to one degree or another, reflected in the prices of most of his coins. If the dealer has substantial operating costs to meet, such as shop rent and employee salaries, his overall pricing structure will reflect this. Yet his prices are not likely to be too much higher than the average, as this class of dealer is intent on quick turnover. Also, there is a certain degree of competitiveness between dealers, particularly those whose advertisements run in the same periodicals. Unfortunately, this competitiveness is sometimes carried to extremes by some dealers, resulting in "bargains" that are sometimes overgraded.

Condition has always played a major role in U.S. coin prices. As of this writing there are no accepted international grading standards for foreign coins.

PUTTING YOUR COIN BUYING KNOWLEDGE TO WORK

1. Deal with someone in whom you can have confidence. The fact that a dealer has been in the business a long period of time may not be an absolute guarantee of his reliability, but it is definitely a point in his favor. Is he a member of coin collector or coin dealer organizations? You do not have to ask about this to find out. If he does hold membership in good standing in any of the more prestigious organizations, that fact will be prominently displayed in his ads, his sales literature, and on the walls of his shop. The leading organization for coin dealers is the PNG, or Professional Numismatists' Guild. Its members are carefully screened and must, after gaining admittance, comply with its code of ethics. Complaints against PNG members are investigated. Those that cannot be easily resolved are brought before an arbitration panel. You are on the safest possible ground when dealing with a PNG member. As the PNG is rather a select group, however, your local dealer may not be a member. This in itself should not make him suspect. One of the requirements of PNG membership is to carry at least $100,000 retail value in coins, and many dealers simply do not maintain that large an inventory. Is your dealer an American Numismatic Association member? A member of the local Chamber of Commerce?

2. Don't expect the impossible, either in a dealer or his coins. The dealers are in business to make a profit and they could not do this by offering bargains on every coin they sell. Treat the dealers fairly. Look at things from their point of view. For example, a long "layaway" on an expensive coin may not be in the dealer's best interest. Dealers will go out of their way for established customers but, even then, they cannot be expected to place themselves at a disadvantage.

BUYING IN PERSON AT A COIN SHOP

1. Plan your visits in advance. Don't shop in a rush or on the spur of the moment. Give yourself time to look, think, examine, and decide.

2. Before entering the shop have a clear idea of the specific coins, or at least the type of coins, you want to see. If more than a few dates and mint marks are involved, do not trust it all to memory. Write a list.

3. Look at everything that interests you before deciding to buy anything.

4. When shopping for rarities, bring along your own magnifier. A small one with attached flashlight is the most serviceable. You may not be able to conduct really in-depth examinations in a shop, but you'll learn more with a magnifier than without one. Don't be reticent about using it. The dealers will not be insulted.

5. If the shop has more than one specimen of the coin that interests you, ask to see them all. Even if all are graded identically and priced identically, you may discover that one seems a shade nicer than the rest.

6. If this is your first visit to the shop, you will want to give some attention to whether or not the shop inspires confidence. An experienced collector tends to get different vibrations from each shop, to the point where he can form an opinion—almost immediately—sometimes before entering. Some coin shops give the distinct impression of being more professional than others. And that impression is usually correct! There are various points on which this can be judged. Do all coins, with the exception of bullion items, have their prices marked on the holder? Is the price accompanied by a statement of condition? Are the holders, and the style of notations on them, fairly uniform from coin to coin? If the coins are housed in various different kinds of holders, with notations that seem to have been made by a dozen different people, they are most likely remnants from the stocks of other dealers or so-called "odd lots." Their condition grades should have been verified and they should have been transferred to uniform holders before being placed on sale. Since the shopkeeper failed to do this, he probably knows very little about their actual condition grades. He merely took the previous owners' word for it. Does the shopkeeper impress you as a person with intimate knowledge of coins? He need not love coins, as his business is selling and not collecting them. But he should appear to regard them a little higher than "just merchandise." He ought to be appreciative of and perhaps even enthusiastic over the finer aspects of a rare coin. Under no circumstances should he treat coins as if he cares nothing about them, such as by handling them roughly or sloppily or touching their surfaces with his fingers.

7. Buying in person gives you an opportunity to converse with the dealer and this can have its advantages. Upon expressing interest in a coin you may discover that the dealer offers a verbal discount from the market price—even without asking for one. If this does not occur, you do, of course, have the right to at least hint at the matter. Just a modest savings can often turn a borderline item into a sound purchase. Don't get the reputation of asking for a discount on every coin you buy. Let the circumstances guide you, and be diplomatic. You are always in a better position to receive a discount when purchasing a number of coins at the same time. Dealers like volume buyers. Never say, "Will you take $300 for this?" or anything that could be construed as making the dealer an offer. The dealers make offers when they buy from the public, and the right to make an offer is something they like to reserve for themselves. You can broach the subject in a more subtle fashion. Instead of mentioning what you would be willing to give for the coins, ask if there is a savings (savings is a much better word than discount) on large purchases. If you pay in cash, you have a better bargaining position as you're saving the dealer the time required in collecting the funds. That is the essence of reasonable discounts; playing fair, not becoming a nuisance, and being willing to accept a small consideration, even if just 5%. At least with the small discounts you are, or should be, getting good coins. If anyone is willing to discount a coin by 50% you can be virtually certain it is a problem item.

BUYING COINS BY MAIL ORDER

There is no reason to shun mail orders. Most coin dealing is done by mail. There are at least a dozen mail-order coin dealers for every one who operates a shop. Your local shop may not specialize in your type of coins, but in dealing by mail you can reach any coin dealer in the country and obtain virtually any coin you may want.

Consider the following before doing any mail-order buying:

1. Compare ads and prices, compare descriptions, compare everything from one ad to another running in the same publication. Look for evidence of the advertiser's professional standing, such as PNG membership. Read his terms of sale. There should be unqualified guarantee of authenticity plus a guarantee of satisfaction. If you are not satisfied with your purchase for any reason, you should have the option of returning it within a specific time period. This time period should be stated in the dealer's terms of sale. (It will usually be ten days or two weeks.) It should likewise be clearly stated that if you do choose to return the coins, you can receive a full refund or credit as you prefer (not as the dealer prefers). Full refund means the sum paid for the coins, with postage and registration fees deducted. Few dealers will refund postage charges. Consequently, when you return a shipment you are paying the postage both ways.

2. Send a small trial order if you haven't previously done business with the advertiser. This will give you the opportunity to judge what sort of coins he supplies. You will also discover how prompt and attentive he is. The results of this trial order should give you a fairly good idea of what you can expect from that dealer when placing large orders.

3. Do not photocopy an ad and circle numbers. Write out your order, simply and plainly. Mention the publication and issue date. The dealer probably has different ads running in different publications.

4. Give second choices only if this is necessary to qualify for a discount. Otherwise don't. Most dealers will send you your first choice if it's available. Some will send the second choice, even if they do still have your first choice. This is called "stock balancing." If they have two remaining specimens of your first choice, and twenty of your second choice, they would much prefer sending you the second choice. Only a relatively small proportion of dealers will ignore your wishes in this manner, but our suggestion still applies: no second choices if you can avoid them. To speed things up, make payment by money order or credit card. A personal check may delay shipment by as much as three weeks.

5. Examine the coins as soon as possible upon receiving them. If a return is necessary, this must be done promptly to be fair to the dealer. Most likely you will not be permitted to remove a coin from its protective holder to examine it. The coins will be in clear mylar (an inert plastic) holders known as "flips" or "flipettes," with a staple at the top. The staple must be in place for return to be honored. While this may seem harsh, it is necessary as a way for the dealer to protect himself against unscrupulous collectors who would switch coins on him. These individuals would replace a high-grade coin with one of lower grade from their collection, and return the lower-grade specimen, asking for a refund. In the unlikely event you receive a coin in a holder which does not permit satisfactory examination, the best course is to simply return it. In making your examination be fair to yourself and to the dealer. Should you have the least doubt about its authenticity, submit the coin to the American Numismatic Association for its opinion and inform the dealer of your action. If the ANA finds the coin to be fake or doctored, you can return it even if the grace period for returns has expired. Under these circumstances many dealers will reimburse you for the ANA's evaluation cost. Chances are, however, that you will never receive a suspect coin.

6. Do not file a complaint against the dealer unless he is clearly in violation of his printed "terms of sale." When it is absolutely necessary to do so, a report of the transaction may be forwarded to the organizations in which he maintains membership, as well as the publications in which he advertises. But even if you place hundreds of mail orders, it is unlikely that the need will ever arise to register a formal complaint against a dealer.

BUYING COINS AT AUCTION SALES

The volume of collector coins sold at auction is enormous. Auction buying is preferred by many collectors, as the opportunity exists to buy coins at somewhat less than their book values. Auctions are covered in detail later in this book.

SELLING COINS TO A DEALER

All coin dealers buy from the public. They must replenish their stock and the public is a much more economical source of supply than buying from other dealers. Damaged, very worn, or common coins are worthless to a dealer. So, too, usually, are sets in which the "key" coins are missing. If you have a large collection or several valuable coins to sell, it might be wise to check the pages of coin publications for addresses of dealers handling major properties, rather than selling to a local shop.

Visit a coin show or convention. There you will find many dealers at one time and place, and you will experience the thrill of an active trading market in coins. You will find schedules of conventions and meetings of regional coin clubs listed in the various trade publications.

To find your local coin dealer, check the Yellow Pages under "Coin Dealers."

Coin collecting offers infinite possibilities as an enjoyable hobby or profitable investment. It need not be complex or problem-laden. But anyone who buys and sells coins—even for the most modest sums—owes it to himself to learn how to buy and sell wisely.

MAIL-ORDER COINS

As stated in the previous chapter, purchasing world coins through mail order will provide you with the greatest opportunity of finding exactly the coins that you are looking for to add to your collection. While working on this book, we have had the opportunity of coming in contact with many dealers as well as collectors. One mail-order dealer that would be of particular interest to the beginning or novice collector would be Edd and Johanne Smith of the Mail Order Company.

Edd and Johanne Smith have been selling foreign coins for about five years. Like most hobby-oriented businesses, theirs started as a coin collection that got out of control. When they first started collecting coins, they found in reading price lists and advertisements that there were very few dealers that sold *only* foreign coins, particularly the lower-end coins, those coins commonly desired by the new or novice collector. By lower-end coins, I am referring to coins in less than Very Fine grades, priced under $2.50. They decided to target their new business to this collector audience. They do not sell coins that have a value over $50 in their regular price list.

Their price lists are printed in four sections, grouping the countries alphabetically. One section is published every other month. They also publish a separate price list that only lists coins from Mexico. *Price lists are sent free upon request.*

Both novice and experienced collectors find their price lists easy to read and well organized. They use large type and a maximum of four columns per page to avoid confusion. Their price lists also have brightly colored covers for easy identification and comb bindings so the lists will lie flat on the table.

Edd and Johanne's philosophy for selling coins is simple—a happy customer *is* their primary goal. They do not question why a coin is returned, and they refund immediately. They also grade very conservatively. Often they under-price a coin or two because the grading of a supplier may be higher than what they feel the grade really should be. Customers prefer their grading over many of the other dealers. Edd and Johanne have customers that send change-of-address cards when they move. Customers even call them when their list is late or not received. They are very proud of their customers' loyalty.

Their policy when refunding an order is to issue a credit memo for anything under $5 and to refund by check anything over $5.

Edd and Johanne Smith offer more coins priced under $1 and in grades lower then Very Fine than most any other dealer. For many collectors on fixed incomes or young collectors who use their allowances to finance their hobby, these coins are quite affordable. Believe it or not, it is difficult to find these types of coins and, as a result, there are many one-of-a-kind coins in their price list.

To better serve their customers Edd and Johanne Smith have a toll-free phone number (1-800-862-6514), a FAX number (1-916-381-2341), and an e-mail address (rgreen@calwb.com). To save on business costs they send their price lists by bulk-rate mail. Edd and Johanne both believe their customers deserve the type of service they would expect to get from any business. Please write or call Edd and Johanne Smith at Mail Order Coins, P.O. Box 160083, Sacramento, CA 95816-0083, to be put on their mailing list for their free price lists.

COINS ONLINE

Courtesy of Brad Reed at Coin World

Welcome to the information universe known as the Internet!

In this essay we'll explore some of the many fascinating sites related to coins and coin collecting to be found on the Internet, especially the World Wide Web. If you're not already hooked into the Internet, write to us at *Coin World*, P.O. Box 150, Sidney, OH 45365, and we'll give you some tips on how to get wired. If you are already surfing on your own and you come across a site that you think is particularly cool, interesting, or useful, please e-mail us at cwbooks@amospress.com.

FIRST THINGS FIRST

Absolutely without a doubt the first thing you should do when you get hooked into the 'Net is to check out the rec.collecting.coins newsgroup (for paper money enthusiasts, there's also the ec.collecting.paper-money newsgroup). Here coin collectors from around the 'Net and around the world gather to exchange questions, ideas, and general chit-chat. *Coin World* answers questions here frequently, and you'll also see posts from the American Numismatic Association and others.

Coin World has its own World Wide Web site, as part of the Collector's SuperMall. You can find us at www.csmonline.com/coinworld.

PIONEERS AND SETTLERS

The Internet has been likened to the great American frontier of the 18th and 19th centuries: more potential than actual riches, and governed by laws of survival rather than civility. This parallel is captured in the pithy phrase, "Pioneers get the glory, but settlers get the land."

While it is entertaining to read the field dispatches from Internet pioneers, some early settlements are being established, and they are beginning to realize the true potential of connectedness.

Many of us coin collectors are history buffs. In fact, the tangible connection to generations past is one of the more alluring elements of this hobby. The ability to conduct historical or archival research online is a tremendous boon. Thanks to the cumulative efforts of government agencies, universities, corporations, and private individuals, the amount of historical information online has been growing at an astounding rate. Almost daily, a new database is made available to the Net-connected researcher.

A few examples may help illustrate what kinds of research are enabled through the Internet.

There is a type of collectible exonumia related to the Civil War called "sutlers' tokens." These are pieces issued privately by sutlers, who were profiteering merchants who followed armies on the move and provided, at dear prices, goods that the Army did not.

A new World Wide Web site operated by the Library of Congress is called "American Memory." Its design is austere, and its depth is revealing. The site, reachable at rs6.loc.gov, maintains collections of personal histories, photographs, and even sound files and movies. Searching for the term "sutler," we find six photographs and two text files. A photograph of a sutler's tent at Petersburg, VA, 2nd Division, 9th Corps is shown; an excerpt from the history of Robert Lee Wright, Salisbury, NC, of one of the histories explains how sutlers were viewed:

> As a sutler Pa [Dexter] had milked both armies. Each desperately needed certain supplies which could be obtained only from the other, so both had shut tired eyes and, with tongue in cheek, had allowed Pa full access behind the lines. At first both sides had tried to extract military information from him; both had employed him as a spy and both had been unsuccessful. He had said that he was willing and had drawn spy's pay from both sides but the only things he saw were the looks and amounts and pieces of goods to be bought, sold or bartered. Finally both armies suffered his mercantile services and avoided him as a source of military information.

Across the Mall from the Library of Congress in Washington, D.C., stands the main building of the National Archives. The homepage of the National Archives and Records Administration can be located at www.nara.gov. NARA is the government agency responsible for overseeing the management of the records of the federal government. NARA publishes the *Federal Register*, the daily official record of the activities of the federal government, as well as the *U.S. Government Manual*. It is in the *Federal Register*, for instance, that we find the Treasury's revised rules governing color illustrations of paper money.

A link out of NARA brings us to GPO Access (***www.access.gpo.gov***), the online service of the Government Printing Office. GPO Access is the Mother Lode for information prospectors on the Internet. From one form you can search by keyword through the Fiscal Year 1997 Budget, bills since 1993, Congressional records since 1994, the Federal Register since 1994, General Accounting Office reports, history of bills, House and Senate legislative calendars, the United States Code and more.

Recently, there was a discussion on the rec.collecting.coins newsgroup about whether "E Pluribus Unum" or "In God We Trust" was the official motto of the United States. A GPO Access search of the United States Code for the phrase "In God We Trust" reveals that, according to Title 36, Chapter 10, Sec. 186, "The national motto of the United States is declared to be 'In God We Trust.' "

As one who has spent literally days at a time wading through "legis-peak" in government documents looking for coin-related rules and legislation, I welcome these new sources of public access with the wide-eyed wonder of the first settlers who gazed upon the Great Plains and were humbled by its potential.

VIRTUAL AUCTIONS

Coin collectors online can participate in auctions without ever leaving their homes. Online auctions provide greater and more immediate feedback than traditional mail-bid sales. Some even provide photographs in the form of gif or jpeg image files of selected lots.

You will find more and more online auctions cropping up as more coin dealers become Internet-savvy. When you first encounter an online auction, and absolutely before you begin bidding, you should read all terms and conditions carefully. These should clearly state who is conducting the sale, who owns the material, what rights you have as a buyer, payment terms, return policies, grading standards, and so on. Do not assume that the terms and conditions of one auction necessarily apply to the next; read each as if it were your first.

I had a look at two types of online auctions in preparing for this essay.

The first type is generally called an "interactive" auction. The web site displays a calendar of auctions with their closing dates, and often a mock auction where "newbies" can practice the steps in examining and bidding on lots.

The term "interactive" may be overstated here. It's not like you see a virtual auctioneer calling off lots and bids, and immediately responding to you raising your bidder's paddle, nor can you read the mannerisms of your competitors as you would in a live auction. Rather, you choose the auction closing date you want, then view a catalog of lots by lot number. You can select particular denominations you are interested in, or just browse through. Each lot is described, and the current high bid is shown. You can enter a higher bid if you choose, and the figure is updated to your price.

Once you leave the site, you will be notified by e-mail if you are outbid on any lot. You may then return and up your bid if you desire. The strategies for success in this type of auction will evolve over time, but it seems that at least initially, you will want to check your e-mail rather frequently, and several hours in advance of the auction closing time, to see how your bids are holding up. That should give you enough time to evaluate your position and enter a new bid, even if network traffic is busy.

The second type of auction is more akin to the traditional and familiar mail-bid sale. In fact, you have the option of phoning in bids, mailing them via "p-mail," or sending an electronic bid sheet to the e-mail address. Essentially, you view lot descriptions, view an occasional photo, check out the estimate, then fill out your bid sheet on the entire sale. You won't get a message sent to you if you are outbid. However, you may be able to arrange for the auctioneer to enter incremental bids up to a maximum level. Again, read the terms of sale carefully.

To find who may be conducting auctions, do a Yahoo search (www.yahoo.com), or use your favorite web search site, or just log on to the rec.collecting.coins newsgroup and check out the postings.

THE U.S. MINT ONLINE

There has been a reciprocal love-hate relationship between the U.S. Mint and coin collectors for a long, long time. On the one hand, we eagerly await each year's new coin offerings. On the other, we can't stand that the designs never change!

From the Mint's perspective, officials in the past have accused coin collectors of causing (or at least exacerbating) coin shortages, but rely on coin collectors to purchase the highly profitable Uncirculated and Proof sets and commemorative issues.

Well, the U.S. Mint's World Wide Web site (www.usmint.gov) isn't going to do much to change that balance. The site itself is well designed and fairly responsive. However, it focuses largely on product marketing, offering little research material. In fact, the site is called the "U.S. Mint Gift Collection" and offers Proof and Uncirculated sets, current commemoratives, coin art (which are framed prints of the sketches of the Civil War Battlefield coin designs), jewelry, bags of Anthony dollars, and special gift boxes.

There are also web pages that recount the history and function of the U.S. Mint; compositions, specifications, and mint marks on coins; and a brief history, quoting the original correspondence, of how the motto "In God We Trust" came to appear on coinage.

Somewhat surprisingly, however, some of the information appears to have been out of date the day they published it on the web. For instance, in the section about mint marks, the text states, "All working dies . . . are manufactured in the Die Manufacturing Division of the Philadelphia Mint," even though the die shop opened at the Denver Mint in May 1996 to great fanfare.

The list of mint marks on modern commemorative coins stops with the 1994 issues, and without note or comment lumps the $10 gold coin from the 1984 Los Angeles Olympic program with the $5 gold commemoratives issued since.

I suspect collectors will demand more accurate information from the source of most of their collectible coins. The site still suffers from a lack of illustrations, missing a big opportunity to take advantage of the web's graphical nature.

To visit the site yourself, go to the Department of the Treasury's home page at www.ustreas.gov and follow the links to bureaus, or go directly to www.ustreas.gov/treasury/bureaus/mint/subintro.html.

Back up a level to the Department of the Treasury's homepage, however, and the situation improves—a little. Among the many graphic files available at www.ustreas.gov are front and back images of the new $100 Federal Reserve note design, in black and white. You can also take a brief "tour" of the Treasury building, with views of the Cash Room and other highlights. The web site is certainly no substitute for a real walking tour, and appropriately you can get the tour schedule and even find out how to make reservations if you'd like to see the real thing.

FAQS

Collectors who may be looking for a coin collection FAQ (for Frequently Asked Questions) can now find a pretty good one at Chuck D'Ambra's web sit. The URL (Uniform Resource Locator) for the FAQ, which is in three parts, is http://www.csn.net/~chuck/coins/faq.html. In addition to a glossary, there's a list of organizations, publications, and of course answers to the most common questions about coin collecting.

Paper money collectors should probably check out the paper money FAQ maintained by Bruce Giese. The FAQ resides on any number of servers, and can be found in the rec.collecting.coins newsgroup. It is also available on the web at http://world.std.com/%7Egiese/pfaq.html.

A FAQ for collectors of ancient Roman and Greek coins can be found at www.math.montana.edu/~umsfwest/numis.

INTERNET SEARCH TOOLS

If you are new to the Internet and the World Wide Web, you may be wondering how to find sites of interest. Well, they don't call it a "web" for nothing. One link leads to another, then to another, and so on, so that eventually every WWW page is linked to every other.

But just roaming around aimlessly is not likely to be productive (especially if you are paying by the hour for access!), so it's wise to acquaint yourself with a few guides to this digital wilderness.

In one sense, the web is a flat, unstructured landscape, with every place connected to every other place. But there is an emerging topology; landmarks and points of reference are growing up out of the flatness. The most visible of these are the major search engines: Alta Vista, HotBot, Yahoo, and so on. They attempt to be all-inclusive in their indexing of the Internet, but in reality the web is growing faster than they can keep up.

My most effective technique is to use the major search services to locate a specialized database or search engine. I watch for references to universities, or to umbrella organizations (the National Academy of Recording Arts and Sciences, for instance). Then use their specialized search engines to tunnel in to the specific information. In time, you will compile quite a collection (remember to "bookmark" the useful sites!) of these specialized search engines, tailored to your own specific needs. Using a two- or even three-level approach to searching on the Internet can save you considerable browse-time over filtering thousands of hits from the general search engines.

My best advice: Follow the links. Soon your own instincts will lead you to the information you want.

A number of services specialize in helping you find information on the Internet. These are known generically as *indexes*. Sometimes you'll hear the term *"search engine,"* although that strictly applies to the software algorithm that processes the information.

Each of the major indexes is a little different, and what you find in each can be different as well. Most rely on someone submitting a URL and a description or keywords for the site to be indexed. A few of the newer services are actively seeking sites and indexing them. At least one major service attempts to index the full text of each site in its database.

What follows is a brief description of some of these services, with the results of an informal test. In each of the services, I entered the word "coin" and performed a simple search—that is, no special filtering criteria were requested. In Internet terms, "coin" is fairly generic, and some services will return "hits" for "COINcidence," for example. Virtually all the services, however, will rank the "hits" according to some relevance scale, so that the first results returned are more likely to satisfy your search.

YAHOO (www.yahoo.com): One of the earliest and still one of the more popular internet indexes. Tries to filter out the less desirable pages. "Coin hits"—184.

Lycos (www.lycos.com): Quite comprehensive, yet fast. Returns hits for graphics files as well as text. "Coin hits"—6,918.

Alta Vista (www.altavista.digital.com): Computer giant Digita Equipment Corporation's Internet giant claims to be the largest. Indexes some 16 million web pages, full text of 13,000 newsgroups. "Coin hits"—about 40,000.

Magellan (www.mckinley.com): Not as extensive as some other search services, but Magellan actually contains reviews by professional writers of the sites it lists. Also green lights (literally) sites suitable for family viewing. "Coin hits"—26.

SEARCH (www.search.com): Search isn't a search engine in itself, but it provides a single screen with windows to the aforementioned services and others, along with a brief description of what each looks for. A decent first stop for those new to Internet searching.

Electric Library (www.elibrary.com): The Electric Library requires users to register, but you can try out the service with no obligation. The Electric Library is a full-text database of more than 1,000 newspapers, magazines, and academic journals, plus images, reference books, literature, and art.

Becoming familiar with the various indexing services will enhance your ability to find collecting-related sites on the Internet. But don't underestimate the serendipity factor.

EFFECTIVE E-MAIL

If you are a regular visitor to *Coin World*'s World Wide Web site at www.csmonline.com/coinworld, then you probably already know that we have been putting the full text of the current week's editorial online.

In the Sept. 16, 1996 issue of *Coin World* (which was online in early September), Editor Beth Deisher called on collectors to write their senators in support of two coinage bills. When we put the editorial online, we linked Sen. Alfonse D'Amato's name in the text to his e-mail address. A person reading the call to action online would see the senator's name highlighted, click on the name, and, providing his browser was properly configured, be presented with a pre-addressed, blank e-mail form, which could then be sent directly to Sen. D'Amato's office.

Another link to the Senate's web site (www.senate.gov) would bring up a list of senators by name or state and hot links to their e-mail. What this means is that an online collector could, with about a half-dozen clicks of the mouse, send a message in support of coinage legislation to both of his home-state senators and the chairman of the Senate Banking Committee.

As I sat back (admittedly rather self-satisfied at this application of new technology to representative democracy), a nagging voice in my head kept asking, "Is it really this easy?"

Do senators really read their e-mail? Well, probably not. It's hard to imagine Kay Bailey Hutchison, R-Texas, hunkered in front of a computer monitor while there are lobbyists in the lobby waiting to, uh, lobby.

But senators' staffs read e-mail. Lots of it. And they compile tallies of public opinion on a wide range of topics, gathering constituent information from e-mail, regular mail, and telephone traffic, as well as opinion polls.

Here are some tips to get your e-mail opinion read (and counted):

- Identify your position in the message header. Use words like "support" or "oppose" and identify the bill number, if you know it.
- Keep to one bill per message. Unless there are two versions of similar legislation (and that happens) use a separate message for different bills. In the recent *Coin World* editorial, for instance, two bills were discussed. Send a separate message for each one.
- Identify yourself as a constituent. Until America Online members get to elect their own representatives to Congress, our legislative branch will continue to be based firmly in geography. Sign your e-mail message with your real name, your city, and state. This lets your senator know that he is representing the interests of the people who put him in office, and not some e-mail savvy activist in another state.
- Keep your message short and to the point. E-mail requires fewer formalities than written mail. Use positive language. If you are against a bill, then say "please oppose" rather than "please do not support."

I don't know of any yet in wide use, but the day is certainly coming when our elected officials will use auto-responders and vote counters to monitor public opinion. These are essentially computer programs or scripts that scan incoming messages for certain text strings, then take an action based on the contents of the message.

For example, let's say Sen. Dianne Feinstein, D-Calif., wants to get a feel for public opinion regarding reopening the Old San Francisco Mint. She instructs her staff to create a vote counter and auto-responder to handle the e-mail. The vote counter would scan for the text "support" or "in favor of" and tally a positive vote, or "oppose" or "against" and tally a negative vote. If you write a message that says "I am not in favor of reopening the Old Mint," your opinion might be tallied as a positive because it contains the text "in favor of"; the computer program ignores the "not" that precedes it.

Similarly, if you write in support of one issue and oppose another, your opinion may be mis-tallied or not counted at all. This is the reason you should limit your e-mail message to a single topic. Even with a human reader, the congressional staff will be making tally sheets. It is far too easy to misconstrue a constituent's opinion if there is more than one issue in the message.

While I don't imagine that soon we will be holding tele-elections as portrayed in the visionary yet short-lived television series "Max Headroom" (http://river.tay.ac.uk/ %7Eccdmlh/max/index.htmlx), it is not much of a stretch to foresee areas of public policy being directed by the electronic winds of the Internet.

SOME COMMON TERMS AND ABBREVIATIONS

Browser: Software that enables you to view World Wide Web documents. The browser you use largely depends on your access provider.

Download: Copying a file from the host to your computer.

E-Mail: A message sent from one computer to another's online address; does NOT include faxes.

Gif: Graphics Interchange Format, a standard file type for displaying pictures online.

Hit: A request from a browser for a web document; each linked element of a web page requires a hit to view it, so accessing one web page may generate several hits.

Homepage: The main orientation screen of a web site, generally a welcome, signup, or map with pointers to other pages or documents.

Internet: A global, loosely configured network of networks. It has come to mean all the linked computers of the world, although that definition is not strictly true.

Keyword Search: The automated lookup of a term or topic by typing in one or a combination of pertinent words.

Links: World Wide Web pages are constructed using HTML, or Hypertext Markup Language. Links, generally displayed with underlines or colors, when activated call up a specified document from the host. This cross-referencing is the "web" part.

Newsgroup: A text-based area where users on many systems can read and post messages, usually on a focused topic.

RCC (rec.collecting.coins): A Usenet newsgroup for coin collectors; rec, for recreation; collecting.coins should be obvious.

Surfing: Somehow this term got applied to what you do on the Internet—akin to "channel surfing" your TV, I guess.

URL: Uniform Resource Locator; it tells the host computer where to look for a document and therefore determines the syntax of Internet addresses; the URL of the Smithsonian Institution is www.si.edu.

Webmaster: The person or persons who create and maintain a web site.

World Wide Web: The graphical side of the Internet, featuring documents linked together with Hypertext Markup Language (HTML).

COMPUTERIZING YOUR COLLECTION

Courtesy of Tom Bilotta, Carlisle Development Corporation

One of the challenges affecting coin collectors is keeping track of your collection. Coin collections tend to contain many items with a significant variation in value. There are many reasons that you will want to maintain an inventory of your collection. There are security concerns such as assuring adequate insurance coverage and your ability to document a loss. You will want to be able to easily identify and list coins that are on your want list. You may wish to monitor the value of your collection. You may want to easily find the location of a coin.

Coin inventory software is designed to minimize the effort needed to create and maintain a coin inventory and also to add to your enjoyment of the collection process by allowing you to work with your collection in a productive manner.

STANDARD DATABASE

One of the most important parts of a coin inventory program is the database. The database contains standard information about coins and saves the user from having to type this information manually. The greater the amount of information in the standard database, the easier the task of data entry. Another important aspect of the standard database is how the coins are organized into groups. Proper grouping allows the user to easily locate an item and also provides guidance as to how to organize a collection. The ability to extend the database is also of significant value, allowing the user to add new coinage immediately or add more specialized coins which are not in the standard database. This is especially important for world coins, which are so numerous that it is very likely that a user will wish to add coins to the database. Recent programs such as those offered by Carlisle Development also incorporate values and pictures in their databases.

FLEXIBILITY OF GROUPING YOUR COINS

There are as many ways of collecting coins as there are collectors and a very important feature of coin inventory software is its ability to organize coins the way the user prefers to do so. Some coin inventory programs require that the user group coins exactly as the database is organized. These programs typically have great difficulty handling duplicates and cause the collector to work in an uncomfortable manner. More advanced programs allow you to group coins from the standard database with complete flexibility. The following are some common examples of how collectors group coins:

Coin Type: Morgan Dollars, Indian Head Cents
Metal: Gold Pounds, Silver Dollars, Old Copper Coins
Period: Year of Birth set, 18th-century silver coins

Often collectors have several types of coin groupings, treating coins in their primary collecting interest differently than duplicates, miscellaneous pieces, or accumulations that they might wish to trade or sell. An advanced program, such as the Coin Collector's Assistant, enables you to use all of these coin groupings and freely move coins between them as your collection interests change and as you buy and sell coins.

VIEWING INFORMATION ABOUT YOUR COLLECTION

Your ability to view information about your collection can significantly contribute to your enjoyment of the hobby as well as your effectiveness as a collector. Coin inventory software allows you to view your collection in many different ways. At one session, you might be focusing on a plan for which coins you are going to acquire over the next year and wanting to look across all of your collections for coins that you are missing. At another session, you might be looking to sell some coins and want to see only coins of a minimum value. You may wish to provide a listing of coins stored at a particular location for insurance purposes. You will sometimes want to view listings on the screen and sometimes print to paper. Most likely, you will want to view both detailed inventory listings and/or summaries of all or selected parts of your collection. Here again, an advanced coin inventory program can allow you to change your view with a few "clicks" of a button. In addition to the ability to determine which coins are to be included in a particular report, you will also want to control the information fields that are included. You might want to produce two versions of your want list, one with your cost goals and one without. An insurance listing might include inventory code numbers. You will want to be able to sort your coins in any manner you wish and to change this frequently.

PICTURES AND SPECIALIZED REPORTS

Availability of picture support provides significant value to the coin collector. In some instances you will want to identify coins which you have not seen before. You might wish to maintain a picture catalog of your collection either to increase your own enjoyment or to share your collection without actually showing the physical coins. Other specialized reports can generate labels to attach to your coins, index cards, or picture reports you can send to other collectors or dealers. An advanced program should offer a full range of specialized reports.

STORAGE AND INSURANCE

Keeping track of where a coin is located requires a two-level approach for most collectors involving locations and containers. There may be several containers and particular locations. Examples of locations would be a bank, office, or desk. Examples of containers would be a safety deposit box, file cabinet, shelf, or safe. The Collector's Assistant supports a two-level storage system where each coin or coin group may be stored in a particular container and easily moved from one to another. It allows as many locations and containers as you need to handle your collection.

SPECIALIZED COIN KNOWLEDGE

Because of the variety of ways that people collect, the more built-in knowledge about coins that a program has, the easier it can adapt to a particular style. For example, the Collector's Assistant knows the contents of government sets and also the date ranges for type coins. This allows the collector of Jefferson Nickels to decide whether coins in government sets are to be considered part of the primary collection and therefore excluded from want lists. Grading is another area in which computer software can help. The first level of assistance is in providing standard grading descriptions. More advanced software provides a standard picture library of high quality digital pictures of all coins at all grades.

EASE OF USE

As with any computer software, ease of use will determine not only your enjoyment of your collection but also your ability to accomplish the task for which you purchased the software. Advanced programs, such as those offered by Carlisle Development, approach this in a combined manner suitable to a wide range of personal preferences.

These include interactive step-by-step instructions, intuitive behavior, context-sensitive help, and a User Manual. Equally important is accessible, competent technical support. This is especially true given the increasing number of applications people are placing on their computers.

A well-designed coin inventory program can both add to your enjoyment of the hobby as well as improve your ability to achieve your collection objectives. Carlisle Development Corporation publishes the most comprehensive line of collector software available, especially with regard to coins and paper money.

Central to Carlisle's product line is the Collector's Assistant, the most advanced and comprehensive collection software available. It is sold in a variety of configurations to serve collectors of over 30 collectibles from autographs to toys. Most extensive is its support for coins and paper money. The Carlisle product family includes:

United States Coin Database—Complete listings of all U.S. Coinage from 1793 to the present by date and mint mark, including government sets, commemoratives, and bullion coins. Also includes Colonial and Hawaiian coinage. This database includes high quality pictures of all U.S. type coins and is available with or without values.

World Coin Database—A listing of over 5,000 coin types from 45 countries which may be extended by the user to additional countries or types.

United States Currency Database—A complete listing of all U.S. Currency including fractionals, confederate, and encased postage stamps.

In addition to the standard databases, Carlisle offers a number of specialized CD's for the coin collector:

Grading Assistant CD—Based on the Official ANA Grading Guide, this CD provides over 1,000 high quality grading pictures of all U.S. coin types in an interactive format.

U.S. Commemoratives CD—A complete color picture library of all U.S. commemorative coins from 1892–1995.

Additional databases and CD's are under development both for world coins and currency, and specialized variety collecting.

To learn more about Carlisle Development's product line, you can contact us by phone (800-219-0257) or e-mail (carlisledc@aol.com). We also have a storefront at the Collector SuperMall which can be accessed at http://www.csmonline.com/carlisledc. This storefront contains an interactive display of our current product line as well as many product screens.

WORLD COINS MINTED BY THE U.S. MINTS (1876–1980)

Courtesy of The Department of The Treasury, The United States Mint

INTRODUCTION

The mints of the United States were first authorized to manufacture coins for foreign governments in 1874.

The first foreign coinage order was executed for the Government of Venezuela during the fiscal year ending June 30, 1876.

Through December 31, 1980, U.S. mints at Philadelphia, Pa., San Francisco, Calif., New Orleans, La., and Denver, Colo., had produced 11,193,348,346 coins for 42 foreign countries.

EXPLANATORY NOTES

In some instances, before 1906, production figures were recorded on a U.S. Government fiscal year basis (July 1 one year through June 30 the following year). Two calendar years combined in the date column of a table indicate that production occurred between July 1 and June 30 of the years stated. The dates appearing on coins may or may not coincide with the production year.

Metallic composition.—The proportions of metals are expressed either in percentages (symbol %) with the proportions adding to 100 percent; or, for gold and silver coins, in thousands with the proportions of precious metal and base metal adding to 1,000 parts.

Gross weight.—This refers to the overall weight of one coin of the specified denomination.

Conversion factors.—Original weight units specified in grains have been converted to grams and diameters specified in inches converted to millimeters. The following conversion factors were used:

Weight units
1 grain=0.0647989182 gram

Measurement units
1 millimeter=0.03937 inch.

Symbols used in tables:

*Not available

P Philadelphia Mint
S San Francisco Mint/Assay Office

D Denver Mint
O New Orleans Mint

Summary of foreign coinage by U.S. mints, by country, through Dec. 31, 1980

Country	*Number of pieces produced*
Argentina (Blanks)	64,058,334
Australia	168,000,000
Belgian Congo	25,000,000
Belgium	25,000,000
Bolivia	30,000,000
Brazil (Blanks)	406,249,266
Canada	85,170,000
China	39,720,096
China, Republic of (Taiwan)	428,172,000
Colombia	133,461,872
Costa Rica	131,798,820
Cuba	496,559,888
Curacao	12,000,000
Dominican Republic	76,954,297
Ecuador	214,451,060
El Salvador	226,695,351
Ethiopia	375,433,730
Fiji	4,800,000
France	50,000,000
Greenland	100,000
Guatemala	7,835,000
Haiti	90,324,000
Hawaii[1]	1,950,000
Honduras	115,929,500
Indo-China	135,270,000
Israel	91,000
Korea	295,000,000
Liberia	56,744,679
Mexico	91,076,840
Mexico (Blanks)	175,714,411
Nepal	195,608
Netherlands	562,500,000
Neth. E. Indies	1,716,368,000
Nicaragua	26,080,000
Panama (Republic)	193,838,428
Peru	761,067,479
Philippines	3,483,718,169
Poland	6,000,000
Saudi Arabia	124,712,574
Siam (Thailand)	20,000,000
Surianam (Netherlands Guiana)	21,195,000
Syria	7,350,000
Venezuela	306,762,944
Total (42 countries)	**11,193,348,346**

[1]Coined prior to Aug. 21, 1959, when Hawaii became the 50th State of the Union.

Summary of foreign coinage by U.S. mints, by calendar year, through Dec. 31, 1980

Calendar year	*Number of pieces produced*	*Calendar year*	*Number of pieces produced*
July 1, 1875– Dec. 31, 1905	155,896,973	1943	186,682,008
1906	10,204,504	1944	788,498,000
1907	45,253,047	1945	1,802,376,004
1908	29,645,359	1946	504,528,000
1909	11,298,981	1947	277,376,094
1910	7,153,818	1948	21,950,000
1911	7,794,406	1949	156,687,940
1912	6,244,348	1950	2,000,000
1913	7,309,258	1951	25,450,000
1914	17,335,005	1952	45,857,000
1915	55,485,190	1953	193,673,000
1916	37,441,328	1954	19,015,000
1917	25,208,497	1955	67,550,000
1918	60,102,000	1956	38,793,500
1919	100,269,195	1957	59,264,000
1920	99,002,334	1958	152,575,000
1921	55,094,352	1959	129,647,000
1922	7,863,030	1960	238,400,000
1923	4,369,000	1961	148,500,000
1924	12,663,196	1962	256,485,000
1925	13,461,000	1963	293,515,000
1926	14,987,000	1964	—
1927	3,650,000	1965	—
1928	16,701,000	1966	7,440,000
1929	34,980,000	1967	176,196,206
1930	3,300,120	1968	416,088,658
1931	4,498,020	1969	348,653,046
1932	9,756,096	1970	483,988,392
1933	15,240,000	1971	207,959,692
1934	24,280,000	1972	392,723,895
1935	109,600,850	1973	295,408,674
1936	32,350,000	1974	373,293,733
1937	26,800,000	1975	762,126,363
1938	48,579,644	1976	562,372,000
1939	15,725,000	1977	13,188,000
1940	33,170,000	1978	30,846,000
1941	208,603,500	1979	15,530,090
1942	307,737,000	1980	19,658,000
		Total	**11,193,348,346**

ARGENTINA—COINAGE BLANKS

Calendar year	U.S. Mint	Denomination	Coinage during year	Metallic composition	Gross weight	Diameter
			Pieces		*Grams*	*mm.*
1919	P	20 centavos	15,175,000	75% copper, 25% nickel	4	21.00
	P	10 centavos	21,840,000	.... do	3	19.00
	P	5 centavos	15,660,000	.... do	2	17.00
			52,675,000			
1920	P	10 centavos	3,443,334	.... do	3	19.00
	P	5 centavos	7,940,000	.... do	2	17.00
			11,383,334			
Total			**64,058,334**			

AUSTRALIA

Calendar year	U.S. Mint	Denomination	Coinage during year	Metallic composition	Gross weight	Diameter
1942	S	Florin	6,000,000	925 silver, 75 copper	11.31	27.00
	S	Shilling	4,000,000	.... do	5.66	23.00
	S	Sixpence	4,000,000	.... do	2.83	19.30
	D	.... do	12,000,000	.... do	2.83	19.30
	S	Threepence	8,000,000	.... do	1.41	16.00
	D	.... do	16,000,000	.... do	1.41	16.00
			50,000,000			
1943	S	Florin	11,000,000	.... do	11.31	27.00
	S	Shilling	16,000,000	.... do	5.66	23.00
	S	Sixpence	4,000,000	.... do	2.83	19.30
	D	.... do	8,000,000	.... do	2.83	19.30
	S	Threepence	8,000,000	.... do	1.41	16.00
	D	.... do	16,000,000	.... do	1.41	16.00
			63,000,000			
1944	S	Florin	11,000,000	.... do	11.31	27.00
	S	Shilling	8,000,000	.... do	5.66	23.00
	S	Sixpence	4,000,000	.... do	2.83	19.30
	S	Threepence	32,000,000	.... do	1.41	16.00
			55,000,000			
Total			**168,000,000**			

BELGIAN CONGO

Calendar year	U.S. Mint	Denomination	Coinage during year	Metallic composition	Gross weight	Diameter
1943	P	2 francs	25,000,000	65% copper, 35% zinc	6	([1])

[1]Hexagonal shaped coin: 29.1 mm. greatest diameter; 24.8 mm. least diameter.

BELGIUM

Calendar year	U.S. Mint	Denomination	Coinage during year	Metallic composition	Gross weight	Diameter
1944	P	2 francs	25,000,000	Zinc-coated steel	2.75	19.05

BOLIVIA

Calendar year	U.S. Mint	Denomination	Coinage during year	Metallic composition	Gross weight	Diameter
			Pieces		Grams	mm.
1942	P	10 centavos.....	**3,500,000**	Zinc..................	1.75	18.0
1943	P	50 centavos.....	10,000,000	95% copper, 5% zinc...........	5.50	24.3
	P	20 centavos.....	10,000,000	Zinc..................	3.25	21.2
	P	10 centavos.....	6,500,000	.... do	1.75	18.0
			26,500,000			
Total			**30,000,000**			

BRAZIL—COINAGE BLANKS

Calendar year	U.S. Mint	Denomination	Coinage during year	Metallic composition	Gross weight	Diameter
1968	D	20 centavos.....	76,335,800	75% copper, 25% nickel.......	7.86	25.00
	D	10 centavos.....	72,463,700	.... do	5.52	23.00
			148,799,500			
1969	D	20 centavos.....	101,781,170	.... do	7.86	25.00
	D	10 centavos.....	108,695,652	.... do	5.52	23.00
			210,476,822			
1970	D	20 centavos.....	20,496,278	.... do	7.86	25.00
	D	10 centavos.....	26,476,666	.... do	5.52	23.00
			46,972,944			
Total			**406,249,266**			

CANADA

Calendar year	U.S. Mint	Denomination	Coinage during year	Metallic composition	Gross weight	Diameter
1968	P	10 cents..........	**42,430,000**	Pure nickel	2.07	17.91
1969	P	10 cents..........	42,740,000	.... do	2.07	17.91
Total			**85,170,000**			

CHINA

Calendar year	U.S. Mint	Denomination	Coinage during year	Metallic composition	Gross weight	Diameter
1938	S	1 dollar	3,240,032	720 silver, 280 copper......	20.00	35.00
	S	½ dollar...........	6,480,064	.... do	10.00	27.00
			9,720,096			
1949	P	1 dollar	20,250,000	880 silver, 120 copper......	26.70	39.37
	S	.... do	3,200,000	.... do	26.70	39.37
	D	.... do	6,550,000	.... do	26.70	39.37
			30,000,000			
Total			**39,720,096**			

CHINA, REPUBLIC OF (TAIWAN)

Calendar year	U.S. Mint	Denomination	Coinage during year	Metallic composition	Gross weight	Diameter
1973	P	5 dollars..........	46,234,000	75% copper, 25% nickel.......	9.50	29.00
	D	1 dollar	67,684,000	55% copper, 27% nickel, 18% zinc..........	6.00	25.00
			113,918,000			

CHINA, REPUBLIC OF (TAIWAN)—CONTINUED

Calendar year	U.S. Mint	Denomination	Coinage during year	Metallic composition	Gross weight	Diameter
			Pieces		Grams	mm.
1974	P	5 dollars	181,938,000	75% copper, 25% nickel	9.50	29.00
	D	1 dollar	132,316,000	55% copper, 27% nickel, 18% zinc	6.00	25.00
			314,254,000			
Total			**428,172,000**			

COLOMBIA

Calendar year	U.S. Mint	Denomination	Coinage during year	Metallic composition	Gross weight	Diameter
1902	P	50 centavos	960,000	835 silver, 165 copper	12.5	30.00
	P	5 centavos	400,000	.... do	2.5	14.00
			1,360,000			
1916	P	50 centavos	**1,300,000**	900 silver, 100 copper	12.5	30.00
1917	P	50 centavos	**142,324**	.... do	12.5	30.00
1920	D	2 centavos	3,855,000	75% copper, 25% nickel	3.0	19.00
	D	1 centavos	7,540,000	.... do	2.0	17.00
			11,395,000			
1921	P	50 centavos	1,000,000	900 silver, 100 copper	12.5	30.00
	D	2 centavos	11,145,000	75% copper, 25% nickel	3.0	19.00
	D	1 centavos	12,460,000	.... do	2.0	17.00
			24,605,000			
1922	P	50 centavos	**3,000,000**	900 silver, 100 copper	12.5	30.00
1933	P	5 centavos	2,000,000	75% copper, 25% nickel	4.0	21.00
	P	2 centavos	3,500,000	.... do	3.0	19.00
	P	1 centavos	3,000,000	.... do	2.0	17.00
			8,500,000			
1934	S	50 centavos	**10,000,000**	900 silver, 100 copper	12.5	30.00
1935	P	5 centavos	10,000,000	75% copper, 25% nickel	4.0	21.00
	P	2 centavos	2,500,000	.... do	3.0	19.00
	P	1 centavos	5,000,000	.... do	2.0	17.00
			17,500,000			
1938	P	5 centavos	3,867,026	.... do	4.0	21.00
	P	2 centavos	3,872,348	.... do	3.0	19.00
	P	1 centavos	7,920,174	.... do	2.0	17.00
			15,659,548			
1946	P	5 centavos	13,423,000	.... do	4.0	21.00
	S	.... do	3,330,000	.... do	4.0	21.00
			16,753,000			

COLOMBIA—CONTINUED

Calendar year	*U.S. Mint*	*Denomination*	*Coinage during year*	*Metallic composition*	*Gross weight*	*Diameter*
			Pieces		*Grams*	*mm.*
1947	S	5 centavos	23,247,000	.... do	4.0	21.00
Total			**133,461,872**			

COSTA RICA

Calendar year	*U.S. Mint*	*Denomination*	*Coinage during year*	*Metallic composition*	*Gross weight*	*Diameter*
1897	P	20 colones[1]	20,000	900 gold, 100 copper	15.56	27.00
	P	10 colones[1]	60,017	.... do	7.78	21.00
			80,017			
1899–1900.	P	20 colones	30,000	.... do	15.56	27.00
	P	10 colones	190,000	.... do	7.78	21.00
	P	5 colones	100,000	.... do	3.89	18.00
			320,000			
1900	P	5 colones	100,000	.... do	3.89	18.00
	P	2 colones	125,000	.... do	1.56	14.00
			225,000			
1903	P	2 centimos	**630,000**	75% copper, 25% nickel	1.00	15.00
1904	P	50 centimos	**250,000**	900 silver, 100 copper	10.00	29.00
1905	P	10 centimos	400,000	.... do	2.00	18.00
	P	5 centimos	500,000	.... do	1.00	15.00
			900,000			
1910	P	10 centimos	400,000	.... do	2.00	18.00
	P	5 centimos	400,000	.... do	1.00	15.00
			800,000			
1912	P	10 centimos	267,783	.... do	2.00	18.00
	P	5 centimos	535,565	.... do	1.00	15.00
			803,348			
1914	P	50 centimos	202,213	.... do	10.00	29.00
	P	10 centimos	150,000	.... do	2.00	18.00
	P	5 centimos	507,212	.... do	1.00	15.00
			859,425			
1915	P	2 colones	**5,000**	900 gold, 100 copper	1.56	14.00
1916	P	2 colones	**5,000**	.... do	1.56	14.00
1921	P	2 colones	**3,000**	.... do	1.56	14.00
1922	P	2 colones	**13,030**	.... do	1.56	14.00
1926	P	2 colones	**15,000**	.... do	1.56	14.00
1928	P	2 colones	**25,000**	.... do	1.56	14.00
1929	P	10 centimos	500,000	95% copper, 4% zinc, 1% tin	2.00	18.00
	P	5 centimos	1,500,000	.... do	1.00	15.00
			2,000,000			
1935	P	50 centimos	700,000	75% copper, 25% nickel	6.25	25.00
	P	25 centimos	1,200,000	.... do	3.45	23.00
			1,900,000			

COSTA RICA—CONTINUED

Calendar year	*U.S. Mint*	*Denomination*	*Coinage during year*	*Metallic composition*	*Gross weight*	*Diameter*
			Pieces		*Grams*	*mm.*
1936	P	1 colon	**350,000**	do	10.00	29.00
1951	P	5 centimos	**3,000,000**	do	1.00	15.00
1952	P	10 centimos	2,500,000	do	2.00	18.00
	P	5 centimos	7,000,000	do	1.00	15.00
			9,500,000			
1953	P	10 centimos	5,290,000	Chromium stainless steel	1.75	18.00
	P	5 centimos	9,040,000	do	.875	15.00
			14,330,000			
1954	P	2 colones	1,028,000	do	12.00	32.00
	P	1 colon	987,000	do	8 2/3	29.00
			2,015,000			
1959	P	10 centimos	10,470,000	do	1.75	18.00
	P	5 centimos	19,940,000	do	.875	15.00
			30,410,000			
1961	P	2 colones	1,000,000	75% copper, 25% nickel	14.00	32.00
	P	1 colon	1,000,000	do	10.00	29.00
			2,000,000			
1967	S	10 centimos	5,500,000	Stainless steel (17% chrome)	1.75	18.00
	S	5 centimos	6,020,000	do	.875	15.00
			11,520,000			
1968	P	1 colon	2,000,000	75% copper, 25% nickel	10.00	29.00
	P	50 centimos	2,000,000	do	7.00	26.00
	S	5 centimos	4,840,000	Stainless steel (17% chrome)	.875	15.00
			8,840,000			
1969	D	10 centimos	10,000,000	75% copper, 25% nickel	2.00	18.00
	D	5 centimos	15,000,000	do	1.00	15.00
			25,000,000			
1970	P	2 colones	1,000,000	do	14.00	32.00
	P	1 colon	2,000,000	do	10.00	29.00
	P	50 centimos	4,000,000	do	7.00	26.00
	D	25 centimos	4,000,000	do	3.45	23.00
	D	5 centimos	5,000,000	do	1.00	15.00
			16,000,000			
Total			**131,798,820**			

[1]Gold planchets.

CUBA

Calendar year	U.S. Mint	Denomination	Coinage during year	Metallic composition	Gross weight	Diameter
			Pieces		Grams	mm.
1915	P	20 pesos	56,770	900 gold, 100 copper	33.44	34.30
	P	10 pesos	95,020	.... do	16.72	26.90
	P	5 pesos	696,050	.... do	8.31	21.50
	P	4 pesos	6,300	.... do	6.69	(*)
	P	2 pesos	10,050	.... do	3.34	(*)
	P	1 peso	6,850	.... do	1.67	14.90
	P	.... do	1,976,100	900 silver, 100 copper	26.73	38.10
	P	40 centavos	2,632,650	.... do	10.00	29.10
	P	20 centavos	7,915,150	.... do	5.00	23.30
	P	10 centavos	5,690,150	.... do	2.50	17.90
	P	5 centavos	5,096,200	75% copper, 25% nickel	5.00	(*)
	P	2 centavos	6,089,700	.... do	3.50	19.30
	P	1 centavo	9,396,200	.... do	2.50	(*)
			39,667,190			
1916	P	20 pesos	10	900 gold, 100 copper	33.44	34.30
	P	10 pesos	1,168,510	.... do	16.72	26.90
	P	5 pesos	1,132,010	.... do	8.36	21.50
	P	4 pesos	128,760	.... do	6.69	(*)
	P	2 pesos	150,010	.... do	3.34	(*)
	P	1 peso	10,600	.... do	1.67	14.90
	P	.... do	843,050	900 silver, 100 copper	26.73	38.10
	P	40 centavos	187,550	.... do	10.00	29.10
	P	20 centavos	2,535,050	.... do	5.00	23.30
	P	10 centavos	560,150	.... do	2.50	17.90
	P	5 centavos	1,714,000	75% copper, 25% nickel	5.00	(*)
	P	2 centavos	5,322,350	.... do	3.50	19.30
	P	1 centavo	9,318,000	.... do	2.50	(*)
			23,070,050			
1920	P	40 centavos	125,000	900 silver, 100 copper	10.00	29.10
	P	20 centavos	4,955,000	.... do	5.00	23.30
	P	10 centavos	3,090,000	.... do	2.50	17.90
	P	5 centavos	10,000,000	75% copper, 25% nickel	5.00	21.20
	P	1 centavo	19,378,000	.... do	2.50	(*)
			37,548,000			
1921	P	40 centavos	415,352	900 silver, 100 copper	10.00	29.10
	P	20 centavos	1,175,000	.... do	5.00	23.30
			1,590,352			

*Not available.

CUBA—CONTINUED

Calendar year	U.S. Mint	Denomination	Coinage during year	Metallic composition	Gross weight	Diameter
			Pieces		*Grams*	*mm.*
1932	P	1 peso	3,550,000	.... do	26.73	38.10
	P	20 centavos.....	184,296	.... do	5.00	23.30
			3,734,296			
1933...........	P	1 peso	**6,000,000**	.... do	26.73	38.10
1934...........	P	1 peso	**10,000,000**	.... do	26.73	38.10
1935...........	P	1 peso	**12,500,000**	.... do	26.73	38.10
1936...........	P	1 peso	**16,000,000**	.... do	26.73	38.10
1937...........	P	1 peso	**11,500,000**	.... do	26.73	38.10
1938...........	P	1 peso	10,800,000	.... do	26.73	38.10
	P	1 centavo	2,000,000	75% copper, 25% nickel.......	2.50	16.80
			12,800,000			
1939...........	P	1 peso	**9,200,000**	900 silver, 100 copper......	26.73	38.10
1943...........	P	5 centavos.......	2,000,000	70% copper, 30% zinc..........	4.60	21.20
	P	1 centavo	2,000,000	.... do	2.30	16.80
			4,000,000			
1944...........	P	5 centavos.......	4,000,000	.... do	4.60	21.20
	P	1 centavo	18,000,000	.... do	2.30	16.80
			22,000,000			
1946...........	P	5 centavos.......	40,000,000	75% copper, 25% nickel.......	5.00	21.20
	P	1 centavo	50,000,000	.... do	2.50	16.80
			90,000,000			
1948...........	P	20 centavos.....	6,830,000	900 silver, 100 copper......	5.00	23.30
	P	10 centavos.....	5,120,000	.... do	2.50	17.90
			11,950,000			
1949...........	P	20 centavos.....	13,170,000	.... do	5.00	23.30
	P	10 centavos.....	9,880,000	.... do	2.50	17.90
			23,050,000			
1952...........	P	40 centavos.....	1,250,000	.... do	10.00	29.10
	P	20 centavos.....	6,700,000	.... do	5.00	23.30
	P	10 centavos.....	10,000,000	.... do	2.50	17.90
	P	1 centavo	2,160,000	70% copper, 30% zinc..........	2.30	16.80
			20,110,000			
1953...........	P	1 peso	1,000,000	900 silver, 100 copper......	26.73	38.10
	P	50 centavos.....	2,000,000	.... do	12.50	30.60
	P	25 centavos.....	19,000,000	.... do	6.25	24.30
	P	20 centavos.....	2,000,000	.... do	5.00	23.30
	P	1 centavo	47,840,000	70% copper, 30% zinc..........	2.30	16.80
			71,840,000			
1958...........	P	1 centavo	**50,000,000**	75% copper, 25% nickel.......	2.50	16.80

CUBA—CONTINUED

Calendar year	U.S. Mint	Denomination	Coinage during year	Metallic composition	Gross weight	Diameter
			Pieces		Grams	mm.
1960...........	P	5 centavos.......	20,000,000	.... do	5.00	21.20
Total			**496,559,888**			

CURACAO

Calendar year	U.S. Mint	Denomination	Coinage during year	Metallic composition	Gross weight	Diameter
1941...........	P	25 centstukken	500,000	640 silver, 360 copper......	3.58	19.00
	P	10 centstukken	300,000	.... do	1.40	15.00
			800,000			
1942...........	P	1 centstukken..	**500,000**	95% copper, 4% zinc, 1% tin	2.50	19.00
1943...........	P	25 centstukken	500,000	640 silver, 360 copper......	3.50	19.00
	P	10 centstukken	500,000	.... do	1.40	15.00
	P	5 centstukken..	500,000	Nickel-silver, 12%	4.50	18.00
			1,500,000			
1944...........	D	Riksdaalder.....	200,000	720 silver, 280 copper......	25.00	38.00
	D	1 gulden	500,000	.... do	10.00	28.00
	D	25 centstukken	1,500,000	640 silver, 360 copper......	3.58	19.00
	D	10 centstukken	1,500,000	.... do	1.40	15.00
	P	5 centstukken.	1,500,000	Nickel-silver, 12%................	4.50	18.00
	D	2½ centstukken	1,000,000	95% copper, 5% zinc...........	4.00	23.50
	D	1 centstukken..	3,000,000	.... do	2.50	19.00
			9,200,000			
Total			**12,000,000**			

DOMINICAN REPUBLIC

Calendar year	U.S. Mint	Denomination	Coinage during year	Metallic composition	Gross weight	Diameter
1896–97	P	1 peso	302,404	Silver-copper...	(*)	(*)
1897–98.....	P	1 peso	251,066	.... do	(*)	(*)
	P	Half peso.........	916,704	.... do	(*)	(*)
	P	20 centavos.....	1,394,557	.... do	5.00	(*)
	P	10 centavos.....	764,387	.... do	2.50	(*)
			3,326,714			
1898–99.....	P	1 peso	**906,089**	.... do	(*)	(*)
1939...........	P	1 peso	15,000	900 silver, 100 copper......	26.73	38.10
	P	25 centavos.....	160,000	.... do	6.25	24.30
	P	10 centavos.....	150,000	.... do	2.50	17.90
	P	5 centavos.......	200,000	75% copper, 25% nickel.......	5.00	21.20
	P	1 centavo	2,000,000	95% copper, 5% zinc and tin	3.11	19.05
			2,525,000			
1941...........	P	1 centavo	**2,000,000**	.... do	3.11	19.05

DOMINICAN REPUBLIC—CONTINUED

Calendar year	U.S. Mint	Denomination	Coinage during year	Metallic composition	Gross weight	Diameter
			Pieces		Grams	mm.
1942	P	25 centavos.....	560,000	900 silver, 100 copper	6.25	24.30
	P	10 centavos.....	2,000,000	.... do	2.50	17.90
	P	1 centavo	2,000,000	95% copper, 5% zinc and tin	3.11	19.05
			4,560,000			
1944	P	1 centavo	**5,000,000**	95% copper, 5% zinc...........	3.11	19.05
1945	P	5 centavos.......	**2,000,000**	560 copper, 350 silver, 90 manganese	5.00	21.20
1947	P	Half peso.........	200,000	900 silver, 100 copper	12.50	30.60
	P	25 centavos.....	400,000	.... do	6.25	24.30
	P	1 centavo	3,000,000	95% copper, 5% zinc and tin	3.11	19.05
			3,600,000			
1949	P	1 centavo	**3,000,000**	.... do	3.11	19.05
1951	P	Half peso.........	200,000	900 silver, 100 copper	12.50	30.60
	P	25 centavos.....	400,000	.... do	6.25	24.30
	P	10 centavos.....	500,000	.... do	2.50	17.90
	P	5 centavos.......	2,000,000	75% copper, 25% nickel.......	5.00	21.20
	P	1 centavo	3,000,000	95% copper, 5% zinc and tin	3.00	19.05
			6,100,000			
1953	P	10 centavos.....	**750,000**	900 silver, 100 copper	2.50	17.90
1955	P	1 peso	50,000	.... do	26.73	38.10
	P	1 centavo	3,000,000	95% copper, 5% zinc and tin	3.00	19.05
			3,050,000			
1956	P	1 centavo	**3,000,000**	.... do	3.00	19.05
1958	P	1 centavo	**5,000,000**	.... do	3.00	19.05
1959		Half peso..............	100,000	900 silver, 100 copper	12.50	30.60
	P	10 centavos....	2,000,000	.... do	2.50	17.90
			2,100,000			
1960	P	5 centavos.......	1,000,000	75% copper, 25% nickel.......	5.00	21.20
	P	1 centavo	5,000,000	95% copper, 5% zinc and tin	3.00	19.05
			6,000,000			

Footnote at end of table.

DOMINICAN REPUBLIC—CONTINUED

Calendar year	U.S. Mint	Denomination	Coinage during year	Metallic composition	Gross weight	Diameter
			Pieces		Grams	mm.
1961	P	Half peso	100,000	900 silver, 100 copper	12.50	30.60
	P	25 centavos	600,000	.... do	6.25	24.30
			700,000			
1978	P	1 peso	80,000	75% copper, 25% nickel	26.70	38.10
	P	50 centavos	732,000	.... do	12.50	30.60
	P	25 centavos	2,580,000	.... do	6.25	24.30
	P	10 centavos	6,490,000	.... do	2.50	17.90
	P	5 centavos	4,984,000	.... do	5.00	21.20
	P	1 centavo	5,980,000	95% copper, 5% zinc	3.00	19.05
			20,846,000			
1979	S	1 peso [1]	5,000	75% copper, 25% nickel	26.70	38.10
	S	.... do [1]	15	900 silver	30.92	38.10
	S	50 centavos [1]	5,000	75% copper, 25% nickel	12.50	30.60
	S	.... do [1]	15	900 silver	14.55	30.60
	P	.... do	300,000	75% copper, 25% nickel	12.50	30.60
	S	25 centavos [1]	5,000	.... do	6.25	24.30
	S	.... do [1]	15	900 silver	7.32	24.30
	P	.... do	200,000	75% copper, 25% nickel	6.25	24.30
	S	10 centavos [1]	5000	.... do	2.50	17.90
	S	.... do [1]	15	900 silver	2.95	17.90
	S	5 centavos [1]	5,000	75% copper, 25% nickel	5.00	21.20
	S	.... do [1]	15	900 silver	5.86	21.20
	S	1 centavo [1]	5,000	95% copper, 5% zinc	3.00	19.05
	S	.... do [1]	15	900 silver	3.58	19.05
			530,090			
1980	P	50 centavos	554,000	75% copper, 25% nickel	12.50	30.60
	P	25 centavos	504,000	.... do	6.25	24.30
	P	10 centavos	600,000	.... do	2.50	17.90
			1,658,000			
Total			**76,954,297**			

ECUADOR

Calendar year	U.S. Mint	Denomination	Coinage during year	Metallic composition	Gross weight	Diameter
1895	P	20 centavos	**5,000,000**	900 silver, 100 copper	5.00	23.00
1914	P	20 centavos	**2,500,000**	.... do	5.00	23.00
1916	P	20 centavos	1,000,000	.... do	5.00	23.00
	P	10 centavos	2,000,000	.... do	2.50	(*)
			3,000,000			

ECUADOR—CONTINUED

Calendar year	U.S. Mint	Denomination	Coinage during year	Metallic composition	Gross weight	Diameter
			Pieces		Grams	mm.
1917	P	5 centavos	1,200,000	75% copper, 25% nickel	3.00	21.00
	P	2½ centavos	1,600,000	do	2.50	19.00
			2,800,000			
1918	P	10 centavos	1,000,000	do	5.00	22.00
	P	5 centavos	7,980,000	do	3.00	21.00
			8,980,000			
1928	P	2 sucres	500,000	720 silver, 280 copper	10.00	28.75
	P	1 sucre	3,000,000	do	5.00	23.50
	P	50 centavos	1,000,000	do	2.50	18.00
	P	5 centavos	5,376,000	Pure nickel	3.00	19.50
			9,876,000			
1929	P	10 centavos	5,000,000	do	4.00	21.50
	P	5 centavos	10,624,000	do	3.00	19.50
	P	2½ centavos	4,000,000	do	2.50	18.50
	P	1 centavo	2,016,000	95% copper, 5% zinc and tin	3.50	20.50
			21,640,000			
1930	P	2 sucres	100,000	720 silver, 280 copper	10.00	28.75
	P	1 sucre	400,000	do	5.00	23.50
	P	50 centavos	155,060	do	2.50	18.00
			655,060			
1934	P	1 sucre	**2,000,000**	do	5.00	23.50
1942	P	20 centavos	2,500,000	80% copper, 20% zinc	4.00	21.00
	P	10 centavos	2,500,000	do	3.00	19.00
	P	5 centavos	1,000,000	do	2.00	17.00
			6,000,000			
1943	P	20 centavos	2,500,000	do	4.00	21.00
	P	10 centavos	2,500,000	do	3.00	19.00
	P	5 centavos	1,000,000	do	2.00	17.00
			6,000,000			
1944	D	20 centavos	15,000,000	do	4.00	21.00
	D	5 centavos	3,000,000	do	2.00	17.00
			18,000,000			
1946	P	5 centavos	**15,888,000**	75% copper, 25% nickel	52.00	17.00
1947	P	1 sucre	18,000,000	Pure nickel	7.00	26.00
	P	20 centavos	30,000,000	75% copper, 25% nickel	4.00	21.00
	P	10 centavos	40,000,000	do	3.00	19.00
	P	5 centavos	24,112,000	do	2.00	17.00
			112,112,000			
Total			**214,451.060**			

*Not available.

EL SALVADOR

Calendar year	U.S. Mint	Denomination	Coinage during year	Metallic composition	Gross weight	Diameter
			Pieces		Grams	mm.
1904	S	1 peso	**400,000**	900 silver, 100 copper	25.00	(*)
1909	S	1 peso	**693,170**	.... do	25.00	(*)
1911	P	1 peso	510,993	90	25.00	(*)
	S	.... do	511,108	.... do	25.00	(*)
			1,022,101			
1914	P	1 peso	2,100,020	.... do	25.00	(*)
	P	25 centavos	1,400,020	835 silver, 165 copper	6.25	24.00
	P	10 centavos	1,500,020	.... do	2.50	(*)
	P	5 centavos	2,000,020	.... do	5.00	23.00
			7,000,080			
1915	P	5 centavos	2,500,000	75% copper, 25% nickel	5.00	23.00
	P	3 centavos	2,700,000	.... do	4.00	(*)
	P	1 centavo	5,008,000	.... do	2.50	16.00
			10,208,000			
1916	P	5 centavos	**1,500,000**	.... do	5.00	23.00
1917	P	5 centavos	**1,000,000**	.... do	5.00	23.00
1918	P	5 centavos	**1,000,000**	.... do	5.00	23.00
1919	P	5 centavos	2,000,000	.... do	5.00	23.00
	P	1 centavo	1,000,000	.... do	2.50	16.00
			3,000,000			
1920	P	5 centavos	2,000,000	.... do	5.00	23.00
	P	1 centavo	1,492,000	.... do	2.50	16.00
			3,492,000			
1921	S	10 centavos	2,000,000	.... do	7.00	26.00
	S	5 centavos	1,780,000	.... do	5.00	23.00
			3,780,000			
1925	S	10 centavos	2,000,000	.... do	7.00	26.00
	S	5 centavos	4,000,000	.... do	5.00	23.00
	S	1 centavo	200,000	.... do	2.50	16.00
			6,200,000			
1926	S	1 centavo	**400,000**	.... do	2.50	16.00
1928	S	1 centavo	**5,000,000**	.... do	2.50	16.00
1936	P	1 centavo	**2,500,000**	.... do	2.50	16.00
1940	P	10 centavos	500,000	.... do	7.00	26.00
	P	5 centavos	800,000	.... do	5.00	23.00
	P	1 centavo	1,000,000	.... do	2.50	16.00
			2,300,000			
1943	S	25 centavos	1,200,000	900 silver, 100 copper	7.50	29.00
	P	1 centavo	5,000,000	95% copper, 5% zinc	2.50	16.00
	S	.... do	5,000,000	.... do	2.50	16.00
			11,200,000			

*Not available.

EL SALVADOR—CONTINUED

Calendar year	U.S. Mint	Denomination	Coinage during year	Metallic composition	Gross weight	Diameter
			Pieces		Grams	mm.
1944..........	S	5 centavos.......	**5,000,000**	Nickel-silver 12%...............	5.00	23.00
1945..........	S	25 centavos.....	1,000,000	900 silver, 100 copper......	7.50	29.00
	P	1 centavo	5,000,000	95% copper, 5% zinc...........	2.50	16.00
			6,000,000			
1947..........	S	1 centavo	**5,000,000**	95% copper, 5% zinc and tin	2.50	16.00
1948..........	S	5 centavos.......	**3,000,000**	Nickel-silver 12%	5.00	23.00
1950..........	S	5 centavos.......	**2,000,000**	.... do	5.00	23.00
1951..........	S	10 centavos.....	1,000,000	75% copper, 25% nickel.......	7.00	26.00
	S	5 centavos.......	2,000,000	.... do	5.00	23.00
	S	1 centavo	10,000,000	95% copper, 5% zinc...........	2.50	16.00
			13,000,000			
1952..........	S	10 centavos.....	336,000	Nickel-silver 12%	7.00	26.00
	S	5 centavos.......	2,000,000	.... do	5.00	23.00
			2,336,000			
1953..........	S	10 centavos.....	1,664,000	.... do	7.00	26.00
	S	5 centavos.......	2,000,000	.... do	5.00	23.00
	S	1 centavo	10,000,000	95% copper, 5% zinc...........	2.50	16.00
			13,664,000			
1954..........	S	50 centavos.....	3,000,000	900 silver, 100 copper......	5.00	21.00
	S	25 centavos.....	14,000,000	.... do	2.50	17.90
			17,000,000			
1956..........	P	5 centavos.......	**6,000,000**	75% copper, 25% nickel.......	5.00	23.00
1957..........	P	5 centavos......	2,000,000	.... do	5.00	23.00
	P	1 centavo	10,000,000	95% copper, 5% zinc...........	2.50	16.00
			12,000,000			
1961..........	P	5 centavos.......	**6,000,000**	75% copper, 25% nickel.......	5.00	23.00
1963..........	P	5 centavos.......	**10,000,000**	.... do	5.00	23.00
1967..........	D	10 centavos.....	2,000,000	.... do	7.00	26.00
	D	5 centavos.......	10,000,000	.... do	5.00	23.00
			3,000,000			
1968..........	D	10 centavos.....	3,000,000	.... do	7.00	26.00
	D	1 centavo	5,000,000	95% copper, 5% zinc...........	2.50	16.00
			8,000,000			
1969..........	D	10 centavos.....	3,000,000	75% copper, 25% nickel.......	7.00	26.00

EL SALVADOR—CONTINUED

Calendar year	*U.S. Mint*	*Denomination*	*Coinage during year*	*Metallic composition*	*Gross weight*	*Diameter*
			Pieces		*Grams*	*mm.*
	D	1 centavo	5,000,000	95% copper, 5% zinc............	2.50	16.00
			8,000,000			
1973...........	S	10 centavos.....	7,000,000	75% copper, 25% nickel.......	7.00	26.00
	S	5 centavos.......	10,000,000	.... do	5.00	23.00
	S	1 centavo	20,000,000	95% copper, 5% zinc............	2.50	16.00
			37,000,000			
Total			**226,695,351**			

ETHIOPIA

Calendar year	*U.S. Mint*	*Denomination*	*Coinage during year*	*Metallic composition*	*Gross weight*	*Diameter*
1944...........	P	50 cents...........	763,000	800 silver, 200 copper......	7.00	25.00
	P	5 cents.............	3,162,000	95% copper, 5% zinc............	4.00	20.00
	P	1 cent	3,000,000	.... do	2.85	17.00
			6,925,000			
1945...........	P	50 cents...........	29,237,000	800 silver, 200 copper......	7.00	25.00
	P	25 cents [1]	10,000,000	95% copper, 5% zinc............	6.80	26.00
	P	10 cents...........	25,000,000	.... do	6.10	23.00
	P	5 cents.............	12,838,000	.... do	4.00	20.00
	P	1 cent	12,000,000	.... do	2.85	17.00
			89,075,000			
1946...........	P	5 cents.............	**10,000,000**	.... do	4.00	20.00
1947...........	P	50 cents...........	20,433,730	700 silver, 300 copper......	7.00	25.00
	P	5 cents.............	12,000,000	95% copper, 5% zinc and tin	4.00	20.00
			32,433,730			
1949...........	P	10 cents...........	16,000,000	95% copper, 5% zinc............	6.10	23.00
	P	5 cents.............	16,000,000	.... do	4.00	20.00
			32,000,000			
1952...........	P	25 cents [1]	1,299,000	.... do	6.80	26.00
	P	10 cents...........	5,000,000	.... do	6.10	23.00
	P	5 cents.............	5,112,000	.... do	4.00	20.00
			11,411,000			
1953...........	P	25 cents [1]	28,701,000	.... do	6.80	26.00
	P	10 cents...........	25,000,000	.... do	6.10	23.00
	P	5 cents.............	34,888,000	.... do	4.00	20.00
			88,589,000			
1957...........	P	10 cents...........	**6,928,000**	.... do	6.10	23.00
1958...........	P	10 cents...........	33,072,000	.... do	6.10	23.00

ETHIOPIA—CONTINUED

Calendar year	U.S. Mint	Denomination	Coinage during year	Metallic composition	Gross weight	Diameter
			Pieces		Grams	mm.
	P	5 cents	10,000,000	do	4.00	20.00
			43,072,000			
1962	P	10 cents	20,000,000	do	6.10	23.00
	P	5 cents	5,000,000	do	4.00	20.00
			25,000,000			
1963	P	10 cents	30,000,000	do	6.10	23.00
Total			**375,433,730**			

*Coin has 14 scallops measuring 26 mm. across scallops.

FIJI

Calendar year	U.S. Mint	Denomination	Coinage during year	Metallic composition	Gross weight	Diameter
1942	S	Florin	250,000	900 silver, 100 copper	11.31	28.50
	S	Shilling	500,000	do	5.66	23.60
	S	Sixpence	400,000	do	2.83	19.40
	S	Penny [1]	1,000,000	65% copper, 35% zinc	6.48	26.00
	S	Half penny [1]	250,000	do	3.24	21.00
			2,400,000			
1943	S	Florin	250,000	900 silver, 100 copper	11.31	28.50
	S	Shilling	500,000	do	5.66	23.60
	S	Sixpence	400,000	do	2.83	19.40
	S	Penny [1]	1,000,000	65% copper, 35% zinc	6.48	26.00
	S	Half penny [1]	250,000	do	3.24	21.00
			2,400,000			
Total			**4,800,000**			

[1]Coin has a central hole measuring 7 mm. in diameter.

FRANCE

Calendar year	U.S. Mint	Denomination	Coinage during year	Metallic composition	Gross weight	Diameter
1944	P	2 francs	50,000,000	70% copper, 30% zinc	8.00	27.00

GREENLAND

Calendar year	U.S. Mint	Denomination	Coinage during year	Metallic composition	Gross weight	Diameter
1944	P	5 kroner	100,000	70% copper, 30% zinc	13.25	31.00

GUATEMALA

Calendar year	U.S. Mint	Denomination	Coinage during year	Metallic composition	Gross weight	Diameter
1925	P	1 quetzal	10,000	720 silver, 280 copper	33 1/3	39.00
	P	50 centavos	400,000	do	16 2/3	34.00
	P	25 centavos	1,160,000	do	8 1/3	27.00
			1,570,000			

GUATEMALA—CONTINUED

Calendar year	U.S. Mint	Denomination	Coinage during year	Metallic composition	Gross weight	Diameter
			Pieces		Grams	mm.
1926	P	20 quetzales....	49,000	900 gold, 100 copper......	33.44	34.00
	P	10 quetzales....	18,000	.... do	16.72	27.00
	P	5 quetzales......	48,000	.... do	8.36	22.00
			115,000			
1943...........	P	25 centavos.....	150,000	720 silver, 280 copper......	8 1/3	27.00
	P	10 centavos.....	600,000	.... do	3 1/3	20.00
	P	5 centavos.......	900,000	.... do	1 2/3	16.00
	P	2 centavos.......	150,000	70% copper, 30% zinc..........	6.00	25.60
	P	1 centavo	450,000	.... do	3.00	20.00
			2,250,000			
1944...........	P	25 centavos.....	750,000	720 silver, 280 copper......	8 1/3	27.00
	S	2 centavos.......	1,100,000	70% copper, 30% zinc..........	6.00	25.60
	S	1 centavo	2,050,000	.... do	3.00	20.00
			3,900,000			
Total			**7,835,000**			

HAITI

Calendar year	U.S. Mint	Denomination	Coinage during year	Metallic composition	Gross weight	Diameter
1949...........	P	10 centimes.....	5,000,000	75% copper, 25% nickel.......	4.00	22.70
	P	5 centimes.......	10,000,000	.... do	2.75	19.90
			15,000,000			
1953...........	P	10 centimes.....	1,500,000	70% copper, 18% zinc, 12% nickel.......	4.00	22.70
	P	5 centimes.......	3,000,000	.... do	2.75	19.90
			4,500,000			
1956...........	P	20 centimes.....	**2,500,000**	.... do	7.50	26.20
1958...........	P	10 centimes.....	7,500,000	.... do	4.00	22.70
	P	5 centimes.......	15,000,000	.... do	2.75	19.90
			22,500,000			
1970...........	D	20 centimes.....	1,000,000	.... do	7.50	26.00
	D	10 centimes.....	2,500,000	.... do	4.00	22.70
	D	5 centimes.......	5,000,000	.... do	2.75	19.90
			8,500,000			
1973...........	S	50 centimes.....	600,000	75% copper, 25% nickel.......	9.88	29.00
	S	20 centimes.....	1,500,000	70% copper, 18% zinc, 12% nickel.......	7.50	26.00
			2,100,000			
1975...........	S	50 centimes.....	1,200,000	70% copper, 18% zinc, 12% nickel.......	9.88	29.00

HAITI—CONTINUED

Calendar year	U.S. Mint	Denomination	Coinage during year	Metallic composition	Gross weight	Diameter
			Pieces		Grams	mm.
	S	20 centimes.....	4,000,000	.... do	7.50	26.20
	S	10 centimes.....	12,000,000	.... do	4.00	22.70
	S	5 centimes.......	16,000,000	.... do	2.75	19.90
			33,200,000			
1976...........	S	50 gourdes......	14,000	925 silver, 75 copper........	16.75	38.00
	S	25 gourdes......	10,000	.... do	8.38	30.00
			24,000			
1979...........	S	50 centimes.....	2,000,000	70% copper, 18% zinc, 12% nickel......	9.88	29.00
Total			**90,324,000**			

HAWAII

Calendar year	U.S. Mint	Denomination	Coinage during year	Metallic composition	Gross weight	Diameter
1883–84.....	S	1 dollar	500,000	900 silver, 100 copper......	26.73	38.00
	S	1/2 dollar...........	700,000	.... do	12.50	(*)
	S	1/4 dollar...........	500,000	.... do	6.25	(*)
	S	dimes...............	250,000	.... do	2.50	(*)
Total			**1,950,000**			

*Not available.

HONDURAS

Calendar year	U.S. Mint	Denomination	Coinage during year	Metallic composition	Gross weight	Diameter
1931...........	P	1 lempira	550,000	900 silver, 100 copper......	12.50	31.00
	P	50 centavos.....	500,000	.... do	6.25	24.00
	P	20 centavos.....	1,000,000	.... do	2.50	18.00
	P	5 centavos.......	2,000,000	75% copper, 25% nickel.......	5.00	21.00
			4,050,000			
1932...........	P	1 lempira	1,000,000	900 silver, 100 copper......	12.50	31.00
	P	50 centavos.....	1,100,000	.... do	6.25	24.00
	P	20 centavos.....	750,000	.... do	2.50	18.00
	P	10 centavos.....	1,500,000	75% copper, 25% nickel.......	7.00	26.00
	P	5 centavos.......	1,000,000	.... do	5.00	21.00
			5,350,000			
1933...........	P	1 lempira	**400,000**	900 silver, 100 copper......	12.50	31.00
1934...........	P	1 lempira	**600,000**	.... do	12.50	31.00
1935...........	P	1 lempira	1,000,000	.... do	12.50	31.00
	P	1 centavo	2,000,000	95% copper, 4% zinc, 1% tin	2.00	15.00
			3,000,000			

HONDURAS—CONTINUED

Calendar year	U.S. Mint	Denomination	Coinage during year	Metallic composition	Gross weight	Diameter
			Pieces		Grams	mm.
1937	P	1 lempira	4,000,000	900 silver, 100 copper	12.50	31.00
	P	50 centavos	1,000,000	.... do	6.25	24.00
			5,000,000			
1939	P	2 centavos	2,000,000	95% copper, 4% zinc, 1% tin	3.00	20.00
	P	1 centavo	2,000,000	.... do	2.00	15.00
			4,000,000			
1949	P	5 centavos	2,000,000	75% copper, 25% nickel	5.00	21.00
	P	2 centavos	3,000,000	95% copper, 5% zinc and tin	3.00	20.00
	P	1 centavo	4,000,000	.... do	2.00	15.00
			9,000,000			
1951	P	50 centavos	500,000	900 silver, 100 copper	6.25	24.00
	P	20 centavos	1,500,000	.... do	2.50	18.00
	P	10 centavos	1,000,000	75% copper, 25% nickel	7.00	26.00
			3,000,000			
1952	P	20 centavos	**2,500,000**	900 silver, 100 copper	2.50	18.00
1956	P	10 centavos	7,559,500	75% copper, 25% nickel	7.00	26.00
	P	5 centavos	10,070,000	.... do	5.00	21.00
	P	2 centavos	7,664,000	95% copper, 5% zinc and tin	3.00	20.00
	P	1 centavo	2,000,000	.... do	1.50	15.00
			27,293,500			
1957	P	2 centavos	12,336,000	.... do	3.00	20.00
	P	1 centavo	28,000,000	.... do	1.50	15.00
			40,336,000			
1958	P	20 centavos	**2,000,000**	900 silver, 100 copper	2.50	18.00
1972	D	5 centavos	**5,000,000**	75% copper, 25% nickel	5.00	21.00
1974	S	50 centavos	4,400,000	.... do	5.67	24.00
Total			**115,929,500**			

INDO-CHINA

Calendar year	U.S. Mint	Denomination	Coinage during year	Metallic composition	Gross weight	Diameter
1920	S	20 centimes	4,000,000	400 silver, 600 copper	6.00	(*)
	S	10 centimes	10,000,000	.... do	3.00	(*)
	S	1 centime	13,290,000	95% copper, 4% tin, 1% zinc	5.00	(*)
			27,290,000			

INDO-CHINA—CONTINUED

Calendar year	U.S. Mint	Denomination	Coinage during year	Metallic composition	Gross weight	Diameter
			Pieces		Grams	mm.
1921	S	1 piastre	4,850,000	900 silver, 100 copper	27.00	(*)
	S	1 centime	1,710,000	95% copper, 4% tin, 1% zinc	5.00	(*)
			6,560,000			
1922	S	1 piastre	**1,150,000**	900 silver, 100 copper	27.00	(*)
1940	S	10 centimes	**25,270,000**	Pure nickel	3.00	18
1941	S	20 centimes	25,000,000	75% copper, 25% nickel	6.00	24
	S	10 centimes	50,000,000	.... do	3.00	18
			75,000,000			
Total			**135,270,000**			

ISRAEL

Calendar year	U.S. Mint	Denomination	Coinage during year	Metallic composition	Gross weight	Diameter
1969	S	10 pounds	[1] 60,000	900 silver, 100 copper	26.00	36.70
	S	.... do	[2] 15,500	.... do	26.00	36.70
			75,500			
1971	S	10 pounds	[3] 15,500	.... do	26.00	36.70
Total			**91,000**			

[1]Commemorative Peace coins, of which 20,000 were proof coins.
[2]Pidyon HaBen commemoratives.
[3]Pidyon HaBen proof coins.

KOREA

Calendar year	U.S. Mint	Denomination	Coinage during year	Metallic composition	Gross weight	Diameter
1959	P	100 hwan	360,000	75% copper, 25% nickel	6.74	26.00
	P	50 hwan	360,000	70% copper, 18% zinc, 12% nickel	3.69	22.86
	P	10 hwan	22,980,000	95% copper, 5% zinc	2.46	19.10
			23,700,000			
1960	P	100 hwan	49,640,000	75% copper, 25% nickel	6.74	26.00
	P	50 hwan	24,640,000	70% copper, 18% zinc, 12% nickel	3.69	22.86
	P	10 hwan	77,020,000	95% copper, 5% zinc	2.46	19.10
			151,300,000			
1961	P	10 hwan	**25,000,000**	95% copper, 5% zinc	2.46	19.10
1962	P	50 hwan	20,000,000	70% copper, 18% zinc, 12% nickel	3.69	22.86

KOREA—CONTINUED

Calendar year	U.S. Mint	Denomination	Coinage during year	Metallic composition	Gross weight	Diameter
			Pieces		Grams	mm.
	P	10 hwan	75,000,000	95% copper, 5% zinc............	2.46	19.10
			95,000,000			
Total			**295,000,000**			

LIBERIA

Calendar year	U.S. Mint	Denomination	Coinage during year	Metallic composition	Gross weight	Diameter
1941...........	P	2 cents.............	812,500	75% copper, 25% nickel.......	8.40	29.00
	P	1 cent	250,000	.... do	5.40	25.50
	P	1/2 cent.............	250,000	.... do	2.50	18.00
			1,312,500			
1959...........	P	50 cents...........	440,000	900 silver, 100 copper......	10.37	29.00
	P	25 cents...........	500,000	.... do	5.18	23.00
	P	10 cents...........	1,000,000	.... do	2.07	17.00
	P	5 cents.............	1,000,000	75% copper, 25% nickel.......	4.15	20.00
	P	1 cent	500,000	95% copper, 5% zinc............	2.59	17.90
			3,440,000			
1960...........	P	50 cents...........	700,000	900 silver, 100 copper......	10.37	29.00
	P	25 cents...........	400,000	.... do	5.18	23.00
			1,100,000			
1961...........	P	1 dollar	11,200,000	.... do	20.74	34.00
	P	50 cents...........	800,000	.... do	10.37	29.00
	P	25 cents...........	1,200,000	.... do	5.18	23.00
	P	10 cents...........	1,200,000	.... do	2.07	17.00
	P	5 cents.............	3,200,000	75% copper, 25% nickel.......	4.15	20.00
	P	1 cent	7,000,000	95% copper, 5% zinc............	2.59	17.90
			14,600,000			
1968...........	D	25 cents...........	**1,600,000**	75% copper, 25% nickel.......	4.49	23.01
1969...........	S	1 dollar	19,454	.... do	17.94	34.00
	S	50 cents...........	19,454	.... do	8.97	29.00
	S	25 cents...........	19,454	.... do	4.49	23.00
	S	10 cents...........	19,454	.... do	1.79	16.99
	S	5 cents.............	19454	.... do	4.15	19.99
	S	1 cent	19,454	95% copper, 5% zinc............	2.59	17.91
			116,724			
1970...........	D	1 dollar	2,000,000	75% copper, 25% nickel.......	17.94	34.00
	S	.... do	3,464	.... do	17.94	34.00
	S	50 cents...........	3,464	.... do	8.97	29.00
	S	25 cents...........	3,464	.... do	4.49	23.00

LIBERIA—CONTINUED

Calendar year	U.S. Mint	Denomination	Coinage during year	Metallic composition	Gross weight	Diameter
			Pieces		Grams	mm.
	D	10 cents	2,500,000	.... do	1.79	16.99
	S	.... do	3,464	.... do	1.79	16.99
	S	5 cents	3,464	.... do	4.15	19.99
	S	1 cent	3,464	95% copper, 5% zinc	2.59	17.91
			4,520,784			
1971	S	1 dollar	3,032	75% copper, 25% nickel	17.94	34.00
	S	50 cents	3,032	.... do	8.97	29.00
	S	25 cents	3,032	.... do	4.49	23.00
	S	10 cents	3,032	.... do	1.79	16.99
	S	5 cents	3,032	.... do	4.15	19.99
	S	1 cent	3,032	95% copper, 5% zinc	2.59	17.91
			18,192			
1972	S	1 dollar	4,866	75% copper, 25% nickel	17.94	34.00
	S	50 cents	4,866	.... do	8.97	29.00
	S	25 cents	4,866	.... do	4.49	23.00
	S	10 cents	4,866	.... do	1.79	16.99
	S	5 cents	4,866	.... do	4.15	19.99
	D	.... do	3,000,000	.... do	4.15	19.99
	S	1 cent	4,866	95% copper, 5% zinc	2.59	17.91
	D	.... do	10,000,000	.... do	2.59	17.91
			13,029,196			
1974	S	5 dollars	28,353	900 silver, 100 copper	35.64	42.50
	S	1 dollar	10,542	75% copper, 25% nickel	17.94	34.00
	S	50 cents	1,010,542	.... do	8.97	29.00
	S	25 cents	2,010,542	.... do	4.49	23.00
	S	10 cents	10,542	.... do	1.79	16.99
	S	5 cents	10,542	.... do	4.15	19.99
	S	1 cent	10,542	95% copper, 5% zinc	2.59	17.91
			3,091,605			
1975	S	5 dollars	29,170	900 silver, 100 copper	35.64	42.50
	S	1 dollar	413,418	75% copper, 25% nickel	17.94	34.00
	S	50 cents	813,418	.... do	8.97	29.00
	S	25 cents	1,613,418	.... do	4.49	23.00
	S	10 cents	4,013,418	.... do	1.79	16.99
	S	5 cents	2,013,418	.... do	4.15	19.99
	S	1 cent	5,013,418	95% copper, 5% zinc	2.59	17.91
			13,909,678			

Footnote at end of table.

LIBERIA—CONTINUED

Calendar year	U.S. Mint	Denomination	Coinage during year	Metallic composition	Gross weight	Diameter
			Pieces		Grams	mm.
1976	S	1 dollar	1,000	75% copper, 25% nickel	17.94	34.00
	S	50 cents	1,000	do	8.97	29.00
	S	25 cents	1,000	do	4.49	23.00
	S	10 cents	1,000	do	1.79	16.99
	S	5 cents	1,000	do	4.15	19.99
	S	1 cent	1,000	95% copper, 5% zinc	2.59	17.91
			6,000			
Total			**56,744,679**			

[1] 200,000 were dated 1961; 1,000,000 were dated 1962.

MEXICO

Calendar year	U.S. Mint	Denomination	Coinage during year	Metallic composition	Gross weight	Diameter
1906	P	10 pesos	1,000,000	900 gold, 100 copper	8 1/3	23.00
	P	5 pesos	4,000,000	do	4.17	19.00
	S	50 centavos	5,000,000	800 silver, 200 copper	12.50	(*)
			10,000,000			
1907	S	50 centavos	7,442,000	do	12.50	(*)
	D	do	6,199,291	do	12.50	(*)
	O	20 centavos	5,434,699	do	5.00	(*)
			19,075,990			
1935	P	50 centavos	25,000,000	420 silver, 580 copper	7.97	27.00
	S	do	18,000,000	do	7.97	27.00
	D	do	17,000,850	do	7.97	27.00
			60,000,850			
1949	S	1 peso	2,000,000	902.7 silver, 97.3 copper	27.07	39.00
Total coins			**91,076,840**			
Blanks:						
1970	D	1 peso	55,843,368	75% copper, 25% nickel	9.20	29.00
	D	50 centavos	119,871,043	do	6.50	24.55
Total blanks			**175,714,411**			
Grand total			**266,791,251**			

*Not available.

NEPAL

Calendar year	U.S. Mint	Denomination	Coinage during year	Metallic composition	Gross weight	Diameter
1970	S	1 rupee	2,187	75% copper, 25% nickel	10.00	27.50
	S	50 pice	2,187	do	5.00	23.50
	S	25 pice	2,187	do	3.00	19.00
	S	10 pice	2,187	66% copper, 34% zinc	4.00	21.00

NEPAL—CONTINUED

Calendar year	U.S. Mint	Denomination	Coinage during year	Metallic composition	Gross weight	Diameter
			Pieces		Grams	mm.
	S	5 pice..............	2,187	100% aluminum	1.20	20.50
	S	2 pice..............	2,187	.... do	.90	18.50
	S	1 pice..............	2,187	.... do	.60	16.50
			15,309			
1972..........	S	1 rupee...........	2,380	75% copper, 25% nickel.......	10.00	27.50
	S	50 pice............	2,380	.... do	5.00	23.50
	S	25 pice............	2,380	.... do	3.00	19.00
	S	10 pice............	2,380	66% copper, 34% zinc..........	4.00	21.00
	S	5 pice..............	2,380	100% aluminum	1.20	20.50
	S	2 pice..............	2,380	.... do	.90	18.50
	S	1 pice..............	2,380	.... do	.60	16.50
			16,660			
1973..........	S	1 rupee...........	3,943	75% copper, 27% nickel.......	10.00	27.50
	S	50 pice............	3,943	.... do	5.00	23.50
	S	25 pice............	3,943	.... do	3.00	19.00
	S	10 pice............	3,943	66% copper, 34% zinc..........	4.00	21.00
	S	5 pice..............	3,943	100% aluminum	1.20	20.50
	S	2 pice..............	3,943	.... do	.90	18.50
	S	1 pice..............	3,943	.... do	.60	16.50
			27,601			
1974..........	S	1 rupee...........	8,891	75% copper, 25% nickel.......	10.00	27.50
	S	50 pice............	8,891	.... do	5.00	23.50
	S	25 pice............	8,891	.... do	3.00	19.00
	S	10 pice............	8,891	66% copper, 34% zinc..........	4.00	21.00
	S	5 pice..............	8,891	100% aluminum	1.20	20.50
	S	2 pice..............	8,891	.... do	.90	18.50
	S	1 pice..............	8,891	.... do	.60	16.50
			62,237			
1975..........	S	1 rupee...........	10,543	75% copper, 25% nickel.......	10.00	27.50
	S	50 pice............	10,543	.... do	5.00	23.50
	S	25 pice............	10,543	.... do	3.00	19.00
	S	10 pice............	10,543	66% copper, 34% zinc..........	4.00	21.00
	S	5 pice..............	10,543	100% aluminum	1.20	20.50
	S	2 pice..............	10,543	.... do	.90	18.50
	S	1 pice..............	10,543	.... do	.60	16.50
			73,801			
Total			**195,608**			

NETHERLANDS

Calendar year	U.S. Mint	Denomination	Coinage during year	Metallic composition	Gross weight	Diameter
			Pieces		Grams	mm.
1944	P	1 gulden	105,125,000	720 silver, 280 copper	10.00	28.00
	P	25 centstukken	40,000,000	640 silver, 360 copper	3.58	19.00
	P	10 centstukken	120,000,000	do	1.40	15.00
	S	do	64,040,000	do	1.40	15.00
	D	do	17,000,000	do	1.40	15.00
			346,165,000			
1945	P	1 gulden	25,375,000	720 silver, 280 copper	10.00	28.00
	P	25 centstukken	92,000,000	640 silver, 360 copper	3.58	19.00
	P	10 centstukken	90,560,000	do	1.40	15.00
	D	do	8,400,000	do	1.40	15.00
			216,335,000			
Total			**562,500,000**			

NETHERLANDS EAST INDIES

Calendar year	U.S. Mint	Denomination	Coinage during year	Metallic composition	Gross weight	Diameter
1941	P	25 centstukken	31,688,000	720 silver, 280 copper	3.18	19.00
	S	do	5,053,000	do	3.18	19.00
	P	10 centstukken	33,800,000	do	1.25	15.00
	S	do	58,150,000	do	1.25	15.00
			128,691,000			
1942	P	25 centstukken	3,259,000	do	3.18	19.00
	S	do	32,000,000	do	3.18	19.00
	P	10 centstukken	8,050,000	do	1.25	15.00
	S	do	75,000,000	do	1.25	15.00
	P	1 centstukken [1]	100,000,000	95% copper, 4% zinc, 1% tin	4.00	23.50
			218,309,000			
1943	D	2½ guilders	2,000,000	720 silver, 280 copper	25.00	38.00
	D	1 gulden	20,000,000	do	10.00	28.00
			22,000,000			
1945	S	25 centstukken	56,000,000	do	3.18	19.00
	P	10 centstukken	100,720,000	do	1.25	15.00
	S	do	19,280,000	do	1.25	15.00
	P	2½ centstukken	117,706,000	95% copper, 5% zinc	12.50	31.00
	P	1 centstukken [1]	184,003,000	do	4.00	23.50
	S	do	59,852,000	do	4.00	23.50
	D	do	133,800,000	do	4.00	23.50
	P	½ centstukken	400,000,000	do	2.30	17.00
			1,071,361,000			
1946	P	2½ centstukken	82,294,000	95% copper, 5% zinc and tin	12.50	31.00

NETHERLANDS EAST INDIES—CONTINUED

Calendar year	U.S. Mint	Denomination	Coinage during year	Metallic composition	Gross weight	Diameter
			Pieces		*Grams*	*mm.*
	P	1 centstukken [1]	150,997,000	.... do	4.00	23.50
	S	.... do	42,716,000	.... do	4.00	23.50
			276,007,000			
Total			**1,716,368,000**			

[1] Coin has a central hole measuring 5.2 mm. in diameter.

NICARAGUA

Calendar year	U.S. Mint	Denomination	Coinage during year	Metallic composition	Gross weight	Diameter
1917...........	P	1 centavo	450,000	95% copper, 5% tin and zinc	4.00	20.30
	P	1/2 centavo.......	720,000	.... do	2.50	17.00
			1,170,000			
1919...........	P	5 centavos.......	100,000	75% copper, 25% nickel.......	5.00	21.20
	P	1 centavo	750,000	95% copper, 5% tin and zinc	4.00	20.30
			850,000			
1920...........	P	5 centavos.......	150,000	75% copper, 25% nickel.......	5.00	21.20
	P	1 centavo	700,000	95% copper, 5% tin and zinc	4.00	20.30
			850,000			
1922...........	P	1 centavo	500,000	95% copper, 5% tin and zinc	4.00	20.30
	P	1/2 centavo.......	400,000	.... do	2.50	17.00
			900,000			
1924...........	P	1 centavo	300,000	.... do	4.00	20.30
	P	1/2 centavo.......	400,000	.... do	2.50	17.00
			700,000			
1927...........	P	10 centavos.....	500,000	800 silver, 200 copper	2.50	17.90
	P	5 centavos.......	100,000	75% copper, 25% nickel.......	5.00	21.20
	P	1 centavo	250,000	95% copper, 5% tin and zinc	4.00	20.30
			850,000			
1928...........	P	25 centavos.....	200,000	800 silver, 200 copper	6.25	24.00
	P	10 centavos.....	1,000,000	.... do	2.50	17.90
	P	5 centavos.......	100,000	75% copper, 25% nickel.......	5.00	21.20
	P	1 centavo	500,000	95% copper, 5% tin and zinc	4.00	20.30
			1,800,000			
1929	P	50 centavos.....	20,000	800 silver, 200 copper	12.50	30.00
	P	25 centavos.....	20,000	.... do	6.25	24.00

NICARAGUA—CONTINUED

Calendar year	U.S. Mint	Denomination	Coinage during year	Metallic composition	Gross weight	Diameter
			Pieces		Grams	mm.
	P	5 centavos.......	100,000	75% copper, 25% nickel.......	5.00	21.20
	P	1 centavo	500,000	95% copper, 5% tin and zinc	4.00	20.30
			640,000			
1930...........	P	25 centavos.....	20,000	800 silver, 200 copper......	6.25	24.00
	P	10 centavos.....	150,000	.... do	2.50	17.90
	P	5 centavos.......	100,000	75% copper, 25% nickel.......	5.00	21.20
	P	1 centavo	250,000	95% copper, 5% tin and zinc	4.00	20.30
			520,000			
1934...........	P	5 centavos.......	200,000	75% copper, 25% nickel.......	5.00	21.20
	P	1 centavo	500,000	95% copper, 5% tin and zinc	4.00	20.30
	P	½ centavo.......	500,000	.... do	2.50	17.00
			1,200,000			
1935...........	P	1 centavo	**500,000**	.... do	4.00	20.30
1936...........	P	25 centavos.....	100,000	800 silver, 200 copper......	6.25	24.00
	P	10 centavos.....	500,000	.... do	2.50	17.90
	P	5 centavos.......	500,000	75% copper, 25% nickel.......	5.00	21.20
	P	1 centavo	500,000	95% copper, 5% tin and zinc	4.00	20.30
	P	½ centavo.......	600,000	.... do	2.50	17.00
			2,200,000			
1937...........	P	5 centavos.......	300,000	75% copper, 25% nickel.......	5.00	21.20
	P	1 centavo	1,000,000	95% copper, 5% tin and zinc	4.00	20.30
	P	½ centavo.......	1,000,000	.... do	2.50	17.00
			2,300,000			
1938...........	P	5 centavos.......	800,000	75% copper, 25% nickel.......	5.00	21.20
	P	1 centavo	2,000,000	95% copper, 5% tin and zinc	4.00	20.30
			2,800,000			
1940...........	P	5 centavos.......	800,000	75% copper, 25% nickel.......	5.00	21.20
	P	1 centavo	2,000,000	95% copper, 5% tin and zinc	4.00	20.30
			2,800,000			
1944...........	P	25 centavos.....	1,000,000	70% copper, 30% zinc..........	7.50	27.00
	P	10 centavos.....	2,000,000	.... do	5.50	24.00

NICARAGUA—CONTINUED

Calendar year	U.S. Mint	Denomination	Coinage during year	Metallic composition	Gross weight	Diameter
			Pieces		Grams	mm.
	P	5 centavos.......	2,000,000	.... do	3.75	21.00
	P	1 centavo	1,000,000	.... do	2.50	18.00
			6,000,000			
Total		....	**26,080,000**			

PANAMA, REPUBLIC OF

Calendar year	U.S. Mint	Denomination	Coinage during year	Metallic composition	Gross weight	Diameter
1904...........	P	1 peso	1,000,000	900 silver, 100 copper......	25.00	36.00
	P	1/2 peso...........	1,500,000	.... do	12.50	30.00
	P	10 centesimos.	1,000,000	.... do	5.00	24.00
	P	5 centesimos...	1,210,138	.... do	2.50	18.00
			4,710,138			
1905...........	P	1 peso	1,800,000	.... do	25.00	36.00
	P	1/2 peso...........	110,000	.... do	12.50	30.00
	P	10 centesimos.	125,000	.... do	5.00	24.00
	P	5 centesimos...	289,862	.... do	2.50	18.00
	P	2 1/2 centesimos	400,000	.... do	1.20	10.00
			2,724,862			
1907...........	P	2 1/2 centesimos	800,000	75% copper, 25% nickel.......	(*)	(*)
	P	1/2 centesimo...	1,000,000	.... do	(*)	(*)
			1,800,000			
1916...........	P	5 centesimos...	100,000	900 silver, 100 copper......	(*)	(*)
	P	2 1/2 centesimos	800,000	75% copper, 25% nickel.......	(*)	(*)
1929...........	P	5 centesimos...	500,000	.... do	5.00	21.00
	P	2 1/2 centesimos	1,000,000	.... do	3 1/3	18.00
			1,500,000			
1930...........	P	1/2 balboa.........	300,020	900 silver, 100 copper......	12.50	30.60
	P	1/4 balboa.........	400,020	.... do	6.25	24.30
	P	1/10 balboa	500,020	.... do	2.50	17.90
			1,200,060			
1931...........	P	1 balboa	200,020	900 silver, 100 copper......	26.73	38.10
	P	1/4 balboa.........	48,000	.... do	6.25	24.30
	P	1/10 balboa	200,000	.... do	2.50	17.90
			448,020			
1932...........	P	1/2 balboa.........	63,000	.... do	12.50	30.60
	P	1/4 balboa.........	126,000	.... do	6.25	24.30
	P	1/10 balboa	150,000	.... do	2.50	17.90
	P	5 centesimos...	332,800	75% copper, 25% nickel.......	5.00	21.00
			671,800			
1933...........	P	1/2 balboa.........	120,000	900 silver, 100 copper......	12.50	30.60

*Not available.

PANAMA, REPUBLIC OF—CONTINUED

Calendar year	*U.S. Mint*	*Denomination*	*Coinage during year*	*Metallic composition*	*Gross weight*	*Diameter*
			Pieces		*Grams*	*mm.*
	P	1/4 balboa.........	120,000	.... do	6.25	24.30
	P	1/10 balboa	100,000	.... do	2.50	17.90
			340,000			
1934...........	S	1 balboa	225,000	.... do	26.73	38.10
	S	1/2 balboa.........	90,000	.... do	12.50	30.60
	S	1/4 balboa.........	90,000	.... do	6.25	24.30
	S	1/10 balboa	75,000	.... do	2.50	17.90
			480,000			
1935...........	P	1 centesimo.....	**200,000**	95% copper, 5% zinc and tin	3.11	19.00
1937...........	P	1 centesimo.....	200,000	.... do	3.11	19.00
1940...........	P	2 1/2 centesimos	1,200,000	75% copper, 25% nickel.......	3 1/3	18.00
	P	1 1/4 centesimos	1,600,000	95% copper, 5% zinc and tin	3.11	20.00
			2,800,000			
1947...........	P	1 balboa	500,000	900 silver, 100 copper......	26.73	38.10
		1/2 balboa.........	450,000	.... do	12.50	30.60
	P	1/4 balboa.........	700,000	.... do	6.25	24.30
	P	1/10 balboa	1,000,000	.... do	2.50	17.90
			2,650,000			
1966...........	S	1/4 balboa.........	**7,440,000**	3-layer composite: outer cladding 75% copper, 25% nickel bonded to core of pure copper.	5.67	24.26
1967: Regular issue:	S	1/2 balboa.........	1,300,000	3-layer composite: outer cladding 800 silver, 200 copper bonded to core of approximately 200 silver, 800 copper......	11.50	30.61
	S	1/10 balboa	1,000,000	3-layer composite: outer cladding 75% copper, 25% nickel bonded to core of pure copper.	5.67	24.26
	S	5 centesimos...	2,600,000	75% copper, 25% nickel.......	5.00	21.21

PANAMA, REPUBLIC OF—CONTINUED

Calendar year	U.S. Mint	Denomination	Coinage during year	Metallic composition	Gross weight	Diameter
			Pieces		Grams	mm.
	S	1 centesimo.....	7,600,000	95% copper, 5% zinc............	3.11	19.05
			12,500,000			
1967: Proof coins:	S	1 balboa	12,701	900 silver, 100 copper......	26.73	38.10
	S	1/2 balboa.........	12,701	3-layer composite: outer cladding 800 silver, 200 copper bonded to core of approximately 200 silver, 800 copper......	11.50	30.61
	S	1/4 balboa.........	12,701	3-layer composite: outer cladding 75% copper, 25% nickel bonded to core of pure copper .	5.67	24.26
	S	1/10 balboa	12,701	.... do	2.27	17.91
	S	5 centesimos...	12,701	75% copper, 25% nickel.......	5.00	21.21
	S	1 centesimo.....	12,701	95% copper, 5% zinc............	3.11	19.00
			76,206			
			12,576,206			
1968: Regular issue:	S	1/2 balboa.........	1,000,000	3-layer composite: outer cladding 800 silver, 200 copper bonded to core of approximately 200 silver, 800 copper......	11.50	30.61
	S	1/4 balboa.........	1,220,000	3-layer composite: outer cladding 75% copper, 25% nickel bonded to core of pure copper .	5.67	24.26
	D	1/10 balboa	5,000,000	.... do	2.27	17.91
	D	5 centesimos...	5,536,000	75% copper, 25% nickel.......	5.00	21.21
	S	.... do	464,000	.... do	5.00	21.21

PANAMA, REPUBLIC OF—CONTINUED

Calendar year	U.S. Mint	Denomination	Coinage during year	Metallic composition	Gross weight	Diameter
			Pieces		Grams	mm.
	D	1 centesimo.....	24,740,000	95% copper, 5% zinc...........	3.11	19.05
	S	.... do	260,000	.... do	3.11	19.05
		....	**38,220,000**			
Proof coins:	S	1 balboa	43,193	900 silver, 100 copper	26.73	38.10
	S	½ balboa.........	43,193	3-layer composite: outer cladding 800 silver, 200 copper bonded to core of approximately 200 silver, 800 copper	11.50	30.61
	S	¼ balboa.........	43,193	3-layer composite: outer cladding 75% copper, 25% nickel bonded to core of pure copper .	5.67	24.26
	S	1/10 balboa	43,193	.... do	2.27	17.91
	S	5 centesimos...	43,193	75% copper, 25% nickel.......	5.00	21.21
	S	1 centesimo.....	43,193	95% copper, 5% zinc...........	3.11	19.05
			259,158			
			38,479,158			
1969: Proof coins:	S	1 balboa	14,000	900 silver, 100 copper	26.73	38.10
	S	½ balboa.........	14,000	3-layer composite: outer cladding 800 silver, 200 copper bonded to core of approximately 200 silver, 800 copper	11.50	30.61
	S	¼ balboa.........	14,000	3-layer composite: outer cladding 75% copper, 25% nickel bonded to core of pure copper .	5.67	24.26
	S	1/10 balboa	14,000	.... do	2.27	17.91
	S	5 centesimos...	14,000	75% copper, 25% nickel.......	5.00	21.21

PANAMA, REPUBLIC OF—CONTINUED

Calendar year	U.S. Mint	Denomination	Coinage during year	Metallic composition	Gross weight	Diameter
			Pieces		Grams	mm.
	S	1 centesimo.....	14,000	95% copper, 5% zinc...........	3.11	19.05
			84,000			
1970 [1].........	S	1 balboa	13,304	900 silver, ... 100 copper	26.73	38.10
	S	1/2 balboa.........	315,528	3-layer composite: outer cladding 800 silver, 200 copper bonded to core of approximately 200 silver, 800 copper	11.50	30.61
	S	1/4 balboa.........	1,089,528	3-layer composite: outer cladding 75% copper, 25% nickel bonded to core of pure copper.	5.67	24.26
	S	1/10 balboa	1,389,528	.... do	2.27	17.91
	S	5 centesimos...	4,417,528	75% copper, 25% nickel.......	5.00	21.21
	S	1 centesimo.....	9,528	95% copper, 5% zinc...........	3.11	19.05
			7,234,944			
1971...........	S	1/2 balboa.........	294,000	3-layer composite: outer cladding 800 silver, 200 copper bonded to core of approximately 200 silver, 800 copper	11.50	30.61
	S	1/4 balboa.........	920,000	3-layer composite: outer cladding 75% copper, 25% nickel bonded to core of pure copper.	5.67	24.26
	S	1/10 balboa	6,120,000	.... do	2.268	17.91
	S	5 centesimos...	592,000	75% copper, 25% nickel.......	5.00	21.21
			7,926,000			
1972 [2].........	S	5 balboas	80,000	900 silver, 100 copper	35.12	39.00
	S	1 balboa	17,559	.... do	26.73	38.10

Footnotes at end of table.

PANAMA, REPUBLIC OF—CONTINUED

Calendar year	*U.S. Mint*	*Denomination*	*Coinage during year*	*Metallic composition*	*Gross weight*	*Diameter*
			Pieces		*Grams*	*mm.*
	S	1/2 balboa.........	10,696	3-layer composite: outer cladding 800 silver, 200 copper bonded to core of approximately 200 silver, 800 copper......	11.50	30.61
	S	1/4 balboa.........	10,696	3-layer composite: outer cladding 75% copper, 25% nickel bonded to core of pure copper.	5.67	24.26
	S	1/10 balboa	10,696	.... do	2.268	17.91
	S	5 centesimos...	10,696	75% copper, 25% nickel.......	5.00	21.21
	S	1 centesimo.....	10,696	95% copper, 5% zinc............	3.11	19.05
			151,039			
1973 [3].........	S	1 balboa	23,413	900 silver, 100 copper......	35.12	39.00
	S	1/2 balboa.........	1,013,332	3-layer composite: outer cladding 75% copper, 25% nickel bonded to core of pure copper.	11.34	30.61
	S	1/4 balboa.........	813,332	.... do	5.67	24.26
	S	1/10 balboa	10,013,332	.... do	2.268	17.91
	S	5 centesimos...	5,013,332	75% copper, 25% nickel.......	5.00	21.21
	S	1 centesimo.....	13,332	95% copper, 5% zinc............	3.11	19.05
			16,890,073			
1974 [4].........	S	1 balboa	30,161	900 silver, 100 copper......	26.73	38.10
	S	1/2 balboa.........	16,946	3-layer composite: outer cladding 75% copper, 25% nickel bonded to core of pure copper.	11.34	30.61
	S	1/4 balboa.........	16,946	.... do	5.67	24.26
	S	1/10 balboa	16,946	.... do	2.268	17.91
	S	5 centesimos...	16,946	75% copper, 25% nickel.......	5.00	21.21

Footnotes at end of table.

PANAMA, REPUBLIC OF—CONTINUED

Calendar year	U.S. Mint	Denomination	Coinage during year	Metallic composition	Gross weight	Diameter
			Pieces		Grams	mm.
	P	2½ centesimos	2,000,000	3-layer composite: outer cladding 75% copper, 25% nickel bonded to core of pure copper .	1.63	15.00
	S	1 centesimo.....	16,946	95% copper, 5% zinc...........	3.11	19.05
			2,114,891			
1975...........	S	1 balboa [5]	29,566	900 silver, 100 copper......	26.73	38.10
	S	½ balboa [5]	17,521	3-layer composite: outer cladding 75% copper, 25% nickel bonded to core of pure copper .	11.34	30.61
	D	.... do	1,200,018	.... do	11.34	30.61
	S	¼ balboa [5]	17,521	.... do	5.67	24.26
	D	.... do	1,500,008	.... do	5.67	24.26
	S	1/10 balboa [5]	17,521	.... do	2.268	17.91
	D	.... do	500,002	.... do	2.268	17.91
	S	5 centesimos [5]	17,521	75% copper, 25% nickel.......	5.00	21.21
	D	.... do	5,000,038	.... do	5.00	21.21
	P	2½ centesimos	1,000,000	3-layer composite: outer cladding 75% copper, 25% nickel bonded to core of pure copper .	1.63	15.00
	S	1 centesimo [5] ..	17,521	95% copper, 5% zinc...........	3.11	19.05
	P	.... do [6]	20,000,000	.... do	3.11	19.05
			29,317,237			
1977...........	P	1 centesimo [7] ..	**10,000,000**	.... do	3.11	19.05
1978...........	P	.... do [7]	**10,000,000**	.... do	3.11	19.05
1979...........	P	½ balboa.........	1,000,000	3-layer composite: outer cladding 75% copper, 25% nickel bonded to core of pure copper .	11.34	30.61
	P	¼ balboa.........	2,000,000	.... do	5.67	24.26
	P	1 centesimo [7] ..	10,000,000	95% copper, 5% zinc...........	3.11	19.05
			13,000,000			

Footnotes at end of table.

PANAMA, REPUBLIC OF—CONTINUED

Calendar year	*U.S. Mint*	*Denomination*	*Coinage during year*	*Metallic composition*	*Gross weight*	*Diameter*
			Pieces		*Grams*	*mm.*
1980	P	1/2 balboa	1,000,000	3-layer composite: outer cladding 75% copper, 25% nickel bonded to core of pure copper	11.34	30.61
	P	1/4 balboa	2,000,000	.... do	5.67	24.26
	P	1/10 balboa	5,000,000	.... do	2.268	17.91
	P	1 centesimo [7]	10,000,000	95% copper, 5% zinc	3.11	19.05
			18,000,000			
Total			**193,838,428**			

[1] Production includes 3,776 proof 1 balboa coins and 9,527 proof sets.
[2] Consists of 10,000 proof coins and 70,000 uncirculated coins.
[3] Production includes 13,332 proof coin sets plus 10,081 proof 1 balboa coins.
[4] Includes 13,215 proof 1 balboa coins and 16,946 proof sets.
[5] Proof coins.
[6] Includes 10 million coins manufactured at U.S. Bullion Depository, West Point.
[7] Manufactured at U.S. Bullion Depository, West Point.
*Not Available.

PERU

Calendar year	*U.S. Mint*	*Denomination*	*Coinage during year*	*Metallic composition*	*Gross weight*	*Diameter*
1916	P	1 libra [1]	500,000	916 2/3 gold, 83 1/3 copper	7.99	22.1
	P	1 sol [2]	1,101,278	900 silver, 100 copper	25.00	36.4
			1,601,278			
1917	P	1 libra [1]	900,000	916 2/3 gold, 83 1/3 copper	7.99	22.1
	P	1/3 pound [1]	10,000	.... do	1.60	14.5
			910,000			
1918	P	20 centavos	2,500,000	75% copper, 25% nickel	7.00	24.0
	P	10 centavos	3,000,000	.... do	4.00	20.0
	P	5 centavos	4,000,000	.... do	3.00	17.0
			9,500,000			
1919	P	1 libra [1]	54,195	916 2/3 gold, 83 1/3 copper	7.99	22.1
	D	.... do	300,000	.... do	7.99	22.1
	P	20 centavos	1,250,000	75% copper, 25% nickel	7.00	24.0
	P	10 centavos	2,500,000	.... do	4.00	20.0
	P	5 centavos	10,000,000	.... do	3.00	17.0
	P	2 centavos	3,000,000	95% copper, 3% tin, 2% zinc	10.00	24.0
	P	1 centavo	4,000,000	.... do	5.00	19.0
			21,104,195			

PERU—CONTINUED

Calendar year	U.S. Mint	Denomination	Coinage during year	Metallic composition	Gross weight	Diameter
			Pieces		Grams	mm.
1920	P	20 centavos	1,464,000	75% copper, 25% nickel	7.00	24.00
	P	10 centavos	3,080,000	.... do	4.00	20.00
			4,544,000			
1921	P	20 centavos	8,536,000	.... do	7.00	24.00
	P	10 centavos	6,920,000	.... do	4.00	20.00
			15,456,000			
1923	P	1 sol	2,369,000	500 silver, 400 copper, 100 nickel	25.00	37.00
	P	5 centavos	2,000,000	75% copper, 25% nickel	3.00	17.00
			4,369,000			
1924	P	1 sol	**3,113,196**	500 silver, 400 copper, 100 nickel	25.00	37.00
1925	P	1 sol	**1,291,000**	.... do	25.00	37.00
1926	P	1 sol	2,157,000	.... do	25.00	37.00
	P	20 centavos	2,500,000	75% copper, 25% nickel	7.00	24.00
	P	10 centavos	3,000,000	.... do	4.00	20.00
	P	5 centavos	4,000,000	.... do	3.00	17.00
			11,657,000			
1942	P	1/2 sol	4,000,000	70% copper, 30% zinc	7.50	27.00
	S	.... do	1,668,000	.... do	7.50	27.00
	P	20 centavos	500,000	.... do	7.00	24.00
	S	.... do	500,000	.... do	7.00	24.00
	P	10 centavos	2,000,000	.... do	4.00	20.00
	S	.... do	2,000,000	.... do	4.00	20.00
	P	5 centavos	4,000,000	.... do	3.00	17.00
	S	.... do	4,000,000	.... do	3.00	17.00
			18,668,000			
1943	S	1/2 sol	6,332,000	.... do	7.50	27.00
	S	20 centavos	500,000	.... do	7.00	24.00
	S	10 centavos	2,000,000	.... do	4.00	20.00
	S	5 centavos	4,000,000	.... do	3.00	17.00
			12,832,000			
1944	P	1 sol	10,000,000	.... do	14.00	33.00
	P	1/2 sol	4,000,000	.... do	7.50	27.00
	P	20 centavos	1,000,000	.... do	7.00	24.00
	P	10 centavos	4,000,000	.... do	4.00	20.00
	P	5 centavos	8,000,000	.... do	3.00	17.00
			27,000,000			
1945	P	50 centavos	4,000,000	.... do	7.50	27.00
1975	P	1 sol	309,697,810	.... do	3.20	21.00
1976	P	1 sol	112,560,000	.... do	3.20	21.00

Footnotes at end of table.

PERU—CONTINUED

Calendar year	U.S. Mint	Denomination	Coinage during year	Metallic composition	Gross weight	Diameter
			Pieces		Grams	mm.
	P	1/2 sol	200,664,000	.... do	2.15	18.00
			313,224,000			
1977	P	1 sol	2,100,000	.... do	3.20	21.00
Total			**761,067,479**			

[1] Gold planchets.
[2] Silver planchets.

PHILIPPINES

Calendar year	U.S. Mint	Denomination	Coinage during year	Metallic composition	Gross weight	Diameter
1903	P	1 peso [1]	2,794,017	900 silver, 100 copper	26.96	38.00
	S	.... do	11,361,000	.... do	26.96	38.00
	P	50 centavos [1]	3,104,177	.... do	13.48	31.00
	P	20 centavos [1]	5,355,347	.... do	5.39	23.00
	S	.... do	150,080	.... do	5.39	23.00
	P	10 centavos [1]	5,105,216	.... do	2.69	18.00
	S	.... do	1,200,000	.... do	2.69	18.00
	P	5 centavos [1]	8,912,558	75% copper, 25% nickel	5.00	21.00
	P	1 centavo [1]	10,792,558	95% copper, 5% zinc and tin	5.18	25.00
	P	1/2 centavo [1]	12,086,558	.... do	2.59	18.00
			60,861,511			
1904	P	1 peso [2]	11,365	900 silver, 100 copper	26.96	38.00
	S	.... do	6,600,000	.... do	26.96	38.00
	P	50 centavos [2]	11,365	.... do	13.48	31.00
	S	.... do	2,160,000	.... do	13.48	31.00
	P	20 centavos [2]	11,365	.... do	5.39	23.00
	S	.... do	2,060,000	.... do	5.39	23.00
	P	10 centavos [2]	11,365	.... do	2.69	18.00
	S	.... do	5,040,000	.... do	2.69	18.00
	P	5 centavos [3]	1,086,355	75% copper, 25% nickel	5.00	21.00
	P	1 centavo [3]	17,051,755	95% copper, 5% zinc and tin	5.18	25.00
	P	1/2 centavo [3]	5,665,355	.... do	2.59	18.00
			39,708,925			
1905	P	1 peso [2]	475	900 silver, 100 copper	26.96	38.00
	S	.... do	6,116,000	.... do	26.96	38.00
	P	50 centavos [2]	475	.... do	13.48	31.00
	S	.... do	852,000	.... do	13.48	31.00
	P	20 centavos [2]	475	.... do	5.39	23.00
	S	.... do	420,000	.... do	5.39	23.00
	P	10 centavos [2]	475	.... do	2.69	18.00
	P	5 centavos [2]	471	75% copper, 25% nickel	5.00	21.00

PHILIPPINES—CONTINUED

Calendar year	U.S. Mint	Denomination	Coinage during year	Metallic composition	Gross weight	Diameter
			Pieces		Grams	mm.
	P	1 centavo [4]	10,000,471	95% copper, 5% zinc and tin	5.18	25.00
	P	½ centavo [2]	471	.... do	2.59	18.00
			17,391,313			
1906 (Coined under act of Mar. 2, 1903)	P	1 peso [2]	501	900 silver, 100 copper	26.96	38.00
	S	.... do	201,000	.... do	26.96	38.00
	P	50 centavos [2]	501	.... do	13.48	31.00
	P	20 centavos [2]	501	.... do	5.39	23.00
	P	10 centavos [2]	501	.... do	2.69	18.00
	P	5 centavos [2]	500	75% copper, 25% nickel	5.00	21.00
	P	1 centavo [2]	500	95% copper, 5% zinc and tin	5.18	25.00
	P	½ centavo [2]	500	.... do	2.59	18.00
			204,504			
1907 (Coined under act of June 23, 1906)	S	1 peso	10,218,000	800 silver, 200 copper	20.00	36.00
	P	50 centavos	1,200,625	750 silver, 250 copper	10.00	27.00
	S	.... do	2,112,000	.... do	10.00	27.00
	P	20 centavos	1,250,651	.... do	4.00	21.00
	S	.... do	3,165,000	.... do	4.00	21.00
	P	10 centavos	1,500,781	.... do	2.00	17.00
	S	.... do	4,930,000	.... do	2.00	17.00
			24,377,057			
1908	P	1 peso	501	800 silver, 200 copper	20.00	36.00
	S	.... do	20,954,944	.... do	20.00	36.00
	P	50 centavos	501	750 silver, 250 copper	10.00	27.00
	S	.... do	1,601,000	.... do	10.00	27.00
	P	20 centavos	501	.... do	4.00	21.00
	S	.... do	1,535,000	.... do	4.00	21.00
	P	10 centavos	501	.... do	2.00	17.00
	S	.... do	3,363,911	.... do	2.00	17.00
	P	centavo	500	75% copper, 25% nickel	5.00	21.00
	P	1 centavo	500	95% copper, 5% zinc and tin	5.18	25.00
	S	.... do	2,187,000	.... do	5.18	25.00
	P	½ centavo	500	.... do	2.59	18.00
			29,645,359			
1909	S	1 peso	7,578,000	800 silver, 200 copper	20.00	36.00
	S	50 centavos	528,000	750 silver, 250 copper	10.00	27.00

Footnotes at end of table.

PHILIPPINES—CONTINUED

Calendar year	U.S. Mint	Denomination	Coinage during year	Metallic composition	Gross weight	Diameter
			Pieces		Grams	mm.
	S	20 centavos.....	450,000	.... do	4.00	21.00
	S	10 centavos.....	312,199	.... do	2.00	17.00
	S	1 centavo	1,737,612	95% copper, 5% zinc and tin	5.18	25.00
			10,605,811			
1910...........	S	1 peso	3,153,559	800 silver, 200 copper......	20.00	36.00
	S	20 centavos.....	500,259	750 silver, 250 copper......	4.00	21.00
	S	1 centavo	2,700,000	95% copper, 5% zinc and tin	5.18	25.00
			6,353,818			
1911...........	S	1 peso	463,000	800 silver, 200 copper......	20.00	36.00
	S	20 centavos.....	505,000	750 silver, 250 copper......	4.00	21.00
	S	10 centavos.....	1,000,505	.... do	2.00	17.00
	S	1 centavo	4,803,800	95% copper, 5% zinc and tin	5.18	25.00
			6,772,305			
1912...........	S	1 peso	680,000	800 silver, 200 copper......	20.00	36.00
	S	20 centavos.....	750,000	750 silver, 250 copper......	4.00	21.00
	S	10 centavos.....	1,010,000	.... do	2.00	17.00
	S	1 centavo	3,001,000	95% copper, 5% zinc and tin	5.18	25.00
			5,441,000			
1913...........	S	20 centavos.....	948,565	750 silver, 250 copper......	4.00	21.00
	S	10 centavos.....	1,360,693	.... do	2.00	17.00
	S	1 centavo	5,000,000	95% copper, 5% zinc and tin	5.18	25.00
			7,309,258			
1914...........	S	20 centavos.....	795,000	750 silver, 250 copper......	4.00	21.00
	S	10 centavos.....	1,180,000	.... do	2.00	17.00
	S	1 centavo	5,000,500	95% copper, 5% zinc and tin	5.18	25.00
			6,975,500			
1915...........	S	20 centavos.....	655,000	750 silver, 250 copper......	4.00	21.00
	S	10 centavos.....	450,000	.... do	2.00	17.00
	S	1 centavo	2,500,000	95% copper, 5% zinc and tin	5.18	25.00
			3,605,000			
1916...........	S	20 centavos.....	1,435,000	750 silver, 250 copper......	4.00	21.00

PHILIPPINES—CONTINUED

Calendar year	U.S. Mint	Denomination	Coinage during year	Metallic composition	Gross weight	Diameter
			Pieces		Grams	mm.
	S	5 centavos......	300,000	75% copper, 25% nickel.......	5.00	21.00
	S	1 centavo	4,330,000	95% copper, 5% zinc and tin	5.18	25.00
			6,065,000			
1917...........	S	50 centavos.....	674,369	750 silver, 250 copper......	10.00	27.00
	S	20 centavos.....	3,150,656	.... do	4.00	21.00
	S	10 centavos.....	5,991,148	.... do	2.00	17.00
	S	5 centavos......	2,300,000	75% copper, 25% nickel.......	5.00	21.00
	S	1 centavo	7,070,000	95% copper, 5% zinc and tin	5.18	25.00
			19,186,173			
1918...........	S	50 centavos.....	2,202,000	750 silver, 250 copper......	10.00	27.00
	S	20 centavos.....	5,560,000	.... do	4.00	21.00
	S	10 centavos.....	8,420,000	.... do	2.00	17.00
	S	5 centavos......	2,780,000	75% copper, 25% nickel.......	5.00	21.00
	S	1 centavo	11,660,000	95% copper, 5% zinc and tin	5.18	25.00
			30,622,000			
1919...........	S	50 centavos.....	1,200,000	750 silver, 250 copper......	10.00	27.00
	S	20 centavos.....	850,000	.... do	4.00	21.00
	S	10 centavos.....	1,630,000	.... do	2.00	17.00
	S	5 centavos......	1,220,000	75% copper, 25% nickel.......	5.00	21.00
	S	1 centavo	4,540,000	95% copper, 5% zinc and tin	5.18	25.00
			9,440,000			
1920...........	S	1 centavo	**2,500,000**	.... do	5.18	25.00
1944...........	S	50 centavos.....	19,187,000	750 silver, 250 copper......	10.00	27.00
	D	20 centavos.....	28,596,000	.... do	4.00	21.00
	D	10 centavos.....	31,592,000	.... do	2.00	17.00
	P	5 centavos......	21,198,000	65% copper, 23% zinc, 12% nickel.......	4.87	21.00
	S	.... do	14,040,000	.... do	4.87	21.00
	S	1 centavo	58,000,000	95% copper, 5% zinc...........	5.18	25.00
			172,613,000			
1945...........	S	50 centavos.....	18,120,000	750 silver, 250 copper......	10.00	27.00
	D	20 centavos.....	82,804,000	.... do	4.00	21.00
	D	10 cenatvos.....	137,208,000	.... do	2.00	17.00

PHILIPPINES—CONTINUED

Calendar year	U.S. Mint	Denomination	Coinage during year	Metallic composition	Gross weight	Diameter
			Pieces		Grams	mm.
	S	5 centavos......	72,796,000	65% copper, 23% zinc, 12% nickel.......	4.87	21.00
	S	1 centavo	78,485,798	95% copper, 5% zinc...........	5.18	25.00
			389,413,798			
1946	S	50 centavos.....	6,288,000	750 silver, 250 copper......	10.00	27.00
	D	20 centavos.....	7,400,000	.... do	4.00	21.00
	D	10 centavos.....	6,384,000	.... do	2.00	17.00
	S	5 centavos......	28,320,000	65% copper, 23% zinc, 12% nickel.......	4.87	21.00
			48,392,000			
1947...........	S	1 peso	100,000	800 silver, 200 copper......	20.00	36.00
	S	50 centavos.....	200,000	750 silver, 250 copper......	10.00	27.00
			300,000			
1958...........	P	50 centavos.....	1,000	70% copper, 18% zinc, 12% nickel.......	10.22	30.60
	P	25 centavos.....	1,000	.... do	5.11	24.30
	P	10 centavos.....	1,000	.... do	2.04	17.90
	P	5 centavos......	10,000,000	80% copper, 20% zinc..........	4.85	21.20
	P	1 centavo	20,000,000	95% copper, 5% zinc...........	3.11	19.10
			30,003,000			
1959...........	P	50 centavos.....	4,999,000	70% copper, 18% zinc, 12% nickel.......	10.22	30.60
	P	25 centavos.....	9,999,000	.... do	5.11	24.30
	P	10 centavos.....	9,999,000	.... do	2.04	17.90
	P	5 centavos.......	10,000,000	80% copper, 20% zinc..........	4.85	21.20
			34,997,000			
1960...........	P	25 centavos.....	10,000,000	70% copper, 18% zinc, and nickel........	5.11	24.30
	P	10 centavos.....	30,000,000	.... do	2.04	17.90
	P	1 centavo	20,000,000	95% copper, 5% zinc...........	3.11	19.10
			60,000,000			
1961...........	P	1 peso	100,000	900 silver, 100 copper......	26.73	38.10
	P	1/2 peso...........	100,000	.... do	12.50	30.60
	P	10 centavos.....	40,000,000	70% copper, 18% zinc, 12% nickel.......	2.04	17.90

PHILIPPINES—CONTINUED

Calendar year	U.S. Mint	Denomination	Coinage during year	Metallic composition	Gross weight	Diameter
			Pieces		Grams	mm.
	P	5 centavos.......	40,000,000	80% copper,		
				20% zinc..........	4.85	21.20
	P	1 centavo	20,000,000	95% copper,		
				5% zinc...........	3.11	19.10
			100,200,000			
1962...........	P	25 centavos.....	40,000,000	70% copper,		
				18% zinc,		
				12% nickel.......	5.11	24.30
	P	10 centavos.....	50,000,000	.... do	2.04	17.90
	P	5 centavos.......	40,000,000	80% copper,		
				20% zinc..........	4.85	21.20
	P	1 centavo	6,485,000	95% copper,		
				5% zinc...........	3.11	19.10
			136,485,000			
1963...........	P	10 centavos.....	50,000,000	70% copper,		
				18% zinc,		
				12% nickel.......	2.04	17.90
	P	5 centavos.......	50,000,000	80% copper,		
				20% zinc..........	4.85	21.20
	P	1 centavo	153,515,000	95% copper,		
				5% zinc...........	3.11	19.10
			253,515,000			
1967...........	S	1 peso [5]	100,000	900 silver,		
				100 copper......	26.73	38.10
	S	25 sentimos.....	40,000,000	70% copper,		
				18% zinc,		
				12% nickel.......	4.00	21.00
	S	10 sentimos.....	50,000,000	.... do	2.00	17.90
	S	5 sentimos.......	40,000,000	60% copper,		
				40% zinc..........	2.50	18.40
	P	1 sentimo	10,000,000	95% aluminum,		
				5% magnesium	.49	15.25
			140,100,000			
1968...........	P	50 sentimos.....	20,000,000	70% copper,		
				18% zinc,		
				12% nickel.......	8.00	27.50
	S	25 sentimos.....	10,000,000	.... do	4.00	21.00
	P	10 sentimos.....	50,000,000	.... do	2.00	17.90
	S	.... do	10,000,000	.... do	2.00	17.90
	S	5 sentimos.......	50,000,000	60% copper,		
				40% zinc..........	2.50	18.40
	P	1 sentimo	27,940,000	95% aluminum,		
				5% magnesium	.49	15.25
			167,940,000			
1969...........	S	1 peso [6]	100,000	900 silver,		
				100 copper......	26.64	38.13
	D	25 sentimos.....	10,000,000	70% copper,		
				18% zinc,		
				12% nickel.......	4.00	21.00

PHILIPPINES—CONTINUED

Calendar year	*U.S. Mint*	*Denomination*	*Coinage during year*	*Metallic composition*	*Gross weight*	*Diameter*
			Pieces		*Grams*	*mm.*
	D	10 sentimos.....	40,000,000	.... do	2.00	17.90
	P	1 sentimo	12,060,000	95% aluminum, 5% magnesium	.49	15.25
			62,160,000			
1970...........	S	1 peso [7]	30,000	900 silver, 100 copper......	26.64	38.13
	S	25 sentimos.....	20,000,000	70% copper, 18% zinc, 12% nickel.......	4.00	21.00
	D	.... do	20,000,000	.... do	4.00	21.00
	D	10 sentimos.....	50,000,000	.... do	2.00	17.90
	S	5 sentimos.......	5,000,000	60% copper, 40% zinc..........	2.50	18.40
	P	1 sentimo	130,000,000	95% aluminum, 5% magnesium	.49	15.25
			225,030,000			
1971...........	D	50 sentimos.....	10,000,000	70% copper, 18% zinc, 12% nickel.......	8.00	27.50
	D	25 sentimos.....	60,000,000	.... do	4.00	21.00
	D	10 sentimos.....	80,000,000	.... do	2.00	17.90
	D	5 sentimos.......	50,000,000	60% copper, 40% zinc..........	2.50	18.40
			200,000,000			
1972...........	D	1 peso	121,821,000	70% copper, 18% zinc, 12% nickel.......	14.50	33.50
	S	25 sentimos.....	59,572,000	.... do	4.00	21.00
	D	10 sentimos.....	121,390,000	.... do	2.00	17.90
	D	5 sentimos.......	71,744,000	60% copper, 40% zinc..........	2.50	18.40
			374,527,000			
1973...........	D	1 peso	28,179,000	70% copper, 18% zinc, 12% nickel.......	14.50	33.50
	D	50 sentimos.....	30,000,000	.... do	8.00	27.50
	S	25 sentimos.....	30,428,000	.... do	4.00	21.00
	D	10 sentimos.....	18,610,000	.... do	2.00	17.90
	D	5 sentimos.......	18,256,000	60% copper, 40% zinc..........	2.50	18.40
			125,473,000			
1974...........	D	1 piso..............	9,127,000	70% copper, 18% zinc, 12% nickel.......	14.50	33.50
	S	.... do	10,244,000	.... do	14.50	33.50
	D	50 sentimos.....	5,000,000	.... do	8.00	27.50
	S	25 sentimos.....	5,000,000	.... do	4.00	21.00

Footnotes at end of table.

PHILIPPINES—CONTINUED

Calendar year	U.S. Mint	Denomination	Coinage during year	Metallic composition	Gross weight	Diameter
			Pieces		Grams	mm.
	D	10 sentimos.....	10,000,000	.... do	2.00	17.90
	D	5 sentimos.......	10,000,000	60% copper, 40% zinc..........	2.50	18.40
			49,371,000			
1975 [8].........	D	1 piso..............	10,875,178	70% copper, 18% zinc, 12% nickel.......	14.50	33.50
	S	.... do	34,766,000	.... do	14.50	33.50
	D	50 sentimos.....	4,000	.... do	8.00	27.50
	S	.... do	5,010,000	.... do	8.00	27.50
	S	25 sentimos.....	10,010,000	.... do	4.00	21.00
	D	10 sentimos.....	207,792	.... do	2.00	17.90
	S	.... do	60,010,000	.... do	2.00	17.90
	D	5 sentimos.......	24,867	60% copper, 40% zinc..........	2.50	18.40
	S	.... do	90,010,000	.... do	2.50	18.40
	S	1 sentimo	105,010,000	95% aluminum, 5% magnesium	.49	15.25
	P	.... do	60,000,000	.... do	.49	15.25
			375,927,837			
1976...........	S	1 piso..............	30,000,000	75% copper, 25% nickel.......	9.50	29.00
	S	25 sentimos.....	10,000,000	.... do	4.00	21.00
	S	10 sentimos.....	50,000,000	.... do	2.00	18.00
	P	5 sentimos.......	98,928,000	60% copper, 40% zinc..........	2.50	(9)
	P	1 sentimo	60,190,000	95% aluminum, 5% magnesium	1.20	(10)
			249,118,000			
1977...........	P	5 sentimos.......	1,088,000	60% copper, 40% zinc..........	2.50	(9)
Total			**3,483,718,169**			

[1] Includes 2,558 proof coins.
[2] Proof coins.
[3] Includes 11,365 proof coins.
[4] Includes 471 proof coins.
[5] In commemoration of the 25th Anniversary of Bataan Day, 1942–67.
[6] Commemorative honoring General Emelio Anguinaldo, bearing years 1869–1969.
[7] In commemoration of Pope Paul's visit to the Philippines.
[8] Includes 10,000 proof sets.
[9] 8 scallops: outside scallops measuring 19 mm. inside scallops measuring 17 mm.
[10] Square coin measuring 19 mm. diagonally and 16.5 mm. across flats.

POLAND

Calendar year	U.S. Mint	Denomination	Coinage during year	Metallic composition	Gross weight	Diameter
1924...........	P	2 zloty.............	**4,400,000**	750 silver, 250 copper......	10	27.00
1925...........	P	2 zloty.............	**1,600,000**	.... do	10	27.00
Total			**6,000,000**			

SAUDI ARABIA

Calendar year	U.S. Mint	Denomination	Coinage during year	Metallic composition	Gross weight	Diameter
			Pieces		Grams	mm.
1944	P	1 riyal	**30,000,000**	$916\frac{2}{3}$ silver, $83\frac{1}{3}$ copper	11.66	30.50
1945	P	Gold disks	91,210	$916\frac{2}{3}$ gold, $83\frac{1}{3}$ copper	31.95	30.60
	P	1 riyal	17,000,000	$916\frac{2}{3}$ silver, $83\frac{1}{3}$ copper	11.66	30.50
			17,091,210			
1946	P	1 riyal	9,288,000	do	11.66	30.50
	P	$\frac{1}{2}$ riyal	1,000,000	do	5.83	24.38
	P	$\frac{1}{4}$ riyal	2,000,000	do	2.92	19.50
			12,288,000			
1947	P	Gold disks	121,364	$916\frac{2}{3}$ gold, $83\frac{1}{3}$ copper	7.99	22.05
	P	1 riyal	14,212,000	$916\frac{2}{3}$ silver, $83\frac{1}{3}$ copper	11.66	30.50
	P	$\frac{1}{2}$ riyal	500,000	do	5.83	24.38
	P	$\frac{1}{4}$ riyal	1,000,000	do	2.92	19.50
	P	1 girsh	7,150,000	75% copper, 25% nickel	6.50	26.75
	P	$\frac{1}{2}$ girsh	10,850,000	do	5.50	23.80
	P	$\frac{1}{4}$ girsh	21,500,000	do	4.25	20.80
			55,333,364			
1949	P	1 riyal	**10,000,000**	$916\frac{2}{3}$ silver, $83\frac{1}{3}$ copper	11.66	30.50
Total			**124,712,574**			

SIAM (THAILAND)

Calendar year	U.S. Mint	Denomination	Coinage during year	Metallic composition	Gross weight	Diameter
1918	P	1 satang [1]	**10,000,000**	95% copper, 4% tin, 1% zinc	5	22.50
1919	P	1 satang [1]	**10,000,000**	do	5	22.50
Total			**20,000,000**			

[1] Coin has a central hole measuring 6 mm. in diameter.

SURINAM (NETHERLANDS GUIANA)

Calendar year	U.S. Mint	Denomination	Coinage during year	Metallic composition	Gross weight	Diameter
1941	P	25 centstukken	300,000	640 silver, 360 copper	3.58	19.00
	P	10 centstukken	500,000	do	1.40	15.00
			800,000			
1942	P	25 centstukken	300,000	do	3.58	19.00
	P	10 centstukken	1,500,000	do	1.40	15.00
	P	1 centstukken	2,000,000	95% copper, 4% zinc, 1% tin	2.50	19.00
			3,800,000			
1943	P	25 centstukken	2,000,000	640 silver, 360 copper	3.58	19.00
	P	10 centstukken	4,000,000	do	1.40	15.00

SURINAM (NETHERLANDS GUIANA)—CONTINUED

Calendar year	U.S. Mint	Denomination	Coinage during year	Metallic composition	Gross weight	Diameter
			Pieces		Grams	mm.
	P	1 centstukken..	4,000,000	70% copper, 30% zinc..........	2.50	19.00
			10,000,000			
1944...........	P	5 centstukken..	**6,595,000**	Nickel-silver 12% and 18%.	4.50	18.00
Total			**21,195,000**			

SYRIA

Calendar year	U.S. Mint	Denomination	Coinage during year	Metallic composition	Gross weight	Diameter
1948...........	P	50 piastres	3,000,000	600 silver, 400 copper......	5.00	24.00
	P	25 piastres	4,000,000	.... do	2.50	20.00
			7,000,000			
1951...........	P	1 pound	250,000	900 gold, 100 copper......	6.76	21.00
	P	1/2 pound.........	100,000	.... do	3.38	19.00
			350,000			
Total			**7,350,000**			

VENEZUELA

Calendar year	U.S. Mint	Denomination	Coinage during year	Metallic composition	Gross weight	Diameter
1875–76.....	P	2 1/2 centavos...	2,000,000	Copper, nickel and zinc...........	(*)	23.00
	P	1 centavo	10,000,000	.... do	(*)	19.00
			12,000,000			
1902...........	P	5 bolivares.......	300,000	900 silver, 100 copper......	25.00	37.00
	P	2 bolivares.......	250,000	835 silver, 165 copper......	10.00	(*)
			550,000			
1903...........	P	5 bolivares.......	400,000	900 silver, 100 copper......	25.00	37.00
	P	1 bolivar..........	800,000	835 silver, 165 copper......	5.00	23.00
	P	1/2 bolivar.........	200,000	.... do	2.50	18.50
	P	1/4 bolivar.........	400,000	.... do	1.25	16.00
			1,800,000			
1904...........	P	2 bolivares.......	**500,000**	.... do	10.00	(*)
1915...........	P	5 centimos.......	**2,000,000**	75% copper, 25% nickel.......	2.50	19.00
1919...........	P	5 bolivares.......	400,000	900 silver, 100 copper......	25.00	37.00
	P	2 bolivares.......	1,000,000	835 silver, 165 copper......	10.00	27.00
	P	1 bolivar..........	1,000,000	.... do	5.00	23.00
	P	1/2 bolivar.........	400,000	.... do	2.50	18.50
	P	1/4 bolivar.........	400,000	.... do	1.25	16.00
			3,200,000			

VENEZUELA—CONTINUED

Calendar year	U.S. Mint	Denomination	Coinage during year	Metallic composition	Gross weight	Diameter
			Pieces		Grams	mm.
1921	P	5 bolivares	500,000	900 silver, 100 copper	25.00	37.00
	P	1/2 bolivar	600,000	835 silver, 165 copper	2.50	18.50
	P	5 centimos	2,000,000	75% copper, 25% nickel	2.50	19.00
			3,100,000			
1922	P	2 bolivares	1,000,000	835 silver, 165 copper	10.00	27.00
	P	1 bolivar	1,000,000	.... do	5.00	23.00
	P	1/4 bolivar	800,000	.... do	1.25	16.00
			2,800,000			
1924	P	5 bolivares	500,000	900 silver, 100 copper	25.00	37.00
	P	2 bolivares	1,250,000	835 silver, 165 copper	10.00	27.00
	P	1 bolivar	1,500,000	.... do	5.00	23.00
	P	1/2 bolivar	800,000	.... do	2.50	18.50
	P	1/4 bolivar	400,000	.... do	1.25	16.00
			4,450,000			
1925	P	12 1/2 centimos	800,000	75% copper, 25% nickel	5.00	23.00
	P	5 centimos	2,000,000	.... do	2.50	19.00
			2,800,000			
1926	P	5 bolivares	800,000	900 silver, 100 copper	25.00	37.00
	P	2 bolivares	1,000,000	835 silver, 165 copper	10.00	27.00
	P	1 bolivar	1,000,000	.... do	5.00	23.00
			2,800,000			
1927	P	12 1/2 centimos	800,000	75% copper, 25% nickel	5.00	23.00
	P	5 centimos	2,000,000	.... do	2.50	19.00
			2,800,000			
1929	P	5 bolivares	800,000	900 silver, 100 copper	25.00	37.00
	P	2 bolivares	1,500,000	835 silver, 165 copper	10.00	27.00
	P	1 bolivar	2,500,000	.... do	5.00	23.00
	P	1/2 bolivar	1,340,000	.... do	2.50	18.50
	P	1/4 bolivar	260,000	.... do	1.25	16.00
	P	12 1/2 centimos	800,000	75% copper, 25% nickel	5.00	23.00
	P	5 centimos	2,000,000	.... do	2.50	19.00
			9,200,000			
1930	P	10 bolivares	500,000	900 gold, 100 copper	3.23	19.00
	P	2 bolivares	425,000	835 silver, 165 copper	10.00	27.00

VENEZUELA—CONTINUED

Calendar year	U.S. Mint	Denomination	Coinage during year Pieces	Metallic composition	Gross weight Grams	Diameter mm.
			925,000			
1935...........	P	5 bolivares.......	1,600,000	900 silver, 100 copper......	25.00	37.00
	P	2 bolivares.......	3,000,000	835 silver, 165 copper......	10.00	27.00
	P	1 bolivar...........	5,000,000	.... do	5.00	23.00
	P	1/2 bolivar.........	1,000,000	.... do	2.50	18.50
	P	1/4 bolivar.........	3,400,000	.... do	1.25	16.00
			14,000,000			
1936...........	P	2 bolivares.......	1,700,000	.... do	10.00	27.00
	P	1 bolivar...........	1,000,000	.... do	5.00	23.00
	P	1/2 bolivar.........	600,000	.... do	2.50	18.50
	P	1/4 bolivar.........	1,800,000	.... do	1.25	16.00
	P	12 1/2 centimos	1,200,000	75% copper, 25% nickel.......	5.00	23.00
	p	5 centimos.......	5,000,000	.... do	2.50	19.00
			11,300,000			
1937...........	P	5 bolivares.......	2,000,000	900 silver, 100 copper......	25.00	37.00
	P	2 bolivares.......	800,000	835 silver, 165 copper......	10.00	27.00
	P	1 bolivar...........	4,000,000	.... do	5.00	23.00
	P	1/4 bolivar.........	1,000,000	.... do	1.25	16.00
			7,800,000			
1938...........	P	12 1/2 centimos.	1,600,000	75% copper, 25% nickel.......	5.00	23.00
	P	5 centimos.......	6,000,000	.... do	2.50	19.00
			7,600,000			
1945...........	D	1/2 bolivar.........	500,000	835 silver, 165 copper......	2.50	18.50
	D	1/4 bolivar.........	1,800,000	.... do	1.25	16.00
	D	12 1/2 centimos.	800,000	70% copper, 30% zinc..........	5.00	23.00
	D	5 centimos.......	4,000,000	.... do	2.50	19.00
			7,100,000			
1946...........	P	1/2 bolivar.........	4,000,000	835 silver, 165 copper......	2.50	18.50
	P	1/4 bolivar.........	8,000,000	.... do	1.25	16.00
	P	12 1/2 centimos	11,200,000	75% copper, 25% nickel.......	5.00	23.00
	P	5 centimos.......	12,000,000	.... do	2.50	19.00
			35,200,000			
1947...........	P	2 bolivares.......	3,000,000	835 silver, 165 copper......	10.00	27.00
	P	1 bolivar...........	8,000,000	.... do	5.00	23.00
	P	1/2 bolivar.........	2,500,000	.... do	2.50	18.50
	P	1/4 bolivar.........	8,000,000	.... do	1.25	16.00
	P	12 1/2 centimos	9,200,000	75% copper, 25% nickel.......	5.00	23.00

Footnote at end of table.

VENEZUELA—CONTINUED

Calendar year	*U.S. Mint*	*Denomination*	*Coinage during year*	*Metallic composition*	*Gross weight*	*Diam-eter*
			Pieces		*Grams*	*mm.*
	P	5 centimos.......	12,000,000	.... do	2.50	19.00
			42,700,000			
1949...........	S	1/4 bolivar.........	8,637,944	835 silver, 165 copper......	1.25	16.00
	S	12 1/2 centimos	6,000,000	75% copper, 25% nickel.......	5.00	23.00
	S	5 centimos.......	18,000,000	.... do	2.50	19.00
			32,637,944			
1955...........	P	1 bolivar...........	13,500,000	835 silver, 165 copper......	5.00	23.00
	P	1/2 bolivar.........	15,000,000	.... do	2.50	18.00
	P	1/4 bolivar.........	36,000,000	.... do	1.25	16.00
			64,500,000			
1959...........	P	12 1/2 centimos	10,000,000	75% copper, 25% nickel.......	5.00	23.00
	P	5 centimos.......	25,000,000	.... do	2.50	19.00
			35,000,000			
Total		....	**306,762,944**			

*Not available.

INTERNATIONAL RATES OF EXCHANGE TABLE

Courtesy of The Monetary Research Institute, "MRI Bankers' Guide to Foreign Currency"

The following is a list of the international exchange fixed rates as of February 24, 1997. The right-hand column indicates the number of units (in that country's currency) that equal $1 USA. Please use these rates as only a guide. Rates may vary, so please check with your local bank before making a transaction.

Country	Currency	U.S.
Afghanistan	Afghani	4750.00
Albania	Lek	128.00
Algeria	Dinar	57.00
Andorra	Spain/France	—
Angola	Kwanza reajustado	230,000
Anguilla	East Carib. dollar	2.67
Antigua & Barbuda	East Carib. dollar	2.67
Argentina	Peso	1.00
Armenia	Dram	462.00
Aruba	Florin	1.79
Australia	Dollar	.7770
Austria	Schilling	11.77
Azerbaijan	Manat	4080
Bahamas	Dollar	1.00
Bahrain	Dinar	3770
Bangladesh	Taka	42.50
Barbados	Dollar	1.98
Belarus	Rubel	29,000
Belgium	Franc	34.40
Belize	Dollar	1.98
Benin	CFA franc West	564.95
Bermuda	Dollar	1.00
Bhutan	Ngultrum	35.75
Bolivia	Boliviano	5.22
Bosnia-Herzegovina	New dinar	167.30
Botswana	Pula	3.55
Brazil	Real	1.05
British Virgin Isl	U.S. dollar	1.00
Brunei	Ringgit	1.4210
Bulgaria	Lev	2450.00
Burkina	CFA franc West	564.95
Burundi	Franc	330.00
Cambodia	Riel	2700
Cameroon	CFA franc Central	564.95
Canada	Dollar	1.3260
Cape Verde	Escudo	82.50
Cayman Islands	Dollar	1.20
Central African Rep Central	CFA franc	564.95
CFA franc-Central		564.95
CFA franc-West		564.95
CFP franc		102.72
Chad	CFA franc Central	564.95
Chile	Peso	414.00
China Peoples Rep	Yuan	8.29
Colombia	Peso	990
Comoros	Franc	424.77
Congo	CFA franc Central	564.95
Cook Islands Dollar		.6970
Costa Rica	Colón	223.00
Croatia	Kuna	6.01
Cuba	Peso	20.00
Cyprus	Pound	1.9820
Czech Republic	Koruna	28.40
Denmark	Krona	6.42
Djibouti	Franc	177.00
Dominica	East Carib. dollar	2.67
Dominican Republic	Peso	14.00
Eastern Caribbean	Dollar	2.67
Ecuador	Sucre	3700
Egypt	Pound	3.37
El Salvador	Colón	8.70
England	Sterling pound	1.8350
Equat Guinea	CFA franc Central	564.95
Eritrea see Ethiopia		
Estonia	Kroon	13.48
Ethiopia	Birr	6.23
European Currency Unit		1.1595
Falklands-Malvinas	Pound	1.6350
Faroes	Krona	6.42
Fiji Is	Dollar	.7055
Finland	Markka	5.03
France	Franc	5.6495
French Polynesia	CFP franc	102.72
Gabon	CFA franc Central	564.95
Gambia	Dalasi	9.80
Georgia	Lari	1.24

Country	Currency	U.S.
Germany	D.Mark	1.6730
Ghana	Cedi	1780
Gibraltar	Pound	1.6350
Greece	Drachma	281.80
Greenland	Denmark	8.42
Grenada	East Carib. dollar	2.67
Guatemala	Quetzal	6.10
Guernsey	Sterling pound	1.6350
Guinea-Bissau	Peso	34,200
Guinea Conakry	Franc	1000
Guyana	Dollar	140.00
Haïti	Gourde	15.90
Honduras	Lempira	12.70
Hong Kong	Dollar	7.74
Hungary	Forint	174.00
Iceland	Krona	70.80
India	Rupee	35.75
Indonesia	Rupiah	2390
Iran	Rial	3000
Iraq	Dinar	1000
Ireland	Punt	1.5875
Isle of Man	Sterling pound	1.6350
Israel	New sheqel	3.34
Italy	Líra	1658
Ivory Coast	CFA franc West	564.95
Jamaica	Dollar	34.70
Japan	Yen	122.10
Jersey	Sterling pound	1.6350
Jordan	Dinar	1.41
Kazakhstan	Tenga	75.50
Kenya	Shilling	54.80
Kiribati	Australian dollar	
Korea PDR	Won	2.15
Korea Republic	Won	867.00
Kuwait	Dinar	.3025
Kyrgyzstan	Som	17.00
Lao PDR	Kip	920.00
Latvia	Lat	.5830
Lebanon	Pound	1540
Lesotho	Maloti	4.42
Liberia	Dollar	1.00
Libya	Dinar	.3555
Liechtenstein	Swiss franc	1.45
Lithuania	Litas	4.00
Luxembourg	Franc	34.40
Macao	Pataca	8.00
Macedonia	New denar	44.00
Madagascar	Franc	4600
Malawi	Kwacha	15.20
Malaysia	Ringgit	2.48
Maldives	Rufiya	11.70
Mali	CFA franc West	564.95
Malta	Lira	2.81
Marshall Isl.	U.S. dollar	
Mauritania	Ougiya	142.50
Mauritius	Rupee	20.00
Mexico	Peso	7.75
Moldova	Lau	4.87
Monaco	French franc	
Mongolia	Tugrik	725
Montenegro	Yugo new dinar	
Montserrat	East Carib. dollar	2.67
Morocco	Dirham	9.36
Mozambique	Metical	11,200
Myanmar	Kyat	8.22
Namibia	Dollar	4.42
Nauru	Australian dollar	
Nepal	Rupee	58.90
Netherlands	Gulden	1.88
Neth Antilles	Gulden	1.79
New Caledonia	CFP franc	102.72
New Zealand	Dollar	.6970
Nicaragua	Córdoba	9.05
Niger	CFA franc West	564.95
Nigeria	Naira	80.00
Northern Ireland	Strling pound	1.6350
Norway	Krone	6.6490
Oman	Rial	.3850
Pakistan	Rupee	40.00
Palau	U.S. dollar	1.00
Panama/Balboa	U.S. dollar	1.00
Papua New Guinea	Kina	1.38
Paraguay	Guarani	2120
Peru	Nuevo sol	2.63
Philippines	Piso	26.30
Poland	New zloty	3.04
Portugal	Escudo	167.80
Oatar	Riyal	3.64
Romania	Lau	8750
Russia	Ruble	5670
Rwanda	Franc	301.00
St Helena	Pound	1.8350
St Kitts & Nevis	E. Carib dollar	2.67
St Lucia	East Caribbean dollar	2.67
St Vincent	East Caribbean dollar	2.67
San Marino	Italian lira	
São Tome e Principe	Dobra	2385
Saudi Arabia	Riyal	3.75
Scotland	Sterling pound	1.8350
Senegal	CFA franc West	564.95
Seychelles	Rupee	5.00
Sierra Leone	Leone	860
Singapore	Dollar	1.4210
Slovakia	Koruna	32.80
Slovenia	Tolar	153.50
Solomon Is.	Dollar	3.63
Somalia	Shillin	7800
Somaliland	Shilin	2500
South Africa	Rand	4.42
Spain	Peseta	141.600
Sri Lanka	Rupee	57.50
Sterling pound		1.6350
Sudan	Dinar	145.00
Surinam	Gulden	410.00
Swaziland	Lilangeni	4.42
Sweden	Krona	7.38
Switzerland	Franc	1.45
Syria	Pound	41.90
Taiwan	NT dollar	27.50
Tajikistan	Tajik ruble	330.00
Tanzenia	Shilling	600.00
Thailand	Baht	25.80
Togo	CFA franc West	564.95
Tonga	Pa'anga	1.28
Transnistria	New ruble	620,000
Trinidad & Tobago	Dollar	6.10
Tunisia	Dinar	1.07
Turkey	Lira	121,500
Turkmenistan	Manat	4100
Turks & Caicos	U.S. dollar	1.00
Tuvalu	Australian dollar	
Uganda	Shilling	1020
Ukraine	Hryvnia	1.76
United Arab Emirates	Dirham	3.67
U.S.A.	Dollar	1.00
Uruguay	Peso uruguayo	8.90
Uzbekistan	Som-Currency	55.00
Vanuatu	Vatu	113.50
Vatican City	Italian lira	
Venezuela	Bolívar	471.00
Vietnam	Dong	11,100
Western Samao	Tala	2.48
Yamen (North)	Rial	130.00
Yugoslavia	Super dinar	5.42
Zaïra	New Zaïra	147,500
Zambia	Kwacha	1290
Zimbabwe	Dollar	11.10

GOLD, SILVER, AND PLATINUM BULLION VALUE CHARTS

The following charts can be used to approximate the bullion or "melt" value of any coin that is made of gold, silver, or platinum. When determining the melt or bullion value of a coin, you will need to take into consideration not only the weight of the coin, but also the purity level of the gold, silver, or platinum, i.e., 18K gold (.921), 14K gold (.771), pure silver (.999), sterling silver (.925), etc. These variables make it difficult for an inexperienced dealer to calculate the bullion value of a coin. We recommend contacting dealers that have experience in dealing in bullion coinage.

SILVER (.999% FINE) BUILLON CHART

Oz. Weight(Troy)	$4.00	$4.50	$5.00	$5.50	$6.00	$6.50	$7.00	$7.50	$8.00	$8.50
.1	.40	.45	.50	.55	.60	.65	.70	.75	.80	.85
.2	.80	.90	1.00	1.10	1.20	1.30	1.40	1.50	1.60	1.70
.3	1.20	1.35	1.50	1.65	1.80	1.95	2.10	2.25	2.40	2.55
.4	1.60	1.80	2.00	2.20	2.40	2.60	2.80	3.00	3.20	3.40
.5	2.00	2.25	2.50	2.75	3.00	3.25	3.50	3.75	4.00	4.25
.6	2.40	2.70	3.00	3.30	3.60	3.90	4.20	4.50	4.80	5.10
.7	2.80	3.15	3.50	3.85	4.20	4.55	4.90	5.25	5.60	5.95
.8	3.20	3.60	4.00	4.40	4.80	5.20	5.60	6.00	6.40	6.80
.9	3.60	4.05	4.50	4.95	5.40	5.85	6.30	6.75	7.20	7.65
1.0	4.00	4.50	5.00	5.50	6.00	6.50	7.00	7.50	8.00	8.50

GOLD AND PLATINUM (.999%) BULLION CHART

Oz. Weight (Troy)	$340.00	$345.00	$350.00	$355.00	$360.00	$365.00	$ 370.00	$375.00	$380.00	$385.00	$390.00
.1	34.00	34.50	35.00	35.50	36.00	36.50	37.00	37.50	38.00	38.50	39.00
.2	68.00	69.00	70.00	71.00	72.00.	73.00	74.00	75.00	76.00	77.00	78.00
.3	102.00	103.50	105.00	106.50	108.00	109.50	111.00	112.50	114.00	115.00	117.00
.4	136.00	138.00	140.00	142.00	144.00	146.00	148.00	150.00	152.00	154.00	156.00
.5	170.00	172.50	175.00	177.50	180.00	182.50	185.00	187.50	190.00	192.50	195.00
.6	204.00	207.00	210.00	213.00	216.00	219.00	222.00	225.00	228.00	231.00	234.00
.7	238.00	241.50	245.00	248.50	252.00	255.50	259.00	262.50	266.00	269.50	273.00
.8	272.00	276.00	280.00	284.00	288.00	292.00	296.00	300.00	304.00	308.00	312.00
.9	306.00	310.50	315.00	319.50	324.00	328.50	333.00	337.50	342.00	346.50	351.00
1.0	340.00	345.00	350.00	355.00	360.00	365.00	370.00	375.00	380.00	385.00	390.00

INTERNATIONAL COIN MINTS AND DISTRIBUTORS

Foreign countries sell their current coinage directly through the government of issue and/or through official U.S. distributors. The following is a list of countries and/or distributors from which current coins can be purchased. Ask to be placed on their mailing lists to receive notification of the most current releases.

ANDORRA
Servei D' Emissions Episcopal
C/. Prat de la Creu
96 4t 5a
Andorra La Vella
PRINCIPAT D' ANDORRA
Telephone: 86 72 80 88 92 80
Fax: +376 869009

(silver coins)
Servei d'Emmisions Vegueria Episcopal
Prata de la Creu 42
PRINCIPA T D' ANDORRA

ARMENIA
Schom-Buchversand
Gerhard Schon
Postfach 71 09 08
D-81459 München
GERMANY

AUSTRALIA *(silver & gold coins)*
North American Office:
Downie's, Ltd. (Royal Australian Mint)
Attn. Craig Whitford
P.O. Box 23064
Lansing, MI 48909
Telephone: (517) 394-4443
Fax: (517) 394-0579

Downie's Ltd. is pleased to announce their appointment as exclusive North American agent for the Royal Australian Mint. Craig Whitford is located in Lansing, Michigan where he manages his own numismatic auction business. He has a long and distinguished history in the American numismatic arena. Craig has been associated with Downie's as their U.S. agent for over 12 years.

Fred Weinberg & Co., Inc.
16311 Ventura Boulevard, Suite 1288
Encino, CA 91436
Telephone: (818) 986-3733
Fax: (818) 986-2153

Gold Corp. (Perth Mint)
30210 Rancho Viejo Road, Suite C
San Juan Capistrano, CA 92675
Telephone: (714) 443-0600
Fax: (714) 443-0901

Universal Coins
(Royal Australian Mint)
47 Clarence Street, Suite 201
Ottawa, Ontario K1N 9K1, Canada
Telephone: (613) 241-1404
Fax: (613) 241-4568

Royal Australian Mint
Denison Street
Canberra, ACT 2600
AUSTRALIA

The Royal Australian Mint in Canberra is the home of Australia's coins and was officially opened by His Royal Highness, The Duke of Edinburgh on Monday, February 22, 1965.

Commissioned to produce Australia's decimal coinage, introduced into circulation on February 14, 1966, the Royal Australian Mint holds a place in history as the first mint in Australia not to be a branch of the Royal Mint in London.

Since its opening in 1965 the Mint has produced over eight billion circulating coins and currently has the capacity to produce over two million coins per day or over six hundred million coins per year, with staff working a single shift only.

Coins are not the only products of the Mint. Medals, medallions, seals, and tokens are produced for a wide range of government, business, sporting, and tourist needs in Australia and overseas. A small selection includes The Order of Australia, Vietnam Medal, New Zealand Commonwealth Games Victory Medals, Third Pacific Conference Games Medallion, Anzac Peace Medallion, Sydney Monorail Token, and Queensland's Jupiters Casino Token.

The Royal Australian Mint strikes coins for a number of South Pacific nations. Export coins were first struck in 1969 for New Zealand, and since then coins have been produced for Papua New Guinea, Tonga, Western Samoa, Cook Islands, Fiji, Malaysia, Thailand, Nepal, Bangladesh, and Tokelau.

Gold Corp.
Perth Mint (Western Australia Mint)
P.O. Box M924
310 Hay Street
East Perth, Western Australia 6004
AUSTRALIA

AUSTRIA *(silver coins)*
North American office:
Universal Coins
47 Clarence Street, Suite 201
Ottawa, Ontario K1N 9K1, Canada
Telephone: (613) 241-1404
Fax: (613) 241-4568

Austrian Mint
Munze Osterreich AG
A-1031 Wien Postfach 181
Am Heumarkt I
AUSTRIA

BANGLADESH *(silver coins)*
MDM, Munzhandelsgesellschaft
Deutsche Munze
Theodor-Heuss-Str 7
38090 Braunschweig
FEDERAL REPUBLIC OF GERMANY

BELGIUM *(silver coins)*
North American office:
Coin & Currency Institute, Inc.
P.O. Box 1057
Clifton, NJ 07014
Telephone: 1 (800) 421-1866
Fax: (201) 471-1062

Back in the 1980s, The Coin & Currency Institute saw that there was a change developing in the way people were collecting their coins. Retail shops were disappearing, coin shows were intimidating for many, and U.S. coins were looked at by many as an expensive investment. There was a general, steady move into the world of foreign coins. This was a world unlike that of U.S. coins. Not only do the first world coins date back to the sixth century B.C.*, but they come in dozens of metals from hundreds of issuers—some extinct, others just starting out.*

It was impossible for all but the

wealthiest and most intrepid of collectors to venture into this vast new world on their own so we decided it was best to bring that world to them. Although we always specialized in foreign coins, the ones most attractive and available were those being offered by the world's mints. But for an American, acquiring these coins was a nightmare! The mints did not take credit cards, did not have toll-free phone numbers, and were scattered about in different time zones. They refused U.S. dollars, which meant that everyone who wanted even one coin had to buy a foreign currency bank draft, which they then had to send overseas. It was just as difficult on the receiving end, where the mints could not efficiently process individual orders to America.

We knew that there was a better way. Through our contacts with many world mints, we established a fulfillment and distribution facility for them here in the states. We offer our toll free number (1-800-421-1866) for anyone wanting to order or who requests information. We have recently added an e-mail address (coincurin@aol.com), and will soon establish an Internet page showing coins of the world's mints. Furthermore, we accept personal checks as well as VISA, MasterCard, and American Express. We handle all importation and customs formalities, and because coins are shipped to us in quantity, we are able to absorb the costs of international freight.

We send information to collectors by mail at least eight times a year and try to have something for every collector's taste and budget: We offer traditional designs by, for example, the Portuguese and Hungarians, as well as the starkly modern new commemoratives of the Netherlands and Finland. Whether gold, silver, or non-precious metal, whether single coins or special proof and mint sets, it is no wonder that legions of collectors are flocking to the world of world coins. We welcome the readers of the Blackbook to come and join them.

Royal Belgian Mint
Monnaie Royale de Belgique
Bd. Pacheco laan 32
1000 Bruxelles
BELGIUM

BERMUDA
Bermuda Monetary Authority
26 Burnaby Street
Hamilton, HM 11
BERMUDA

BRAZIL *(silver & gold coins)*
Casa de Moeda do Brasil
Rua Rene Bitten-Court 371
23565 Distrito Industrial de
Santa Cruz
Rio de Janeiro
BRAZIL

BULGARIA *(silver coins)*
Bulgarian Mint
6 Boulevard Russky
Sofia
BULGARIA

CANADA *(silver & gold coins)*
North American office:
Fred Weinberg & Co., Inc.
16311 Ventura Boulevard,
Suite 1288
Encino, CA 91436
Telephone: (818) 986-3733
Fax: (818) 986-2153

Universal Coins
47 Clarence Street, Suite 201
Ottawa, Ontario K1N 9K1, Canada
Telephone: (613) 241-1404
Fax: (613) 241-4568

Royal Canadian Mint
320 Sussex Drive
Ottawa, Ontario K1A 0G8
CANADA

CUBA *(silver & gold coins)*
Empresa Cubana de Acunaciones
Calle 18 No. 306 e
3ra y 5ta Avenue Miramar
Ciudad de La Habana
CUBA

CYPRESS
Schom-Buchversand
Gerhard Schon
Postfach 71 09 08
D-81459 München
GERMANY

CZECH REPUBLIC *(silver coins)*
Ceska Mincovna
Czech Mint
Jablonec nad Nisou
CZECH REPUBLIC

Czech National Bank
Currency Department
Na prikope 28, 110, 03
Prague 1
CZECH REPUBLIC

Ivo Cerny
POB 19
695 04 Hodonfn
CZECH REPUBLIC
Telephone: 420 68 26489
Fax: 420 631 322023

(gold coins)
Czechoslovia State Bank
Na Prikope 28
CS-100 03 Praha 1
CZECH REPUBLIC

DENMARK *(silver & gold coins)*
Den Kongelige Mont
Solmarksvej 5
2605 Brondy
DENMARK

EGYPT *(silver & gold coins)*
Egyptian Mint House
Abbessia, Cairo
EGYPT

(silver coins)
Egyptian Coin Center
41 Ramses Street
P.O. Box 77
Mohamed Farid
Cairo
EGYPT

FEDERAL REPUBLIC OF GERMANY
(silver & gold coins)
B.H. Mayer Mint
Turnplatz 2
D-75172 Pforzheim
FEDERAL REPUBLIC OF GERMANY

(silver coins)
Bayerisches Hauptmunzamt
Zamdorfer Strabe 92
81677 Munchen
FEDERAL REPUBLIC OF GERMANY

Staatliche Muenze Hamburg
Bei de neuen Muenze 19
2000 Hamburg
FEDERAL REPUBLIC OF GERMANY

Staatliche Munze Stuttgart
70372 Stuttgart
Reichhaller Strasse 58
W-7500 Stuttgart 50
FEDERAL REPUBLIC OF GERMANY

FEDERAL REPUBLIC OF KOREA
(silver coins)
Korea Security Printing and
Minting Corp.
90 Kajong-dong
Taejon 305-350
FEDERAL REPUBLIC OF KOREA

FINLAND *(silver coins)*
North American office:
Coin & Currency Institute, Inc.
P.O. Box 1057
Clifton, NJ 07014
Telephone: 1 (800) 421-1866
Fax: (201) 471-1062

Mint of Finland
PL 13
SF-01671 Vantaa
FINLAND

(gold coins)
Suomen Pankki-Findlands Bank
P.O. Box 160
00101 Helsinki 10
FINLAND

FRANCE
North American office:
Universal Coins
47 Clarence Street, Suite 201
Ottawa, Ontario K1N 9K1, Canada
Telephone: (613) 241-1404
Fax: (613) 241-4568

Monnaie de Paris
11 quai de Conti
75270 Paris Cedex 06
FRANCE

HUNGARY *(silver coins)*
North American office:
Coin & Currency Institute, Inc.
P.O. Box 1057
Clifton, NJ 07014
Telephone: 1 (800) 421-1866
Fax: (201) 471-1062

Hungarian State Mint
H-1450
Budapest
HUNGARY

IRAN *(gold coins)*
Bank Markazi Iran
P.O. Box 3362
Teheran
ISLAMIC REPUBLIC OF IRAN

IRELAND
Central Bank of Ireland
P.O. Box 61
Dublin 16
IRELAND
Telephone: 01 2955666
Fax: 01 2956536

ISRAEL *(gold coins)*
North American office:
Coin & Currency Institute, Inc.
P.O. Box 1057
Clifton, NJ 07014
Telephone: 1 (800) 421-1866
Fax: (201) 471-1062

J.J. Van Grover, LTD.
P.O. Box 123
Oakland Gardens, NY
11364-0123
Telephone: 1-800-56-COINS

Israel Coins & Medals Gallery of
New York
7 East 35th Street, Suite 1013
New York, NY 10016

Israel Government Coins &
Metals Corp.
5 Ahad Ha'am Street
P.O. Box 2270
Jerusalem 91022
ISRAEL

ITALY *(silver & gold coins)*
Instituto Poligrafico e
Zecca Dello Stato
Piazza Giuseppe Verdi, 10
00100 Roma
ITALY

(silver coins)
Stabilimento Stefano Johnson SpA
ViaTerraggio, 15
20123 Milan
ITALY

LITHUANIA
Lithuanian Mint
Eiguliu g. 4
2015 Vilnius
REPUBLIC OF LITHUANIA
Telephone: +370 2 26 23 90
Fax: +370 2 26 24 00

MALTA
Emmanuel Said
43/2 Zachery Street

PO Box 345
Vallette VLT 04
MALTA
Telephone: +356 23 68 53
Fax: +356 246960
E-mail: emsaid@dream.vol.net.mt

MEXICO *(silver & gold coins)*
North American office:
Coin & Currency Institute, Inc.
P.O. Box 1057
Clifton, NJ 07014
Telephone: 1 (800) 421-1866
Fax: (201) 471-1062

Casa de Moneda de Mexico
Paseo de la Reforma 295, 5° Piso
Colonia Cuahtemoc
06500 Mexico, D.F.
MEXICO

NAMBIA *(silver coins)*
E.D.J. Van Roekel B.V.
P.O. Box 1400 AA
Bussom
HOLLAND

NETHERLANDS *(silver & gold coins)*
North American office:
Coin & Currency Institute, Inc.
P.O. Box 1057
Clifton, NJ 07014
Telephone: 1 (800) 421-1866
Fax: (201) 471-1062

Rijks Munt
Leidsweg 90, 3531 BG
Postbus 2407
3500 GK Utrecht
THE NETHERLANDS

NEW ZEALAND
Collectors Coin Division, Banking & Currency Dept.
Reserve Bank of New Zealand
P.O. Box 2498
Wellington
NEW ZEALAND

NIUE *(silver coins)*
MDM, Munzhandelsgesellschaft
Deutsche Munze
Theodor-Heuss-Str 7
38090 Braunschweig
FEDERAL REPUBLIC OF GERMANY

NORWAY *(silver & gold coins)*
Royal Mint of Norway
Hyttegt I
N-3600 Kongsberg
NORWAY

OMAN *(silver coins)*
Central Bank of Oman
Attn. Mr. Ali Khamis, Vice President
P.O. Box 1161
Ruwi, OM 112
SULTANATE OF OMAN

PALAU *(silver & gold coins)*
E.D.J. Van Roekel B.V.
P.O. Box 1400 AA
Bussom
HOLLAND

PEOPLE'S REPUBLIC OF CHINA *(silver & gold coins)*
North American office:
Fred Weinberg & Co., Inc.
16311 Ventura Boulevard, Suite 1288
Encino, CA 91436
Telephone: (818) 986-3733
Fax: (818) 986-2153

Universal Coins
47 Clarence Street, Suite 201
Ottawa, Ontario K1N 9K1, Canada
Telephone: (613) 241-1404
Fax: (613) 241-4568

China Gold Coin, Inc.
Information Division
Room 1103, ACFTU Hotel
No. 1 Zhen Wu Miao Road
XI Cheng District
PEOPLE'S REPUBLIC OF CHINA

PERU *(silver & gold coins)*
Banco Central de Reserva del Peru
Apartado 1958, Correo Central
Lima 1
PERU

POLAND *(silver & gold coins)*
Mint of Poland
MINT-POL S.A.
Pereca Street, 21
00 958 Warsaw
POLAND

(gold coins)
Narodow Bank Polski
Swietokrzyska Street 11/21
00 950 Warszawa
POLAND

PORTUGAL *(silver coins)*
North American office:
Coin & Currency Institute, Inc.
P.O. Box 1057
Clifton, NJ 07014
Telephone: 1 (800) 421-1866
Fax: (201) 471-1062

Portugal State Mint
Impresa Nacional—Casa da Moeda
Av. Dr. Antonio Jose de Almeida
P-1092 Lisboa, Codex
PORTUGAL

(gold coins)
Portugal State Mint
Tua de D. Francisco Manuel de
Menlo 5
P-1092 Lisboa, Codex
PORTUGAL

ROMANIA *(silver coins)*
Romania State Mint
The National Bank of Romania
25 Lipscani Street
Bucharest
ROMANIA

SALOMON ISLANDS *(silver coins)*
MDM, Munzhandelsgesellschaft
Deutsche Munze
Theodor-Heuss-Str 7
38090 Braunschweig
FEDERAL REPUBLIC OF GERMANY

SINGAPORE *(silver coins)*
North American office:
Universal Coins
47 Clarence Street, Suite 201
Ottawa, Ontario K1N 9K1, Canada
Telephone: (613) 241-1404
Fax: (613) 241-4568

BCCS Depot Singapore
10 Depot Walk
SINGAPORE 04 10

(gold coins)
Singapore Mint Pte. Ltd.
249 Jalan Boon Lay
SINGAPORE 2261

SLOVENIJE
Bank of Slovenia
Slovenska 35
1505 Ljubjana
SLOVENIJA
Telephone: +386 61 17 19 000
Fax: +386 61 215 516

Ivo Cerny
POB 19
695 04 Hodonfn
CZECH REPUBLIC
Telephone: 420 68 26489
Fax: 420 631 322023

SOUTH AFRICA
(silver & gold coins)
North American office:
Coin & Currency Institute, Inc.
P.O. Box 1057
Clifton, NJ 07014
Telephone: 1 (800) 421-1866
Fax: (201) 471-1062

South African Mint
P.O. Box 464
Pretoria 000 1
SOUTH AFRICA

(silver coins)
Numismatic Sales
P.O. Box 5580
Hennopsmeer 0046
SOUTH AFRICA

SPAIN *(silver & gold coins)*
Fabrica Nacional de Moneda y Timbre
Jorge Juan, 106
28009 Madrid
SPAIN

SWEDEN *(silver & gold coins)*
AB Tumba Bruk Myntverket
Swedish Mint
Box 401
S-63 1 06 Eskilstuna
SWEDEN

SWITZERLAND *(silver & gold coins)*
Huguenin Medailleurs, S.A.
rue Henry-Grandjean, 5
2400 Le Locle
SWITZERLAND

(silver coins)
Valcambi S.A.
Via Passeggiata
CH-6828 Balerna
SWITZERLAND

THAILAND *(silver coins)*
Royal Thai Mint
The Treasury Department
Rama VI Road
Bankok 10400
THAILAND

TURKEY *(silver & gold coins)*
Turkish State Mint
Darphane Mudurlugu
Yildiz-Istanbul
TURKEY

UNITED KINGDOM
(silver & gold coins)
North American office:
British Royal Mint
RR2, Box 59A South Road
Millbrook, NY 12545
Telephone: 1 (800) 822-2748

Fred Weinberg & Co., Inc.
16311 Ventura Boulevard, Suite 1288
Encino, CA 91436
Telephone: (818) 986-3733
Fax: (818) 986-2153

Universal Coins
47 Clarence Street, Suite 201
Ottawa, Ontario K1N 9K1, Canada
Telephone: (613) 241-1404
Fax: (613) 241-4568

Royal Mint
Llantrisant, Pontyclun
Mid-Glamorgan CF7 8YT
UNITED KINGDOM

UNITED STATES OF AMERICA
(silver & gold coins)
United States Mint
633 Third Street, N.W.
Washington, D.C. 20220
USA

(silver coins)
Sunshine Mint
7405 N. Government Way
Coeur d' Alene, ID 83814
USA

(gold coins)
Franklin Mint
Franklin Center, PA 19091
USA

Liberty Mint
651 Columbia Lane
Provo, UT 84604
USA

VATICAN CITY
North American office:
Universal Coins
47 Clarence Street, Suite 201
Ottawa, Ontario K1N 9K1, Canada
Telephone: (613) 241-1404
Fax: (613) 241-4568

INTERNATIONAL ASSOCIATION OF PROFESSIONAL NUMISMATISTS

OBJECT OF THE ASSOCIATION

The I.A.P.N. was constituted at a meeting held in Geneva in 1951 to which the leading international numismatic firms had been invited. There were 28 foundation members. The objects of the Association are the development of a healthy and prosperous numismatic trade conducted according to the highest standards of business ethics and commercial practice, the encouragement of scientific research and the propagation of numismatics, and the creation of lasting and friendly relations amongst professional numismatists throughout the world.

Membership is vested in numismatic firms, or in numismatic departments of other commercial institutions, and *not* in individuals. Today there are 100 numismatic firms in membership, situated in five continents and twenty-one countries. The General Assembly is the supreme organ of the Association, and this is convened annually, normally in a different country.

The Executive Committee is composed of twelve to fifteen persons from at least six different countries and includes the President, two Vice-Presidents (one from each Hemisphere), the General Secretary and the Treasurer. There are subcommittees dealing with membership, discipline, publications and anti-forgery work.

In pursuit of the objective to encourage numismatic research the Association has published or assisted in the publication of a number of important numismatic works. In particular it maintains a close liaison with the International Numismatic Commission, and individual members take an active interest in the work of their national numismatic organizations.

In 1965 the I.A.P.N. held an international congress in Paris to consider the study of and defence against counterfeit coins, and in 1975 the Association established the International Bureau for the Suppression of Counterfeit Coins (I.B.S.C.C.) in London. This Bureau maintains close links with mints, police forces, museums, collectors and dealers, publishing both a half-yearly Bulletin on Counterfeits and specialized reports on counterfeits. It will give an opinion as to authenticity and further details may be had on application to the Bureau.

International Bureau for the Suppression of Counterfeit Coins.

Mr. Stefan Sonntag
Münzen und Medaillenhandlung Stuttgart
Charlottenstrasse 4
D-70182 Stuttgart
T: ++49 711 24 44 57

The members of the I.A.P.N. guarantee the authenticity of all the coins and medals which they sell—this is a condition of membership—so collectors may purchase numismatic material from any of the firms listed in the following pages in the full knowledge that if any item did prove to be counterfeit or not as described the piece could be returned, the purchase price would be refunded, without regard to date of purchase.

Membership of the Association is not lightly acquired as applicants have to be sponsored by three members, and the vetting of applications involves a rigorous and sometimes protracted procedure. In order to be admitted the applicants must have been established in business as numismatists for at least four years and must be known to a number of members, and the Committee need to be satisfied that they have carried on their business in an honourable manner and that they have a good general knowledge of numismatics as well as expertise in whatever field is their speciality.

The Medal of Honour of the Association was established in 1963 in memory of its first president, Leonard S. Forrer, and is awarded by the President to persons of distinction whom the Association wishes to honour or for distinguished services to the Association.

The Association is a non-profit making organization established within the terms of paras. 60 *et seq* of the Swiss Civil Code. Its registered office is at P.O. Box 3647, CH-4002 Basle (Switzerland). Further enquiries about the Association may be made to the General Secretary.

AUSTRALIA

NOBLE NUMISMATICS Pty Ltd
(Jim and Anky Noble, Bob Climpson)
229 Macquarie Street,
SYDNEY NSW 2000
PH: (61) 612 223 4578
FX: (61) 612 233 6009
Auctions
Specialties: *Australian and World Coins, Banknotes, Commemorative and War Medals, Tokens. Branch Office in Melbourne (Gerhard Reimann-Basch and Jill Pearson)*

AUSTRIA

HERINEK, G.
Josefstädterstrasse 27,
A-1082 WIEN VIII
PH: (43) (01) 40 64 396
FX: (43) (01) 40 64 396
Publications

MOZELT, Erich
(Erich und Christine Mozelt)
Vienna Marriott Hotel,
Parkring 12a, A-1010 WIEN
PH: (43) (01) 512 9807
FX: (43) (01) 512 9783
List
Specialties: *Münzen des Römisch Deutschen Reiches, Weltmünzen und Antike*

BELGIUM

ELSEN SA, Jean
(Jean Elsen, Olivier Elsen, Roselyne Dus)
Avenue de Tervuren 65,
B-1040 BRUXELLES
PH: (32) (02) 734 6356; 736 0712
FX: (32) (02) 735 7778
List Publications Auctions
Specialties: *Ancient, Oriental and Medieval coins, Low Countries, World coins, Medals and Books*

FRANCESCHI & Fils, B.
10, Rue Croix-de-Fer,
B-1000 BRUXELLES
PH: (32) (02) 217 9395
List Publications Auctions

VAN DER SCHUEREN, Jean-Luc
14, Rue de la Bourse,
B-1000 Bruxelles
PH: (32) (02) 513 3400
FX: (32) (02) 512 2528
List
Specialties: *Ancient and medieval coins, Low Countries, World coins and Tokens*

CANADA

WEIR NUMISMATICS LTD., Randy
PO Box 64577, UNIONVILLE,
Ont. L3R 0M9
PH: (905) 764 7999
FX: (905) 764 0628
List Mail Bid Sales
Specialties: *British Colonial coins, Canadian Tokens*

EGYPT

BAJOCCHI JEWELLERS
(Cav. Pietro Bajocchi)
45 Abdel Khalek Sarwat Street,
11111 CAIRO
PH: (20) 391 9160 / 390 0030
FX: (20) (02) 393 1696
Specialties: *Ptolemaiques, Romaines, Greco-Romaines d'Alexandrie*

FRANCE

ANTIKA 1 (Marcel Pesce)
33, Rue Sainte-Hélène,
F-69002 Lyon
PH: (33) 78 37 23 90+
FX: (33) 78 42 28 10
List Auctions
Specialties: *Monnaies antiques, françaises, médailles, jetons, décorations et papier monnaie*

BOURGEY, Sabine
7, Rue Drouot, F-75009 PARIS
PH: (33) (01) 47 70 88 67 / 47 70 35 18
FX: (33) (01) 42 46 58 48
List Publications Auctions
Specialties: Monnaies, médailles, jetons, éditions numismatiques

BURGAN, Claude - Maison Florange
(Claude et Isabelle Burgan)
68, Rue de Richelieu, F-75002 PARIS
PH: (33) (01) 42 96 95 57
FX: (33) (01) 42 86 92 43
List Publications Mail Bid Sales
Specialties: Monnaies royales françaises, monnaies antiques, librairie numismatique

MAISON PLATT SA (Gérard Barré, Daniel Renaud)
49, Rue de Richelieu, F-75001 PARIS
Postal address: PB 2616, F-75026 Paris Cedex 01
PH: (33) (01) 42 96 50 48
FX: (33) (01) 42 61 13 99
List Publications Auctions
Specialties: Monnaies antiques, françaises, médailles, jetons, papier-monnaie. Ordres et décorations, librairie numismatique

NUMISMATIQUE et CHANGE DE PARIS
(Annette Vinchon)
3, Rue de la Bourse, F-75002 PARIS
PH: (33) (01) 42 97 53 53 / 42 97 46 85
FX: (33) (01) 42 97 44 56
Publications Mail Bid Sales Auctions
Specialties: Monnaies modernes. Monnaies d'or cotées en bourse. Lingots. Billets, assignats. Ourvages de Référence

O.G.N.
(Pierre Crinon, François Mervy)
64, rue de Richelieu, F-75002 Paris
PH: (33) (01) 42 97 47 50
FX: (33) (01) 42 60 01 37
List Publications Auctions
Specialties: Monnaies antiques, françaises, étrangères, médailles, jetons

A. POINSIGNON-NUMISMATIQUE
4, Rue des Francs Bourgeois, F-67000 STRASBOURG
PH: (33) 88 32 10 50
FX: (33) 88 75 01 14
List Auctions
Specialties: Monnaies antiques, françaises, alsaciennes et islamiques, librairie numismatique

SILBERSTEIN, Claude
39, Rue Vivienne, F-75002 PARIS
PH: (33) (01) 42 33 19 55
FX: (33) (01) 42 33 16 15
Specialties: Monnaies, médailles, jetons

VINCHON-NUMISMATIQUE, Jean
(Jean Vinchon et Françoise Berthelot-Vinchon)
77, Rue de Richelieu, F-75002 PARIS
PH: (33) (01) 42 97 50 00
FX: (33) (01) 42 86 06 03
List Publications Auctions
Specialties: Monnaies, médailles, décorations, pierres gravées, cylindres, bijoux anciens, antiquités

WEIL, Alain-SPES NUMISMATIQUE
54, Rue de Richelieu, F-75001 PARIS
PH: (33) (01) 47 03 32 12
FX: (33) (01) 42 60 14 18
List Auctions
Specialties: Monnaies antiques et françaises, jetons et médailles, documents sur la numismatique, billets de banque

GERMANY

DILLER, Johannes
(Ohlstadter Str. 21) PO Box 700429,
D-81304 MÜNCHEN
PH: (49) (089) 760 3550
FX: (49) (089) 769 8939
List
Specialties: *Münzen (900-1800), Medaillen (1500-1933), Kelten von Süddeutschland, Numism, Antiquariat*

FRANKFURTER MÜNZHANDLUNG GmbH
(Anders Ringberg, Helmut Stapf, Peter R. Hiltbrunner, Lutz Neumann-Lysloff)
Grosse Bockenheimer Strasse 44,
D-60313 FRANKFURT
PH: (49) (069) 28 77 77
FX: (49) (069) 71 40 11 72
List Auctions
Specialties: *Mittelalter und Neuzeit*

GARLICH, Kurt B.
Albert Schweitzer Str. 24a,
D-63303 DREIEICH-GÖTZENHAIN
PH: (49) (06103) 8 59 70
FX: (49) (06103) 83 01 85
List Auctions
Specialties: *Deutsche Gold- und Silbermünzen ab 1800.*

GIESSENER MÜNZHANDLUNG DIETER GORNY GmbH
Maximiliansplatz 20,
D-80333 MÜNCHEN
PH: (49) (089) 226876
FX: (49) (089) 2285513
List Auctions
Specialties: *Münzen und Medaillen der Antike und der Neuzeit*

HIRSCH, NACHF., Gerhard
(Dr. Francisca Bernheimer)
Promenadeplatz 10/II,
D-80333 MÜNCHEN
PH: (49) (089) 29 21 50 and 290 7390
FX: (49) (089) 228 36 75
List Auctions
Specialties: *Münzen und Medaillen der Antike, Mittel-alter und Neuzeit, Kunstwerke der Antike*

JACQUIER, Paul-Francis
Honsellstrasse 8, D077694 KEHL
PH: (49) (07851) 12 17
List
Specialties: *Keltische, Griechische, Römische, Byzantinische Münzen, Antike Kleinkunst. Celtic, Greek, Roman, Byzantine coins. Classical Art.*

KRICHELDORF Nachf., H.H.
(Volker Kricheldorf)
Günterstalstrasse 16,
D-79102 FREIBURG i.Br.
PH: (49) (0761) 739 13
FX: (49) (0761) 70 96 70
List Publications Auctions

KÜNKER, Fritz Rudolf, Münzenhandlung
(F.R. Künker, H.-R. Künker, P.N. Schulten, U. Helmig)
Gutenbergstrasse 23,
D-49076 OSNABRÜCK
PH: (49) (0541) 96 20 20
FX: (49) (0541) 96 20 222
List Auctions
Specialties: *Mittelalter und Neuzeit, Goldmünzen*

KURPFÄLZISCHE MÜNZENHANDLUNG-KPM
(H. Gehrig, G. Rupertus)
Augusta-Anlage 52, D-68165 MANNHEIM
PH: (49) (0621) 44 88 99 / 44 95 66
FX: (49) (0621) 40 37 52
Auctions
Specialties: *The antiquity, Germany, France, Benelux, paper money*

KAISER, Rüdiger,
Münzfachgeschäft
Mittelweg 54, D-60318 FRANKFURT
PH: (49) (069) 597 11 09
FX: (49) (069) 55 38 16
Specialties: *Antike, Europäische Münzen und Medaillen bis 1900*

Numismatik LANZ (Dr. Hubert Lanz, Ingrid Franke, Walter Schantl, Florian Eggers)
Luitpoldblock-Maximiliansplatz 10, D-80333 MÜNCHEN
PH: (49) (089) 29 90 70
FX: (49) (089) 22 07 62
Auctions
Specialties: *Antike, Mittelalter, Neuzeit, Literatur, Münzen und Medaillen*

MENZEL, Niels
Beckerstrasse 6A, D-12157 BERLIN
PH: (49) (030) 855 52 96
FX: (49) (030) 855 04 90
List Auctions

MÜNZEN- UND MEDAILLENHANDLUNG STUTTGART
(Dr. Michael Brandt, Stefan Sonntag)
Charlottenstrasse 4, D-070182 STUTTGART
PH: (49) (0711) 24 44 57
FX: (49) (0711) 23 39 36
List Publications

OLDENBURG, H.G.
Holstenstrasse 22, Postfach 3546, D-24034 KIEL
PH: (49) (0431) 9 46 76
FX: (49) (0431) 9 66 56
List Auctions
Specialties: *Antike, Mittelalter und Neuzeit*

Bankhaus PARTIN & Co. (Klaus Partin)
Numismatische Abt., Bahnhofplatz 1, D-97980 BAD MERGENTHEIM
PH: (49) (07931) 59 25 00 / 501
FX: (49) (07931) 59 24 45
List Auctions
Specialties: *Neuzeit und Goldmünzen*

PEUS NACHF., Dr. Busso (Dieter Raab)
Bornwiesenweg 34, D-60322 FRANKFURT/M.
PH: (49) (069) 597 02 81
FX: (49) (069) 55 59 95
Publications Mail Bid Sales Auctions

Münzhandlung RITTER GmbH
(E. & J. Ritter und Klaus Fleissner)
Immermannstr. 19,
D-40210 Düsseldorf
Postal address: Postfach 24 01 26,
D-40090 Düsseldorf
PH: (49) (0211) 367 80-0
FX: (49) (0211) 367 80-25
List
Specialties: *Münzen der Antike und Deutschlands. Grosshandel/ Wholesale*

SCHRAMM GmbH, H.J.
Scheinerstrasse 9, D-81679 MÜNCHEN
PH: (49) (089) 98 12 43
FX: (49) (089) 98 12 43
Auctions

TIETJEN + CO.
Spitalerstrasse 30, D-20095 HAMBURG
PH: (49) (040) 33 03 68
FX: (49) (040) 32 30 35
Publications Auctions
Specialties: *Coins, medals, paper money and books*

IRELAND

COINS & MEDALS (Redg.)
(Emil Szauer)
10 Cathedral Street, DUBLIN 1
PH: (353) (01) 874 4033
VAT: (353) IE 9Y50349S
Specialties: *Ancient, medieval, modern coins of the world*

ISRAEL

EIDELSTEIN, Adolfo
61 Herzl St., HAIFA
Postal address: POB 5135,
31051 Haifa
PH: (972) (04) 8645 035
Specialties: Ancient and modern coins, Judaica

QEDAR, Shraga
3, Granot Street, Entrance 6,
JERUSALEM
Postal address: PO Box 520, 91004
Jerusalem
PH: (972) (02) 791 273, (Home:
(972) (03) 641 9897)
FX: (972) (02) 790 912
Specialties: Numismatic consulting: Ancient and Islamic coins, Ancient weights

ITALY

BERNARDI, Giulio
(G. Bernardi, G. Paoletti)
Via Roma 3 & 22c, PO Box 560,
I-34121 TRIESTE
PH: (39) (040) 639 086
FX: (39) (040) 630 430
List Publications
Specialties: Greek, Roman, Medieval, Islam, medallions, numismatic books

CARLO CRIPPA s.n.c.
(Carlo e Paolo Crippa)
Via degli Omenoni 2
(angolo Piazza Belgioioso),
I-20121 MILANO
PH: (39) (02) 878 680
FX: (39) (02) 878 680
List Publications
Specialties: Grecques et romaines. Italiennes médiévales et modernes, surtout de l'atelier de Milan

DE FALCO (Alberto de Falco)
Corso Umberto 24, I-80138 NAPOLI
PH: (39) (081) 55 28 245
FX: (39) (081) 55 28 245
List
Specialties: Monete dell'Italia meridionale e della Sicilia

FALLANI (Dr. Carlo-Maria Fallani)
Via del Babuino 58a, I-00187 ROMA
PH: (39) (06) 320 7982
FX: (39) (06) 320 7645
Specialties: Grecques, romaines et byzantines. Archéologie

MARCHESI GINO & Figlio
(Giuseppe Marchesi)
V. le Pietramellara 35,
I-40121 BOLOGNA
PH: (39) (051) 255 014
FX: (39) (051) 255 014
List (Trimestrale) Publications
Specialties: Greek, Roman and Medieval Italian coins

PAOLUCCI, Raffaele
Via San Francesco 154,
I-35121 PADOVA
PH: (39) (049) 651 997
FX: (39) (049) 651 552
Specialties: Medieval Italian coins, especially Venetian

RATTO, Mario
Via A. Manzoni 14 (Palazzo
Trivulzio), I-20121 MILANO
PH: (39) (02) 79 93 80
FX: (39) (02) 79 64 93
List Publications Auctions
Specialties: Grecques, romaines, italiennes, médiévales et modernes

RINALDI O. & Figlio,
(Alfio e Marco Rinaldi)
Via Cappello 23 (Casa di Giulietta),
I-37121 VERONA
PH: (39) (045) 803 40 32
FX: (39) (045) 803 40 32
List Publications
Specialties: Greche, romane, italiane, estere e medaglie

JAPAN

DARUMA INTERNATIONAL GALLERIES
(Yuji Otani)
2-16-32-301, Takanawa,
Minato-ku, JP-TOKYO 108
PH: (81) (03) 3447 5567
FX: (81) (03) 3449 3344
List Publications Auctions
Specialties: World gold and silver coins, Japanese coins and Banknotes Chinese coins

LUXEMBOURG

LUX NUMIS (Romain Probst)
Galerie Mercure, 41, Av. de la Gare,
L-1611 LUXEMBOURG
PH: (352) 48 78 77 / 34 04 87
FX: (352) 40 55 17
List Publications Auctions
Specialties: Luxembourg, Monnaies du monde, Monnaies de nécessité, gauloises

MONACO

LE LOUIS D'OR
(Romolo Vescovi, Claude Bouveron)
9, Ave. des Papalins,
MC-98000 MONACO
PH: (33) 92 05 35 81
FX: (33) 92 05 35 82
List Publications
Specialties: Monnaies Italiennes, Antiques, Médiévales et Françaises

NETHERLANDS

MEVIUS NUMISBOOKS INTERNATIONAL BV
(Johan Mevius, Gabriel Munoz)
Oosteinde 97,
NL-7671 AT VRIEZENVEEN
PH: (31) (0546) 561 322
FX: (31) (0546) 561 352
List Publications
Specialties: Numismatic books, coins & medals of the Netherlands

SCHULMAN BV, Laurens
(Laurens and Carla Schulman)
Brinklaan 84a, NL-1404 GM BUSSUM
PH: (31) (035) 691 6632
FX: (31) (035) 691 0878
List Publications Auctions
Specialties: Coins of the Netherlands, Europe, Historical medals, Numismatic books and paper money

VAN DER DUSSEN BV, A.G.
(Pauline van der Dussen)
Hondstraat 5, NL-6211 HW MAASTRICHT
PH: (31) (043) 321 51 19
FX: (31) (043) 321 60 14
Publications Auctions
Specialties: Coins of the world, medals; numismatic books

WESTERHOF, Jille Binne
Trekpad 38-40,
NL-8742 KP BURGWERD
PH: (31) (0515) 573 364
FX: (31) (0515) 573 364
Auctions
Specialties: Coins of the Netherlands, Europe, Historical medals

NORWAY

OSLO MYNTHANDEL AS
(Jan Olav Aamlid, Gunnar Thesen)
Kongens gate 31, Sentrum, N-OSLO 1
PO Box 355,
Sentrum, N-0101 Oslo 1
PH: (47) 22 41 60 78
FX: (47) 22 33 32 36
List Publications Auctions
Specialties: Scandinavian coins, Thailand, Ancient coins

SINGAPORE

TAISEI STAMPS & COINS (S) PTE LTD.
(B.H. Lim, S.L. Ang, T.W. Ma, Lim Ming Lim)
12 Aljunied Rd, #06-02 SCN-Centre, SINGAPORE 389801
PH: (65) 841 2355
FX: (65) 841 7680
Auctions
Specialties: Chinese coins, coins of Asia, Banknotes, World gold and silver coins

SPAIN

CALICO, X. & F. (Xavier Jr. Calicó)
Plaza del Angel 2, E-08002 BARCELONA
PH: (34) (3) 310 55 12 / 310 55 16
FX: (34) (3) 310 27 56
Publications Auctions
Specialties: Espagne, possessions espagnoles en Europe, Amérique latine, Editeurs de médailles

CAYON, Juan R., JANO S.L.
Alcala 35, E-28014 MADRID
PH: (34) (1) 522 8030 / 523 3585
FX: (34) (1) 522 0967
List Publications
Specialties: Spanish World, Ancient coins, Crowns and Numismatic Books

VICO SA, Jesus
(Jesus Vico and Julio Chico)
Lope de Rueda 7, E-28009 MADRID
PH: (34) (1) 431 88 07
FX: (34) (1) 431 01 04
Publications Auctions
Specialties: Spain, Latin America, Roman, Banknotes

SWEDEN

AHLSTRÖM MYNTHANDEL AB
(Bjarne Ahlström)
Norrmalmstorg 1, I, PO Box 7662, S-103 94 STOCKHOLM
PH: (46) (08) 10 10 10
FX: (46) (08) 678 77 77
List Publications Auctions
Specialties: Scandinavian coins

NORDLINDS MYNTHANDEL AB, ULF
(Hans Hirsch, Ulf Nordlind)
Karlavägen 46, PO Box 5132, S-102 43 STOCKHOLM
PH: (46) (08) 662 62 61
FX: (46) (08) 661 62 13
List
Specialties: Scandinavian coins, medals, numismatic literature

SWITZERLAND

HESS-DIVO AG (J.P. Divo, Françoise Divo-Page, Juliet Divo)
Löwenstrasse 55, CH-8001 ZÜRICH
Postal address: Postfach, CH-8023 Zürich
PH: (41) (01) 225 4090
FX: (41) (01) 225 4099
List Auctions Publications
Specialties: Swiss coins. Coins of the world, medals; ancient coins

LEU NUMISMATIK AG
(S. Hurter, H. Stotz, Dr. A.S. Walker)
In Gassen 20, CH-8001 ZÜRICH
Postal address: Postfach 4738, CH-8022 Zürich
PH: (41) (01) 211 47 72
FX: (41) (01) 211 46 86
List Publications Auctions
Specialties: Münzen, Medaillen; Antike, Mittelalter und Neuzeit, Schweiz

MONETARIUM-SCHWEIZ. KREDITANSTALT
(Dr. G. Giacosa, J. Richter, K. Zimmermann)
Bahnhofstrasse 89, 4. Stock, CH-8021 ZÜRICH
PH: (41) (01) 333 25 26
FX: (41) (01) 212 07 15
List (Monetarium Katalog)
Specialties: Antike, griechische, römische und byzantinische Münzen, Gold- und Silbermünzen des Mittelalters und der Neuzeit. CH- Banknoten

MÜNZEN UND MEDAILLEN AG
(Dr. H. Voegtli,
Dr. U. Kampmann, A. Kirsch,
Dr. B. Schulte)
Malzgasse 25, BASEL
Postal address: Postfach 3647,
CH-4002 Basel
PH: (41) (061) 272 7544
FX: (41) (061) 272 7514
List (monatlich) *Publications*
Auctions
Specialties: *Antike, mittelalterliche und neuzeitliche Münzen*

NUMISMATICA ARS CLASSICA AG
(Paolo del Bello, Roberto Russo,
Arturo Russo)
Niederdorfstrasse 43, Postfach 745,
CH-8025 ZÜRICH
PH: (41) (01) 261 1703
FX: (41) (01) 261 5324
List *Publications* *Mail Bid Sales* *Auctions*
Specialties: *Greek, Roman, Byzantine and Medieval coins*

STERNBERG AG, Frank
Schanzengasse 10
(Bhf. Stadelhofen), CH-8001 ZÜRICH
PH: (41) (01) 252 30 88
(tel. Voranmeldung erwünscht)
privat (41) (01) 391 47 53
FX: (41) (01) 252 40 67
List *Auctions*
Specialties: *Münzen und Medaillen aller Zeiten und Länder. Numismatische Literatur, Antike Kleinkunst*

UNITED KINGDOM

BALDWIN & SONS LTD., A.H.
(P.D. Mitchell, A.H.E. Baldwin,
B.T. Curtis)
11 Adelphi Terrace,
GB-LONDON WC2N 6BJ
PH: (44) (0171) 930 6879
FX: (44) (0171) 930 9450
Publications *Auctions*

FORMAT OF BIRMINGHAM LTD.
(Garry Charman, David Vice)
18, Bennetts Hill,
GB-BIRMINGHAM B2 5QJ
PH: (44) (0121) 643 2058
FX: (44) (0121) 643 2210
List
Specialties: *World Coins and medals 1500-1960*

KNIGHTSBRIDGE COINS
(Stephen C. Fenton)
43, Duke Street, St. James's,
GB-LONDON SW1.Y.6DD
PH: (44) (0171) 930 7597 /
930 8215
FX: (44) (0171) 930 8214
Specialties: *English coins, Coins from USA, Australia and Thailand*

LUBBOCK & SON LTD.
(Richard M. Lubbock)
315 Regent Street,
GB-LONDON W1R 7YB
PH: (44) (0171) 580 9922 /
323 0676 / 637 7922
FX: (44) (0171) 637 7602
List
Specialties: *Gold coins of the world and rare banknotes*

SPINK & SON LTD.
(M. Rasmussen, J. Pett),
D. Saville, B. Faull, May Sinclair)
5/7 King Street, St. James's,
GB-LONDON SW1 Y 6QS
PH: (44) (0171) 930 7888
FX: (44) (0171) 839 4853
Auctions *List (10 a year)* *Publications*
Specialties: *Ancient, British, Islamic and World coins*

UNITED STATES OF AMERICA

BERK, LTD., Harlan J.
31 North Clark Street,
CHICAGO, IL 60602
PH: (001) (312) 609 0016
FX: (001) (312) 609 1309
List (bimonthly)
Specialties: All coins 700 BC to 1990's; Classical Antiquities

BOWERS AND MERENA GALLERIES, INC.
(Q. David Bowers, Raymond N. Merena)
PO Box 1224, WOLFEBORO, NH 03894
PH: (001) (603) 569 5095
FX: (001) (603) 569 5319
List Publications Auctions
Specialties: US coins and currency, foreign coins, ancient coins, publishers of numismatic books

BULLOWA, C.E. (Mrs. Earl E. Moore). COINHUNTER
1616 Walnut Street,
PHILADELPHIA, PA 19103
PH: (001) (215) 735 5517 / 5518
FX: (001) (215) 735 5517
List Auctions
Specialties: US, ancient and foreign coins and books.

COIN AND CURRENCY INSTITUTE INC.
(Arthur and Ira Friedberg)
PO Box 1057, CLIFTON, NJ 07014
PH: (001) (201) 471 1441
FX: (001) (201) 471 1062
Publications

COIN GALLERIES
(Robert Archer, Jan Eric Blamberg)
123 West 57 Street, NEW YORK, NY 10019
PH: (001) (212) 582 5955
FX: (001) (212) 582 1945 / 245 5018
List Mail Bid Sales Auctions
Specialties: European, ancient, medieval

CRAIG, Freeman
(Freeman and Marney Craig)
PO Box 4176, SAN RAFAEL, CA 94913
PH: (001) (415) 883 5336
FX: (001) (415) 382 1008
Specialties: Latin American coinage in gold, silver and minor metals from 1536–1950, including medals

DAVISSON'S LTD.
(Allan Davisson, Ph.D., Marnie Davisson)
COLD SPRING, MN 56320
PH: (001) (612) 685 3835
after 1.3.96: (001) (320) 685 3835
FX: (001) (612) 685 8636
after 1.3.96: (001) (320) 685 8636
List (bimonthly) Publications
Mail Bid Sales
Specialties: British, ancient and classical European coins, books

FORD JR., John J.
PO Box 10317, PHOENIX, AZ 85064
PH: (001) (602) 957 6443
FX: (001) (602) 957 1861
Specialties: US colonial coins, US silver, gold medals

FREEMAN + SEAR (David R. Sear, Robert D. Freeman, Tory Fleming Freeman)
PO Box 5004, CHATSWORTH, CA 91313
PH: (001) (310) 202 0641 and (001) (818) 993 7607
FX: (001) (310) 202 0641 and (001) (818) 993 6119
List Mail Bid Sales Auctions
Specialties: Ancient Greek, Roman and Byzantine coins

FROSETH INC., K.M. (Kent Froseth)
PO Box 23116,
MINNEAPOLIS, MN 55423
PH: (001) (612) 831 9550

FX: (001) (612) 835 3903
Telex 857006 KMFROSETH UD
Specialties: *US, foreign gold and silver coins*

GILLIO INC., Ronald J. (Ronald Gillio)
Goldmünzen International
1103 State Street, SANTA BARBARA, CA 93101
PH: (001) (805) 963 1345
FX: (001) (805) 962 6659
List Publications Auctions
Specialties: *US Gold, especially rare dates and proofs, US type coins. All Oriental and Asian numismatics, especially Japan, Korea and Taiwan*

HINDERLING, Wade
PO Box 606, MANHASSET, NY 11030
PH: (001) (516) 365 3729
Specialties: *Coins of the U.S. and France*

KOLBE, George Frederick
Fine Numismatic Books
PO Drawer 3100, CRESTLINE, CA 92325-3100
PH: (001) (909) 338 6527
FX: (001) (909) 338 6980
List Publications Auctions
Specialties: *Numismatic literature*

KOVACS, Frank L.
PO Box 25300, SAN MATEO, CA 94402
(suburb of San Francisco)
PH: (001) (415) 574 2028
FX: (001) (415) 574 1995
Specialties: *Ancient and Byzantine coins and antiquities*

MALTER & CO. INC., Joel L.
(Joel and Michael Malter)
17005 Ventura Blvd., ENCINO, CA 91316
PH: (001) (818) 784 7772 / 784 2181
FX: (001) (818) 784 4726
List (quarterly) Publications Auctions
Specialties: *Ancient and medieval coins, classical antiquities, numismatic books and literature*

MARGOLIS, Richard
(Richard and Sara Margolis)
PO Box 2054, TEANECK, NJ 07666
PH: (001) (201) 848 9379
FX: (001) (201) 847 0134
Publications
Specialties: *Foreign coins, medals, tokens, patterns*

PONTERIO & ASSOCIATES, Inc.
(Richard Ponterio, Stewart Westdal, M. Rennie, M. Fletcher, Kent Ponterio)
1818 Robinson Ave., SAN DIEGO, CA 92103
PH: (001) (619) 299 0400
FX: (001) (619) 299 6952
Auctions
Specialties: *Coins, medals and banknotes of Mexico and Latin America, World paper money, gold coins and crowns. Ancient coins*

RARE COIN COMPANY OF AMERICA, Inc.
(E. Milas, J. Bernberg)
6262 South Route 83, WILLOWBROOK, IL 60514
PH: (001) (708) 654 2580
FX: (001) (708) 654 3556
Auctions
Specialties: *US, foreign type coins and paper money*

ROSS, John G.
55 West Monroe Street, Suite 1070, CHICAGO, IL 60603
PH: (001) (312) 236 4088
Specialties: *US coins, coins of the world*

RYNEARSON, Dr. Paul
PO Box 4009, MALIBU, CA 90264
PH: (001) (310) 457 7713
FX: (001) (310) 457 6863
List Publications Mail Bid Sales
Specialties: Ancient and world coinage

STACK'S
(Harvey and Lawrence Stack)
123 West 57 Street, NEW YORK, NY 10019
PH: (001) (212) 582 2580
FX: (001) (212) 245 5018
List Publications Auctions
Specialties: United States, European, ancient, medieval

STEPHENS Inc., Karl (Karl Stephens)
PO Box 458, TEMPLE CITY, CA 91780
PH: (001) (818) 445 8154
FX: (001) (818) 447 6591
List
Specialties: Foreign coins, medals, tokens, eastern Europe US Type and copper coins

SUBAK Inc.
(Carl and Jon Subak, Peter Klem)
22 West Monroe Street,
Room 1506, CHICAGO, IL 60603
PH: (001) (312) 346 0609 / 346 0673
FX: (001) (312) 346 0150
Specialties: Roman, Byzantine, medieval

TELLER NUMISMATIC ENTERPRISES
(M. Louis Teller, Ph.D., A. Wing)
16027 Ventura Blvd., Suite 606,
ENCINO, CA 91436
PH: (001) (818) 783 8454
FX: (001) (818) 783 9083
Specialties: Gold and Silver coins of the World. Specialist in Russia, China, 19th Century Oriental Coins, and choice foreign paper money

WADDELL, Ltd., Edward J.
(Edward J. Waddell Jr.)
Suite 316, 444 N. Frederick Ave.,
GAITHERSBURG, MD 20877
(Suburb of Washington D.C.)
PH: (001) (301) 990 7446
FX: (001) (301) 990 3712
List
Specialties: Greek, Roman, Byzantine and Medieval coins; numismatic literature

WORLD-WIDE COINS OF CALIFORNIA
(James F. Elmen)
PO Box 3684,
SANTA ROSA, CA 95402
PH: (001) (707) 527 1007
FX: (001) (707) 527 1204
List Auctions
Specialties: World coins and medals 1500 to date

INTERNATIONAL NUMISMATIC ORGANIZATIONS

The following is a list of international numismatic organizations. This information is current as of the publication date. It is suggested that you write, call, or fax for more up-to-date membership information. If your organization is not listed, please send information to the author for inclusion in subsequent editions.

AUSTRALIA

• NUMISMATIC ASSOCIATION OF AUSTRALIA, P.O. Box 1920 R, GPO Melbourne, Victoria 3001 AUSTRALIA

• TASMANIAN NUMISMATIC SOCIETY, INC., 1 Fern Court, Clarmont, Tasmania 7011 AUSTRALIA. PH: 2-278825

BELGIUM

• SOCIETE ROYALE DE NUMISMATIQUE DE BELGIQUE, Musee de la Banque Natl.e, 14, Blvd. de Berlaymont, B-1000 Brussels, BELGIUM. Contact: Luc Smolderen

CANADA

• CANADIAN NUMISMATIC ASSOCIATION, P.O. Box 226, Barrie, ONTARIO L4M 4T2. Contact: Kenneth B. Prophet, PH: 705-737-0845, FX: 705-737-0293

The CNA is a non-profit educational and social body incorporated by Dominion Charter in 1963. It has grown by leaps and bounds from an idea of dedicated numismatists to form the world's second largest numismatic association.

Their present membership is basically located in Canada and the United States but we do have additional members around the world. They all have one common interest and that is Canadian numismatics.

As a member of the Association you will be eligible to receive the CNA/NESA Numismatic Correspondence Course at a reduced cost. You will receive the Journal *which carries articles, advertisements by dealers/members, and information about other CNA activities.*

The Journal *has been published since 1966 and has carried many of the most important papers relating to Canadian numismatics.*

CHINA

• CHINA NUMISMATIC SOCIETY, 32 Chengfang Street, Xicheng District, Bejing 100800, PEOPLE'S REPUBLIC OF CHINA. Contact: Zhi qiang Dai, Sec. Gen., PH: 86-1-6069935, FX: 86-1-6016414

• ORIENTAL NUMISMATIC SOCIETY (ONS), 30 Warren Road, Woodley, Reading, Berks RG5 3AR, England. Contact: Michael R. Broome, Sec. Gen., PH: 44-1734-693528 *American Region, P.O. Box 356, New Hope, PA. Contact: W.B. Warden, Sec.

The aims of the Society are to promote the systematic study of the coins, medals, and currency, both ancient and modern, of India, the Far East, the Islamic countries and their non-Western predecessors. It was founded in 1970 and its membership of some 650 people is spread over 40 countries.

CROATIA

• CROATIAN NUMISMATIC SOCIETY, RR1, P.O. Box 729-F, Rockville, IN 47872.

A current price list for Bosnian, Croatian, Macedonian, Serbian, Slovenian, and Yugoslavian bank notes and coins is available from the society. This list is free to all interested collectors when accompanied by a stamped, self-addressed envelope from the U.S.A., or cost of postage from other countries. Also available from the society is a limited number of large geographic maps of the Independent State of Croatia, 1941–45, in color.

DENMARK

• DANISH TOKEN CLUB, Støden 3, DK- 4000 Roskilde, DENMARK. Contact: Viktor Søndergaard, PH: 0045-46-35-88-63

• FUNEN NUMISMATIC SOCIETY, Odense Söhusvej, DK- 5270 Odense N., DENMARK. Contact: Ole Halkjaer Nielsen, FX: 45-65978628, E-Mail: ohn@post6.tele.dk

• NORDIC NUMISMATIC UNION, Royal Collection of Coins & Medals, National Museet, DK-1220 Copenhagen K DENMARK. Contact: Jorgen Steen Jensen, Exec. Officer, PH: 45-33134411, FX: 45-33155521

FRANCE

• LA SOCIETE AMERICANINE POUR L' ETUDE DE LA NUMISMATIQUE FRANCAISE, 5140 East Boulevard N.W., Canton, OH 44718

GERMANY

• DEUTSCHE NUMISMATISCHE GESELLSCHAFT, Dr. R. Albert H. Ehrend, Leharstr. 17,6720 Speyer GERMANY

• VERBAND DER DEUTSCHEN MUNZVEREINE, Assoc. of German Numismatic Societies, Reisenbergstr 58A, 8000 Munich 60 GERMANY

GREECE

• HELLENIC NUMISMATIC SOCIETY, Elleniki Nomismatiki Etaireia, Didotou 45, 106 8 Athens, GREECE. PH: 30-1-3615-585, FX: 30-1-3934-296

ISRAEL

• AMERICAN ISRAEL NUMISMATIC ASSOCIATION, P.O. Box 940277, Rockaway Park, NY 11694-0277. Contact: Edward Schuman, PH: 718-634-9266, FX: 718-318-1455

• ISRAEL NUMISMATIC SOCIETY, P.O. Box 750, Jerusalem, ISRAEL. TELEX: 26598, FX: 972-2-249779

• I.N.S.L.A./I.C.C.L.A. ISRAEL NUMISMATIC SOCIETY/ISRAEL COIN CLUB OF LOS ANGELES, 432 South Curson Avenue, Los Angeles, CA 90036. Contact: Murray Singer

The INSLA has been active in the Israel numismatic field over 28 years. Activities are devoted to the study and collection of numismatic items (both ancient and modern) related to Israel in particular and the Holy Land area in general.

Meetings feature educational programs covering coins, medals, paper money, and exonumia, as well as the material of the Palestine Mandata era.

Each meeting of INSLA/ICCLA is affilliated with the ANA, AINA, NASC, and CSNA.

INDIA

• NUMISMATIC SOCIETY OF INDIA, P.O. Box Banaras Hindu University, Varanasi, 221-005 INDIA

LITHUANIA

• LITHUANIAN NUMISMATIC ASSOCIATION—The Knight, P.O. Box 612, Columbia, MD 21045

MALAYSIA

• MALAYSIA NUMISMATIC SOCIETY, P.O. Box 12367, Kuala Lumpur, 50776 MALAYSIA

MEXICO

• SOCIEDAD NUMISMATICA DE MEXICO A. C., Eugena No. 13-301, Col. Nápoles, C. P. 03810, MEXICO. PH: 536-4440, FX: 543-1791

The society publishes a trimestral bi-lingual journal. The society periodically organizes auctions. Members receive catalogs and prices realized of these auctions and may also place numismatic items of their own for auction sale.

• SOCIEDAD NUMISMATICA DE MONTERREY C. A., Apartado Postal No. 422, Monterrey, N. L. MEXICO, C. P. 64000. Contact: Ing. Carlos Olivares Guzmá, PH: 8-331-1331, FX: 8-351-3444, E-Mail: fscagonz@vto.com

The society is a scientific and cultural institution, founded in 10/15/70, for promotion, increasing and divulgation of numismatic concerns for the numismatic and mainly for the Mexican numismatic, through research and knowledge of coins, medals, tokens and bills.

NEW ZEALAND

• ROYAL NUMISMATIC SOCIETY OF NEW ZEALAND, G.P.O., Box 2023, Wellington, NEW ZEALAND

PORTUGAL

• CLUBE NUMISMATIC DE PORTUGAL, Rua Angelina Vidal 40, 1100 Lisbon, PORTUGAL

• SOCIEDADE PORTUGUESA DE NUMISMATICA, Rua De Costa Cabral, 664, 4200 Porto PORTUGAL

RUSSIA

• RUSSIAN NUMISMATIC SOCIETY, P.O. Box 3013, Alexandria, VA 22302. Contact: Sec. Treas., PH: 703-920-2043, FX: 703-920-9345.

The Society was established in 1979. Since 1981 the Society's journal, the JRNS, is published three times a year and is the principle element holding the Society to its course. In support of its editorial work, the Society maintains a very comprehensive library of standard and specialized works on Russian numismatics, many of which are available on loan to the members. The Society provides advice and support on research resources.

SOUTH AFRICA

• SOUTH AFRICAN NUMISMATIC SOCIETY, P.O. Box 1689, Cape Town, 8000 SOUTH AFRICA

SPAIN

• ASOCIACION NUMISMATICA ESPAÑOLA, Gran via de las Corts Catalanes 627, 08010 Barcelona, SPAIN. FX: 34-3-3189062

SWITZERLAND

• COMMISSION INTERNATIONAL NUMISMATIQUE (CIN), Rutimeyer Strasse 12, CH-4054 Basel SWITZERLAND

• INTERNATIONAL ASSOCIATION OF PROFESSIONAL NUMISMATISTS (INAP), Loewenstrasse 65, CH-8001 Zurich, SWITZERLAND. Contact: Mr. Jean-Paul Divo, Gen. Sec., PH: 41-1-2211885, FX: 41-1-2112976

• NUMISMATISCHER VEREIN ZURICH, Postfach 4584, 8022, Zurich SWITZERLAND

• SOCIETE SUISSE de NUMISMATIQUE, Schweizerische Numismatische Gesellschaft, c/o Regie de Fribourg, 24 rue de Romong, CH-3701 Fribourg SWITZERLAND

THAILAND

• NUMISMATIC ASSOCIATION OF THAILAND, Royal Mint, 11017 Pradipat Road, Bangkok THAILAND

TURKEY

• TURKISH NUMISMATIC SOCIETY, P.K. 258, Osmanbey, Istanbul TURKEY

UKRAINE

• UKRAINIAN PHILATELIC & NUMISMATIC SOCIETY, P.O. Box 303, Southfields, NY 10975-0303

The Society was founded in 1952 and concentrates on collectibles (coins, banknotes, stamps, etc.) of Ukrainian themes. The Society publishes a bi-monthly newsletter and quarterly journal.

UNITED KINGDOM

• BRITISH ASSOCIATION OF NUMISMATIC SOCIETIES, c/o Bush Boake Allen, LTD., Blackhorse Lane, London E17 5QP, ENGLAND. Contact: P.H. Mernick, PH: 44-181-5236531, FX: 44-181-5318162

• BRITISH NUMISMATIC SOCIETY, c/o Hunterian Museum, Glasgow University, Glasgow G12 8QQ, SCOTLAND. Contact: J.D. Bateson, PH: 44-141-3304221, FX: 44-141-3078059

The British Numismatic Society was founded in 1903. The Society's terms of reference extend to cover all coins struck or used in Great Britain and Ireland from the introduction of coinage into Britain in the first century B.C. *down to modern times. It also concerns itself with medals, tokens, etc., and with coinage of present or former British overseas territories and dependencies.*

The British Numismatic Journal, *published annually by the Society and distributed to all paid-up members, provides the results of the most recent scholarly research into the history of the coinage, and records significant new numismatic discoveries. It is issued cloth-bound.*

Applications for membership from individuals or corporate bodies should be addressed to the Hon. Sec., Dr. J.D. Bateson, at the Hunterian Museum, University of Glasgow, University Avenue, Glasgow G128QQ.

• BRITISH SOCIETY, c/o Hunterian Museum, Glasgow University, Glasgow G12 8QQ SCOTLAND

• INTERNATIONAL NUMISMATIC COMMISSION, Dept. of Coins and Medals, British Museum, London WC1B 3DG, ENGLAND. Contact: Dr. A.M. Burnett, Sec., PH: 44-171-3238227, FX: 44-171-3238171

• ROYAL NUMISMATIC SOCIETY, Dept. Coins/Medals, British Museum, Great Russell Street, London WC1B 3DG, ENGLAND. Contact: V. Hewitt, PH: 44-171-3238173

The Society was founded in 1836 as the Numismatic Society of London and received the title of the Royal Numismatic Society by Royal Charter in 1904. The Society is an academic body of charitable status concerned with research into all branches of numismatics. Its lectures and publications deal with classical, oriental, medieval, and modern coins, as well as paper money, tokens, and medals.

• THE IPSWICH NUMISMATIC SOCIETY, PO BOX 104, Ipswitch, IP5, 7QL, UNITED KINGDOM. Contact: S. E. Sewell, PH: 01473-626950, FX: Same

U.S.A.

• AMERICAN NUMISMATIC ASSOCIATION, 818 North Cascade Avenue, Colorado Springs, CO 80903-3279. Contact: Robert Leuver, Exec. Dir., PH: 719-632-2646, FX: 719-634-4085, Internet: Leuver@Money.org

• AMERICAN NUMISMATIC SOCIETY, Broadway at 155th Street, New York, NY 10032, PH: 212-234-3130, FX: 212-234-3381

• ANCIENT COIN CLUB OF LOS ANGELES, P.O. Box 227, Canoga Park, CA 91305. Contact: Ralph J. Marx.

This club was established in 1966 and features highly informative and enjoyable programs on ancient Greek or Roman numismatics and cultures, as well as afternoons of coin trading exhibits and door prizes. Visitors are cordially invited to attend their meetings and meet others who share the same numismatic interests.

The club publishes a monthly newsletter and is a member of COIN and NASC.

• CALIFORNIA EXONUMIST SOCIETY, P.O. Box 6909, San Diego, CA 92166-0909. Contact: Kay Lenker, Sec.

Established in 1960, the California Exonuist Society (CES) encourages the study and collecting of exonumia—medals, tokens, script, orders and decorations, and all non-governmental items used for barter or trade.

CES meets and conducts educational forums in conjunction with the major conventions of GSCS and CSNA (Northern Calif.). CES sponsors an All-Day Collectibles Show with bourse dealers specializing in exonumia items and invitational.

CES's current president is Dorothy Baker. CES publishes a quarterly newsletter, The Medallion.

• COUNCIL OF INTERNATIONAL NUMISMATICS, P.O. Box 3637, Thousand Oaks, CA 91359. Contact: Sally Marx, President, PH: 805-495-1930

The Council of International Numismatics (COIN) was founded in 1963. Their goal is to promote interest in the collecting of foreign and ancient coins, foreign currency, medals, tokens, and other means of exchange.

At the present time there are seven clubs making up the council membership; there is no individual membership in COIN.

• INTERNATIONAL NUMISMATIC SOCIETY AUTHENTICATION BUREAU, P.O. Box 33134, Philadelphia, PA 19142. Contact: Charles R. Hoskins, Treas., PH: 215-365-0752, FX: 215-365-0752

• INTERNATIONAL NUMISMATIC SOCIETY OF SAN DIEGO, P.O. Box 6909, San Diego, CA 92166. Contact: Kay Lenker, Sec.

The International Numismatic Society of San Diego pursues the interest of foreign numismatics.

The club is affilliated with the American Numismatic Association (ANA) and California State Numismatic Association (CSNA).

• NUMISMATICS INTERNATIONAL, P.O. Box 670013, Dallas, TX 75367-0013. Contact: Jack Lewis, Membership Chair., PH: 214-361-7543

Numismatics International was formed in Dallas, Texas, in July 1964 and now has well over 800 members worldwide.

Their objectives are to encourage and promote the science of numismatics by specializing in areas and nations other than the United States; to cultivate fraternal relations among collectors and numismatic students; to encourage and assist new collectors; to foster the interest of youth in numismatics; to stimulate and advance affiliations among collectors and kindred organizations; and to acquire, share, and disseminate numismatic knowledge.

• SOCIETY FOR ANCIENT NUMISMATICS (SAN), P.O. Box 4085, Panarama City, CA 91412-4095. Contact: Dr. Lawrence A. Adams.

The Journal *of the Society for Ancient Numismatics (SAN) is published twice yearly. The SAN* Journal *supports the field of ancient numismatics with its wide range of articles and illustrations by scholars, professional numismatists, collectors, and amateurs with special perspectives. The* Journal *may be found in many of the world's foremost university and museum libraries.*

• SOCIETY FOR INTERNATIONAL NUMISMATICS, P.O. Box 943, Santa Monica, CA 90406. Contact: Barry Lapes, PH: 310-399-1085

The Society for International Numismatics is an international organization dedicated to the promotion of serious numismatic studies, endeavoring to bring to the collecting fraternity special items of interest and fundamental information. They hope their work will stimulate the individual study of numismatics from a practical as well as historical and economic viewpoint.

The Society's publications are: SINformation, *the Society's news journal;* COIN *(Compendium of International Numismatics), composed of original articles by Society members; and* NUMOGRAM, *a "Reader's Digest" of numismatic articles.*

The Society also publishes papers from its various bureaus on a periodic basis and presents educational forums and lecture programs for the collecting fraternity.

• WORLD PROOF NUMISMATIC ASSOCIATION, P.O. Box 4094, Pittsburgh, PA 15201. Contact: Gail P. Gray, PH: 412-782-4477, FX: 412-782-0227

INTERNATIONAL NUMISMATIC PUBLICATIONS

AUSTRALIA

• TASMANIAN NUMISMATIST, Tasmanian Numismatic Society, Inc., 1 Fern Court, Claremont, Tasmania 7011, AUSTRALIA. PH: 2-278825.

AUSTRIA

• NUMISMATIK SPEZIAL, Zeitungsverlag Kuhn und Co.GmbH, Kutschkergasse 42, A-1180 Vienna, AUSTRIA. PH: 01-47686, FX: 01-4768621. **Document type:** Consumer publication.

BELGIUM

• REVUE BELGE DE NUMISMATIQUE ET DE SIGILLOGRAPHIE, Royale de Numismatique de Belgique, c/o J.A. Schoonheit, Treas., 1 av. G. van Nerom, 1160 Brussels, BELGIUM. PH: 32-2-6728904. **Document type:** Academic/scholarly publication.

CANADA

• CANADIAN NUMISMATIC JOURNAL, Canadian Numismatic Association, P.O. Box 226, Barrie, Ontario L4M 4T2, CANADA. PH: 705-737-0845, FX: 705-737-0293. **Summary of content:** Aims to encourage and promote the science of numismatics by the study of coins, paper money, medals, tokens, and all other numismatic items, with special emphasis on material pertaining to Canada.

• CANADIAN COIN NEWS, Trajan Publishing Corp., 202–103 Lakeshore Road, Saint Catherines, Ontario L2N 2T6, CANADA. PH: 905-646-7744, FX: 905-646-0995. **Summary of content:** Whether numismatist or novice, it brings the collector the most complete, most authoritative, and most timely news available, with features on tokens and paper money to the finest coverage of Canadian decimal coinage.

CHINA

• ZHONGGUO QIANBI/CHINA NUMISMATICS (Zhongguo Qianbi Xuehui), Zhongguo Qianbi Bianjibu, 32 Chengfang Jie, Xicheng, Bejing 100800, PEOPLE'S REPUBLIC OF CHINA. PH: 86-10-6015522, FX: 86-10-6016414. **Document type:** Academic/scholarly publication. **Summary of content:** Publishes research on numismatics or the history of coins, news of excavations, and interesting anecdotes about coins; introduces historic coins, presents the experiences of coin collectors, and reports on related events in China and the world. Text in Chinese.

CZECH REPUBLIC

• NUMISMATICKE LISTY, Narodni Muzeum, Vaclavske nan.68, 115 79 Prague 1, CZECH REPUBLIC. Text in Czech; summaries in English, French, German, and Russian.

DENMARK

• NORDISK NUMISMATISK UNION MEDLEMSBLAD, Nordisk Numismatisk Union, c/o Royal Collection of Coins and Medals, National Museum, DK-1220 Copenhagen K, DENMARK. FX: 45-33-15-55-21.

ENGLAND

• COINS MARKET VALUES, Link House Magazines, Ltd, Link Hse, Dingwall Avenue, Croydon, Surrey, CR9 2TA ENGLAND. PH: 0180-686-2599, FX: 0181-760-0973. **Summary of Content:** Numismatics, all British coinage: medieval and modern.

• COIN NEWS, Token Publishing, Ltd., P.O. Box 20, Axminister, Devon, EX13 7YT ENGLAND. PH: 01404-831878, or 01404-831895. **Summary of content:** General magazine for collectors covering coins, medals, and banknotes.

• COIN NEWS COIN YEARBOOK, Token Publishing, Ltd, P.O. Box 20, Axminister, Devon, EX13 7YT ENGLAND. PH: 01401-831878, FX: 01401-831895. **Summary of content:** Yearbook covering all aspects of coin collecting, and price guide to coins, banknotes, and medallions.

• NUMISMATIC CIRCULAR, Spink and Son, Ltd., 5 King Street, St. James's, London, ENGLAND. PH: 44-171-930-7888, FX: 44-171-839-4853. **Document type:** Catalog.

FINLAND

• NUMISMAATIKKO, Suomen Numismaatikkoliitto, P.O. Box 895, FIN-00101 Helsinki, FINLAND. PH: 358-31-631-480, FX: 358-31-631-480.

FRANCE

• NUMISMATIQUE & CHANGE, SEPS, 12 rue Poincare, 55800 Revigny, FRANCE. PH: 29-70-56-33, FX 29-70-57-44.

• REVUE NUMISMATIQUE (Societe Francaise de Numismatique), Societe d'Edition les Belles Lettres, 95 Boulevard Raspail, 75006 Paris, FRANCE. PH: 1-45485826, FX: 1-45485860. **Document type:** Academic/scholarly publication.

GERMANY

• DER GELDSCHEINSAMMLER, H. Gietl Verlag and Publikations Service GmbH, Postfach 166, 93122 Regenstauf, GERMANY. PH: 49-9402-5856, FX: 49-9402-6635. **Document type:** Newsletter.

• NUMISMATISCHES NACHRICHTENBLATT, Deutsche Numismatische Gesellchaft, Hans-Purrmann-Allee 26, 67346 Speyer, GERMANY. PH: 49-6232-35752. **Document type:** Newsletter.

GREECE

• NOMISMATIKA KHRONIKA, Hellenic Numismatic Society-Elleniki Nomismatiki Etaireia, Didotou 106 80 Athens, GREECE. PH: 30-1-3615-585, FX: 30-1-3634-296. **Document type:** Academic/scholarly publication, monographic series. **Summary of content:** Covers Greek and related numismatics of all periods. Translations or summaries in English.

INDIA

• JOURNAL NUMISMATIC SOCIETY OF INDIA, Numismatic Society of India, Banaras Hindu University, Varanasi 221005, INDIA. PH: 311074. Text in English.

IRAQ

• AL-MASKUKAT, Ministry of Culture and Information, State Organization of Antiquities and Heritage, Jamal Abdul Nasr Street Baghdad, IRAQ. PH: 4158355.

ISRAEL

• ISRAEL NUMISMATIC JOURNAL, Israel Numismatic Society, P.O. Box 750, Jerusalem, ISRAEL. PH: 26598, FX: 972-2-249779. **Document type:** Academic/scholarly publication. Text in English.

ITALY

• ISTITUTO ITALIANO DI NUMISMATICA, Istituto Italiano di Numismatica, Palazzo Barberini, Via Quattro Fontane 13, 00195 Rome, ITALY. PH: 39-6-4743603, FX: 39-6-4743603. **Document type:** Academic/scholarly publication. **Summary of content:** Presents research on numismatic subjects.

• NUMISMATICA, Gino Manfredini, Ed. & Pub., Via Ferramola 1-A, 25121 Brescia, ITALY. PH: 030-3756211. **Document type:** Newsletter.

• PANORAMA NUMISMATICO, 75000, Via Grimau 6-A, 46029 Suzzara (MN), ITALY. PH: 39-376-532063, FX: 39-376-521304. **Document type:** Academic/scholarly publication. **Summary of content:** Covers ancient and Italian numismatics for collectors and scholars.

• WORLD COLLECTIONS NEWS, World Wide Collections S.r.l., Corso Buenos Aires, 20-4, 16129 Genoa, ITALY. PH: 39-10-581463, FX: 39-10-561855. **Document type:** Newspaper.

NETHERLANDS

• EUROPEAN NUMISMATICS, Uitgeverij Numismatica Nederland N.V., Darwinplantsoen 26, Amsterdam 6, NETHERLANDS. Text in Dutch and English.

• JAARBOEK VOOR MUNT-EN PENNINGKUNDE, Koninklijk Nederlands Genootschap voor Munt-en Penningkunde-Royal Dutch Society of Numismatics, c/o The Netherlands Bank, Postbus 98, 1000 AB Amsterdam, NETHERLANDS. **Document type:** Academic/scholarly publication. Text in Dutch, occasionally in English, French, German; summaries in English.

POLAND

• LODZKI NUMIZMATYK, Polskie Towarzystwo Archeologiczne i Numizmatyczne, Oddzial w Lodzi, Plac Wolnosci 14, Lodz, POLAND.

• WIADOMOSCI NUMIZMATYCZNE/NUMISMATIC NEWS, Ossolineum Publishing House, Foreign Trade Department, Rynek 9, 50-106 Wroclaw, POLAND.

SLOVAKIA

• SLOVENSKA NUMIZMATIKA (Slovenska Akademia Vied) Veda, Publishing House of the Slovak Academy of Sciences, Klemensova 19, 814, 30 Bratislava, SLOVAKIA. Text in Slovak.

SPAIN

• GACETA NUMISMATICA, Asociacion Numismatica Espanola, Gran Via de les Corts Catalanes, 627, 08010 Barcelona, SPAIN. FX: 34-3-3189062. **Document type:** Academic/scholarly publication.

SWEDEN

• NUMISMATISKA MEDDELANDEN NUMISMATIC COMMUNICATIONS, Svenska Numismatiska Foereningen, Banergatan 17 nb, S-115 22 Stockholm, SWEDEN. PH: 46-8-667-55-98, FX: 46-8-6670771. **Document type:** Academic/scholarly publication.

SWITZERLAND

• GAZETTE NUMISMATIQUE SUISSE/SCHWEIZER MUENZBLAETTER, Alexander Wild, Rathausgasse 30, CH-3011 Bern, SWITZERLAND. **Document type:** Newsletter.

• HAUTES ETUDES NUMISMATIQUES (Ecole Pratique des Hautes Etudes, Centre de Recherches d'Histoire et de Philologie, FR), Librairie Droz S.A., 11, rue Massot, CH-1211 Geneva 12, SWITZERLAND. PH: 41-22-3466666, FX: 41-22-3472391, E-mail: drozsa@dial.eunet.ch; URL:http://www.eunet.ch/customers/droz. circ.500. **Document type:** Monographic series. **Summary of content:** Examines ancient coins.

• MUENZEN-REVUE, International Coin Trend Journal, Verlag Muenzen-Revue AG, Blotzheimerstr.40, CH-4055 Basel, SWITZERLAND. PH: 41-61-3825504, FX: 41-61-3825542. **Document type:** Trade publication. **Summary of content:** Feature news, history, values, new coins, trade, as well as reports of events and auctions for coin hobbyists.

• NUMISMATICA E ANTICHITA CLASSICHE, Amici dei Quaderni Ticinesi di Numismatica e Antichita Classiche, Secretariat, C.P.3157, CH-6901 Lugano, SWITZERLAND. PH: 41-91-6061606. **Document type:** Academic/scholarly publication. Text in English, French, German, and Italian.

• REVUE SUISSE DE NUMISMATIQUE/SCHWEIZERISCHE NUMISMATISCHE RUNDSCHAU, Societe Suisse de Numismatique-

Schweizerische Numismatische Gesellschaft, Niederdorfstr. 43, CH-8001 Zurich, SWITZERLAND. **Document type:** Newsletter.

USA

• AMERICAN JOURNAL OF NUMISMATICS, SERIES 2, American Numismatic Society, Broadway at 155th Street, New York, NY 10032. PH: 212-345-3130, FX: 212-234-3381. **Summary of content:** Academic analysis of numismatic objects contributing to the understanding and interpretation of history, political science, archaeology, and art history.

• CLASSICAL NUMISMATIC REVIEW, Classical Numismatic Group, Inc., P.O. Box 479, Lancaster, PA 17608-0479. PH: 717-390-9194, FX: 717-390-9978.

• PROOF COLLECTORS CORNER, World Proof Numismatic Association, Box 4094, Pittsburgh, PA 15201. PH: 412-782-4477, FX: 412-782-0227. **Document type:** Trade publication. **Summary of content:** Provides current coverage of numismatic issues, with information on the history and background of coins.

• SHEKEL, American Israel Numismatic Association, P.O. Box 940277, Rockaway Park, NY 11694-0277. PH: 718-634-9266, FX: 718-318-1455. **Document type:** Academic/scholarly publication. **Summary of content:** Presents collection of Israel and Judaic coins, medals, and currency from antiquity to the present.

• SINFORMATION, Society for International Numismatics, Box 943, Santa Monica, CA 90406. PH: 213-396-4662. **Document type:** Newsletter.

• THE CELATOR, Journal of Ancient and Medieval Art and Artifacts, Celator, Inc., P.O. Box 123, Lodi, WI 53555. PH: 608-592-4684, FX: 608-592-4684, E-mail: celator@aol.com. **Document type:** Consumer publication. **Summary of content:** Articles and features about ancient coins and artifacts, connoisseurship, and market news.

VIRGIN ISLANDS

• MONETA INTERNATIONAL, Coins and Treasures Monthly, Vernon W. Pickering, P.O. Box 704, Road Town—Tortola, BRITISH VIRGIN ISLANDS, W.I. PH: 809-49-43510, FX: 809-494-4540. **Summary of content:** Covers coin collecting and numismatic research from ancient to modern coins.

COIN AUCTION SALES

$99,000 for an 1825 Russian Ruble of Constantine! $143,000 for an 1862 British Columbia $20! $18,150 for an 1839 British gold 5-pound piece!

by Q. David Bowers

Auctions are a vital part of the coin hobby. Indeed, from the standpoint of news value, auction action captures more headlines than any other field of commercial activity. Just recently Bowers and Merena Galleries (which advertises as America's most successful rare coin auctioneer), sold at auction the finest collection of Canadian coins ever to cross the block—the fabulous Norweb cabinet. The total realization exceeded $2,000,000 (U.S. funds) and many records were set in the meantime. Highlighting the event was a beautiful gold $20 piece struck in British Columbia in 1862, which crossed the block at a record-breaking $143,000.

Representative of the field of world coins in general, the collection formed over a long period of years by Ambassador and Mrs. R. Henry Norweb was echoed in headlines around the United States, indeed all over the world. Records are made to be broken, and this sale had its share. Focusing for a moment on Canadian pieces, the Norweb Collection included the following, giving the highest price in each of various denominations in the Canadian series:

NORWEB COLLECTION CANADIAN COIN HIGHLIGHTS

1.	1925 one-cent piece with special Proof finish	$3630
2.	1885 five-cent piece. Gem Uncirculated	27,500
3.	1921 five-cent piece. Known as the "Prince of Canadian Coins"	24,200
4.	1875 ten-cent piece with H mintmark, gem Proof	17,600
5.	1886 twenty-five cent piece, Proof	34,100
6.	1921 fifty-cent piece, Gem Uncirculated "King of Canadian Coins"	82,000
7.	1935 silver dollar, Gem Proof	12,100
8.	1916 sovereign struck at the Ottawa Mint, Gem Uncirculated	16,500

WORLD WIDE ACTIVITY

In America, while Bowers and Merena Galleries was busy selling the Norweb Collection, other firms such as Superior Galleries, Stack's, Ponterio & Wyatt, Sotheby's, Christie's, Heritage, and others were preparing catalogues or scheduling events which often showcased coins of the world, in addition to United States issues. Also important in the program of most auctioneers are Ancient coins of Greece and Rome, some of which have exquisite beauty and extraordinary values.

In Canada, Australia, England, Germany, Switzerland, France, and elsewhere, several dozen other auctioneers were and are active. Scarcely a week goes by on the calendar without an important auction of world coins being held somewhere or other on the globe.

A TRUE TEST OF VALUE

Auctions are perhaps the truest test of coin values world wide. One can talk about "bid" and "ask" prices in various numismatic publications, and general market guides, but do actual transactions occur at these figures? The bottom line is that a coin is worth what someone will pay for it. An auction price, assuming that the sale is conducted in a professional manner, that "reserves" are disclosed, that the catalogue is widely distributed and that the sale is publicized, represents what a given coin, token, medal, or piece of paper money is worth in a given moment of time. For example, if I were to state to you that a certain coin in Very Fine grade fetched $1,200 at a recent sale, you would be hard pressed to argue that it was only worth $500 or, conversely, it was worth $3,000. Rather, $1,200 represents the current market value at the moment.

However, sometimes in the case of "name" sales, coins will bring more than their normal prices at auctions. Let me explain:

AUCTION "FEVER"

There are a lot of interesting stories that can be told with regard to auction sales. One of my favorites treats the incredible collection of Stanislaw Herstal which was catalogued by Karl Stephens of our staff, and showcased at auction in February 1974. Herstal, a citizen of Poland, was born in 1908. He grew up in a very artistic family; his mother was a poetess, his sister a pianist, and his brother an actor and producer. This artistic background fostered an early interest in numismatics. During the great European conflict, a great part of his collection—some 11,000 coins in all—disappeared, never to be returned to him. Still his enthusiasm continued, and new areas of study and collecting were explored. The collection grew again. Years later, we were given the privilege of handling his estate. This came on the heels of a major United States collection. For the first event, the United States coins, the gallery was filled to capacity, excitement prevailed, and records were broken. Then the scene shifted to the specialized offering of Polish pieces. At that time, February 7–9, 1974, Poland was solidly behind the Iron Curtain, and few people in that country had the means or opportunity to bid on their own coins. I mention this as often if there is an active coin collecting community within a country, this strengthens prices. United States citizens mainly want to buy United States coins, Canadian citizens mainly want to buy Canadian coins, British citizens mainly want to buy British coins and so on. However, in the present instance, while Polish citizens may have wanted to buy Polish coins, they were not able to do so. Thus, the market was left to those in other countries. As the last United States coin was sold, the chairs emptied one by one. Finally, just a handful of people remained. Panic! What will happen? These thoughts ran through my mind. Not to worry. It takes only two bidders to run up the price of a coin at auction, or even to set record prices. It turned out that a small group of bidders, while not impressive in numbers, had very well endowed bank accounts and were determined to buy these coins. A bidding war ensued, and when the dust settled, many pieces sold for five to ten times their previously estimated market values! I will never forget this occurrence.

In another time a beautiful proof silver ruble of Constantine of Russia, 1825, was consigned to one of our sales. This issue is especially desirable as only a few pieces are known with the portrait of this ruler. Even major collections are apt to lack an example, and many specialists have never *seen* a Constantine ruble, let alone have had the opportunity to buy one.

What was the coin worth? When it was catalogued for sale by us in 1994 as an additional consignment to the collection of the Massachusetts Historical Society, no one was sure. $20,000? That figure seemed too low, but certainly a bid at that level would have been competitive. $40,000? Certainly a strong bid, but again there were no answers. The sale day came, and the audience rippled with excitement as the chance of a lifetime was about to occur. Many hands went in the air as the auctioneer called the opening of the lot, and as the bidding progressed a thousand dollars at a time, then in larger jumps, competition narrowed. Finally, midst applause, the coin was sold for a record $99,000—the buyer being a representative of a financial institution in Russia (which by this time had secured a degree of financial freedom).

The foregoing also illustrates the appeal of world coins. In today's market, American collectors are more active than are those of any other country. Accordingly, United States coins are bid to much higher levels than coins of comparable rarity from other countries. The 1825 Constantine ruble of Russia is rarer than a United States silver dollar of 1804 (15 pieces being known of the latter). The 1804 dollar has sold in the hundreds of thousands of dollars on several occasions, and is valued at about the $1 million mark for a really outstanding specimen. This is about ten times the price of a Constantine ruble! Similarly, gold coins of the United States sell for many multiples than comparable rarities among gold coins of France, England, Australia, or other areas. While Americans will probably always have preference for United States coins, there are certainly interesting purchase opportunities in the price levels of other numismatic specialties.

HOW TO BE A SMART BIDDER

How should one participate in an auction? In my opinion, it is best to plan in advance. I recommend contacting different auction firms requesting sample copies of their catalogues, but please bear in mind that often a charge must be paid as catalogues can be very expensive to publish. Review the catalogues, paying particular attention to the Terms of Sale as they fluctuate from firm to firm. Issues to be concerned with are buyer's fees, return privileges, bidding options, etc. You are legally bound to those terms, and they are put into the catalogue for a specific purpose—not just for entertaining reading. Do not take them lightly or fail to read them! Please bear in mind that certain countries may have different regulations from those in effect in the United States. There is such things as export taxes to be considered, customs, duties, overseas postage, insurance or lack thereof, and so on. If you are bidding in an auction held in the United States, and are a United States citizen, the situation is fairly straightforward. However, if you are bidding elsewhere, be sure to seek specific advice as to the items just discussed. Some procedures are exceedingly complicated!

As a collector of world coins, you have many purchase possibilities. There are dozen of auction houses all over the globe, some of whom conduct major sales on a fairly regular basis, and others who have only occasional offerings. It probably is not practical to subscribe to every auction catalogue published. A good alternative is to sign up as a subscriber to a periodical on the subject, for example *World Coin News* (Krause Publications, Iola, WI 54945). Such a publication contains information as to forthcoming auctions, catalogue ordering information, etc. In this way you can specifically order the catalogues that interest you most.

Beyond this, certain firms have specialties. As an example, in London there are a number of auction houses specializing in British coins. If such are your forte, you may wish to become acquainted with these houses, whereas an auctioneer in Germany, for example, would be apt to have only minor offerings of British coins.

When bidding in a sale, it is also important to learn a bit about exchange rates. While some overseas firms may accept bids in American dollars, usually bids are wanted in the currency of the country in which the sale occurs. Conversion rates change from time to time, and while changes during a period of a few weeks—while your bids are on the way to the sale—will probably not be significant, still there might be a few percentage points. Be careful, and take this into consideration if you are watching your bids closely.

A typical auction firm will issue a catalogue describing each lot in detail. If you have a question about a piece, that question can often be answered on the telephone—assuming you wish to pay international telephone rates and you can find an operator in English. More practical may be the use of a fax. In that way time can be given for the other party to reply. Be sure to include instructions as to your fax number so that they can return the information. Of course, you need to have a personal or office fax address to do this (using a commercial fax service in a public facility may be unsatisfactory, as you may not receive the reply for a few days).

Terms in catalogues issued outside the United States may have different meanings. The numerical system of grading so common here in America has no counterparts elsewhere. Instead, adjectives are typically used, sometimes with descriptions that can mean different things to different buyers. For example, in France *flurde coin*, abbreviated fdc, is the equivalent of "gem." However, gem quality is often in the eye of the beholder. As is true anywhere, grading interpretations can vary.

If you plan to spend a large amount of money in a sale held outside the borders of the United States, you may wish to contact an American foreign coin specialist and commission him or her to exercise your bids. A fee will be charged for this service, but you will have a pair of expert eyes representing you, and this may answer some of your questions about grades, price levels, and so on. The investment would seem to be well worth it. Of course, arrangements have to be made in advance, and you will have to establish your credit with the agent. If an agent spends, say, $10,000 on your behalf at a London auction or one in Paris, he or she will expect you to immediately pay for these coins upon notification. If you don't like the grade of the coins, or have changed your mind about buying them, that is too bad, as the coins are yours and you are obligated to pay for them. This is a responsibility, and it should be carefully considered in advance. Your agent is representing you, not bidding on his or her own account.

Price estimates are sometimes given in auction catalogues, but actual results are apt to vary. While printed estimates can be used as a general guide, it is better to do your homework and see what comparable coins have sold for at other auctions, or ask some friends or dealer acquaintances for suggestions. It is sometimes the policy of auction houses to low-ball the estimates. For example, a coin that a dealer might readily pay $5,000 for in order to buy for stock, might be estimated in a catalogue at the equivalent of $3,000–$4,000. When the auction takes place, such a piece would naturally sell for more than $5,000. Those who are not "in the know" and who observe the prices realized would think that a record price was being set, for the $3,000–$4,000 estimate has been far exceeded. However, the facts of life are that the estimate was too low to begin with. This is a particularly popular practice with art auction houses and general auctioneers, less so with advanced coin specialists. After this particular sale takes place, order a copy of the "prices realized." Bear in mind that it is a practice of some houses not to state whether or not a coin has been sold, and the price might be listed, but may represent a buy-in by the owner. Nevertheless, a listing of prices will have some general value and will certainly guide you to your bids the next time around.

Many firms will gladly accommodate your request for a phone description. Furthermore, if you are an established collector with a history of successful coin buying, and are known to the auctioneer, an arrangement may be made whereby the coin can be sent to you for inspection, providing that the coin is returned the same day and that you pay postage and insurance both ways. This courtesy is commonly referred to as "mail inspection."

Participation in an auction sale can be by mail or in person. Before each auction, there is a lot viewing period during which each lot can be personally inspected. Most auctioneers firmly state that anyone who has had a chance to view lots beforehand, or anyone who is a floor bidder, cannot return a coin for any reason whatsoever, with the exception of authenticity. So do your homework earlier, not later!

BIDDING BY MAIL

If you plan to bid by mail, send in your bid sheet as early as you can. Remember that overseas delivery can be very erratic, and it is not unusual for mail to take a week or more to reach many places on the globe, even large cities. Fax is a better option. Request a return fax verifying the receipt of your bids. In that way you will be secure in the knowledge that the information has been received on a timely basis. If you are unknown to the auction house, start at an early date to establish credit, contacting the auction house as to the amount you wish to spend, and how credit should be arranged. Quite probably, a deposit will be required or excellent bank reference will be needed. If you employ an agent in America to bid for you, this point becomes moot, as the agent will establish his or her own credit.

As a general bidding strategy, while compiling your bids, first determine the lots you are interested in and the amount which you are willing to pay for each. Be aware of current price levels. If a certain variety of Morgan silver dollar generally brings $500 on the retail market, the chances aren't very good that a bid of $300 will make you the owner. Conversely, there is no particular point in bidding $800 for it if you can buy one somewhere else for $500, unless you like the pedigree, toning, or some other aspect which differentiates the piece.

Many auction houses offer a reduction in the top bid if competition permits, but not all companies follow this practice. In any event, it is best not to count on this for if you bid $1,000, you may very well be charged $1,000. I reiterate that bids may need to be submitted in another currency, and it would be devastating to bid a figure in American dollars if the auction is to be conducted in British pounds—your dollar bids might be mistaken for pound bids, and you'll pay far too much! Conversely, if you are bidding in an auction in Belgium, where the franc is worth very little, a bid inadvertently submitted in dollars would have virtually no chance of success.

Once your bids are compiled, you can determine whether to utilize some of the special bidding options offered by the auction house. These special options help the mail bidder place as many potentially winning bids as possible.

Extreme care must be taken when bidding in overseas auctions, and again I suggest that employing an agent may be the most practical method, at least until you gain auction experience.

FLOOR BIDDING

At the sale itself, coins awarded to floor bidders are usually final. If a coin is overgraded, damaged, or even counterfeit, often that is simply too bad for the buyer—there is no recourse. (In the United States, rare coin auctioneers generally guarantee the authenticity of what they sell, but this is not always the case in foreign countries.) It is important to study each piece carefully during lotviewing time permitted before the sale, or have your agent do so. If you attend in person, I suggest viewing some coins that are not in the mainstream. And so forth. For example, if you are bidding on British coins, there is nothing more frustrating than to specialize in silver crown-size coins and look only at these, only to find at the sale itself that there are some wonderful bargains in, say, half crowns or copper pennies. If your numismatic appetite is versatile, be sure to check a few other series as well.

Bidding strategy at the sale itself has furnished the topic for endless discussions. Should I sit in the front? Or, will I better know what is going on if I sit in the back? Or, perhaps on the side would be best. There are no rules. Pick your favorite. In the case of foreign auctions, it's probably best not to decide until the sale itself begins. Watch what is going on, then determine what would be a position advantageous to your best interest.

Most auction houses furnish bidders with paddles or cards with printed numbers. Some bidders flick their paddles almost unnoticeably while others hold them up in the air like a banner. Personal preference is the key, but be sure the auctioneer knows what you are doing. If the auctioneer misses your bid, call out right at the time the lot is being sold. Generally the auctioneer at his discretion may reopen a lot if he feels that a legitimate mistake has been made on the auction floor, but he will not do this on a consistent basis for the same bidder who isn't paying attention.

After the sale, you will be required to make payment, probably on a draft from your bank to the bank of the auctioneer. Relatively few foreign auction firms want to take personal checks from the United States, except perhaps from dealers or other long-established accounts. If your purchases are nominal, you may to take the coins with you, but be sure to have appropriate documents for customs. Alternatively, you may wish to have the auctioneer ship the coins to your United States address. Again, some forms will probably need to be filled out and regulations followed.

YOUR ROLE AS A SELLER— FINDING THE RIGHT AUCTIONEER

If you have a group of scarce and rare foreign (non-American) coins to sell, and the coins are valued at several thousand dollars or more in total, auction may be the route for you. By exposing your coins in an auction catalogue, thousands of potential bidders can become acquainted with them. On the other hand, if you have miscellaneous coins of low value, or bullion-type coins, a dealer with an over-the-counter business may offer a better price to buy such items for store stock.

If you live in the United States you can, of course, consign your coins to an auctioneer in a foreign country. However, it is far more practical to pick someone here in America. In that way the seller will talk your language, carefully answer any questions you may have and so on.

As a caveat at this point, I suggest that the vast majority of "miscellaneous foreign coins" owned by American citizens have very low values. In general, coins brought back as souvenirs from an overseas war or a grand tour of Europe, or a cruise to the orient have very little value in the United States. Time and again I have seen little value. For starters, before spending a great amount of emotional energy, if you feel you have coins of value, either have them appraised by a local coin shop (which may involve paying a fee), or secure a copy by purchase or loan of the Krause-Mischler reference, *The Standard Catalog of World Coins.* This immense volume, larger than most metropolitan phone books, lists just about everything.

If you find you have coins that are worth several thousand dollars or more, and the group consists of scarce and rare pieces (rather than bulk), then give some thought to choosing an auctioneer. Here are some questions you should ask:

What is the commission rate? What is the buyer's fee? Some auction houses will offer a reduced commission rate but an increased buyer's fee.

What do I get for this rate? Are there any extra charges? Are catalogue illustrations extra? What about photography? What about advertising? It is a practice for some auction houses to give a "minimum price" or cut-rate fee, and then charge extra to bring the service up to "normal" Find this out in advance.

Once the auction takes place, when will the settlement date be? How will I receive payment? Can I receive a portion of the expected realization in advance? If so, what interest rates are charged? What is the financial reputation of the company? Does the company have adequate insurance? How can I be sure that my valued coins and other numismatic items are in truly safe hands?

Does the auction house allow reserves? Can I bid on my own coins? What is the anticipated market for my consignment? What happens is someone bidding on my coins fails to pay his auction bill?

What type of coins has the firm handled in the past? Does the company specialize only in certain areas or does it offer many different services? How large is the staff and what are the qualifications of the individual staff members?

What is the reputation of the firm? What do past consignors think of the performance of the auction house? Is the company familiar with die-varieties, great rarities, and obscure coins in addition to ones normally seen? Does the firm have a specialty such as Mexican coins, British coins, Oriental coins, or any other niche that might correspond to the coins you have?

What do the firm's catalogues look like? Are the descriptions appealing? Are the descriptions authoritative? What is the quality of the mailing list? Does it contain proven bidders? What type of advertising will be done for the catalogue featuring my coins?

In what town or city will the event be held? What are the facilities like?

I suggest that each of the preceding questions be answered with care and you may well think of other questions in addition.

IT'S THE BOTTOM LINE THAT COUNTS

Several years ago, I and another member of the Auctions by Bowers and Merena staff traveled to visit with the heirs to a very large collection of United States and world coins. Our firm offered a 10% commission rate to sell the pieces, stating that they would be presented in a Grand Format™ color-illustrated catalogue with no expense spared when it came to advertising, publicity and the like.

While the owners of the coins seemed to be very impressed with our track record, the appearance of our past catalogues, our reputation, and other factors, there was one problem: a competitor had offered to do it for no commission rate at all! It was stated that the competitor's profit would be determined only by the buyer's fee.

To make a long story short, the coins were awarded to a company whose main expertise was not in coins but rather, in art and furniture. The sale came and went, and instead of realizing the approximately $1.5 million that the heirs hoped for, (and which I felt could be achieved with proper presentation), only about half that amount was obtained! Dealers at the sale had a field day, for few collectors had received a copy of the catalogue. I later reviewed a copy of the prices realized and noted that many issues sold for fractions of what I felt they could be sold for by my firm or, for that matter, by other leading *rare coins* auctioneers. Virtually no advertising was placed by the other auction firm. And, apparently many of the catalogues went to people who were not proven buyers of the type of coins being offered.

To expand upon this further, if an auctioneer sells a coin for $1,000 hammer price and charges you 10%, thus netting you $900, it might be a much better deal than if another auctioneer sells your coin for $600 and charges you no fee at all—netting you $600. If you were considering having surgery done, or having an architect design your house, or having your portrait painted, I cannot envision you saying "I am looking for the cheapest rate." Rather such considerations as past performance would be more important. So it should be with coins as well. As I believe John Ruskin said, "the bitterness of poor quality last much longer than the sweetness of low price."

A LASTING TRIBUTE

There are some aesthetic considerations to selling at auction. A finely prepared catalogue can be a memorial to you and your collecting activities. Although the coins once owned by you are in new hands, the catalogue will remain a lasting tribute to your collection for you to enjoy. In addition, most people who have spent many years collecting coins enjoy the pride and satisfaction that comes with the recognition a beautiful catalogue provides when their collections are sold.

If you form a collection over a long period of years, and if you enjoy numismatics to its fullest extent, selling your collection by auction can be the high point of your accomplishments.

Meanwhile, as you build your collection, auctions provide an interesting and exciting way to acquire pieces that you need.

Have fun!

AUCTIONS BY BOWERS AND MERENA

Auctions by Bowers and Merena, Inc., has had the good fortune of being in the forefront of numismatics for many years. Not only have we been market leaders in United States coins, we have handled many important world and ancient properties as well. Along the way we have received more "Catalogue of the Year" honors awarded by the Numismatic Literary Guild than all of our competitors combined. Of the top three most valuable U.S. coin collections every to be sold at auction, we have catalogued and sold all three—the $25,000,000 Garrett Collection, the $20,000,000 Norweb Collection, the $12,400,000 Eliasberg Collection of U.S. Gold coins, as well as the $11,600,000 Louis E. Eliasberg Sr., Collection Part I.

Values of world coins are less than United States coins, due to market demand as mentioned earlier. That is, a given Canadian rarity will sell for less than a United States rarity, ditto for a British rarity. Even so, many incredible realizations have been accomplished, including the landmark Guia collection of world gold coins auctioned by us in 1988 on behalf of an overseas client. Many records from this sale still echo today. Sample realizations include:

Spain: Charles III Gold 8 Escudos, 1762 JV. Seville. About Uncirculated. $77,000.

Spain: Ferdinand II (V of Spain). 10 Ducats (quadruple ducado), n.d. Choice Very Fine. $58,300.

Sweden: John III (1568–1592). 2 Rosenobles, or 5 Ducats, n.d. About Uncirculated. $57,200.

Italian States: John Galeazzo Maria Sforza, under the Regency of Lodovico il Moro (1481–1494). 2 Ducats, n.d. About Uncirculated. $55,000.

Italian States: Philip IV. 20 Zecchini, 1643. Extremely Fine. $82,500.

Italian States: Charles Emanuel II. 10 Scudi d'Oro, 1663. Very Fine. $61,600.

Italian States: Republic of Italy. Pattern Doppia, an II (=1803). Milan. Uncirculated, prooflike. $77,000.

If you would like an "World Coin Auction Kit" which includes a current auction catalogue and a full color brochure on consigning your coins to auction, please send a certified check or money order in the amount of $10 to World Auction Kit, Auctions by Bowers and Merena, Inc., PO Box 1224, Wolfeboro, NH 03894.

We regret that we cannot engage in correspondence or appraisals of miscellaneous world coins, except for a fee of $5 or more per coin, payable in advance. An easy alternative is to acquire a copy of the aforementioned Krause-Mischler catalog, and develop estimates on your own, or have a coin store in your own area offer information.

Note: There is no appraisal fee for established numismatists who have carefully formed *numismatic collections* with rarities, proofs, and other delicacies. The fee applies only to common issues without numismatic importance.

If you'd like immediate information on the most profitable way to sell your coins call Dr. Richard A. Bagg, our Director of Auctions, at 1-603-569-5095 ext.53. Contacting us today may be the most financially rewarding decision you have ever made.

HOW TO USE THIS BOOK

This book was written as a guide to the world's most popular coins. To list every coin that was ever minted by every country in the world would fill a book many times this size. We, therefore, have chosen to list the coins that are readily available to the average collector, with prices that would accommodate the largest number of collectors. Considerable effort was expended to consolidate and verify the information listed. Should you have any questions or corrections, the authors would be grateful to hear your comments. Please write to: Blackbooks, P.O. Box 690312, Orlando, FL 32869.

The prices listed in this book represent the current collector values at the time of printing. Since some of the types and varieties of coinage fluctuate in price more than others, it would be wise to consult several sources, i.e. coin dealers and trade publications, before any transaction.

Apart from the chapter immediately following titled "Ancient Coins," each coin listing in this guide contains the following information:

DATE or DATE RANGE—Date ranges were used to conserve space. Likewise, listings for coins later that 1980 were generally omitted because of their minimal collector value.

COIN TYPE—This is the unit of measure of the face value of the coin.

VARIETY—This information usually describes the images that appear on either the obverse (front) or the reverse (back) of the coin. Please note that some varieties of the same denomination may command a higher price than others of the same denomination.

METAL—When known, the metallic content of the coin is listed.

ABP—This is the average buy price that coin dealers are buying from the public. Readers should understand that the actual prices paid by any given dealer will vary based on the dealer's inventory and the market demand in the dealer's specific area. Remember that this book is presented merely as a guide.

There are two reasons for not listing an ABP price for a particular coin. The first concerns *coins that* are not *made from a precious metal* (gold, silver, or platinum). If there is no price listed for this kind of coin, it means that the price that a dealer would pay would be minimal.

ABP prices are also not listed for *coins that* are *made of gold, silver, or platinum.* The reason for this is that the dealers usually buy this kind of coin based on its bullion value. In most cases they will pay you for the amount of gold, silver, or platinum that the coin contains plus a premium, i.e. the bullion "spot" price plus a percentage. When determining the melt or bullion value of the coin, the dealer not only will have to consider the weight of the coin, but he will also have to determine the purity level of the gold, silver, or platinum, i.e. pure silver (.999), sterling silver (.925), etc. These variables make it difficult for an inexperienced dealer to calculate the bullion value of a coin. We recommend contacting dealers that have experience in dealing in bullion coinage. We have included a bullion value chart in this book which you can use to approximate the bullion value, assuming the coin is made from gold, silver, or platinum. Don't forget that the purity level of the gold, silver, or platinum will affect the bullion value.

CURRENT RETAIL VALUES—These prices are listed in either average fine or average UNC (uncirculated) condition. It is of utmost importance that a coin be accurately graded before a value can be determined. Although *there is no universally accepted grading standards for world coinage,* we have adopted the two U.S. grading conditions of AVERAGE FINE and AVERAGE UNC for the purposes of this book.

AVERAGE FINE condition would be represented by a coin that exhibited a moderate amount of wear, but still had visible signs of all of the detail that could be found on a coin of UNC condition. Usually the higher relief areas on the coin show the most wear.

AVERAGE UNC condition or uncirculated condition would be a coin that was never in general circulation. Current issues of uncirculated coins can be purchased directly from the mints where they are made, or from dealers or other collectors. Usually the finish of an uncirculated coin is much brighter, with very few surface scratches. When building a collection with the more current issues, you should try to collect UNC specimens when possible.

PRICES—The prices that are listed are average prices for coins that were minted in that particular date range. The price for a coin of a specific date in that particular date range will vary slightly from the price indicated. This variation in price is based on several variables. Some of the factors that affect the price of a coin are: 1) the amount of coins that were minted, 2) the amount of coins in circulation, 3) the demand for that coin in your geographic area, and 4) the condition in which the coin is generally found.

INVENTORY CHECKLIST—For the purposes of record keeping, we have included a ☐ at the beginning of each listing. Write a check mark or darken the ☐ in front of each coin in your collection. By doing this you will have a portable record of your collection to take with you to coin shows and dealers.

We hope that you enjoy using this book and invite you to become familiar with the other books in the *Official Blackbook Price Guide* series.

There is the best-selling *Official Blackbook Price Guide of U.S. Coins* which lists more than 16,000 prices for every U.S. coin minted, including colonial tokens, farthings, halfpennies, and gold pieces, plus sections on varieties and errors. It is fully illustrated.

There is also the *Official Blackbook Price Guide of U.S. Paper Money* which lists more than 6,000 prices for every national note issued from 1861 to date, including demand notes, national bank notes, silver and gold certificates, treasury notes, federal reserve notes, and confederate currency. It too is fully illustrated.

And finally, there is the *Official Blackbook Price Guide of U.S. Postage Stamps* which lists more than 20,000 prices for general U.S. postage stamps issued from 1847 to date, plus revenue, stock transfer and hunting permit stamps, United Nations issues, mint sheets, and first day covers. It is fully illustrated *in color.*

These books are available from your local bookstores, coin shops, and from the publisher.

ANCIENT COINS: COLLECTING HISTORICAL COINS

Courtesy of Victor England, Jr., Senior Director of Classical Numismatic Group, Inc.

Coins are the most important form of money. For over 2,000 years these small pieces of metal have represented units of intrinsic value.

Today we take coins for granted; but since coinage emerged in the late 7th century B.C. it has played an important role in the economics of many cultures. Today we are fortunate to have coins as records of past history.

Through the collecting of coins you can acquire significant historical artifacts that can lead you down many paths of research and exploration. If only these small objects could talk—I am sure they would tell many interesting tales.

The collecting of historical coins from the Greek, Roman, and Byzantine periods is an affordable pastime that can provide many hours of enjoyment. The collecting of ancient coins is perhaps the oldest part of numismatics. Once only the hobby of kings, it is now a rewarding field readily open to all.

A recently published book, *Ancient Coin Collecting* by Wayne G. Sayles, is a must for anyone wanting to look over this fascinating area of numismatics. This book, published in 1996, now in its second printing, is available from your favorite bookstore or numismatic book seller. As of this writing it is only $24.95.

Over the next few pages I will introduce you to 30 ancient coins that might form the beginnings of your collection. Condition, strike, and style play important roles in the price of ancient coins. I have provided price ranges you might expect to pay for some of these coins. The price categories in the order they appear on the following pages are as follows:

Fine–Very Fine   Very Fine–Good   Very Fine—Extremely Fine

Over 2,600 years ago in Lydia (Western Turkey), small lumps of metal were stamped with a simple design. These lumps of metal, made from a natural alloy of silver and gold, were called electrum. They represent one of the earliest coins.

1. Uncertain Kings of Lydia. Before 561 B.C. Electrum Third Stater. Obverse: Head of a roaring lion, knob on forehead. Reverse: Double incuse punch. Average weight 4.70 grams.

500–700 800–1200 1500–2000

Croesus, the last King of the Lydians, lived from 560–546 B.C. He was an extremely powerful ruler who subjected many lands in the area. From the spoils of successful war and a rich supply of bullion in his native land, he became fabulously wealthy. The expression "rich as Croesus" still has meaning today. Croesus introduced us to coins made of refined metals of gold and silver.

2. LYDIA, King Croesus. 560–546 B.C. Silver Siglos. Obverse: Confronted foreparts of lion and bull. Reverse: Double incuse punch. Average weight 5.30 grams.

250–350 500–600 700–1000

Over the next hundred years that followed, coinage became the accepted medium of exchange. People in Greece and other nearby countries soon started making use of coins. The designs on the coins reflected the heritage of the many diverse cities that surrounded the Mediterranean. As a result of commerce and war the coinage of the greatest cities of the ancient world became the trade coins of the day. Many Greek coins were very skillfully made and extremely beautiful. Designs often incorporated the patron deity of the city or the badge of the city itself.

Tarentum was the most important city in Southern Italy in the 5th and 4th centuries before Christ. The foundation myth of the city relates the story of a dolphin saving Taras from a shipwreck at sea. In the place where he came ashore, the city of Tarentum was founded.

3. TARENTUM in Calabria. Circa 334–330 B.C. Silver Nomos. Obverse: Naked horseman on horse right. Taras astride of dolphin left. Average weight 7.80 grams.

150–200 250–400 500–1000

On the island of Sicily, Syracuse became the dominant city. Coinage developed on the island in the 6th century B.C. and reached its height in the 5th century. Some of the finest examples of the engravers' art are found on the coins of Syracuse.

4. SYRACUSE on the island of Sicily. Circa 480–475 B.C. Silver Tetradrachm. Obverse: Charioteer driving slow quadriga to the right, Nike above placing a wreath on the horse's head. Diademed head of Arethusa right, four dolphins swimming around. Average weight 17.00 grams.

300–500 600–800 1500–2500

Throughout most of the 5th century B.C. after the defeat of the Persians, Athens was mistress of the Aegean. She became the cultural and political center of the Greek world.

5. ATHENS in Attica. After 449 B.C. Silver Tetradrachm. Obverse: Helmeted head of Athena. Reverse: Owl standing right in shallow incuse, olive spray behind. Average weight 17.00 grams.

200–300 400–600 800–1200

Corinth, situated in central Greece, was one of the great commercial centers in her day. Coins of Corinth were widely imitated by other cities. The flying Pegasus is seen on the coins of many of her trading partners.

6. CORINTH in Corinthia. Circa 345–307 B.C. Silver Stater. Obverse: Pegasus flying left. Reverse: Helmeted head of Athena left. Average weight 8.50 grams.

150–200 250–400 500–750

In Asia Minor we find the important port and naval base of Aspendos. Her coins depict two naked wrestlers grappling in contest. Sporting events were an integral part of life in ancient Greece. The modern day Olympics trace their origins to Greece and her culture.

7. ASPENDOS in Pamphylia. Circa 370–330 B.C. Silver Stater. Obverse: Two wrestlers grappling. Reverse: Slinger standing right in throwing pose, triskeles in the field. Average weight 10.50 grams.

150–200 250–400 500–750

Along the north coast of Africa we find the important maritime trading city of Carthage. Due to the great natural harbor and favorable geographical location, Carthage became one of the great powers of the Greek world.

8. CARTHAGE in Zeugitania. Circa 350–260 B.C. Gold/Electrum Stater. Obverse: Wreathed head of Tanit left. Reverse: Horse standing right. Average weight 7.50 grams.

400–500	600–700	1000–1500

In the late 4th century a ruler came to power who would change the shape of the world as it was known at the time. At the age of 20, in 336 B.C., Alexander III (the Great) became ruler of the small kingdom of Macedonia. By the time he died 13 years later at the age of 33, he had conquered an empire that stretched from Greece to India. Alexander's coinage played an important role in his eastern conquests. Local coinages were replaced with his tetradrachms. Over 200 mints produced coins in his name.

9. Alexander III, King of Macedon. 336–323 B.C. Silver Tetradrachm. Obverse: Head of Herakles right, wearing a lion skin. Reverse: Zeus enthroned left, holding an eagle in his outstretched hand. Average weight 17.00 grams.

150–200	250–400	500–750

Alexander was one of the most successful generals who ever lived. Upon his death his Kingdom was divided amongst several of his generals. Many of the kings who came after Alexander put his picture on their coins. They believed he was a god.

10. Lysimachos, King of Thrace. 323–281 B.C. Silver Tetradrachm. Obverse: Head of deified Alexander the Great right. Reverse: Athena seated left holding Nike in her outstretched hand. Average weight 17.00 grams.

200–250 300–450 800–1200

As the successors of Alexander established power in their own rights, several powerful kingdoms formed. One of the most powerful of the new kingdoms was the Ptolemaic kingdom in Egypt. Under Ptolemy and his successors, this kingdom would survive until the death of Cleopatra VII, lover of Julius Caesar and Mark Antony. The coins of Ptolemaic Egypt provide us with portraits of important historical rulers.

11. Ptolemy I, King of Egypt. 323–283 B.C. Silver Tetradrachm. Obverse: Diademed bust of Ptolemy right. Reverse: Egyptian eagle standing left on thunderbolt. Average weight 14.50 grams.

100–200 250–350 450–600

12. Cleopatra VII, Queen of Egypt. 51–30 B.C. Bronze 80 Drachmae. Obverse: Diademed bust of Cleopatra right. Reverse: Eagle standing left on thunderbolt. Average weight 18.00 grams.

100–200 300–600 1000–1500

To the east of Egypt was the province of Judaea. The area was under the rule first of the Persians, then Alexander the Great, and later the Ptolemaic kings followed by the Seleucids. During the late 2nd century B.C., Judaea achieved a measure of independence under the Hasmoneans and finally under Alexander Jannaeus, 103–76 B.C., full autonomy. This impoverished area gave birth to two of the world's greatest religions—Judaism and later Christianity.

13. Alexander Jannaeus, Hasmonean King of Judaea. 103–76 B.C. Bronze Prutah. Obverse: Anchor, legend around. Reverse: Wheel with eight spokes. Average weight 1.00 gram.

20–30 40–75 100–200

Late in the 2nd century B.C., the port city of Tyre regained her autonomy in the waning days of Ptolemaic and Seleucid influence. A remarkable silver coinage was struck at Tyre from about 126 B.C. until well into Roman times. The famous tetradrachms (shekels) of this series have achieved some notoriety as the most likely coinage with which Judas was paid his "30 pieces of silver" for the betrayal of Christ.

14. TYRE in Phoenicia. After 126 B.C. Silver Tetradrachm (shekel). Obverse: Laureate bust of Melkart. Reverse: Eagle standing left on prow. Average weight 14.00 grams, declining later to 13.00 grams.

200–300 300–500 600–800

"And when they had bound him, they led him away, and delivered him to Pontius Pilate the governor." Matthew 27:2

This coin speaks for itself.

15. Pontius Pilate, Roman Prefect of Judaea under Tiberius, Emperor of Rome. 26–29 A.D. Bronze Prutah. Obverse: Lituus with inscription around. Reverse: Date within wreath. Average weight 1.00 gram.

30–50 75–100 200–300

While the Hellenistic kingdoms were vying for control in the east another power was slowly emerging in the west. On the banks of the river Tiber in Italy in a small village called Rome, a new empire was taking shape. According to legend, twins called Romulus and Remus founded Rome in the middle of the 8th century B.C. By the 3rd century B.C. this small agricultural community had grown and began building one of the greatest empires the world has ever seen.

At first the Romans used coins that were struck on the Greek system that was already in place in Italy.

16. ROMAN REPUBLIC. Circa 225–212 B.C. Silver Didrachm (Quadrigatus). Obverse: Laureate head of Janus. Reverse: Jupiter in a quadriga moving to the right being driven by Victory. Average weight 6.50 grams.

100–200 300–400 600–1000

One of the main reasons the Romans struck coins was to pay the soldiers. As the Roman army expanded the boundaries of the

Empire, a new denomination emerged that would become the standard for many centuries. The Roman silver denarius was struck from the 2nd century B.C. until the 3rd century A.D. In the latter days of the Republic and early days of the Empire a Roman soldier received an annual salary of 225 denarii.

17. ROMAN REPUBLIC. After 200 B.C. Issued by various moneyers. Silver Denarius. Obverse: Helmeted head of Roma right, X below chin. Reverse: The Dioscuri riding right. Average weight 3.85 grams.

40–60 100–150 250–400

As the Empire expanded, the political system in Rome suffered. No longer able to govern itself under rules of just a Senate, influential people began to try and take control of the reins of power. In 59 B.C., Caius Julius Caesar was elected to be a governing consul. He spent the next eight years campaigning in Britain and Gaul. A power struggle ensued amongst other ruling members of the ruling Roman triumvirate, and, after defeating Pompey in 48 B.C. Caesar marched into Rome as her undisputed master. After only a short period of supreme power he was assassinated on the Ides (15th) of March in 44 B.C.

18. Julius Caesar. Struck 49 B.C. Silver Denarius. Obverse: Elephant right trampling a serpent, CAESAR below. Reverse: Priestly implements. Average weight 4.00 grams.

125–200 250–350 500–700

After the assassination of Caesar, another triumvirate was formed to try and govern Rome. Two of the members of this group, Mark Antony and Octavian (Augustus), were to play important roles in the advancement of the Roman empire. Antony was given command of the province of Asia. It was here that he met and was captivated by the last of the Ptolemaic dynasty, Cleopatra VII. Antony then quarrelled with Octavian in a struggle for ultimate power. He was defeated at the battle of Actium and fled with Cleopatra to Egypt where he committed suicide in 30 B.C. During this struggle with Octavian he struck a series of denarii for each of the legions under his command.

19. Mark Antony. 32–31 B.C. Silver Legionary Denarius. Obverse: Manned galley right. Reverse: Aquila surmounted by an eagle and flanked by two standards, the legend LEG followed by a Roman numeral representing the legion. Average weight 3.50 grams.

75–100 150–200 400–600

Having achieved undisputed mastery of the Roman world in 30 B.C., Octavian returned stability to the Roman state. In 27 B.C. the Senate acknowledged his mastery and bestowed upon him the title of Augustus, by which he is best known. Augustus ruled long and prosperously, dying at the age of 77. He left behind the foundations for one of the world's greatest empires.

20. Augustus. 27 B.C.–14 A.D. Silver Denarius. Obverse: Laureate head of Augustus right. Reverse: Caius and Lucius Caesars standing facing, shields and spears between them. Average weight 3.60 grams.

75–100 150–200 350–500

Augustus' long life and treachery within his household resulted in his stepson Tiberius succeeding him. Tiberius proved himself an able administrator. The ministry and crucifixion of Jesus Christ occurred during his reign.

The Tribute Penny. *"Is it lawful to give tribute to Caesar, or not? Shall we give or shall we not give? But he knowing their hypocrisy, said unto them, Why tempt ye me? Bring me a penny, that I may see it. And they brought it. And He said unto them, Whose is this image and superscription? And they said unto Him, Caesar's. And Jesus, answering, said unto them, Render to Caesar the things that are Caesar's, and to God the things that are God's."* Mark 12:14–17

21. Tiberius. 14–37 A.D. Silver "Tribute" Denarius. Obverse: Laureate head right, inscription around. Reverse: Livia as pax seated right on throne. Average weight 3.60 grams.

125–200 250–300 500–700

When no clear line of succession to an emperor was apparent, it was often the Praetorian guard who helped choose a successor. Upon the death of the infamous Caligula, the guard raised Claudius to the purple giving him the title of Augustus. The story of these turbulent times has been re-created on video under the title of *I, Claudius.*

22. Claudius. 41–54 A.D. Bronze As. Obverse: Bare head of Claudius left. Reverse: Minerva standing right hurling javelin. Average weight 11.00 grams.

100–175 250–350 500–700

Nero, the adopted son of Claudius, was one of Rome's most colorful emperors. His unbridled enthusiasm, love of the finer things in life, passion for sporting events, and rumored love of fire, lead him to commit suicide.

23. Nero. 54–68 A.D. Bronze As. Obverse: Laureate head of Nero right. Reverse: View of the front of the Temple of Janus. Average weight 11.00 grams.

100–175	250–350	500–700

By the 2nd century A.D. the Roman Empire had reached gargantuan proportions. One of Rome's best administrators was the emperor Hadrian. He spent much of his career travelling the vast empire. His most lasting legacy is Hadrian's Wall in northern England.

24. Hadrian. 117–138 A.D. Silver Denarius. Obverse: Laureate head of Hadrian right. Reverse: Concordia seated left. Average weight 3.35 grams.

50–75	100–200	300–500

In 248 A.D. Rome celebrated the 1000th anniversary of its foundation. Philip I, emperor of Rome, celebrated this anniversary with magnificent games featuring many wild beasts collected especially for this celebration. By the middle of the 3rd century, the denarius had lost much of its value. A larger silver piece was introduced called the antoninianus.

25. Philip I. 244–249 A.D. Silver Antoninianus. Obverse: Radiate bust of Philip right. Reverse: SAECVLARES AVG around various different animals used in the celebration of the 1000th anniversary. Average weight 3.65 grams.

30–50 75–100 125–200

Christianity was a persecuted religion for much of its first 300 years. The first Roman emperor to embrace Christianity was Constantine I, the Great. It is said that he converted on his deathbed.

26. Constantine I, the Great. 307–337 A.D. Bronze Follis. Obverse: Helmeted and cuirassed bust right. Reverse: Roma seated right holding shield. (Many obverse and reverse variations). Average weight 3.00–4.00 grams.

20–30 40–60 75–125

Christianity did not gain immediate acceptance after the death of Constantine. The "Philosopher" Julian II outlawed Christianity 30 years after the death of Constantine, preferring the old pagan religions.

27. Julian II, the Philosopher. 360–363 A.D. Bronze (uncertain denomination). Obverse: Diademed, draped, and cuirassed bust right. Reverse: Apis bull standing right, two stars above. Average weight 8.50 grams.

150–200 300–400 700–1000

By the 5th century A.D., the Roman empire had split into two empires. The empire in the west was tangled in political upheaval. The center of the empire had moved from Rome to Constantinople. In contrast to the problems in the West, the Eastern division of the Empire enjoyed comparative peace under the leadership of Theodosius II. His most notable achievement was the compilation of the legal code known as the Codex Theodosianus. By the 5th century, silver and bronze coins had been replaced by the gold solidus as the coin of the realm.

28. Theodosius II. 402–450 A.D. Gold Solidus. Obverse: Helmeted and cuirassed three-quarter facing bust, spear over far shoulder. Reverse: Constantinopolis enthroned left, holding globus cruciger and sceptre. Average weight 4.45 grams.

200–300 350–500 700–1000

By the 6th century the last vestiges of the Roman Empire had faded into obscurity. While the west was still in turmoil the east found leadership under the religious successors to the Romans. The Byzantine Empire would last until the fall of Constantinople in 1453.

The Byzantine Empire found solid leadership under Justinian I. He ruled for almost four decades. He consolidated the empire, regaining territory lost to the Goths and Vandals. At home in Constantinople, he built the great church of St. Sophia. This is still standing as one of the great architectural achievements of its time in modern day Istanbul. Justinian is also remembered for his final codification of Roman law. He consolidated the best of Roman law for generations to come.

29. Justinian I. 527–565 A.D. Bronze Follis. Obverse: Helmeted facing bust of Justinian holding globus cruciger. Reverse: Large M, flanked by ANNO on the left, numbers on the right indicating the year of his reign and a mint mark below. Average weight 22.00 grams declining to 15.00 grams.

20–30 75–100 200–350

By the 7th century, new nations were emerging in the West and the Byzantine Empire was locked in perpetual struggle with the Arab world. Justinian II showed his devotion to God by placing the image of Christ on his coinage. He was the first emperor to do this. However, his attempts at introducing his doctrines into the policies of the Church were rejected. In the old city of Rome, the papacy was in its infancy. But once again a gradual shift of power was beginning to occur.

30. Justinian II. 685–695 A.D. Gold Solidus. Obverse: Facing bust of bearded Christ imposed over a cross, hand raised in benediction. Reverse: Justinian standing crowned, wearing loros and holding cross potent on steps. Average weight 4.30 grams.

600–800 900–1200 1500–2000

This is only an abbreviated list of the many thousands of different coins one can purchase. Hopefully this list will start you on the road to discovery and collecting in this fascinating field.

The following is a list of six suggested titles for further reading:

Foss, Clive. *Roman Historical Coins.* 1990
Howgego, Christopher. *Ancient History From Coins.* 1995
Jenkins, G. K. *Coins in History—Ancient Greek Coins.* 1990
Lorber, Cathy. *Treasures of Ancient Coinage: From the Private Collections of American Numismatic Society Members.* 1996
Sayles, Wayne G. *Ancient Coin Collecting.* 1996.
Sear, David. *Byzantine Coins and Their Values.* 1987

One of the best general publications on ancient coins is The Celator, Ed. Steven A Sayles, published monthly. Contact the publication at P.O. Box 123, Lodi WI 53555.

Two organizations that are active in the field of ancient numismatics are the American Numismatic Society (ANS) (contact at Broadway at 155th

St., New York, NY 10032), and the Society for Ancient Numismatics (SAN) (contact at P.O. Box 4095, Panorama City, CA 91412).

I am one of the Directors of the Classical Numismatic Group, Inc. (CNG). For the past 22 years we have been quietly building a full-service numismatic firm dedicated to serving the needs of our customers in the fields of ancient, world, and British numismatics. Each year we conduct four auctions, publish three fixed-price lists, attend numerous shows around the world, and even occasionally publish a book. If you would like to know more about us or the field of ancient numismatics, please get in touch. We would like to be of service. Write, call, or e-mail us at Classical Numismatic Group, Inc., P.O. Box 479, Lancaster, PA 17608–0479. Phone (717) 390-9194, fax (717) 390-9978, e-mail: cng4ve@aol.com.

ANTILLES (NETHERLANDS)

DATE	COIN TYPE/VARIETY/METAL	ABP FINE	AVERAGE FINE
□ 1952–1968	1 Cent, Juliana, Bronze	$ .40	$ .80

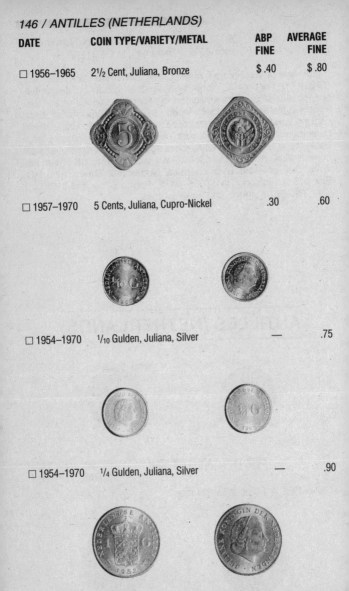

DATE	COIN TYPE/VARIETY/METAL	ABP FINE	AVERAGE FINE
□ 1956–1965	$2^1/_2$ Cent, Juliana, Bronze	$ .40	$ .80
□ 1957–1970	5 Cents, Juliana, Cupro-Nickel	.30	.60
□ 1954–1970	$^1/_{10}$ Gulden, Juliana, Silver	—	.75
□ 1954–1970	$^1/_4$ Gulden, Juliana, Silver	—	.90
 □ 1952–1970	1 Gulden, Juliana, Silver	—	1.00

DATE	COIN TYPE/VARIETY/METAL	ABP FINE	AVERAGE FINE
□ 1964	2½ Gulden, Juliana, Silver	—	$1.50

ARGENTINA

The first coins were used in 1813, followed by silver reales in 1815, and the copper centavos and gold pesos in the mid-1800s. Cupronickel pesos and aluminum-bronze pesos were used in the 1900s. Decimal coins were used in 1881. The currency today is the peso.

Argentina—Type Coinage

DATE	COIN TYPE/VARIETY/METAL	ABP FINE	AVERAGE FINE
□ 1882–1896	1 Centavo, Bronze	$ .45	.75
□ 1939–1944	1 Centavo, Bronze	.12	.20
□ 1945–1948	1 Centavo, Copper	.10	.18

DATE	COIN TYPE/VARIETY/METAL	ABP FINE	AVERAGE FINE
□ 1882–1896	2 Centavos, Bronze	$.45	$.75
□ 1939–1947	2 Centavos, Bronze	—	.12
□ 1947–1950	2 Centavos, Copper	—	.18
□ 1896–1942	5 Centavos, Cupro-Nickel	.16	.28

DATE	COIN TYPE/VARIETY/METAL	ABP FINE	AVERAGE FINE
□ 1942–1950	5 Centavos, Aluminum-Bronze	—	.12
□ 1950	5 Centavos, Death of San Martin Centennial, Cupro-Nickel	—	.22
□ 1951–1953	5 Centavos, Cupro-Nickel	—	.22
□ 1953–1956	5 Centavos, Copper-Nickel Clad Steel	—	.16
□ 1957–1959	5 Centavos, Nickel Clad Steel	—	.16
□ 1881–1883	10 Centavos, Silver	3.00	5.00

DATE	COIN TYPE/VARIETY/METAL	ABP FINE	AVERAGE FINE
□ 1896–1942	10 Centavos, Cupro-Nickel	.28	.50
□ 1942–1950	10 Centavos, Aluminum-Bronze	—	.18
□ 1950	10 Centavos, Death of San Martin Centennial, Cupro-Nickel	—	.32
□ 1951–1953	10 Centavos, Cupro-Nickel	—	.32

DATE	COIN TYPE/VARIETY/METAL	ABP FINE	AVERAGE FINE
☐ 1952–1956	10 Centavos, Copper-Nickel Clad Steel	—	$ .12
☐ 1957–1959	10 Centavos, Nickel Clad Steel	—	.12
☐ 1881–1883	20 Centavos, Silver	—	12.00
☐ 1896–1942	20 Centavos, Cupro-Nickel	$ .28	.40
☐ 1942–1950	20 Centavos, Aluminum-Bronze	—	.18
☐ 1950	20 Centavos, Death of San Martin Centennial, Cupro-Nickel	.22	.30
☐ 1951–1953	20 Centavos, Cupro-Nickel	—	.18
☐ 1952–1956	20 Centavos, Copper-Nickel Clad Steel	—	.18
☐ 1957–1961	20 Centavos, Nickel Clad Steel	—	.18
☐ 1881–1883	50 Centavos, Silver	—	30.00
☐ 1941	50 Centavos, Nickel	.65	1.00
☐ 1952–1956	50 Centavos, Copper-Nickel Clad Steel	—	.18
☐ 1957–1961	50 Centavos, Nickel Clad Steel	—	.12
☐ 1881–1883	1 Peso, Silver	—	75.00
☐ 1957–1962	1 Peso, Nickel Clad Steel	—	.12
☐ 1960	1 Peso, Sesquicentennial of Provisional Government, Nickel Clad Steel	.16	.28
☐ 1884	½ Argentino, Gold	—	—
☐ 1881–1896	Argentino, Gold	—	—

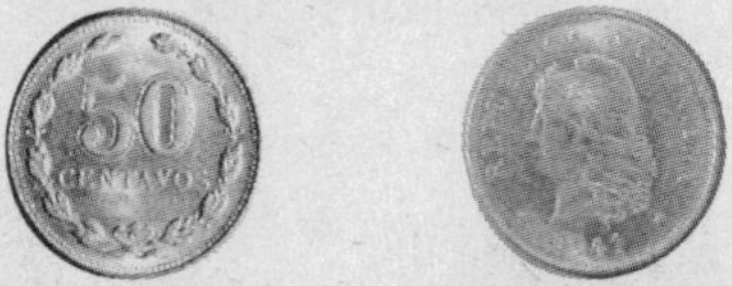

DATE	COIN TYPE/VARIETY/METAL	ABP FINE	AVERAGE FINE
□ 1961–1968	5 Pesos, Nickel Clad Steel	—	$ .12

DATE	COIN TYPE/VARIETY/METAL	ABP FINE	AVERAGE FINE
□ 1962–1968	10 Pesos, Nickel Clad Steel	—	.12
□ 1966	10 Pesos, Sequicentennial of Independence, Nickel Clad Steel	—	.12

DATE	COIN TYPE/VARIETY/METAL	ABP FINE	AVERAGE FINE
□ 1964–1968	25 Pesos, Nickel Clad Steel	—	.12
□ 1968	25 Pesos, Death of Sarmiento, Nickel Clad Steel	$ .18	.30

Argentina—Current Coinage

DATE	COIN TYPE/VARIETY/METAL	ABP FINE	AVERAGE FINE
□ 1970–1975	1 Centavo, Aluminum	—	.10
□ 1983	1 Centavo, Aluminum	—	.11
□ 1970–1975	5 Centavos, Aluminum	—	.12
□ 1985–1988	5 Centavos, Brass	—	.12

DATE	COIN TYPE/VARIETY/METAL	ABP FINE	AVERAGE FINE
□ 1970–1976	10 Centavos, Brass	—	$ .12
□ 1983	10 Centavos, Aluminum	—	.16

DATE	COIN TYPE/VARIETY/METAL	ABP FINE	AVERAGE FINE
□ 1970–1976	20 Centavos, Brass	—	.12
□ 1970–1976	50 Centavos, Brass	—	.12
□ 1983–1984	50 Centavos, Aluminum	—	.26
□ 1974–1976	1 Peso, Aluminum-Brass	—	.12
□ 1984	1 Peso, National Congress, Aluminum	—	.18
□ 1976–1977	5 Pesos, Aluminum-Bronze	—	.12
□ 1977	5 Pesos, Bicentennial of Admiral Brown, Aluminum-Bronze	—	.12
□ 1984–1985	5 Pesos, Buenos Aires City Hall, Brass	—	.25
□ 1976–1978	10 Pesos, Aluminum-Bronze	—	.12
□ 1977	10 Pesos, Bicentennial of Admiral Brown, Aluminum-Bronze	—	.20
□ 1984–1985	10 Pesos, Independence Hall, Brass	—	.40
□ 1978	50 Pesos, Birth of San Martin 200th Anniversary, Aluminum-Bronze	—	.12
□ 1979	50 Pesos, Jose de San Martin, Aluminum-Bronze	—	.12

DATE	COIN TYPE/VARIETY/METAL	ABP FINE	AVERAGE FINE
□ 1977–1978	50 Pesos, World Soccer Championship, Aluminum-Bronze	$ .18	$ .30
□ 1980–1981	50 Pesos, Jose de San Martin, Brass-Steel	—	.18
□ 1980–1981	50 Pesos, Conquest of Patagonia Centennial, Aluminum-Bronze	—	.18
□ 1985	50 Pesos, Central Bank 50th Anniversary, Aluminum-Bronze	—	.20

DATE	COIN TYPE/VARIETY/METAL	ABP FINE	AVERAGE FINE
□ 1977–1978	100 Pesos, World Soccer Championship, Aluminum-Bronze	.18	.30
□ 1978	100 Pesos, Death of San Martin 200th Anniversary, Aluminum-Bronze	.32	.60
□ 1979	100 Pesos, Conquest of Patagonia Centennial, Aluminum-Bronze	—	.18
□ 1979–1981	100 Pesos, San Martin, Aluminum-Bronze	—	.18
□ 1980–1981	100 Pesos, Brass-Steel	—	.18
□ 1977	1000 Pesos, World Soccer Championship, Silver	—	10.00
□ 1978	1000 Pesos, World Soccer Championship, Silver	—	10.00
□ 1977	2000 Pesos, World Soccer Championship, Silver	—	15.00
□ 1978	2000 Pesos, World Soccer Championship, Silver	—	15.00
□ 1977	3000 Pesos, World Soccer Championship, Silver	—	25.00
□ 1978	3000 Pesos, World Soccer Championship, Silver	—	25.00

Argentina—Latest Coinage

DATE	COIN TYPE/VARIETY/METAL	ABP FINE	AVERAGE FINE
□ 1985	½ Centavo, Brass	.15	.26
□ 1985–1987	1 Centavo, Ostrich, Brass	—	.28
□ 1992	1 Centavo, Brass	—	.28

DATE	COIN TYPE/VARIETY/METAL	ABP FINE	AVERAGE FINE
□ 1985–1988	5 Centavos, Wildcat, Brass	—	$ .35
□ 1992	5 Centavos, Radiant Sun, Brass	—	.35

DATE	COIN TYPE/VARIETY/METAL	ABP FINE	AVERAGE FINE
□ 1985–1988	10 Centavos, Radiant Sun, Brass	$ .28	.50
□ 1992	10 Centavos, Radiant Sun, Aluminum-Bronze	—	.20
□ 1992	25 Centavos, Building, Brass	.75	1.00

DATE	COIN TYPE/VARIETY/METAL	ABP FINE	AVERAGE FINE
□ 1985–1988	50 Centavos, Brass	.75	1.20
□ 1992	50 Centavos, Tucuman Capitol Building, Brass	—	1.00
□ 1989	1 Austral, Buenos Aires City Hall, Aluminum	—	.18

DATE	COIN TYPE/VARIETY/METAL	ABP FINE	AVERAGE FINE
☐ 1989	5 Australes, Tucuman Independence Hall, Aluminum	$ .18	$ .30

DATE	COIN TYPE/VARIETY/METAL	ABP FINE	AVERAGE FINE
☐ 1989	10 Australes, Casa del Acuerdo, Aluminum	.28	.40
☐ 1990–1991	100 Australes, Aluminum	.18	.25
☐ 1990–1991	500 Australes, Aluminum	.18	.25

DATE	COIN TYPE/VARIETY/METAL	ABP FINE	AVERAGE FINE
☐ 1990–1991	1000 Australes, Aluminum	.40	.65
☐ 1991	1000 Australes, Ibero American Series, Silver	—	45.00

AUSTRALIA

Australia's currency is based on the decimal system: one hundred cents (100c) equals one Australian dollar ($1). Decimal currency was introduced in Australia on 14 February 1966 and replaced the imperial system of pounds, shillings, and pence.

Like most national currencies, Australia's currency consists of both coins and currency notes. At various times Australian coins have been made in San Francisco, London, Birmingham, Bombay, and Calcutta but, today, all Australian circulating coins are produced at the Royal Australian Mint in Canberra.

All Australian currency notes are produced by Note Printing Australia, an autonomous division of the Reserve Bank of Australia, located at Craigieburn, just outside Melbourne.

BRIEF HISTORY OF AUSTRALIA'S COINS

The early inhabitants of the penal colony of New South Wales brought with them English coins as well as those from ports of call on the long voyage. Many different coins and tokens were traded in the colony for differing values, sometimes based vaguely on the value of the coin's metal content.

As this was an unsatisfactory way of conducting transactions, Governor King, in 1800, issued a proclamation to establish a uniform value for the most common coins. The lowest value of two pence was given to a copper coin of one ounce. Various other coins such as rupees, ducats, guilders, and guineas were assigned higher values.

Front: Portuguese Johanna
Back: Ducat

The chronic shortage of coin bedevilled several of the colony's early governors (namely, Phillip, Hunter, King, and Bligh). Rum was more freely available and became the common medium of exchange, earning for New South Wales the name, "the rum colony."

Governor Lachlan Macquarie recognized the role of rum in the colony's affairs but also realized that something had to be done about the acute shortage of coin. He overcame the problem, at least partially, when His Majesty's Sloop *Samarang* arrived in 1812 carrying 40,000 Spanish dollars. Macquarie had the ingenious idea of cutting the centre out of the dollars and overstamping the two separate pieces with "New South Wales 1813" to make coins of two different denominations, the so-called "holey dollar" and its centrepiece, the "dump." These coins remained in circulation until 1829. Silver coins from England were used from about 1824.

Holey dollar

The Gold Rush of the 1850s led to the belief that some of Australia's coins could be locally produced. In 1855 the Sydney Mint opened—its first coin was the Sydney gold sovereign. Mints were also established in Melbourne (1872) and Perth (1899).

The first federally commissioned coins were issued in 1910. In 1916, numbers of threepence, sixpence, one shilling and two shilling (florin) coins were minted in Melbourne.

The Sydney Mint closed in 1926 and the Melbourne Mint closed in 1968 when its functions were transferred to the newly established Royal Australian Mint in Canberra. The Royal Australian Mint is the first Australian mint not to be a branch of the Royal Mint in London. It has produced more than 10 billion Australian coins. It has also made circulating coins or collector (numismatic) coins for such countries as Bangladesh, the Cook Islands, Tonga, New Zealand, Papua New Guinea, and Thailand.

TYPE OF COINS

Australia produces three categories of coins:

Circulating Coins: Standard day-to-day currency and used in normal commercial transactions.

Adelaide ingot

Collector Coins: Commemorative or other coins not in general circulation. They are, however, legal tender and may be used for commercial transactions. Collector coins are classified as "proof" or "uncirculated" coins.

Bullion Coins: Gold, silver, or platinum coins. The bullion value of the metal used in the manufacture of each coin is greater than its face value. These are classified as "non-circulating legal tender" (NCLT).

Circulating coins

The denominations of the new decimal currency coins introduced in 1966 were: 1c, 2c, 5c, 10c, 20c, and 50c. All were round in shape.

Round 50c coin (reverse)

There were no mintings of the 50c coin in the next two years and, when it next appeared, in 1969, its shape was changed to dodecagonal (12 sided). The round 50c was made in a silver alloy (80%). As the price of silver rose in the late 1960s, the metal value of the coin rose above its face value. It was a loss-maker for the government as well as confusing to consumers because of its size similarity to the 20c coin.

A $1 coin was introduced in 1984 and a $2 coin was introduced in 1988 to replace $1 and $2 currency notes which were gradually withdrawn.

Composition of circulating coins

The 1c and 2c (bronze) coins are made from copper (97%), zinc (2.5%), and tin (0.5%).

The 5c, 10c, 20c, and 50c coins are made of cupro-nickel; that is, 75% copper and 25% nickel.

The $1 and $2 coins are aluminum-bronze: 92% copper, 6% aluminum, and 2% nickel.

Withdrawal of coins

In 1990 the Australian government announced that from 1992 all 1c and 2c coins would be withdrawn. This is because of the changing worth of small denominations generally. These two coins, however, remain legal tender.

The demand for circulating coins has dropped steadily since the 1970s due mainly to the wider availability and acceptance of credit cards. As a result, the Royal Australian Mint has not only stopped making some coins (for instance, 1c and 2c pieces) but also it has reduced production of others. An unexpected side effect of the withdrawal of 1c and 2c coins, as from February 1992, has been the large number of other coins that have been returned to banks, most particularly 5c and 10c coins. This phenomenon has been called the "money box effect"—because of people emptying their money boxes on bank counters and handing in all their "loose change."

Dodecagonal 50c coin (obverse)

Coin designs

Coins have an obverse side and a reverse side. The obverse side of all Australian decimal coins carries an effigy of Her Majesty Queen Elizabeth II, as she is the Queen of Australia. This side of all coins also carries the year the coin was minted. Designs are approved by the Australian Treasurer.

The theme selected in 1966 for Australia's first decimal coins was Australian native fauna (except for the 50c coin which shows the Australian Coat of Arms). Later coins have featured different subjects.

from left to right, 1c coin: the feather tail glider (a type of possum) also known as the "flying squirrel"

2c coin: the frill-necked lizard

5c coin: the echidna or spiny ant eater

10c coin: the lyrebird

(below) 20c coin: the platypus

(above) 50c coin: Australia's Coat of Arms with a kangaroo on the left side of the coin and an emu on the right. The Coat of Arms shows a shield with six parts, each containing the badge of one of Australia's six states. The same design applies to the 1966 round version of this coin and the later 12-sided one.

$1 coin: the kangaroo

The 1993 $1 coin has water quality as its theme. It features a tree sculpted in flowing water to show the link between water and the environment.

$2 coin: a bust of an Aborigine, taken from an engraving by Ainslie Roberts and set against a background of the Southern Cross and Australian flora. The flora is Xanthorrhoea, *commonly known as the grass tree, which is found throughout Australia.*

Collector coins

In addition to proof and uncirculated sets of coins, which are issued each year, the Royal Australian Mint issues commemorative coins on a regular basis.

The $5 coin is aluminium-bronze: 92% copper, 6% aluminum, and 2% nickel. The first $5 coin was issued to commemorate the opening of Australia's new federal Parliament building. Parliament House in Canberra was officially opened on 9 May 1988 by Her Majesty Queen Elizabeth II. Two $5 coins were released in 1990 in a joint program with New Zealand to celebrate the 75th anniversary of the landing at Gallipoli by Australian and New Zealand forces in 1915. In 1992 a $5 commemorative coin was issued to mark the International Year of Space.

The $10 coin is made of sterling silver (that is, 92.5% silver and the balance made up of copper). The first $10 coin was released in 1982 to commemorate the XII Commonwealth Games, held in Brisbane. Subsequent designs have carried the theme of the Coat of Arms of each of Australia's six states and two territories: Victoria (1985); South Australia (1986); New South Wales (1987); First Fleet Bicentennial design (1988); Queensland (1989); Western Australia (1990); Tasmania (1991), and Northern Territory (1992). The Australian Capital Territory is featured on the 1993 coin.

Tasmania's $10 commemorative coin

A "Birds of Australia" series was introduced in 1989 on a double thickness (piedfort) $10 coin and on a standard proof $10 coin. The first bird featured was a kookaburra—others in the series are a sulphur crested cockatoo (1990), a jabiru (1991), an emperor penguin (1992), and a palm cockatoo for 1993.

The $200 coin is manufactured from 22K gold (that is, 91.66% gold).

The first $200 coin showed a koala on the reverse and was minted in 1980. Subsequent $200 coins have depicted the wedding of the Prince of Wales and Lady Diana Spencer in 1981; the Commonwealth Games in Brisbane (1982); the embarkation of the First Fleet to Australia in 1787 (1987); and the landing by Captain Arthur Phillip at Sydney Cove in 1788 (1988).

Australia's first $200 coin

The "Pride of Australia" series, which began in 1989, adopted Australia's unique wildlife as its theme and has so far shown a frilled-neck lizard (1989), platypus (1990), emu (1991), echidna (1992), and feather-tail glider (1993).

Bullion (or investment) coins

Since 1986 the Perth Mint has produced various gold, silver, and platinum coins for collectors and investors.

Gold coins, called nuggets, have been produced in various denominations based on the metal content of the individual coins. Similar conditions apply to silver and platinum coins.

The coins are non-circulating legal tender (NCLT) because the value of the metal used in the minted coin is greater than the coin's face value. For example, a $100 gold nugget coin costs considerably more than $100 to buy and depends on the international gold price. The Australian gold nugget coin is 9999 fine, that is 99.99% pure.

Australia—Type Coinage

DATE	COIN TYPE/VARIETY/METAL	ABP FINE	AVERAGE FINE
□ 1911–1936	½ Penny, George V, Bronze	$ .18	$ .40
□ 1938–1939	½ Penny, George VI, Bronze	.16	.25
□ 1939–1948	½ Penny, George VI, Bronze	.16	.25
□ 1949–1952	½ Penny, George VI, Bronze	—	.18
□ 1953–1956	½ Penny, Elizabeth II, Bronze	—	.18
□ 1959–1964	½ Penny, Elizabeth II, Bronze	—	.12

DATE	COIN TYPE/VARIETY/METAL	ABP FINE	AVERAGE FINE
□ 1911–1936	1 Penny, George V, Bronze	.60	1.00
□ 1938–1948	1 Penny, George VI, Bronze	.25	.65
□ 1949–1952	1 Penny, George VI, Bronze	.18	.25
□ 1953	1 Penny, Elizabeth II, Bronze	.18	.25
□ 1955–1964	1 Penny, Elizabeth II, Bronze	—	.12
□ 1910	3 Pence, Edward VII, Silver	—	1.85
□ 1911–1936	3 Pence, George V, Silver	—	1.75

DATE	COIN TYPE/VARIETY/METAL	ABP FINE	AVERAGE FINE
□ 1938–1944	3 Pence, George VI, Silver	—	.75
□ 1947–1948	3 Pence, George VI, Silver	—	1.00
□ 1949–1952	3 Pence, George VI, Silver	—	1.00

DATE	COIN TYPE/VARIETY/METAL	ABP FINE	AVERAGE FINE
☐ 1953–1954	3 Pence, Elizabeth II, Silver	—	$1.50
☐ 1955–1964	3 Pence, Elizabeth II, Silver	—	.30

DATE	COIN TYPE/VARIETY/METAL	ABP FINE	AVERAGE FINE
☐ 1910	6 Pence, Edward VII, Silver	—	8.00
☐ 1911–1936	6 Pence, George V, Silver	—	3.50
☐ 1938–1945	6 Pence, George VI, Silver	—	1.85
☐ 1946–1948	6 Pence, George VI, Silver	—	1.75
☐ 1950–1952	6 Pence, George VI, Silver	—	2.00
☐ 1953–1954	6 Pence, Elizabeth II, Silver	—	2.10
☐ 1955–1963	6 Pence, Elizabeth II, Silver	—	.80
☐ 1910	1 Shilling, Edward VII, Silver	—	11.00
☐ 1911–1936	1 Shilling, George V, Silver	—	6.00

DATE	COIN TYPE/VARIETY/METAL	ABP FINE	AVERAGE FINE
☐ 1938–1944	1 Shilling, George VI, Silver	—	3.50
☐ 1946–1948	1 Shilling, George VI, Silver	—	3.00
☐ 1950–1952	1 Shilling, George VI, Silver	—	3.50
☐ 1953–1954	1 Shilling, Elizabeth II, Silver	—	2.50
☐ 1955–1963	1 Shilling, Elizabeth II, Silver	—	2.10
☐ 1910	1 Florin, Edward VII, Silver	—	60.00
☐ 1911–1936	1 Florin, George V, Silver	—	20.00

DATE	COIN TYPE/VARIETY/METAL	ABP FINE	AVERAGE FINE
☐ 1938–1945	1 Florin, George VI, Silver	—	$6.00
☐ 1946–1947	1 Florin, George VI, Silver	—	6.25
☐ 1951–1952	1 Florin, George VI, Silver	—	3.00
☐ 1953–1954	1 Florin, Elizabeth II, Silver	—	5.00
☐ 1956–1963	1 Florin, Elizabeth II, Silver	—	3.00

DATE	COIN TYPE/VARIETY/METAL	ABP FINE	AVERAGE FINE
☐ 1937–1938	1 Crown, George VI, Silver	—	8.00
☐ 1871–1887	½ Sovereign, Victoria, Young Head, Gold	—	100.00
☐ 1887–1893	½ Sovereign, Victoria, Jubilee Head, Gold	—	110.00
☐ 1893–1901	½ Sovereign, Victoria, Old Head, Gold	—	75.00
☐ 1902–1910	½ Sovereign, Edward VII, Gold	—	65.00
☐ 1911–1918	½ Sovereign, George V, Gold	—	60.00
☐ 1871–1887	1 Sovereign, Victoria, Young Head, Rev: Shield, Gold	—	100.00
☐ 1871–1887	1 Sovereign, Victoria, Young Head, Rev: St. George, Gold	—	110.00
☐ 1887–1893	1 Sovereign, Victoria, Jubilee Head, Gold	—	60.00
☐ 1893–1901	1 Sovereign, Victoria, Old Head, Gold	—	80.00
☐ 1902–1910	1 Sovereign, Edward VII, Gold	—	100.00
☐ 1911–1931	1 Sovereign, George V, Gold	—	200.00

Australia—Commemorative Coinage

DATE	COIN TYPE/VARIETY/METAL	ABP FINE	AVERAGE FINE
□ 1927	Commemorative Florin, Establishment of Parliament at Canberra, Silver	—	$5.00
□ 1934	Commemorative Florin, Victoria & Melbourne Centennial, Dated 1934–35, Silver	—	110.00
□ 1951	Commemorative Florin, Fifty-year Jubilee, Silver	—	2.75
□ 1954	Commemorative Florin, Royal Visit, Silver	—	2.20

Australia—Decimal Coinage

□ 1966 to Date	1 Cent, Elizabeth II, Ring-tailed Opossum, Bronze	—	.12
□ 1966 to Date	2 Cents, Elizabeth II, Frilled Lizard, Bronze	—	.14

□ 1966 to Date	5 Cents, Elizabeth II, Spiny Anteater, Cupro-Nickel	—	.15

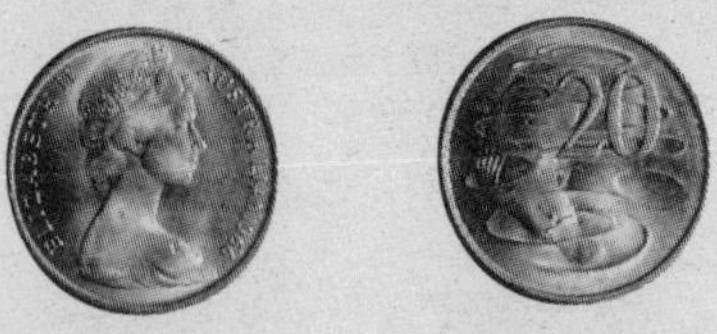

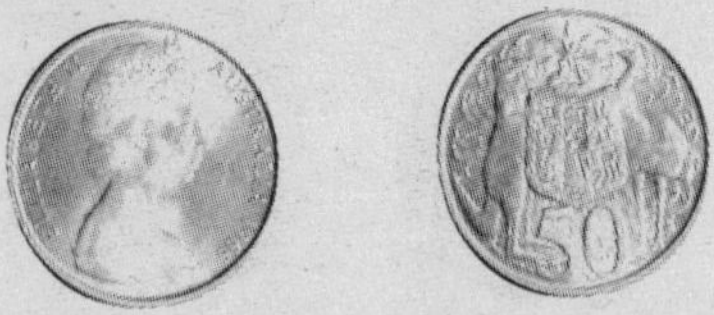

DATE	COIN TYPE/VARIETY/METAL	ABP FINE	AVERAGE FINE
☐ 1966 to Date	10 Cents, Elizabeth II, Lyre bird, Cupro-Nickel	—	$ .12
☐ 1966 to Date	20 Cents, Elizabeth II, Duckbill Platypus, Cupro-Nickel	—	.20
☐ 1966	50 Cents, Elizabeth II, Silver	—	8.00
☐ 1969–1984	50 Cents, Elizabeth II, Cupro-Nickel	—	.50
☐ 1970	50 Cents, Elizabeth II, Cook's Voyage—200th Anniversary, Cupro-Nickel	—	.18
☐ 1977	50 Cents, Elizabeth II, Queen's Silver Jubilee, Cupro-Nickel	—	.30
☐ 1981	50 Cents, Elizabeth II, Wedding of Prince Charles and Lady Diana, Cupro-Nickel	—	.30
☐ 1982	50 Cents, Elizabeth II, 12th Commonwealth Games, Cupro-Nickel	—	.30
☐ 1985 to Date	50 Cents, Elizabeth II, Cupro-Nickel	—	.30
☐ 1988	50 Cents, Elizabeth II, Australian Bicentennial, Cupro-Nickel	—	.20
☐ 1988	50 Cents, Elizabeth II, Australian Bicentennial, Silver	—	15.00
☐ 1989	50 Cents, Elizabeth II, 12th Commonwealth Games, Silver	—	15.00
☐ 1989	50 Cents, Elizabeth II, Cook's Voyage—200th Anniversary, Silver	—	15.00
☐ 1989	50 Cents, Elizabeth II, Wedding of Prince Charles & Lady Diana, Silver	—	15.00

DATE	COIN TYPE/VARIETY/METAL	ABP FINE	AVERAGE FINE
☐ 1989	50 Cents, Elizabeth II, Queen's Silver Jubilee, Silver	—	$15.00
☐ 1991	50 Cents, Elizabeth II, Decimal Currency—25th Anniversary, Cupro-Nickel	—	1.00

DATE	COIN TYPE/VARIETY/METAL	ABP FINE	AVERAGE FINE
☐ 1984 to Date	1 Dollar, Elizabeth II, Kangaroos, Nickel-Aluminum-Copper	—	.50
☐ 1986	1 Dollar, Elizabeth II, International Year of Peace, Aluminum-Bronze	—	.40
☐ 1988	1 Dollar, Elizabeth II, Aboriginal Art, Aluminum-Bronze	$1.75	3.00
☐ 1988–1990	1 Dollar, Elizabeth II, Masterpieces in Silver—Aboriginal Art, Silver	—	40.00
☐ 1990	1 Dollar, Elizabeth II, Masterpieces in Silver—International Year of Peace, Silver	—	40.00
☐ 1990	1 Dollar, Elizabeth II, Masterpieces in Silver—Kangaroos, Silver	—	40.00
☐ 1992	1 Dollar, Elizabeth II, Olympics—Javelin Thrower, Aluminum-Bronze	2.25	5.00

DATE	COIN TYPE/VARIETY/METAL	ABP FINE	AVERAGE FINE
☐ 1988–1991	2 Dollars, Elizabeth II, Male Aborigine, Aluminum-Bronze	2.25	5.00
☐ 1988	5 Dollars, Elizabeth II, House of Parliament, Aluminum-Bronze	2.75	6.00
☐ 1988	5 Dollars, Elizabeth II, House of Parliament, Silver	—	25.00

DATE	COIN TYPE/VARIETY/METAL	ABP FINE	AVERAGE FINE
□ 1990	5 Dollars, Elizabeth II, ANZAC Memorial, Aluminum-Bronze	$3.25	$7.00
□ 1992	5 Dollars, Elizabeth II, Australian Space Industry, Aluminum-Bronze	5.75	12.00
□ 1982	10 Dollars, Elizabeth II, 12th Commonwealth Games, Silver	—	30.00
□ 1985	10 Dollars, Elizabeth II, State of Victoria—150th Anniversary, Silver	—	20.00
□ 1986	10 Dollars, Elizabeth II, South Australia—150th Anniversary, Silver	—	20.00
□ 1987	10 Dollars, Elizabeth II, New South Wales, Silver	—	25.00
□ 1988	10 Dollars, Elizabeth II, Governor Philip Landing, Silver	—	30.00
□ 1989	10 Dollars, Elizabeth II, Queensland, Silver	—	20.00
□ 1989	10 Dollars, Elizabeth II, Kookaburra, Silver	—	35.00
□ 1990	10 Dollars, Elizabeth II, Cockatoo, Silver	—	40.00
□ 1990	10 Dollars, Elizabeth II, Western Australia, Silver	—	20.00
□ 1991	10 Dollars, Elizabeth II, Birds of Australia—Jabiru Stork, Silver	—	20.00
□ 1991	10 Dollars, Elizabeth II, Tasmania, Silver	—	35.00
□ 1992	10 Dollars, Elizabeth II, Northern Territory, Silver	—	20.00
□ 1992	10 Dollars, Elizabeth II, Emperor Penguin, Silver	—	45.00
□ 1992	25 Dollars, Elizabeth II, Queen's 40th Anniversary of Reign—Princess Diana, Silver	—	35.00
□ 1992	25 Dollars, Elizabeth II, Queen's 40th Anniversary of Reign—Queen Mother, Silver	—	35.00
□ 1992	25 Dollars, Elizabeth II, Queen's 40th Anniversary of Reign—Princess Margaret, Silver	—	35.00
□ 1980	200 Dollars, Elizabeth II, Koala, Gold	—	175.00
□ 1981	200 Dollars, Elizabeth II, Wedding of Prince Charles & Lady Diana, Gold	—	160.00
□ 1982	200 Dollars, Elizabeth II, 12th Commonwealth Games, Gold	—	160.00
□ 1985	200 Dollars, Elizabeth II, Koala, Gold	—	175.00
□ 1986	200 Dollars, Elizabeth II, Koala, Gold	—	175.00
□ 1987	200 Dollars, Elizabeth II, Arthur Philip, Gold	—	185.00
□ 1988	200 Dollars, Elizabeth II, Australia Bicentennial, Gold	—	185.00

DATE	COIN TYPE/VARIETY/METAL	ABP FINE	AVERAGE FINE
☐ 1989	200 Dollars, Elizabeth II, Pride of Australia—Frilled-Neck Lizard, Gold	—	$185.00
☐ 1990	200 Dollars, Elizabeth II, Pride of Australia—Platypus, Gold	—	185.00
☐ 1991	200 Dollars, Elizabeth II, Pride of Australia—Emu, Gold	—	185.00
☐ 1992	250 Dollars, Elizabeth II, Queen's 40th Anniversary of Reign—Princess Diana, Gold	—	400.00
☐ 1992	250 Dollars, Elizabeth II, Queen's 40th Anniversary of Reign—Princess Anne, Gold	—	400.00
☐ 1992	250 Dollars, Elizabeth II, Queen's 40th Anniversary of Reign—Queen Mother, Gold	—	400.00
☐ 1992	250 Dollars, Elizabeth II, Queen's 40th Anniversary of Reign—Princess Margaret, Gold	—	400.00

BELGIUM

The first coins appeared in the 2nd century. The silver Denier was popular through the 12th century. During the 1400s, most of the coins produced were gold. In the 1500s, large copper coins were introduced. A new coin system was established in 1612. Most of the coins then included liards, patards, schellings, patagons, ducatons, and sovereigns. The currency used today is based on the franc.

Belgium—Type Coinage

DATE	COIN TYPE/VARIETY/METAL	ABP FINE	AVERAGE FINE
☐ 1869–1907	1 Centime, Leopold II—1st Coinage, Copper	$1.40	$3.00
☐ 1912–1914	1 Centime, Albert I, Copper	1.40	3.00
☐ 1869–1909	2 Centimes, Leopold II—1st Coinage, Copper	.60	1.50
☐ 1910–1919	2 Centimes, Albert I, Copper	.12	.30
☐ 1894–1901	5 Centimes, Leopold II—1st Coinage, Cupro-Nickel	.60	1.50

DATE	COIN TYPE/VARIETY/METAL	ABP FINE	AVERAGE FINE
☐ 1901–1907	5 Centimes, Leopold II—2nd Coinage, Cupro-Nickel	$ .12	$ .30
☐ 1910–1932	5 Centimes, Albert I, Cupro-Nickel	—	.12
☐ 1915–1916	5 Centimes, German Occupation, Zinc	—	.15
☐ 1930–1932	5 Centimes, Albert I, Nickel-Brass	—	.12
☐ 1938–1940	5 Centimes, Leopold III—Belgie-Belgigue, Nickel-Brass	—	.12
☐ 1941–1943	5 Centimes, German Occupation, Zinc	—	.12
☐ 1894–1901	10 Centimes, Leopold II—1st Coinage, Cupro-Nickel	.80	2.00
☐ 1901–1906	10 Centimes, Leopold II-2nd Coinage, Cupro-Nickel	.12	.30
☐ 1915–1917	10 Centimes, German Occupation, Zinc	—	.20
☐ 1920–1929	10 Centimes, Albert I, Cupro-Nickel	—	.20
☐ 1930–1932	10 Centimes, Albert I, Nickel-Brass	1.75	4.00
☐ 1938–1939	10 Centimes, Leopold III—Belgie-Belgigue, Nickel-Brass	.12	.30
☐ 1941–1946	10 Centimes, German Occupation, Zinc	—	.20

DATE	COIN TYPE/VARIETY/METAL	ABP FINE	AVERAGE FINE
□ 1953–1963	20 Centimes, Baudouin I, Bronze	—	$ .10
□ 1908–1909	25 Centimes, Leopold II—2nd Coinage, Cupro-Nickel	—	.60
□ 1910–1929	25 Centimes, Albert I, Cupro-Nickel	—	.20
□ 1915–1918	25 Centimes, German Occupation, Zinc	$ .12	.30
□ 1938–1939	25 Centimes, Leopold III—Belgie-Belgigue, Nickel-Brass	.80	2.00
□ 1942–1947	25 Centimes, German Occupation, Zinc	—	.10

DATE	COIN TYPE/VARIETY/METAL	ABP FINE	AVERAGE FINE
□ 1964–1976	25 Centimes, Cupro-Nickel	—	.10
□ 1866–1899	50 Centimes, Leopold II—1st Coinage, Silver	—	5.00
□ 1901	50 Centimes, Leopold II—2nd Coinage, Silver	—	1.50
□ 1907–1909	50 Centimes, Leopold II—2nd Coinage, Silver	—	3.00
□ 1910–1914	50 Centimes, Albert I, Silver	—	1.50
□ 1918	50 Centimes, German Occupation, Zinc	.28	.60
□ 1922–1934	50 Centimes, Albert I, Nickel	.20	.50

DATE	COIN TYPE/VARIETY/METAL	ABP FINE	AVERAGE FINE
□ 1952–1980	50 Centimes, Baudouin I, Bronze	—	.10
□ 1866–1887	1 Franc, Leopold II—1st Coinage, Silver	—	4.00
□ 1880	1 Franc, Leopold II—50th Anniversary of Independence, Silver	—	4.25
□ 1904–1909	1 Franc, Leopold II—2nd Coinage, Silver	—	1.50
□ 1910–1918	1 Franc, Albert I, Silver	—	1.25

DATE	COIN TYPE/VARIETY/METAL	ABP FINE	AVERAGE FINE
☐ 1922–1935	1 Franc, Albert I, Nickel	—	$ .30
☐ 1939–1940	1 Franc, Leopold III—Belgie-Belgigue, Nickel	—	.20
☐ 1941–1947	1 Franc, German Occupation, Zinc	—	.30
☐ 1950	1 Franc, Postwar Issue, Cupro-Nickel	—	.12
☐ 1866–1887	2 Francs, Leopold II—1st Coinage, Silver	—	20.00
☐ 1880	2 Francs, Leopold II—50th Anniversary of Independence, Gold	—	12.00
☐ 1904–1909	2 Francs, Leopold II—2nd Coinage, Silver	—	10.00
☐ 1910–1912	2 Francs, Albert I, Silver	—	6.00
☐ 1923–1930	2 Francs, Albert I, Nickel	—	18.00

DATE	COIN TYPE/VARIETY/METAL	ABP FINE	AVERAGE FINE
☐ 1944	2 Francs, Allied Issue, Steel	—	.40

DATE	COIN TYPE/VARIETY/METAL	ABP FINE	AVERAGE FINE
☐ 1865–1876	5 Francs, Leopold II—1st Coinage, Silver	—	10.00
☐ 1930–1934	5 Francs, 1 Belga, Albert I, Nickel	$ .80	1.50
☐ 1938–1939	5 Francs, Leopold III—Belgie-Belgigue, Nickel	—	5.00

DATE	COIN TYPE/VARIETY/METAL	ABP FINE	AVERAGE FINE
□ 1941–1947	5 Francs, German Occupation, Zinc	—	$35.00
□ 1948	5 Francs, Postwar Issue, Cupro-Nickel	$ .16	.25
□ 1930	10 Francs, 2 Belgas, Albert I: Independence Centennial, Nickel	1750.00	2000.00
□ 1867–1882	20 Francs, Leopold II—1st Coinage, Gold	—	300.00
□ 1914	20 Francs, Albert I, Gold	—	120.00
□ 1931–1932	20 Francs, 4 Belgas, Albert I, Nickel	28.00	40.00
□ 1933–1934	20 Francs, Albert I, Silver	26.00	38.00
□ 1934–1935	20 Francs, Leopold III, Silver	—	5.00
□ 1949–1955	20 Francs, Postwar Issue, Silver	—	3.00

DATE	COIN TYPE/VARIETY/METAL	ABP FINE	AVERAGE FINE
□ 1980–1992	20 Francs, Bronze	—	.80
□ 1987–1988	5 ECU, European Currency Units, Silver	—	25.00
□ 1935	50 Francs, Brussels Exposition/ Railway Centennial, Silver	—	50.00

DATE	COIN TYPE/VARIETY/METAL	ABP FINE	AVERAGE FINE
□ 1939–1940	50 Francs, Leopold III, Silver	—	25.00
□ 1948–1954	50 Francs, Postwar Issue, Silver	—	12.00
□ 1958	50 Francs, Brussels Fair, Silver	—	12.00
□ 1960	50 Francs, Marriage Commemorative, Silver	—	5.00
□ 1987	50 Francs, Belgigue, Nickel	2.75	5.00
□ 1989–1990	10 ECU, European Currency Units, Gold	—	200.00
□ 1948–1954	100 Francs, Postwar Issue, Silver	—	12.00
□ 1990–1991	20 ECU, European Currency Units, Gold	—	300.00
□ 1989	25 ECU, European Currency Units, Gold	—	200.00

DATE	COIN TYPE/VARIETY/METAL	ABP FINE	AVERAGE FINE
☐ 1976	250 Francs, Jubilee of King Baudouin, Silver	—	$10.00
☐ 1987–1988	50 ECU, European Currency Units, Gold	—	250.00
☐ 1980	500 Francs, Independence—150th Anniversary, Silver Clad	—	25.00
☐ 1989	100 ECU, European Currency Units—Maria Theresa, Gold	—	600.00
☐ 1990	500 Francs, King Baudouin—60th Birthday, Silver	—	25.00

BERMUDA

The first coins were used in 1616. The copper sixpence was followed by the copper penny in the 1700s and the silver crown and bronze cent in the 1900s. The first decimal coins were used in 1970. Today's currency is the dollar.

Bermuda—Bullion Coinage*

DATE	COIN TYPE/VARIETY/METAL	ABP FINE	AVERAGE FINE
☐ 1980	1/10 Krugerrand, Gold	—	—
☐ 1980	1/4 Krugerrand, Gold	—	—
☐ 1980	1/2 Krugerrand, Gold	—	—
☐ 1967	1 Krugerrand, Gold	—	—

Bermuda—Bullion/Bermuda*

DATE	COIN TYPE/VARIETY/METAL	ABP FINE	AVERAGE FINE
☐ 1987	5 Dollars, Sailing Ship—Sea Venture Wreck, Silver	—	—
☐ 1988	5 Dollars, Sailing Ship—San Antonio, Silver	—	—
☐ 1992	5 Dollars, Olympic Rings, Silver	—	—

*Since these coins were manufactured and sold primarily for their bullion value, their current value is determined by the current spot price of gold.

DATE	COIN TYPE/VARIETY/METAL	ABP FINE	AVERAGE FINE
□ 1987	25 Dollars, Ship—Sea Venture, Palladium	—	—
□ 1988	25 Dollars, Ship—San Antonio Wreck, Palladium	—	—

Bermuda—Type Coinage

DATE	COIN TYPE/VARIETY/METAL	ABP FINE	AVERAGE FINE
□ 1970–1990	1 Cent, Wild Boar, Bronze	—	$ .10
□ 1991–1992	1 Cent, Wild Boar, Zinc	—	.10
□ 1970–1990	10 Cents, Bermuda Lily, Cupro-Nickel	—	.12
□ 1970–1988	25 Cents, Tropical Bird, Cupro-Nickel	$ .18	.28
□ 1984	25 Cents, 375th Anniversary, Cupro-Nickel	.28	.60
□ 1959	1 Crown, 350th Anniversary, Silver	—	7.00
□ 1964	1 Crown, Silver	—	5.00

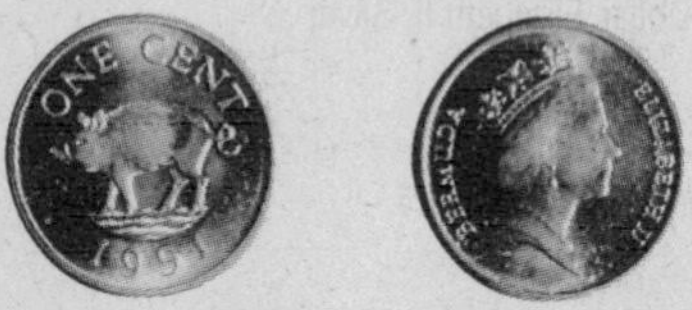

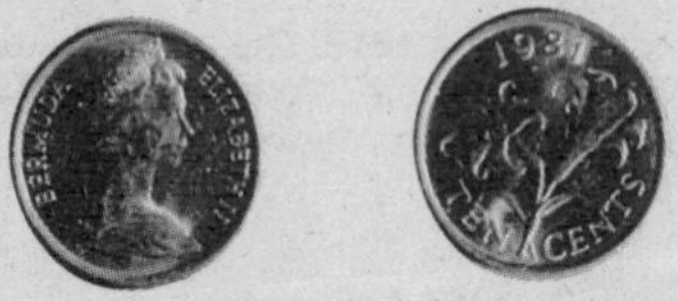

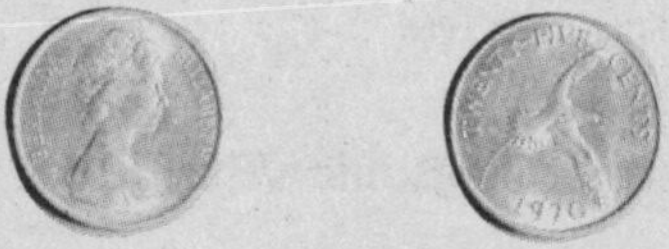

DATE	COIN TYPE/VARIETY/METAL	ABP FINE	AVERAGE FINE
□ 1970–1988	50 Cents, Arms of the Bermudas, Cupro-Nickel	$ .40	$ .75
□ 1970	1 Dollar, Elizabeth II, Silver	—	8.00

DATE	COIN TYPE/VARIETY/METAL	ABP FINE	AVERAGE FINE
□ 1972	1 Dollar, Silver Wedding Anniversary, Silver	—	8.00
□ 1981	1 Dollar, Royal Wedding, Cupro-Nickel	1.75	4.00
□ 1981	1 Dollar, Royal Wedding, Silver	—	20.00
□ 1983	1 Dollar, Cahow Over Bermuda, Brass	1.40	3.00
□ 1985	1 Dollar, Cruise Ship Tourism, Silver	—	18.00
□ 1985	1 Dollar, Cruise Ship Tourism, Copper-Nickel	1.75	4.00
□ 1986	1 Dollar, World Wildlife Fund—Sea Turtle, Cupro-Nickel	2.25	5.00
□ 1986	1 Dollar, World Wildlife Fund—Sea Turtle, Silver	—	20.00
□ 1986	1 Dollar, World Wildlife Fund—Sea Turtle, Brass	9.75	20.00
□ 1987	1 Dollar, Commercial Aviation—50th Anniversary, Cupro-Nickel	2.25	5.00
□ 1987	1 Dollar, Commercial Aviation—50th Anniversary, Silver	—	25.00
□ 1988	1 Dollar, Railroad, Silver	—	25.00
□ 1988	1 Dollar, Sailboat, Brass	1.40	3.00
□ 1988	1 Dollar, Railroad, Cupro-Nickel	2.25	5.00
□ 1989	1 Dollar, Monarch Conservation Project, Silver	—	30.00

DATE	COIN TYPE/VARIETY/METAL	ABP FINE	AVERAGE FINE
□ 1989	1 Dollar, Monarch Conservation Project, Cupro-Nickel	$2.75	$6.00
□ 1990	1 Dollar, 90th Birthday of Queen Mother, Silver	—	75.00
□ 1990	1 Dollar, 90th Birthday of Queen Mother, Cupro-Nickel	2.75	6.00
□ 1992	1 Dollar, Olympic Rings, Bronze	18.00	30.00
□ 1990	2 Dollars, Cicada Insects, Silver	—	60.00
□ 1990	2 Dollars, Tree Frog, Silver	—	60.00
□ 1991	2 Dollars, Yellow-crowned Night Heron, Silver	—	60.00
□ 1991	2 Dollars, Spiny Lobster, Silver	—	60.00
□ 1992	2 Dollars, Cedar Tree, Silver	—	60.00
□ 1992	2 Dollars, Bluebird, Silver	—	60.00
□ 1983–1986	5 Dollars, Onion Over Map of Bermuda, Brass	4.75	10.00
□ 1983–1986	10 Dollars, Hogge Money—Ship, Gold	—	90.00
□ 1983–1986	10 Dollars, Wildlife—Tree Frog, Gold	—	75.00
□ 1983–1986	10 Dollars, Hogge Money—Wild Pig, Gold	—	90.00
□ 1970	20 Dollars, Seagull in Flight, Gold	—	300.00
□ 1975	25 Dollars, Papal Visit, Silver	—	35.00
□ 1975	25 Dollars, Royal Visit, Cupro-Nickel	28.00	40.00
□ 1977	25 Dollars, Queen's Silver Jubilee, Silver	—	50.00
□ 1989	25 Dollars, Hogge Money—Ship, Gold	—	225.00
□ 1990	25 Dollars, Hogge Money—Wild Pig, Gold	—	225.00
□ 1977	50 Dollars, Queen's Silver Jubilee, Gold	—	150.00
□ 1989	50 Dollars, Hogge Money—Wild Pig, Gold	—	450.00
□ 1990	50 Dollars, Hogge Money—Ship, Gold	—	450.00
□ 1975	100 Dollars, Royal Visit, Gold	—	175.00
□ 1977	100 Dollars, Queen's Silver Jubilee, Gold	—	175.00
□ 1989	100 Dollars, Hogge Money—Ship, Gold	—	1000.00
□ 1990	100 Dollars, Hogge Money—Wild Pig, Gold	—	1000.00
□ 1981	250 Dollars, Wedding of Prince Charles & Lady Diana, Gold	—	500.00

BOLIVIA

The first coins were used in 1574, and nearly all were silver for the following 250 years. The silver "cob" Spanish reales was in use in the 1700s, followed by the silver melgarejo. The cupro-nickel centavos were in evidence in the 1800s, and the cupro-nickel pesos bolivianos in the 1970s. Decimal coins were used in 1864. The currency today is the peso boliviano.

Boliva—Type Coinage

DATE	COIN TYPE/VARIETY/METAL	ABP FINE	AVERAGE FINE
☐ 1864	1 Centecimo, 1st Coinage, Copper	$30.00	$75.00
☐ 1878	1 Centavo, 3rd Coinage, Obv: Date, Rev: Wreath Containing, Copper	25.00	60.00
☐ 1878	1 Centavo, 3rd Coinage, Obv: Value, Rev: Wreath Containing Legend, Copper	110.00	250.00
☐ 1883	1 Centavo, 3rd Coinage, Obv: Value, Rev: Wreath Containing Legend, Bronze	70.00	200.00

DATE	COIN TYPE/VARIETY/METAL	ABP FINE	AVERAGE FINE
☐ 1864	2 Centecimos, 1st Coinage, Copper	40.00	100.00
☐ 1878	2 Centavos, 3rd Coinage, Obv: Value, Rev: Wreath Containing Legend, Copper	25.00	70.00
☐ 1878	2 Centavos, 3rd Coinage, Obv: Date, Rev: Wreath Containing Value, Copper	100.00	200.00

DATE	COIN TYPE/VARIETY/METAL	ABP FINE	AVERAGE FINE
□ 1883	2 Centavos, 3rd Coinage, Obv: Value, Rev: Wreath Containing Legend, Bronze	$5.00	$10.00
□ 1864–1865	1/20 Boliviano, 1st Coinage, Silver	—	18.00

DATE	COIN TYPE/VARIETY/METAL	ABP FINE	AVERAGE FINE
□ 1871–1872	5 Centavos, 2nd Coinage, Obv: 11 Stars at Bottom, Rev: Without Weight, Silver	—	10.00
□ 1871	5 Centavos, 2nd Coinage, Obv: 11 Stars at Bottom, Rev: With Weight, Silver	—	10.00
□ 1872–1884	5 Centavos, 3rd Coinage, La Union Es La Fuerza, Silver	—	2.50
□ 1872	5 Centavos, 2nd Coinage, Obv: 9 Stars at Bottom, Rev: Without Weight, Silver	—	10.00
□ 1883	5 Centavos, 3rd Coinage, Center Hole; Obv: Value, Rev: Wreath Containing Legend, Cupro-Nickel	1.00	2.00
□ 1883	5 Centavos, 3rd Coinage, Obv: Value, Rev: Wreath Containing Legend, Cupro-Nickel	1.00	2.00
□ 1885–1900	5 Centavos, 3rd Coinage, La Union Es La Fuerza, Silver	—	1.00
□ 1892	5 Centavos, 3rd Coinage, Obv: Value, Rev: Wreath Containing Legend, Cupro-Nickel	1.00	2.00
□ 1893–1919	5 Centavos, 3rd Coinage, Cupro-Nickel	1.00	2.00

DATE	COIN TYPE/VARIETY/METAL	ABP FINE	AVERAGE FINE
☐ 1864–1866	1/5 Boliviano, 1st Coinage, Silver	—	$3.00
☐ 1864–1867	1/10 Boliviano, 1st Coinage, Silver	—	3.00
☐ 1870–1871	10 Centavos, 2nd Coinage, Obv: 11 Stars at Bottom, Rev: With Weight, Silver	—	2.00
☐ 1871	10 Centavos, 2nd Coinage, Obv: 11 Stars at Bottom, Rev: Without Weight, Silver	—	1.50
☐ 1872	10 Centavos, 2nd Coinage, Obv: 9 Stars at Bottom, Rev: Without Weight, Silver	—	1.25
☐ 1872–1884	10 Centavos, 3rd Coinage, La Union Es La Fuerza, Silver	—	1.00
☐ 1883	10 Centavos, 3rd Coinage, Obv: Value, Rev: Wreath Containing Legend, Cupro-Nickel	$4.00	10.00
☐ 1883	10 Centavos, 3rd Coinage, Center Hole; Obv: Value, Rev: Wreath Containing Legend, Cupro-Nickel	1.00	2.50
☐ 1885–1900	10 Centavos, 3rd Coinage, La Union Es La Fuerza, Silver	.50	1.00

DATE	COIN TYPE/VARIETY/METAL	ABP FINE	AVERAGE FINE
☐ 1892	10 Centavos, 3rd Coinage, Obv: Value, Rev: Wreath Containing Legend, Cupro-Nickel	1.00	2.00
☐ 1893–1919	10 Centavos, 3rd Coinage, Cupro-Nickel	1.00	1.50
☐ 1870–1871	20 Centavos, 2nd Coinage, Obv: 11 Stars at Bottom, Rev: With Weight, Silver	—	30.00
☐ 1871	20 Centavos, 2nd Coinage, Obv: 11 Stars at Bottom, Rev: Without Weight, Silver	—	9.00
☐ 1871–1872	20 Centavos, 2nd Coinage, Obv: 9 Stars at Bottom, Rev: Without Weight, Silver	—	12.00

DATE	COIN TYPE/VARIETY/METAL	ABP FINE	AVERAGE FINE
☐ 1872–1885	20 Centavos, 3rd Coinage, La Union Es La Fuerza, Silver	—	$2.50
☐ 1879	20 Centavos, Daza, Daza, President 1876–1880, Silver	—	20.00

DATE	COIN TYPE/VARIETY/METAL	ABP FINE	AVERAGE FINE
☐ 1885–1907	20 Centavos, 3rd Coinage, La Union Es La Fuerza, Silver	—	3.00
☐ 1870–1871	Boliviano-2nd Coinage obv: 11 stars at bottom, rev: with weight, Silver	—	15.00
☐ 1871–1872	Boliviano, 2nd Coinage, obv: 9 stars at bottom, rev: without weight, Silver	—	15.00
☐ 1872–1893	Boliviano, 3rd Coinage, La Union Es La Fuerza, Silver	—	15.00

BRAZIL

The first coins were used in 1645 and included the gold guilders, followed by the gold "Johannes," gold reis, silver reis, and the copper reis. The stainless steel centavos was issued in 1975. The decimal system was established in 1942. Today's currency is the real.

Brazil—Type Coinage

DATE	COIN TYPE/VARIETY/METAL	ABP FINE	AVERAGE FINE
☐ 1868–1870	10 Reis, Pedro II, Bronze	$.28	.60

DATE	COIN TYPE/VARIETY/METAL	ABP FINE	AVERAGE FINE
☐ 1868–1870	20 Reis, Pedro II, Bronze	$1.75	$2.00
☐ 1889–1912	20 Reis, Republic, Bronze	.35	.60
☐ 1918–1935	20 Reis, Republic, Cupro-Nickel	.20	.35
☐ 1873–1880	40 Reis, Pedro II, Bronze	.85	1.25
☐ 1889–1912	40 Reis, Republic, Bronze	.75	1.00
☐ 1886–1888	50 Reis, Pedro II, Cupro-Nickel	.85	1.50
☐ 1918–1935	50 Reis, Republic, Cupro-Nickel	.35	.50
☐ 1871–1875	100 Reis, Pedro II, Cupro-Nickel	.85	1.50

DATE	COIN TYPE/VARIETY/METAL	ABP FINE	AVERAGE FINE
☐ 1886–1889	100 Reis, Pedro II, Cupro-Nickel	$ .40	$1.00
☐ 1889–1900	100 Reis, Republic, Cupro-Nickel	2.75	4.00
☐ 1901	100 Reis, Republic, Cupro-Nickel	.28	.50
☐ 1918–1935	100 Reis, Republic, Cupro-Nickel	.18	.30
☐ 1932	100 Reis, Republic, Colonization 400th Anniversary, Cupro-Nickel	.28	.50
☐ 1936–1938	100 Reis, Republic, National Heroes Series—Tamandare, Cupro-Nickel	—	.25
☐ 1938–1942	100 Reis, Republic, Vargas, Cupro-Nickel	—	.12
☐ 1942–1943	10 Centavos, Republic, Cupro-Nickel	.22	.40

DATE	COIN TYPE/VARIETY/METAL	ABP FINE	AVERAGE FINE
☐ 1947–1955	10 Centavos, Republic, Obv: Bonifacio, Aluminum-Bronze	.12	.20
☐ 1956–1962	10 Centavos, Republic, Aluminum	—	.12
☐ 1854–1867	200 Reis, Pedro II, Silver	—	4.00
☐ 1867–1869	200 Reis, Pedro II, Silver	—	5.00
☐ 1871–1874	200 Reis, Pedro II, Cupro-Nickel	.80	1.50
☐ 1886–1889	200 Reis, Pedro II, Cupro-Nickel	.80	1.50
☐ 1889–1900	200 Reis, Republic, Cupro-Nickel	2.00	3.00
☐ 1901	200 Reis, Republic, Cupro-Nickel	.60	1.00

DATE	COIN TYPE/VARIETY/METAL	ABP FINE	AVERAGE FINE
☐ 1918–1935	200 Reis, Republic, Cupro-Nickel	.28	.40
☐ 1932	200 Reis, Republic, Colonization 400th Anniversary, Silver	—	—
☐ 1936–1938	200 Reis, Republic, National Heroes Series—Maua, Cupro-Nickel	.18	.30
☐ 1938–1942	200 Reis, Republic, Vargas, Cupro-Nickel	.18	.30
☐ 1942–1943	20 Centavos, Republic, Cupro-Nickel	.18	.30

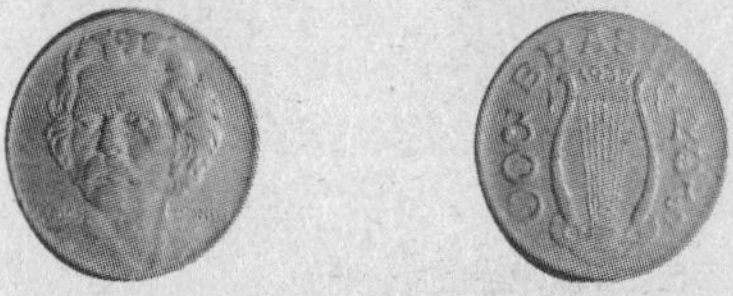

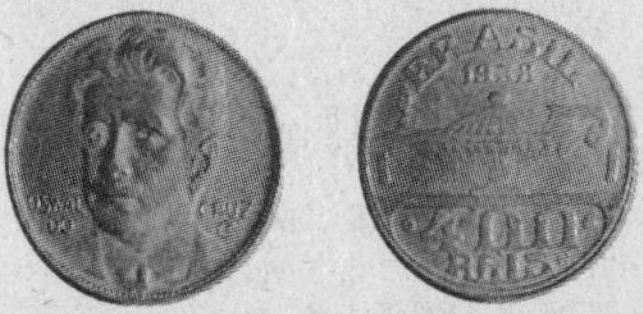

DATE	COIN TYPE/VARIETY/METAL	ABP FINE	AVERAGE FINE
□ 1948–1956	20 Centavos, Republic, Obv: Barbosa, Aluminum-Bronze	$ .10	$ .18
□ 1948–1956	20 Centavos, Republic, Obv: Dutra, Aluminum-Bronze	.10	.18
□ 1956–1962	20 Centavos, Republic, Aluminum	—	.12
□ 1936–1938	300 Reis, Republic, National Heroes Series—Carlos Gomes, Cupro-Nickel	.20	.30
□ 1938–1942	300 Reis, Republic, Vargas, Cupro-Nickel	.22	.35
□ 1900	400 Reis, Republic, Discovery 400th Anniversary, Silver	—	12.00
□ 1901	400 Reis, Republic, Cupro-Nickel	1.00	1.50
□ 1918–1935	400 Reis, Republic, Cupro-Nickel	.60	1.00
□ 1932	400 Reis, Republic, Colonization 400th Anniversary, Cupro-Nickel	.80	1.50
□ 1936–1938	400 Reis, Republic, National Heroes Series—Oswaldo Cruz, Cupro-Nickel	.18	.40

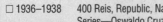

DATE	COIN TYPE/VARIETY/METAL	ABP FINE	AVERAGE FINE
☐ 1938–1942	400 Reis, Republic, Vargas, Cupro-Nickel	—	$ .20
☐ 1922	500 Reis, Republic, Independence Centennial, Aluminum-Bronze	$ .18	.30
☐ 1932	500 Reis, Republic, First Settler, Aluminum-Bronze	—	—
☐ 1939	500 Reis, Republic, Famous Men Series—de Assis, Aluminum-Bronze	1.00	2.00
☐ 1849–1852	500 Reis, Pedro II, Silver	—	10.00
☐ 1853–1867	500 Reis, Pedro II, Silver	—	6.00
☐ 1867–1868	500 Reis, Pedro II, Silver	—	8.00
☐ 1868–1869	500 Reis, Pedro II, Silver	—	5.00
☐ 1889	500 Reis, Republic, Silver	—	60.00

DATE	COIN TYPE/VARIETY/METAL	ABP FINE	AVERAGE FINE
☐ 1906–1913	500 Reis, Republic, Silver	—	4.00
☐ 1924–1930	500 Reis, Republic, Aluminum-Bronze	.18	.40
☐ 1935	500 Reis, Republic, National Heroes Series—Diego Feijo, Aluminum-Bronze	1.40	3.00
☐ 1942–1943	50 Centavos, Republic, Cupro-Nickel	.28	.50

DATE	COIN TYPE/VARIETY/METAL	ABP FINE	AVERAGE FINE
☐ 1956	50 Centavos, Republic, Aluminum-Bronze	.12	.20
☐ 1849–1852	1000 Reis, Pedro II, Silver	—	7.00
☐ 1853–1866	1000 Reis, Pedro II, Silver	—	8.00
☐ 1869	1000 Reis, Pedro II, Silver	—	20.00
☐ 1876–1869	1000 Reis, Pedro II, Silver	—	10.00
☐ 1889	1000 Reis, Republic, Silver	—	12.00
☐ 1900	1000 Reis, Republic, Discovery 400th Anniversary, Silver	—	50.00

DATE	COIN TYPE/VARIETY/METAL	ABP FINE	AVERAGE FINE
☐ 1922	1000 Reis, Republic, Independence Centennial, Aluminum-Bronze	$ .20	$ .50

DATE	COIN TYPE/VARIETY/METAL	ABP FINE	AVERAGE FINE
☐ 1906–1913	1000 Reis, Republic, Silver	—	4.00
☐ 1924–1931	1000 Reis, Republic, Aluminum-Bronze	.28	.60
☐ 1932	1000 Reis, Republic, First Governor, Aluminum-Bronze	1.40	3.00
☐ 1935	1000 Reis, Republic, National Heroes Series—Jose de Anchieta, Aluminum-Bronze	.60	1.50
☐ 1939	1000 Reis, Republic, Famous Men Series—Barreto, Aluminum-Bronze	.12	.30

DATE	COIN TYPE/VARIETY/METAL	ABP FINE	AVERAGE FINE
☐ 1942–1956	Cruzeiro, Republic, Aluminum-Bronze	.12	.30
☐ 1956	Cruzeiro, Republic, Aluminum-Bronze	—	.20
☐ 1957–1961	Cruzeiro, Republic, Aluminum	—	.12
☐ 1851–1852	2000 Reis, Pedro II, Silver	—	12.00
☐ 1853–1867	2000 Reis, Pedro II, Silver	—	12.00
☐ 1868–1869	2000 Reis, Pedro II, Silver	—	25.00
☐ 1886–1889	2000 Reis, Pedro II, Silver	—	12.00
☐ 1891–1897	2000 Reis, Republic, Silver	—	200.00
☐ 1900	2000 Reis, Republic, Discovery 400th Anniversary, Silver	—	75.00

DATE	COIN TYPE/VARIETY/METAL	ABP FINE	AVERAGE FINE
□ 1906–1913	2000 Reis, Republic, Silver	—	$5.00
□ 1924–1934	2000 Reis, Republic, Silver	—	2.00
□ 1932	2000 Reis, Republic, King Joao III, Aluminum-Bronze	$1.40	3.00
□ 1935	2000 Reis, Republic, National Heroes Series—Caxias, Aluminum-Bronze	—	—
□ 1936–1938	2000 Reis, Republic, National Heroes Series—Duke of Caxias, Aluminum-Bronze	.60	1.00
□ 1939	2000 Reis, Republic, Famous Men Series—Peixoto, Aluminum-Bronze	.28	.60

DATE	COIN TYPE/VARIETY/METAL	ABP FINE	AVERAGE FINE
□ 1942–1956	2 Cruzeiros, Republic, Aluminum-Bronze	.18	.30
□ 1956	2 Cruzeiros, Republic, Aluminum-Bronze	.18	.30
□ 1957–1961	2 Cruzeiros, Republic, Aluminum	—	.20
□ 1900	4000 Reis, Republic, Discovery 400th Anniversary, Silver	—	150.00
□ 1854–1869	5000 Reis, Pedro II, Gold	—	100.00

DATE	COIN TYPE/VARIETY/METAL	ABP FINE	AVERAGE FINE
☐ 1936–1938	5000 Reis, Republic, National Heroes Series—Santos Dumont, Silver	—	$3.00
☐ 1942–1943	5 Cruzeiros, Republic, Aluminum-Bronze	$ .35	.80
☐ 1849–1851	10000 Reis, Pedro II, Gold	—	150.00
☐ 1853–1889	10000 Reis, Pedro II, Gold	—	150.00
☐ 1889–1922	10000 Reis, Republic, Gold	—	175.00
☐ 1965	10 Cruzeiros, Republic, Aluminum	—	.12
☐ 1849–1851	20000 Reis, Pedro II, Gold	—	300.00
☐ 1851–1852	20000 Reis, Pedro II, Gold	—	275.00
☐ 1853–1889	20000 Reis, Pedro II, Gold	—	300.00
☐ 1889–1922	20000 Reis, Republic, Gold	—	350.00
☐ 1965	20 Cruzeiros, Republic, Aluminum	.18	.25
☐ 1965	50 Cruzeiros, Republic, Cupro-Nickel	—	.20

CANADA

The first coins, sols, and deniers in silver, bullion, and copper were used in 1670. In the 1800s the bronze penny token was in use. The first decimal coins were used in 1858. The currency today is the dollar.

CANADIAN NUMISMATIC CHRONOLOGY

Courtesy of Q. David Bowers, Bowers and Merena Galleries, Inc.

Decimal Issues 1857–1967

The following listing comprises some of the many events that played a part in Canadian numismatics, leading to the discipline as we know it today. The study begins with the authorization of decimal coins in 1857 and concludes with the end of production of circulating silver coins in 1967. The study relates to decimal coin issues, with an acknowledgment that many other noteworthy events relating to paper money, tokens, and medals took place before and during the same time period.

1857: Decimal coinage system is adopted, and government records are now required to be kept in dollars and cents. This follows legislative action dating back to 1850 when Canadian coinage was proposed, but British authorities objected. Circulating coinage consists of a rich mixture of private copper tokens, United States coins, English coins, Spanish-American silver, and other issues. Forthcoming Canadian decimal coins are to be on par with United States coins. Although Canadian coins are to be denominated in dollars and fractions thereof, no one-dollar coins will be made for circulation until 1935.

1858: First decimal coins are struck for the Province of Canada: 1¢, 5¢, 10¢, and 20¢, Circulation strikes as well as a few Specimens are made, all at the Royal Mint, London, which will continue to be the main facility for striking Canadian coins until the Ottawa Mint opens in 1908. Coins feature the portrait of Queen Victoria, reigning monarch of England.

1859: Bronze cents are struck in large quantities for the Province of Canada, but no silver coins will be produced in this or any other year. By the time silver coinage is resumed in 1870, the Dominion of Canada will have been formed. So many bronze cents are made in 1859 that there will be a glut of them in the channels of commerce until the mid-1870s. Nova Scotia adopts a decimal system based upon the pound sterling rated at an exact $5.

1860: At the Royal Mint in London, bronze replaces copper for minor coins, and a revised portrait of Queen Victoria is created as is a new border style featuring tiny dots instead of the previous toothed-denticle format. The beaded border causes problems with the rim of the die breaking off, and denticles are reverted to. Meanwhile, both the new portrait of Victoria and the beaded border are used for a time in the early 1860s on certain bronze coins and patterns relating to Canadian maritime provinces. On April 9 New Brunswick approves a decimal coinage. The Heaton Mint begins construction of a new facility on Icknield Street, Birmingham, which will be ready in 1862 at which time 11 screw presses and one lever press will be used.

1861: First decimal coins are struck for Nova Scotia and New Brunswick at the Royal Mint, London, using the British farthing (1/4 penny) and halfpenny dies for the obverses. Bronze half cents and cents will be struck for Nova Scotia through 1864. New Brunswick half cents are struck by mistake and apparently mixed in with Nova Scotia coinage; obverse die of British farthing utilized. Other New Brunswick coins will be struck through 1864. Now as in future years, coinage orders from various entities in British North America placed with the Royal Mint will receive secondary attention in comparison to domestic coinage for England.

1862: In New Westminster, British Columbia, a few $10 and $20 gold coins are struck using gold from the Fraser River district, these being Canada's first gold coinage. Examples of these pieces are sent to London for exhibit in the International Exposition there; one each of the gold $10 and $20 from this showing will be presented to the British Museum in due course. The Numismatic Society of Montreal is founded on December 6 and will publish *The Canadian Antiquarian*. Adélard J. Boucher (born in 1835; secretary beginning in 1854 of the Montreal & Bytown Railway Co.) is named as its first president. In England, George William Wyon, young resident engraver at the Royal Mint since 1860, dies at the age of 26 years, and the Royal Mint strikes a memorial medal utilizing a reverse device that is also found on the New Brunswick 20-cent pieces of this year, creating a curiosity that will delight future generations of collectors. Vancouver adopts a decimal currency system. Ralph Heaton II dies in the same year that his new facility is ready for business. The firm becomes known as Ralph Heaton & Sons.

1863: United States coins are rare in circulation in the United States itself—which is in the middle of its Civil War—but are in oversupply in Canada. Particularly numerous are the old U.S. copper "large" cents dated from about the 1820s through 1857, with some worn earlier issues as well. During the decade Devins & Bolton, Montreal pharmacists, will counterstamp thousands of these American cents with their advertising message. Newfoundland adopts an exchange rate under which a Newfoundland dollar is worth one Spanish silver dollar, the latter being worth four shillings two pence in sterling; thus £1 sterling is worth $4.80 in Newfoundland decimal currency. This rate will be maintained until the banking crisis of 1894; in 1895 Newfoundland money will be at par with Canadian. The Numismatic Society of Montreal appoints a committee to prepare a catalogue of Canadian coin varieties, but the project will lapse.

1864: At the Royal Mint, London, Master Thomas Graham (who served in the post from April 27, 1856, until his death on September 16, 1869) discontinues the practice, considered wasteful, of scrapping dated English coin dies at the end of the calendar year. However, post-date use of *colonial* coin dies until they wore out is already the norm and is continued. This will wreak havoc with the accuracy of certain Royal Mint yearly coinage figures as related to coin dates. The Dominion of Canada is formed by the union of Nova Scotia, Quebec, and Ontario.

1865: Newfoundland bronze half cents are struck for circulation. Coins for Newfoundland will be produced by various mints through 1947. Newfoundland $2 gold coins are inaugurated this year and will be made intermittently through 1888, sometimes using the identical obverse dies employed to strike 10-cent pieces. These $2 pieces will become the only widely circulating Canadian gold coins of the 19th century and will be a delight to numismatists of generations to come. The mainland of British Columbia adopts a decimal system (but does not strike coins); Vancouver has been on the decimal system since 1862.

1866: United States coins remain a glut in the channels of commerce in Canada, but are the standard of trade. Liberty Seated half dimes, dimes, quarter dollars, and half dollars are ubiquitous in Montreal, Quebec, Vancouver, and other cities. They sell at varying discounts from face value, engendering a lively trade for money brokers of which there are dozens in the larger eastern cities, Montreal being a special center of activity. In January the collectors' group there changes its name to the Numismatic and Antiquarian Society of Montreal, reflecting members' interest in history as well as coins. The Boucher Collection, which had been awarded first prize at the Provincial Exhibition in 1863, is the first major numismatic property to be sold by public auction. John J. Arnton conducts the event, and the 726 lots—including many rare Canadian tokens—realize about $400. In November the James Rattray Collection is auctioned.

1867: The British North America Act unites the Confederation (New Brunswick, Nova Scotia, Quebec, and Ontario) as the Dominion of Canada. The government begins to take action to decrease United States coins in circulation. There are abundant Liberty Seated silver coins just about everywhere in Canada—as there have been since the 1850s—while in the United States itself they still are not seen in circulation, and transactions are conducted with paper Fractional Currency notes, bronze Indian cents, and some new issues including two-cent, nickel three-cent, and nickel five-cent pieces. The collections of William V. B. Hall and H. Laggatt (the latter cabinet known as the Bronsdon Collection) cross the auction block.

1868: Charles W. Fremantle becomes deputy director and comptroller of the Royal Mint; his tenure would last through 1894. A numismatist, Fremantle will see to it that Proofs (Specimens) were struck of many dates so that the British Museum and others will have some for display purposes.

1869: A catalogue, *Coins, Tokens and Medals of the Dominion of Canada,* by Alfred Sandham, is published by the Numismatic and Antiquarian Society of Montreal. Thomas Graham passes away on September 16; he had been master of the Royal Mint since April 27, 1856, and had been important in the contract coinage for the Province of Canada, 1858 and 1859. Graham insisted that all British coins struck in a given calendar year be dated correctly, but no such rule applied to colonial coinages (which were nearly always given second shrift at the mint).

1870: Silver coins for the Dominion of Canada are minted for the first time, by the Royal Mint in London. Denominations include the bronze 1¢ and the silver 5¢, 10¢, 25¢ (instead of the 20¢ used in the 1858 Province of Canada coinage), and 50¢. Dies of the decade will be made by hand by entering various elements such as Victoria's portrait, inscription letters, etc., by single punches, yielding a wealth of minor die varieties such as repunched and misaligned letters and numerals. Legislation provides for the revision of value of the millions of copper bank and provincial tokens in circulation, currently passing at 120 to the dollar for the halfpenny size; henceforth they will be worth one cent each, or 100 to the dollar. The fewer large copper tokens such as the copper pennies are to be worth two cents each. Minister of Finance Sir Francis Hincks and William Weir are two important government figures in the campaign to get rid of Liberty Seated silver coinage from the United States. Weir is put in charge and decides to export vast quantities. Meanwhile, as the new 25-cent pieces for Canada have not arrived from England, an issue of 25¢ paper currency is floated. Years later, Weir will write a book about his experiences during this era. In 1880 a consortium of commercial interests will recognize his service and give him a silver tea service in which United States silver coins are embedded. The Royal Mint, London, publishes its first annual report. Beginning in 1884 it will include technical information about Canadian and related foreign coinages.

1871: The Royal Mint in London, too busy to take on outside work, subcontracts certain Dominion of Canada coinage to a private facility, Ralph Heaton & Sons, simply known as the "Heaton Mint." Birmingham, more than any other city in the entire world, has a rich history of private coinage facilities, these being especially active in the previous century and dominated by the famous Soho Mint operated by Boulton and Watt. On an intermittent basis from now until 1903 the Heaton Mint will produce Canadian coins from cents to 50-cent pieces, each bearing an H mintmark. Dies for Dominion coinage are made at the Royal Mint and shipped to Heaton. On

December 18 the first Canadian coins are struck by Heaton and consists of 1,000 50-cent pieces made under the watch of personnel from the Royal Mint, with special security precautions. This year the Heaton Mint also produces bronze cents for Prince Edward Island, but the H is inadvertently omitted; this picturesque coin with its arboreal theme will remain as that island's only official decimal coinage. Heaton coinage for Newfoundland ranges from the cent to the 50-cent piece. The Dominion Currency Act is passed and helps standardize exchange values within British North America. British Columbia becomes part of the Dominion of Canada on July 20. The Assay Office in British Columbia is closed.

1872: The *Canadian Antiquarian and Numismatic Journal* makes its debut and will continue to be published through 1933. Canadian coinage was accomplished exclusively at the Heaton Mint, Birmingham, as it will be for the next several years. The Royal Mint, using machinery that was modern 60 years earlier when it was installed, but which is now obsolete, struggles to keep pace with orders for British coins and leans upon Heaton to supply planchets for bronze issues.

1873: Prince Edward Island becomes part of the Dominion of Canada, thus isolating its 1871 cent as the only decimal coinage of that province. Canadian circulating coinage continues to be accomplished exclusively at the Heaton Mint.

1874: Canadian circulating coinage is accomplished exclusively at the Heaton Mint, thus contributing to a cluster of issues of this era with H mintmarks.

1875: Silver coinage this year continues to be concentrated at the Heaton Mint, typically in small quantities—thus delighting numismatists of a later generation who will consider most of the 1875-H issues to be objects of great desire. At the suggestion (it is said) of Charles W. Fremantle the Royal Mint strikes a few mintmarkless coins for cabinet purposes. In due course these will become numismatic rarities.

1876: Bronze cents, not minted since 1859, are again produced, this year at the Heaton Mint plus a few Specimen strikings at the Royal Mint where all dies are produced. Old provincial and private copper tokens, mostly of the one-cent trading value, begin to be gradually withdrawn from circulation. For the numismatists of the era, such copper pieces provide a rich area for collecting, and most emphasis in numismatic circles was on the tokens. There are not enough decimal coin varieties by this time to attract much attention. In this year Canadian circulating coinage production continues exclusively at the Heaton Mint, Birmingham. From time to time the Heaton Mint sets aside samples of the Canadian coinage for possible showing to other world countries and entities that might like to have their coinage made by the same factory. Not all of these will be passed out, and circa 1975 they will be mentioned to an executive of Paramount International Coin Corporation of Dayton, Ohio, U.S.A., who will recognize their importance. In due course over the next 10 years—1975 to the early 1980s—Raymond N. Merena and David W. Akers of Paramount, followed by Spink & Son, Ltd., London, will distribute these pieces in numismatic channels. Joseph LeRoux, M.D. (born April 9, 1849), of Montreal begins to collect coins with great enthusiasm, and in the next decade he will publish several numismatic guides including a catalogue of Canadian coins (1882), the *Numismatic Atlas for Canada* (1883), *The Collectors' Vade Mecum* (1885), the monthly *Collectionneur* magazine (beginning in 1996), and the *Canadian Coin Cabinet* (1888 with a supplement in 1890 and new edition in 1890).

1877: Canadian circulating coinage is once again only made at the Heaton Mint.

1878: The Royal Mint, London, source for all Canadian decimal coin dies, adopts a new steam hammer method of die forging to replace the former tedious hand forging. New dies will be stronger and last longer, yielding more coins per die. Continuing what is becoming a tradition, Canadian circulating coinage is struck exclusively at the Heaton Mint.

1879: R.W. McLachlan's detailed study of Canadian coins, begun in 1877, first appears in the *American Journal of Numismatics* and will run for several years. A pioneer in the field, McLachlan gave much information that was new to his general audience, including mintage figures. Canadian circulating coinage continues to be made only at the Heaton Mint. Charles W. Fremantle, in charge of the Royal Mint, becomes a member of the Numismatic Society in London. His interest in coins is hardly new, for earlier in the decade he had tapped numismatist William Webster to catalogue the Mint's own collection. Gaps in the holdings were found, and Fremantle obtained permission from the Treasury to produce impressions from old dies (*i.e.,* restrikes) of the past century or so, from King George III through Queen Victoria, along the way creating some "restrikes" of which there were no "originals" (*e.g.,* certain 1870-, 1871-, and 1875-dated silver coins).

1880: Canadian circulating coinage is once again exclusively struck at the Heaton Mint, Birmingham. Gerald E. Hart, Montreal numismatist, sells a collection of Canadian coins, tokens, and medals to the Canadian government for $2,500 and writes a catalogue of it; the government states its intention to publish and distribute the catalogue and pay him an extra $500, but the project eventually lapses.

1881: Canadian circulating coinage is accomplished exclusively at the Heaton Mint. In banking and exchange circles $72.75 in British Columbia money is worth $73 in Canadian money. In April the Canadian government ships $50,000 face value in 1858 20-cent pieces to the Heaton Mint to be converted into other coins (also see note under Lot 279 in the present catalogue).

1882: No surprise: Canadian circulating coinage is again struck only with H mintmarks. The Royal Mint, London, is being renovated and updated, and Heaton produces all Imperial bronze coins and all British colonial issues. Certain presses obtained decades earlier from Matthew Boulton are replaced by new models made in Birmingham by Heaton, capable of striking 90 coins per minute (5,400 per hour), giving the Royal Mint a capacity of about 75,000 coins per hour when all facilities are running. During this era the *American Numismatic Journal*, published by the American Numismatic and Archaeological Society (founded 1858), continues to include important articles by R.W. McLachlan on Canadian coins. The Heaton Mint strikes Newfoundland $2 gold coins this year only, creating the only Canadian-related gold coins to bear an H mintmark. Other Newfoundland $2 coins from 1865 through 1888 are made at the Royal Mint, London.

1883: Canadian circulating coinage is again accomplished exclusively at the Heaton Mint.

1884: The *Fifteenth Annual Report of the Deputy Master of the Mint* includes much technical information about Canadian coinage made under contract. Such detailed information will continue to be a part of report until 1907. After a lapse of over a decade during which time the Heaton Mint did all of the coinage, the Royal Mint, now with expanded facilities, begins once again striking coins for Canada, although the Heaton Mint will be called upon from time to time to do work.

1885: Mintage quantities for certain Canadian and Newfoundland coins are low this year, creating varieties that numismatists yet unborn will venerate as rarities, especially if in high grades. The government of Canada redeems $18,000 face value in old 1858 20-cent pieces and causes them to be melted.

1886: In this year at least three significant date punch variations occur on the 10-cent piece. On the 25-cent piece the 1886/3 overdate is made, one of the relatively few overdates in Canadian coinage of this or any other era.

1887: There is little call for silver 50-cent pieces in the eastern provinces, although they are popular in British Columbia on the West Coast, hardly a new situation and one that will continue into the 1890s.

1888: Joseph LeRoux publishes a reference on Canadian coins and will continue to update it through 1892. At the Royal Mint, London, maker of all dies for Dominion of Canada decimal coins, a new method is adopted whereby dies would be forged to their approximate finished size, rather than being made much larger and then machined to smaller dimensions. This results in greater efficiency. Canadian coins are becoming increasingly stereotyped, with die varieties being minor and mostly limited to date repunching and numeral size variations. In Monroe, Michigan, Dr. George F. Heath launches the *American Numismatist*, name soon changed to *The Numismatist*. In due course it will attract many Canadian subscribers and will publish many articles on Canadian coinage. The government redeems $17,174 worth of 1858 20-cent pieces for the melting pot.

1889: Despite a published high mintage the 1889 10-cent piece will prove to be a major rarity in the Canadian series. A later generation of numismatists will conclude that while many coins were struck in calendar year 1889, most pieces were dated earlier. Twenty-cent pieces continue to be called in, and $16,585 face value goes to the melting pot. The Heaton minting facility changes its name to The Mint, Birmingham, Ltd. Ralph Heaton III retires, and a contract with the newly renamed firm, now a public company, specifies the hiring of Ralph Heaton IV (1864-1930) as general manager.

1890: Pierre Napoleon Breton publishes the *Illustrated Canadian Coin Collector.* Breton, born in Montreal on June 10, 1858, just in time to be on hand for the first Canadian decimal coins, became interested in coins at the age of 15, and in 1889 he opened a store to sell books, numismatic items, and curios (in those days few coin dealers anywhere in North America dealt exclusively in numismatics). His first love was the copper "bouquet sou" token series, many of which were struck by Gibbs in Belleville, New Jersey. Meanwhile, as the father of 15 children, he must have been busy as well with family matters. Breton will live until 1917 and at that time will be widely mourned. In the Canadian Parliament a proposal for a domestic mint is introduced on March 4 as a measure to help gold-mining interests convert metal to coin. However, nothing comes of the idea at the time, which is viewed as being primarily beneficial to interests in the western part of the Dominion. In Newfoundland the dollar is revalued to place it on a par with Canadian and American dollars. It is found that two Royal Mint staff members are shareholders in the Heaton Mint, an uncomfortable situation in view of the Royal Mint giving contracts to the Birmingham coiner; the offending staffers sell their shares. Moreover, Royal Mint superintendent Robert Anderson Hill is connected by marriage to the Heaton family.

1891: In this year several date and leaf variations on the reverse of the bronze cent are created, but are of little notice at the time, but decades later will loom large when two of the several major varieties will be determined as being quite hard to find. The American Numismatic Association is formed in Chicago and will go on to become the world's largest organization of coin collectors, to hold annual conventions including in Canada in 1909 and 1923, and years later in 1941-1942 to have a Canadian, J. Douglas Ferguson, serve as president.

1892: In this year there is no coinage for Nova Scotia, nor had there been in 1891, nor will there be in 1893. In numismatic circles the most popular discipline was the acquisition of early 19th-century tokens, a trend that would continue until well into the 20th century.

1893: Joseph Hooper, of Ontario, is one of the most active writers and researchers of the era and contributes many items to *The Numismatist.* Canadian numismatic activity is intense and is focused almost exclusively on private tokens and related issues.

1894: P.N. Breton's *Illustrated History of Coins and Tokens Related to Canada* is published and in due course becomes the standard reference in the field. Over a period of time "Breton numbers" will be used to identify the multitudinous varieties of early 19th-century tokens as well as later ones. To a much lesser extent information is given on decimal coins. Breton notes that R.W. McLachlan, born in 1845 and who began collecting coins in 1857, has the largest numismatic cabinet in Canada, numbering over 8,000 pieces and ranging from ancient Greek issues to modern coins. Meanwhile, J.W. Scott & Co., New York City, publishes its *Standard Catalogue* series on various coins and treats Canadian tokens extensively, but gives very little detail on Canadian decimal coins. Serious collectors view the widely-distributed Scott catalogues to be beneficial for the popularization of the hobby, but to be rather superficial in numismatic content. The Canadian government causes $14,518 worth of 1858 20-cent pieces to be melted. By now, they are becoming elusive in circulation and have long since been replaced by the 25-cent pieces. However, the denomination circulates actively in Newfoundland, with inscriptions pertaining to that island, and will continue to be minted for Newfoundland for years in the future. A major financial crisis occurs in Newfoundland, the island's two banks collapse, and four banks from the Canadian mainland set up facilities to provide financial services. Newfoundland residents hoard "hard" money including the gold $2 coins of the island minted 1865-1888, which soon become virtually nonexistent in circulation. Charles W. Fremantle, now at the age of 60, retires from the Royal Mint, having made many technological improvements during his watch and having encouraged the production of many Proof issues for museum and other cabinet purposes.

1895: Newfoundland money is set at par with Canadian money. Many fishermen and traders under foreign flags stop at Newfoundland, with the result that during this time the circulating coinage of the island is a varied mixture of world denominations, much more so than in the Dominion of Canada. In the United States the most active dealer in tokens and medals of Canada is Lyman H. Low.

1896: Gold is discovered in the Klondike, Yukon Territory. In the next year the "north to Alaska" slogan will draw thousands of fortune hunters through the Chilkoot Pass on their way north. Seattle, Washington, becomes the main jumping-off place for debarkation.

1897: Klondike fever is in full force and is the first gold rush to attract a press corps. Novelist Jack London is among those on the scene. This new find of gold revives interest (see 1890) in establishing a domestic mint, and discussion continues for several years thereafter, but no firm steps will be taken until 1901.

1898: The J.W. Scott & Co. series of *Standard Catalogues*, published in multiple editions during this era, continues to list and illustrate coins and tokens (mainly) of Canada and the provinces, but provides virtually nothing in the way of historical material. Nevertheless, their wide circulation continues to draw collectors to the Canadian series, mostly to the area of tokens, but rarely decimal coinage.

1899: The Canadian government redeems $18,895 face value in obsolete silver coins including 5-, 10-, and 20-cent pieces.

1900: Various proposals are made for the institution of a Canadian gold coinage, including one from a government accountant in Winnipeg who suggests that these be called the "beaver" and to be of "bold and active" appearance and be decorated with seven stars to represent the different provinces. By this time, the last year of the 19th century, the once ubiquitous provincial and private copper tokens have largely disappeared from circulation, even in remote areas. In larger cities they have been scarce for most of the decade. Many private coin collectors, and dealers too, issue their own brass tokens, and many bear Canadian addresses.

1901: The visage of Queen Victoria, familiar on British coins since 1838 and Canadian decimal issues since 1858, appears for the last time. By this time British coinage uses the "Old Head" or "Veiled Head," adopted in 1893, but Canadian coinage portrays her as somewhat younger. On May 21 the Ottawa Mint Act is introduced to provide for a Canadian branch of the Royal Mint, London, following efforts of Hon. W.S. Fielding, minister of finance. It is anticipated that this will provide a facility to coin vast quantities of gold from British Columbia and the Yukon, the latter being the site of the Klondike gold rush. Otherwise, the gold would be shipped to foreign mints. In July the Department of the Interior opens an assay office in Vancouver. Meanwhile, the Royal Mint, London, is in the midst of a modernization program which in 1907 will result in the replacement of steam power by electricity.

1902: The coinage now depicts the heir to Victoria's throne, King Edward VII. Construction of the new mint is anticipated to begin, but does not.

1903: Only one million 10-cent pieces are coined, which will stand as the low water mark for mintage of this denomination during the current reign.

1904: The mintage of 400,000 25-cent pieces is the lowest of this denomination during the reign of Edward VII. This and other silver coins of Edward are not well detailed on the obverse and become quickly abraded, creating issues that numismatists decades later will find to be rarities in Mint State, even if large numbers of pieces are made for circulation.

1905: Construction of the Ottawa Mint begins. Only 40,000 50-cent pieces are struck at the Royal Mint, London, which will prove to be the smallest mintage of the reign of Edward VII.

1906: The Canadian government redeems $7,461 face value in obsolete silver coins including 5-, 10-, and 20-cent pieces. By now the 1858 Canadian 20-cent piece is very scarce in circulation, except in Newfoundland where they are mixed in with Newfoundland coins of the same denomination (which continue to be minted). United States silver coins are accumulating in commercial channels, reminiscent of the Liberty Seated coinage nuisance of decades earlier. Canadian banks act as depots to receive United States coins and ship them to the New York City office of the Bank of Montreal.

The Finance Department in Canada reimburses the banks for shipping charges and pays a commission of 3/8ths of one percent to reimburse the institutions for their handling expenses. From March 1 through August 1 over $500,000 worth of silver coins is exported. However, quantities remained north of the border, and in January 1908 when Deputy Minister of Finance T.C. Boville sought to determine the situation, he learned that in British Columbia—always a heavy user of larger silver denominations—about 75% of circulating coinage was from the United States.

1907: The Ottawa Mint is completed. The mintage of only 800,000 1907-H cents is at once the only Heaton Mint coin of this denomination, the lowest cent mintage of the Edwardian era, and the last H-mintmarked coinage ever made for the Dominion of Canada.

1908: Ottawa Mint opens on January 2. Governor General Earl Grey strikes the first coin, a silver 50-cent piece, and a few minutes later his wife, Countess Grey, strikes a bronze cent. Production of business strike silver coins commences on February 19. Specimen sets are issued for sale to the public. From this point onward, nearly all Dominion of Canada coins will be minted here, as will some contract coinage for other entities, notably Newfoundland. Dies continue to be made at the Royal Mint, London. Gold sovereigns (worth £1 sterling) are struck for the first time, bear a C mintmark (the first such use), and will be made continuously through 1919. Few circulate within Canada, however, and they are mainly used in international trade. Unfortunately the gold production of British Columbia and the Yukon, which provided a reason in 1901 to begin steps to establish the mint, has diminished greatly.

1909: The American Numismatic Association holds its annual convention for the first time in Canada. Montreal furnishes the venue for a lot of in-fighting and bickering which had begun in 1908 and would continue through 1910. Numismatic entrepreneur Farran Zerbe was the controversial focal point of much dissension, with not many approving of his recent purchase of *The Numismatist* from the widow of its founder, Dr. George F. Heath of Monroe, Michigan. Just about everyone expected that it would be sold to the ANA, but, apparently, Zerbe sweet-talked Mrs. Heath into a private sale. Enter prominent Canadian collector W.W.C. Wilson, who will soon become the main factor in smoothing things when he purchases *The Numismatist* from Zerbe (who finds that running the magazine was a lot of work and not profitable) and presents it to the American Numismatic Association.

1910: Edward VII dies on May 6. This year is the swan song for his portrait on coins.

1911: The new coinage depicts King George V who is crowned on June 22. Specimen sets are issued for sale to the public, but not many find buyers. Dominion of Canada coins omit mention of the Deity (DEI GRA., for DEI GRATIA, "by the grace of God") on the obverse inscription, causing some public outcry (in 1907 a similar situation had occurred in the United States with the new gold $10 and $20 designs which omitted IN GOD WE TRUST, partway through 1908 President Theodore Roosevelt restored the motto). A separate gold refinery is set up at the Ottawa Mint; earlier refining had been done by the Assay Office at the same institution.

1912: Canadian $5 and $10 gold pieces are struck for the first time. This attractive coinage will continue for two more years, after which the government will have ideas of its own about controlling the gold supply, and this does not include the minting of coins (see 1914). The last 20-cent pieces are struck for Newfoundland; the denomination had been first minted in 1865. Meanwhile, the ephemeral 20-cent coinages for the Province of Canada (1858) and the United States (1875-1878) have been largely forgotten. In 1917 the Newfoundland 20-cent piece will be superseded in its silver series by a 25-cent piece, a value not coined earlier for this island.

1913: Interest in collecting early tokens of Canada, exceedingly popular in the 1890s (especially after the publication of Breton's 1894 book) and continuing past the turn of the century, begins to fade. The same happens on the United States token series as such scholars as Low and Wright are no longer on the scene. Thomas L. Elder will become a minority voice when he states that token collecting is a basic foundation stone of numismatics.

1914: $5 and $10 gold coins are minted for the last time. The Finance Department of the government seeks to control gold, and early in 1915 it decrees that henceforth it will prefer gold bars to coins of these denominations, but gold sovereigns, minted under a different authorization and supplied on demand to depositors of gold bullion, will continue to be made for the next several years. In August the World War commences after an unfortunate incident in Sarajevo. Canadians respond to the call, and volunteers assemble the First Canadian Division and go to France.

1915: Boom times begin in Canada and the United States as factories work overtime to provide material for the war in Europe. The economy expands, and for the next several years mintage quantities will increase.

1916: The Ottawa Mint strikes only 6,111 gold sovereigns, thus creating a coin that decades later would be recognized as a classic rarity. Apparently, most went to the United States Treasury and were melted.

1917: Newfoundland taps the Ottawa Mint to produce coins for it, and the 25-cent piece replaces the old 20-cent denominations; the Ottawa Mint would strike coins for Newfoundland through 1947, but 25-cent pieces were made only once again, in 1919. Coins bear a C mintmark. The Ottawa Mint does its part for the World War effort and makes sights and eyepieces for guns and also helps the Royal Mint (London) by making six million planchets for shillings.

1918: World War I ends in Europe, but over 50,000 Canadian soldiers will never come home. The momentum of the boom economy lingers and good times and high coinage quantities continue through 1920. The Ottawa Mint strikes coins under contract for Jamaica, these being in copper-nickel metal, the first quantity coinage of that alloy made in Ottawa.

1919: The last Canadian gold sovereign drops from the press, ending a series which started in 1908. The government has preferred gold bars for a long time (see 1914), and newly refined gold often goes to government vaults as security for gold-backed paper currency. A slightly modified bronze alloy is adopted for cents part way through the year, this making the planchets somewhat easier to strike and less susceptible to defects.

1920: The old-style "large cent" format, first used in 1858, gives way to the new small cent. Both types of cents are coined. Silver is high-priced on the international market, playing havoc with certain coinages in this metal. To forestall any problems, the fineness of the alloy in Canadian silver coins is reduced from 92.5% silver (sterling standard) to 80%.

1921: It is a tough year for the economy. The boom times engendered by the World War in Europe and the position of Canada as a supplier of material comes to an end. Times are tough, and commerce is slow. Although quite a few coins are minted as a result of the kinetic energy remaining from preceding good years, it turns out that there is an oversupply of coins, and in succeeding years many will be melted, including nearly all of the 1921-dated silver five-cent and 50-cent coins, which in time will become famous rarities. It turns out that this is the last year the silver five-cent piece would be minted.

1922: The format of the five-cent piece is changed to pure nickel and of larger diameter, with a new reverse design. This will use up a lot of nickel, a metal with which Canada is well endowed, but which is a bit scarce in the United Sattes. Mintage of the cent will total just 1,243,635, the smallest since the opening of the Ottawa Mint. Production quantities of coins will remain low for the next several years and will be non-existent for silver denomination.

1923: The American Numismatic Association holds its annual convention in Montreal, the second (and final) time a Canadian venue is selected. Years later the ANA Board of Governors will strongly reconsider the idea at the behest of John Jay Pittman, but border-crossing rules will make it virtually impossible for collectors and dealers to take coins back and forth easily. However, in 1962 a joint convention of the ANA and the Canadian Numismatic Association will be held in Detroit.

1924: No silver coinage is produced this year, nor has there been any since 1921, nor will there be any more until 1928. There is not a great deal of demand in the eastern provinces for silver, and British Columbia, where such pieces are widely used, apparently has enough.

1925: It is a good *numismatic* year for cents and nickels, what with their low mintages. Still no new silver coins. In November in

New York City at the Anderson Galleries, Wayte Raymond conducts a three-day sale of the W.W.C. Wilson Collection, strong in Canadian Proofs and patterns (but with few circulation strikes and hardly complete by date) and many other important pieces. The catalogue notes: "No such assemblage of numismatic material pertaining to [Canada] has ever before been offered for sale. He bought many collections belonging to Canadian amateurs of his time, perhaps the most important being that of the late Thomas Wilson. . . . Canadian collectors will no doubt be appreciative of the opportunity to acquire rarities seldom offered."

1926: Some nickel five-cent pieces are struck with "Far 6," a minor date position variation. In later years some numismatists will consider it to be highly important, others will dismiss it as trivial.

1927: Supplies of silver coins minted 1921 and earlier are still adequate, and no new issues are produced.

1928: New issues of gold are contemplated. $5 and $10 denominations have not been struck since 1914, and base metal patterns with new designs are made, but no circulating coinage materializes. Silver coinage is resumed as more pieces are needed, especially by the central provinces.

1929: A new commercial demand arises for 50-cent pieces, which have not been minted since 1921. Many undistributed earlier coins are melted and recoined into currently dates pieces, creating a supply of this denomination that will suffice until 1931. Newfoundland silver five-cent and 10-cent pieces are coined for the first time since 1919, but will not be made again until 1938.

1930: Welcome to the first full year of the Depression. Although 50-cent pieces had been needed in 1929, enough were made then to fill all demand, and none are made in 1930.

1931: The Ottawa Mint changes its name to Royal Canadian Mint on December 1 and is put under the management of the Department of Finance of the Canadian government. It now operates independently, rather than as a small branch of the Royal Mint, London.

1932: The record high mintage of one-cent pieces, 21,316,190, will not be exceeded until 1939.

1933: Economic times continue to be difficult, and interest in Canadian numismatics is sluggish.

1934: In October, Prime Minister R.B. Bennett proposes issuing a silver dollar, and plans are made for implementation in the following year. Interest in coin collecting increases somewhat, perhaps reflective of the growing interest in hobbies to occupy one's spare time when jobs were scarce, and also in view of renewed strength in the United States coin market.

1935: Silver dollars are struck for the first time as circulating coinage, the purpose being to observe the 25th year on the throne of King George V. This becomes Canada's first commemorative coin. Like other commemoratives of the next several decades will be, it is made for circulating purposes and not sold at a premium.

The new dollar is widely admired and attracts many to Canadian numismatics.

1936: King George V dies, and Edward VIII is expected to assume the throne and does on December 11. However, his complex personal life and intended marriage to an American divorcée precludes his remaining there, and he abdicates. George VI becomes king and in the next year is crowned. Meanwhile, early in 1937 it will be desired to make new Canadian coins featuring George VI, but dies will not be ready. Old dies of George V dated 1936 will be pressed (literally) into service, and to signify that the 1936-dated coins were actually made in calendar year 1937, a tiny dot will be placed on the bottom of the reverse of the cent, 10 cents, and 25 cents. In time these will become known as the "1936 Dot" issues, although no notice or account will be published of them at the time. The Toronto Coin Club is formed. This is the last year of the large-size bronze cent for Newfoundland, to be replaced in 1938 (there being no 1937 coinage for this island) by a small-diameter version.

1937: The year's coinage is the first to depict King George VI. Specimen sets are issued for sale to the public, drawing from an inventory of 1,295 struck. Designs of Canadian coins become distinctive and feature new reverses for the cent (maple leaf), five cents (beaver), 10 cents (fishing schooner), 25 cents (caribou), and 50 cents (arms of Canada). However, the Royal Mint in London is too busy to make the masters, and the work is farmed out to the Paris Mint. The dollar reverse continues the voyageur motif first used in 1935. In early 1937, "1936 Dot" coins (see preceding year) are minted and quietly released by the hundreds of thousands into circulation. For some unexplained reason, "Dot" cents and 10-cent pieces prove to be numismatic rarities, perhaps because the holes drilled into the dies to create the dot filled with debris, rendering the dot invisible. In New York City, Wayte Raymond, who deals in numismatic items and sells popular "National" brand albums, who recently distributed Oregon Trail commemorative half dollars, and who published the *Standard Catalogue of United States Coins*, issues *The Coins and Tokens of Canada*. This little guide will come out in later editions in 1947 and 1952 (and in the 1952 edition the rarity of the 1921 50-cents will be recognized for the first time). Before this time collectors have had no guide as to which decimal coins had been minted and which had not, which were rarities and which were common, and how many were minted. This paves the way for collecting decimal coins on a widespread basis. Raymond's "National" brand coin albums could be adapted for Canadian coins, thus making them easy to collect, and quite a few are sold for this purpose. In coming years it will be discovered that many "common" decimal coins are, in face, great rarities if in Uncirculated preservation. However, right now no one has a clue that the 1921 five-cent and 1921 50-cent pieces are rarities, for their high mintage figures suggest otherwise. Further on the 1937 coinage of Canada, this is from the *Royal Canadian Mint*

Report: "From a numismatic point of view, 1937 will long be remembered for the first important change since Confederation in the general type of Canadian subsidiary coins which now, in addition to the new series of reverse designs . . . have on the obverse the uncrowned Royal effigy, hitherto reserved for the coins of Great Britain, instead of the crowned effigy of former reigns. When in 1935 consideration was being given to the design of the first silver dollar, the legend on the obverse of which included a reference to the 25th anniversary of the accession of His late Majesty King George V, an informal suggestion that the Royal effigy on the new coin should be uncrowned was not favorably received, but I may now be permitted to say that the portrait of His former Majesty, King Edward VIII, approved for the new series of Canadian coins, but never actually used, was uncrowned. The uncrowned portrait now appears on the coinage of Great Britain, Canada, Australia, New Zealand, and South Africa, the crowned effigy [of George VI] being retained for the coinage of British India and of the British colonies and possessions."

1938: The mintage of only 90,304 silver dollars this year is a tiny fraction of the previous two years' quantity. The voyageur reverse is used this year, but will not be seen again until 1945.

1939: The "Royal Visit" by English monarchy in late spring furnishes the occasion to create a new reverse for the silver dollar, representing a view of the main section of the Canadian Parliament. This becomes Canada's second commemorative coin. On September 1 the Nazis invade Poland, and soon thereafter England and other countries including Canada (on September 10) declare war on Germany. The Canadian economy goes into overdrive and with it there is a tremendous additional demand for coins.

1940: Ottawa numismatist James Hector notices that some 1936 25-cent pieces have a strange little "dot" on the reverse. An inquiry is set into motion that eventually leads to the story of the "1936 Dot" coinage. G.R.L. Potter, prominent numismatist, eventually will publish the facts after consulting with Maurice Lafortune, an employee at the Mint when the "Dot" coinage was made. The Royal Mint, London, can no longer handle contract coinage for Newfoundland, and punches and masters for the island's denominations are shipped to the Royal Canadian Mint in Ottawa.

1941: Mintage of the 1941-C Newfoundland 10-cents is 483,630, far and away the highest production figure before or after for this island and denomination. A record is also set for the 1941-C silver five-cent piece with 612,641 made.

1942: Five-cent pieces are struck in tombac alloy, a kind of brass, to conserve nickel needed for war efforts; this alloy will also be used in 1944. To prolong die life the Mint chrome-plates one- and five-cent dies, thus giving the finished coins a mirrorlike appearance in many instances. Some die pairs of this and other years through 1944 are transitional, with one die being chrome-plated and the other not, thus resulting in one side of the coins being frosty and the other mirrorlike. Canadian Bankers Association proposes that a three-cent piece be coined, but the idea does not go beyond the idea stage.

1943: The "Victory" design adopted for the reverse of the five-cent piece bears a Morse Code inscription around the border. WE WIN WHEN WE WORK WILLINGLY. The World War II effort is in full swing. The Victory motif will be used through the last year of the war, 1945.

1944: Five-cent pieces are struck in steel for the first time and will continue in this metal through 1945, after which nickel will be re-instituted.

1945: Silver dollars are coined for the first time since 1939. The voyageur reverse, first used in 1935, is employed, as it will be on most other dollars for the next two decades. *Royal Canadian Mint Report:* "Every effort has been made during the last few years to increase the number of coins struck by each die or pair of dies. After much study and research more satisfactory results in lengthened die life are at last being achieved. Careful selection of the most suitable die steel for Mint work; efficient heat-treatment of the steel die in progress and proper hardening and tempering of the finished die; chromium plating the design of all dies; correct annealing of the silver and copper blanks for coinage; and constant training of the press operators, appears responsible for the increase of over 150% in the number of pieces struck per pair of dies. One pair of one-cent dies struck over 5,000,000 coins before being discarded through the wearing away of the design."

1946: Only 2,041 (estimated, per account of Mint official) 1946-C silver five-cent are pieces struck for Newfoundland, crating a modern day rarity. Actually, these will not be made until January 1947, but from 1946-C dies.

1947: It is déjà vu, and the "1936 Dot" scenario will be replayed, this time early in 1948 using 1947-dated dies marked with a tiny raised maple leaf for identification. The occasion will be the need for a new obverse die omitting mention of India, which is no longer a part of the British Empire. New dies will not be ready for 1948 coinage, so 1947 dies will be pressed (that pun again) into service in early 1948. An instant collectible will be created, and 1947 Maple Leaf coins from the cent to the dollar will become all the rage among what relatively few Canadian collectors there are at the time. This will set the scene for more numismatic excitement in 1948 (which see). In the date 1947 on certain coins, varieties are created in the shape and size of the downward tail. In this year the last coinage made specifically for Newfoundland leaves the presses at the Royal Canadian Mint. Fred Bowman's article, "The Decimal Coinage of Canada," appears in the March 1947 issue of *The Numismatist* and is the first detailed treatment of the subject ever to be published.

1948: The low mintage for the silver dollar this year creates a flurry of numismatic and investment interest, and buyers scurry to banks to buy all they can find.

1949: Newfoundland joins the Dominion of Canada, and the year's silver dollar, nearly all of which were made with prooflike surfaces, features on the reverse the ship that Henry Cabot used when he "discovered" Newfoundland in the 18th century. Dr. William H. Sheldon's grading system for United States large cents of the 1793–1814 era is published as part of *Early American Cents* (which will be retitled *Penny Whimsy* when an updated version is published in 1958). Years later, Sheldon's numerical system of numbers 1 to 70 will spread to Canada, and soon such designations as MS-60, MS-62, MS-65, etc., will be used, with most thinking that at long last, grading would be precise. Coin clubs are started in Ottawa, Regina, and Vancouver. This is a great era for coin clubs—the ideal forum to while away an evening discussing numismatics, in an era when television was not yet popular and no one had ever heard of personal computers, both of which will in due course absorb a lot of recreational time, to the detriment of sedentary hobbies.

1950: The Canadian Numismatic Association is formed. Numismatist Leslie C. Hill takes a survey in an effort to determine the relative rarity of certain classic Canadian rarities and finds these coins: 1936 Dot cent (located the whereabouts of 2); 1921 five cents (36) 1946-C Newfoundland five-cent piece (26); 1889 10 cents (16); 1936 Dot 10 cents (2); 1921 50 cents (5). While others would come to light later, this listing does serve to illustrate which varieties were on the "most wanted" lists of collectors at the time.

1951: In addition to the regular five-cent piece of the year, a special commemorative is made to observe the 200th anniversary of the isolation of nickel as a metal. Nickel, found in large quantities in Ontario, is a major factor in the Canadian economy. The Windsor Coin Club is formed.

1952: James E. Charlton, quiet-spoken dealer who operates the Canada Coin Exchange, issues his first guide. The *Catalogue of Canadian Coins, Tokens & Fractional Currency*, will become the standard for the hobby and do much to advance it. G.R.L. Potter writes "Variations in Re-Engraved Dates of Canada's Large Cent of 1859," for the Canadian Numismatic Association *Bulletin*. Potter, active in the hobby for many years, is widely viewed as *the* old timer to consult about technical and historical numismatic matters, and he shares some of his views about rarity with New York City dealer John J. Ford, Jr., among others. From the *Royal Canadian Mint Report*, 1952, relative to the coming year's coinage: "Canada has adopted for its coins the same uncrowned or classical effigy as the United Kingdom, Australia, New Zealand, the Union of South Africa, Southern Rhodesia and Ceylon. Canadian coins, however, will continue to use the form of inscription or royal title adopted some years ago. This inscription will read: 'Elizabeth II Dei Gratia Regina.' Her Majesty's profile on the coins is facing towards the right. It is a tradition in coinage practice that the royal effigy of a new sovereign should face in the direction opposite to that used on coins issued in the reign of the preceding sovereign. . . . Seventeen artists sent in models for the design for the uncrowned effigy of the Queen and that of Mrs. Mary Gillick was finally selected. Mrs. Gillick was accorded the privilege of sittings by Her Majesty. For the first time in the history of Canadian coinage, the master dies are being made at the Royal Canadian Mint, Ottawa. The plaster model of the uncrowned royal effigy was sent to Canada from the Royal Mint, London. The inscription was cut in the plaster model surrounding the Effigy and an electrotype made, from which the dies are being reduced to the dimensions of all denominations of Canadian coins."

1953: This is the first year of coinage depicting Queen Elizabeth II. James E. Charlton, who is rapidly becoming recognized as the standard authority on Canadian coin prices, creates the word "prooflike," as the Royal Canadian Mint disavows that it ever made any Proof coins. A coin club is formed in London, Ontario. Many others will be formed in the 1950s and will do much to spur the hobby. On the United States side of the border John Jay Pittman is the most active collector of Canadian coins, having started his cabinet in the 1940s; later he became the first American to be president of the Canadian Numismatic Association. In Cleveland, Ohio, Emery May Holden Norweb, one of the leading collectors of American coins, begins in a serious way her specialty in Canadian coins by the acquisition of the remarkable William B. Tennant Collection through the efforts of John J. Ford, Jr. A Teletype service links Canadian and United States dealers. "Specimen" sets are widely sold to collectors for the first time, but some coins seem to be more mirrorlike than others. James E. Charlton will suggest later that only about 10% of the sets are prooflike enough to be equivalent to United States Proof coins.

1954: The Mint solves some of its quality control problems, and beginning this year all of the sets sold to collectors at a premium are fully prooflike. In Cairo, Egypt, the collections of deposed King Farouk are sold at auctions; the coin holdings include many rarities. Among those attending from the United States are Hon. and Mrs. R. Henry Norweb and John Jay Pittman, who make many purchases including Canadian coins. Other Americans on hand include James P. Randall, Abe Kosoff, Sol Kaplan, Maurice Storck, and Hans M.F. Schulman, the last being on hand to try to collect from the Egyptian military junta some unpaid bills of the exiled king. The Canadian Numismatic Association holds its first convention; this will become an annual event. No Charlton catalogue is issued this year, the only break in the annual series.

1955: A shipment of silver dollars to the Playtex factory in Arnprior, Ontario, is found to contain coins which have the "error" of only two and one-half water lines to the right of the canoe, rather than the requisite four, an anomaly due to die preparation, not to any design change. The search is on for "Arnprior dollars," and, eventually, other earlier dates of silver dollars will be examined closely and found to have a shortage of water lines too, giving rise to the strange name, for example, "1950 Arnprior dollar"; Arnprior, although it remains capitalized, becomes an adjective meaning "two and one-half water lines," although some suggest that three waterlines are okay, and still others yawn at the idea of being concerned at all about the little ripple lines. Interest in die varieties of all kinds increases.

1956: United States Proof sets rise in value to unprecedented heights, to peak in the spring. Meanwhile, Canadian prooflike sets seem ridiculously cheap by comparison, and investors in the United States start buying up some of these Canadian "Proof sets," as most called them. The *Canadian Numismatic Journal* makes its debut as successor to the *Bulletin* published by the Canadian Numismatic Association.

1957: Fred Bowman publishes his study on Canadian pattern coins, superseding R.W. McLachlan's earlier works. Jerome H. Remick is among the relatively few who research and publish about die varieties; his byline will extend over many years.

1958: "Totem Pole dollars" are struck with motifs pertaining to British Columbia. These catch the fancy of United States dealers, and Wilson Pollard (of Indiana) and other professionals buy large quantities of them for sale to collector and investors.

1959: The Canadian market is very active and prooflike sets are in special demand.

1960: The boom in the Canadian coin market starts in earnest.

1961: Through articles in the *Canadian Numismatic Journal* that will continue to be published over a long period of succeeding years, R.C. Willey describes many technical die varieties of Canadian and provincial coinage and explores Canadian numismatic history.

1962: The investment market for Canadian coins is very active, and many United States collectors review mintage figures and coin availability of Canadian issues and conclude there are many good buys to be found. Bags and other quantities of newly minted Canadian coins are hoarded. Mint errors and oddities became popular, and it is found that significant errors are much rarer than in the United States series—remember all of those rejected coins in the 19th-century Royal Mint reports? In Detroit, Michigan, the 71st annual convention of the American Numismatic Association is held in cooperation with the ninth annual Canadian Numismatic Association convention, the first joint show of the two groups.

1963: The Canadian market for investment coins continues to be extremely active. The Canadian Numismatic Research Society is formed. J. Douglas Ferguson (1901-1982), one of the most prominent figures on the collecting scene, begins the transfer of his vast holdings of coins, currency, and tokens to the Bank of Canada, thus making strong the foundation for the National Currency Collection.

1964: New Netherlands Coin Co.'s 58th Sale, September 22-23, includes many Canadian rarities and other issues and attracts a lot of attention. Cataloguer John J. Ford, Jr., is perhaps the most technically knowledgeable United States dealer in the Canadian field, although many others are active. Canadian silver dollar features Charlottetown motif. The coin market reaches its apex—more dealers, more investors, higher prices than ever before. The Canadian Paper Money Society is formed.

1965: The "investor market" for Canadian coins all but disappears, and eventually many old-time numismatists who were sitting on the sidelines, checkbook in pocket, will reappear and became active buyers.

1966: The softening of the market continues as its hoped-for quick revival (and that of the related United States coin market) fail to materialize.

1967: New products at the Mint this year including a $20 gold coin give the market an upbeat pulse, but the stimulus is brief.

1968: The Royal Canadian Mint is extremely busy, and the work of coining some five-cent pieces is farmed out to the Philadelphia Mint. James A. Haxby publishes articles on Canadian decimal coinage and their history. In 1971 Haxby will join with researcher R.C. Willey to publish the first issue of *Coins of Canada*, a guide to information and prices. The Canadian coin market lapses back into relative desuetude, but in the 1970s it will revive with a new group of collectors.

	ABP FINE	AVERAGE FINE
Large Cent, Victoria, Copper, 1858–1901		
☐ 1858	$31.00	$52.00
☐ 1859, Bronze	2.40	4.10
☐ 1859, Brass	650.00	1100.00
☐ 1859, Double Strike 9/8	150.00	250.00
☐ 1859, Double Strike 9/9	24.00	40.00
☐ 1876H	2.40	4.00
☐ 1881H	3.00	5.50
☐ 1882H	2.75	4.50
☐ 1884	2.75	4.50
☐ 1886	4.00	6.50
☐ 1887	4.00	6.00
☐ 1888	2.75	4.50

	ABP FINE	AVERAGE FINE
☐ 1890H	$6.00	$10.00
☐ 1891, Large Date	6.00	10.00
☐ 1891, Small Date, Large Leaves Reverse	45.00	75.00
☐ 1891, Small Date, Small Leaves Reverse	36.00	60.00
☐ 1892	4.00	6.75
☐ 1893	2.50	4.50
☐ 1894	6.50	11.00
☐ 1895	4.50	7.50
☐ 1896	2.50	4.00
☐ 1897	2.50	4.00
☐ 1898H	5.50	9.00
☐ 1899	2.75	4.50
☐ 1900	7.20	12.00
☐ 1900H	2.75	4.75
☐ 1901	2.00	3.50

Large Cent, Edward VII, Copper, 1902–1910

	ABP FINE	AVERAGE FINE
☐ 1902	1.80	3.00
☐ 1903	1.80	3.00
☐ 1904	1.95	3.25
☐ 1905	4.80	8.00
☐ 1906	1.50	2.60
☐ 1907	2.70	4.50
☐ 1907H	10.00	16.00
☐ 1908	3.20	5.50
☐ 1909	1.80	3.00
☐ 1910	1.80	3.00

Large Cent, George V, Copper, 1911–1920

	ABP FINE	AVERAGE FINE
☐ 1911	$1.05	$1.75
☐ 1912	1.05	1.75
☐ 1913	1.05	1.75
☐ 1914	2.10	3.50
☐ 1915	1.20	2.00
☐ 1916	.60	1.00
☐ 1917	.60	1.00
☐ 1918	.60	1.00
☐ 1919	.60	1.00
☐ 1920	.60	1.00

Small Cent, George V, Copper, 1920–1936

	ABP FINE	AVERAGE FINE
☐ 1920	.90	1.50
☐ 1921	1.25	2.10
☐ 1922	9.20	15.50
☐ 1923	15.00	25.00
☐ 1924	6.00	10.00
☐ 1925	14.50	24.00
☐ 1926	3.00	5.10
☐ 1927	1.60	2,75
☐ 1928	.65	1.30
☐ 1929	.65	1.30
☐ 1930	1.80	3.00
☐ 1931	1.20	2.10
☐ 1932	.40	.75
☐ 1933	.40	.75
☐ 1934	.75	1.25
☐ 1935	.75	1.25
☐ 1936	.75	1.25

	ABP FINE	AVERAGE FINE
Small Cent, George VI, Copper, 1937–1952		
☐ 1937	$ .60	$1.00
☐ 1938	.45	.75
☐ 1939	.45	.75
☐ 1940	.30	.50
☐ 1941	.30	.50
☐ 1942	.30	.50
☐ 1943	.30	.50
☐ 1944	.45	.75
☐ 1945	.30	.50
☐ 1946	.30	.50
☐ 1947	.30	.50
☐ 1947, Reverse Change	.30	.50
☐ 1948	.42	.70
☐ 1949	.15	.25
☐ 1950	.15	.25
☐ 1951	.15	.25
☐ 1952	.15	.25

Small Cent, Elizabeth II, Copper, 1953 to Date		
☐ 1953	1.50	2.50
☐ 1953, No Shoulder Mark Obverse	.30	.50
☐ 1954	.36	.60
☐ 1954, No Shoulder Mark Obverse	(Proof Only)	
☐ 1955	.18	.30
☐ 1955, No Shoulder Mark Obverse	100.00	175.00
☐ 1956	.18	.30

	ABP FINE	AVERAGE FINE
☐ 1957	$ .18	$ .30
☐ 1958	.18	.30
☐ 1959	.18	.30
☐ 1960	.18	.30
☐ 1961	.18	.30
☐ 1962	.18	.30
☐ 1963	.18	.30
☐ 1964	.18	.30
☐ 1965, Small Dots, Pointed 5 Reverse	.60	1.00
☐ 1965, Small Dots, Flat 5 Reverse	.18	.30
☐ 1965, Large Dots, Flat 5 Reverse	.18	.30
☐ 1965, Large Dots, Pointed 5 Reverse	6.00	10.00
☐ 1966–1969	—	.10
☐ 1970–1979	—	.10
☐ 1980 to Date	—	.05

Five Cents, Victoria, Silver, 1858–1901

	ABP FINE	AVERAGE FINE
☐ 1858, Small Date	—	40.00
☐ 1858, Large Date/Small Date	—	375.00
☐ 1870	—	35.00
☐ 1871	—	35.00
☐ 1872H	—	26.00
☐ 1874, Small Date	—	58.00
☐ 1874, Large Date	—	35.00
☐ 1875H, Small Date	—	300.00
☐ 1875H, Large Date	—	375.00
☐ 1880H	—	16.00
☐ 1881H	—	20.00
☐ 1882H	—	20.00
☐ 1883H	—	45.00
☐ 1884	—	310.00
☐ 1885, Small 5	—	26.00
☐ 1885, Large 5	—	50.00
☐ 1886, Small 5	—	25.00
☐ 1886, Large 5	—	20.00
☐ 1887	—	50.00
☐ 1888	—	16.00
☐ 1889	—	75.00

	ABP FINE	AVERAGE FINE
☐ 1890H	—	$20.00
☐ 1891	—	11.50
☐ 1892	—	20.00
☐ 1893	—	14.00
☐ 1894	—	50.00
☐ 1896	—	16.00
☐ 1897	—	16.00
☐ 1898	—	35.00
☐ 1899	—	10.00
☐ 1900, Large Date, Round 0 Reverse	—	10.00
☐ 1900, Small Date, Condensed 0 Reverse	—	75.00
☐ 1901	—	12.00

Five Cents, Edward VII, Silver, 1902–1910

	ABP FINE	AVERAGE FINE
☐ 1902	—	5.50
☐ 1902H, Small Mint Mark	—	35.00
☐ 1902H, Large Mint Mark	—	6.50
☐ 1903	—	20.00
☐ 1903H	—	9.50
☐ 1904	—	9.00
☐ 1905	—	9.00
☐ 1906	—	6.00
☐ 1907	—	6.00
☐ 1908	—	20.00
☐ 1909	—	10.00
☐ 1910	—	5.00

Five Cents, George V, Silver, 1911–1921

	ABP FINE	AVERAGE FINE
☐ 1911	—	$6.50
☐ 1912	—	4.50
☐ 1913	—	4.50
☐ 1914	—	5.00
☐ 1915	—	25.00
☐ 1916	—	9.00
☐ 1917	—	3.50
☐ 1918	—	3.50
☐ 1919	—	3.50
☐ 1920	—	3.50
☐ 1921	—	2500.00

Five Cents, George V, Nickel, 1922–1936

	ABP FINE	AVERAGE FINE
☐ 1922	$1.50	2.75
☐ 1923	2.60	4.50
☐ 1924	2.00	3.50
☐ 1925	55.00	90.00
☐ 1926, 6 Close To Leaf Reverse	9.50	16.00
☐ 1926, 6 Far From Leaf Reverse	110.00	170.00
☐ 1927	1.50	2.75
☐ 1928	1.50	2.75
☐ 1929	1.50	2.75
☐ 1930	1.50	2.75
☐ 1931	1.50	2.75
☐ 1932	1.50	2.75
☐ 1933	2.60	4.50
☐ 1934	2.00	3.50
☐ 1935	2.00	3.50
☐ 1936	2.00	3.50

	ABP FINE	AVERAGE FINE
Five Cents, George VI, Nickel, 1937–1942		
☐ 1937	$1.20	$2.25
☐ 1938	1.80	3.00
☐ 1939	1.20	2.25
☐ 1940	.80	1.50
☐ 1941	.80	1.50
☐ 1942	.80	1.50
☐ 1942, Beaver Reverse, Brass, 12 Sided	1.20	2.00
☐ 1943, Brass, 12 Sided	.60	1.00
☐ 1944, Steel, 12 Sided	.60	1.00
☐ 1945, Steel, 12 Sided	.60	1.00
☐ 1946, Resume Nickel, 12 Sided	.48	.80
☐ 1947	.48	.80
☐ 1948	1.00	1.75
☐ 1949	.48	.80
☐ 1950	.48	.80
☐ 1951	.48	.80
☐ 1951, Commemorative Reverse	.60	1.00
☐ 1952	.48	.80

	ABP FINE	AVERAGE FINE
Five Cents, Elizabeth II, Nickel Clad Steel, 1953 to Date		
☐ 1953	.30	.50
☐ 1954	.30	.50
☐ 1955, Nickel	.60	1.00
☐ 1956	.30	.50
☐ 1957	.30	.50
☐ 1958	.30	.50
☐ 1959	.30	.50

	ABP FINE	AVERAGE FINE
☐ 1960	$ .30	$ .50
☐ 1961–1969	.30	.50
☐ 1970–1979	.20	.40
☐ 1980 to Date	—	.20

Ten Cents, Victoria, Silver, 1870–1901

	ABP FINE	AVERAGE FINE
☐ 1858	—	85.00
☐ 1870, Condensed 0 Release	—	50.00
☐ 1870, Round 0 Reverse	—	82.00
☐ 1871	—	100.00
☐ 1871H	—	100.00
☐ 1872H	—	240.00
☐ 1874H	—	45.00
☐ 1875H	—	825.00
☐ 1880H	—	45.00
☐ 1881H	—	52.00
☐ 1882H	—	45.00
☐ 1883H	—	200.00
☐ 1884	—	820.00
☐ 1885	—	140.00
☐ 1886, Small Date 6	—	72.00
☐ 1886, Large Date 6	—	80.00
☐ 1887	—	210.00
☐ 1888	—	38.00
☐ 1889	—	1800.00
☐ 1890H	—	70.00
☐ 1891	—	74.00
☐ 1892	—	45.00
☐ 1893	—	110.00
☐ 1894	—	85.00
☐ 1896	—	42.00
☐ 1898	—	42.00
☐ 1899, Small Date 9	—	40.00
☐ 1899, Large Date 9	—	50.00
☐ 1900	—	34.00
☐ 1901	—	40.00

	ABP FINE	AVERAGE FINE
Ten Cents, Edward VII, Silver, 1902–1910		
☐ 1902	—	$ 20.00
☐ 1902H	—	16.00
☐ 1903	—	55.00
☐ 1903H	—	23.00
☐ 1904	—	34.00
☐ 1905	—	40.00
☐ 1906	—	19.00
☐ 1907	—	16.00
☐ 1908	—	42.00
☐ 1909, Victorian Leaf Reverse	—	22.00
☐ 1909, Wide Leaf Reverse	—	40.00
☐ 1910	—	20.00

	ABP FINE	AVERAGE FINE
Ten Cents, George V, Silver, 1911–1936		
☐ 1911	—	20.00
☐ 1912	—	9.00
☐ 1913, Small Leaf Reverse	—	9.00
☐ 1913, Large Leaf Reverse	—	375.00
☐ 1914	—	7.75
☐ 1915	—	28.00
☐ 1916	—	5.50
☐ 1917	—	4.50
☐ 1918	—	4.50
☐ 1919	—	4.50
☐ 1920	—	4.50
☐ 1921	—	5.50
☐ 1928	—	4.50

	ABP FINE	AVERAGE FINE
☐ 1929	—	$4.50
☐ 1930	—	5.50
☐ 1931	—	5.50
☐ 1932	—	8.00
☐ 1933	—	11.50
☐ 1934	—	25.00
☐ 1935	—	24.00
☐ 1936	—	4.50

Ten Cents, George VI, Silver, 1937–1952

☐ 1937	—	4.50
☐ 1938	—	4.50
☐ 1939	—	3.50
☐ 1940	—	2.25
☐ 1941	—	4.50
☐ 1942	—	2.25
☐ 1943	—	2.25
☐ 1944	—	2.25
☐ 1945	—	2.25
☐ 1946	—	3.50
☐ 1947	—	4.50
☐ 1947, Date Leaf Reverse	—	2.50
☐ 1948	—	10.00
☐ 1949	—	1.00
☐ 1950	—	1.00
☐ 1951	—	1.00
☐ 1952	—	1.00

	ABP FINE	AVERAGE FINE
Ten Cents, Elizabeth II, Silver, 1953–1968		
☐ 1953	—	$2.00
☐ 1954	—	3.10
☐ 1955	—	1.20
☐ 1956	—	1.20
☐ 1957	—	1.20
☐ 1958	—	1.20
☐ 1959	—	1.20
☐ 1960	—	1.00
☐ 1961	—	1.00
☐ 1962	—	1.00
☐ 1963	—	1.00
☐ 1964	—	1.00
☐ 1965	—	1.00
☐ 1966	—	1.00
☐ 1967, 50% Silver	—	.80
☐ 1968, 50% Silver	—	.80

	ABP FINE	AVERAGE FINE
Ten Cents, Elizabeth, Nickel, 1969 to Date		
☐ 1969	—	.30
☐ 1970–1979	—	.20
☐ 1980–1989	—	.20
☐ 1990 to Date	—	.15

	ABP FINE	AVERAGE FINE
Twenty Cents, Victoria, Silver, 1858		
☐ 1858	—	140.00

	ABP FINE	AVERAGE FINE
Twenty-five Cents, Victoria, Silver, 1870–1901		
☐ 1870	—	$75.00
☐ 1871	—	100.00
☐ 1871H	—	125.00
☐ 1872H	—	38.00
☐ 1874H	—	40.00
☐ 1875H	—	1600.00
☐ 1880H, Condensed 0 Reverse	—	450.00
☐ 1880H, Wide 0 Reverse	—	500.00
☐ 1881H	—	80.00
☐ 1882H	—	100.00
☐ 1883H	—	75.00
☐ 1885	—	460.00
☐ 1886	—	90.00
☐ 1887	—	410.00
☐ 1888	—	72.00
☐ 1889	—	460.00
☐ 1890H	—	110.00
☐ 1891	—	275.00
☐ 1892	—	70.00
☐ 1893	—	400.00
☐ 1894	—	100.00
☐ 1899	—	40.00
☐ 1900	—	40.00
☐ 1901	—	40.00

Twenty-five Cents, Edward VII, Silver, 1902–1910

	ABP FINE	AVERAGE FINE
☐ 1902	—	$44.00
☐ 1902H	—	28.00
☐ 1903	—	40.00
☐ 1904	—	100.00
☐ 1905	—	45.00
☐ 1906	—	40.00
☐ 1907	—	40.00
☐ 1908	—	58.00
☐ 1909	—	48.00
☐ 1910	—	34.00

Twenty-five Cents, George V, Silver, 1911–1936

	ABP FINE	AVERAGE FINE
☐ 1911	—	38.00
☐ 1912	—	16.00
☐ 1913	—	16.00
☐ 1914	—	18.00
☐ 1915	—	140.00
☐ 1916	—	15.00
☐ 1917	—	12.00
☐ 1918	—	12.00
☐ 1919	—	12.00
☐ 1920	—	14.00
☐ 1921	—	75.00
☐ 1927	—	100.00
☐ 1928	—	15.00
☐ 1929	—	15.00
☐ 1930	—	15.00
☐ 1931	—	17.50
☐ 1932	—	18.50
☐ 1933	—	20.00
☐ 1934	—	22.50
☐ 1935	—	24.00
☐ 1936	—	9.00

	ABP FINE	AVERAGE FINE
Twenty-five Cents, George VI, Silver, 1937–1952		
☐ 1937	—	$5.10
☐ 1938	—	7.75
☐ 1939	—	7.20
☐ 1940	—	5.10
☐ 1941	—	5.10
☐ 1942	—	5.10
☐ 1943	—	5.10
☐ 1944	—	6.10
☐ 1945	—	5.10
☐ 1946	—	6.75
☐ 1947	—	8.50
☐ 1947, Date Leaf Reverse	—	140.00
☐ 1948	—	6.50
☐ 1949	—	3.50
☐ 1950	—	3.50
☐ 1951	—	3.50
☐ 1952	—	3.50

	ABP FINE	AVERAGE FINE
Twenty-five Cents, Elizabeth II, Silver, 1953–1968		
☐ 1953	—	3.10
☐ 1954	—	4.20
☐ 1955	—	8.50
☐ 1956	—	3.25
☐ 1957	—	3.25
☐ 1958	—	2.20

	ABP FINE	AVERAGE FINE
☐ 1959	—	$2.20
☐ 1960	—	1.50
☐ 1961	—	1.50
☐ 1962	—	1.50
☐ 1963	—	1.50
☐ 1964	—	1.50
☐ 1965	—	1.50
☐ 1966	—	1.50
☐ 1967	—	1.50
☐ 1968, 50% Silver	—	1.50

Twenty-five Cents, Elizabeth II, Nickel, 1969 to Date

☐ 1969	—	1.50
☐ 1970–1980	—	.50
☐ 1980 to Date	—	.35

Fifty Cents, Victoria, Silver, 1870–1901

☐ 1870	—	2800.00
☐ 1870, Initial LCW Obverse	—	300.00
☐ 1871	—	400.00
☐ 1871H	—	600.00
☐ 1872H	—	300.00
☐ 1872H, A/V Obverse	—	650.00
☐ 1881H	—	275.00
☐ 1888	—	620.00
☐ 1890	—	3000.00
☐ 1892	—	400.00
☐ 1894	—	1500.00

	ABP FINE	AVERAGE FINE
□ 1898	—	$450.00
□ 1899	—	600.00
□ 1900	—	300.00
□ 1901	—	300.00

Fifty Cents, Edward VII, Silver, 1902–1910

	ABP FINE	AVERAGE FINE
□ 1902	—	120.00
□ 1903	—	150.00
□ 1904	—	400.00
□ 1905	—	600.00
□ 1906	—	100.00
□ 1907	—	100.00
□ 1908	—	180.00
□ 1909	—	180.00
□ 1910	—	90.00

Fifty Cents, George V, Silver, 1911–1936

	ABP FINE	AVERAGE FINE
□ 1911	—	290.00
□ 1912	—	100.00
□ 1913	—	125.00
□ 1914	—	205.00
□ 1916	—	72.00
□ 1917	—	50.00
□ 1918	—	30.00
□ 1919	—	34.00
□ 1920	—	40.00
□ 1921	—	20,000.00

	ABP FINE	AVERAGE FINE
☐ 1929	—	$34.00
☐ 1931	—	100.00
☐ 1932	—	280.00
☐ 1934	—	100.00
☐ 1936	—	80.00

Fifty Cents, George VI, Silver, 1937–1952

	ABP FINE	AVERAGE FINE
☐ 1937	—	11.00
☐ 1938	—	30.00
☐ 1939	—	20.00
☐ 1940	—	6.00
☐ 1941	—	7.50
☐ 1942	—	7.50
☐ 1943	—	6.50
☐ 1944	—	6.50
☐ 1945	—	6.50
☐ 1946	—	10.00
☐ 1947, Straight 7 Reverse	—	14.00
☐ 1947, Curved 7 Reverse	—	14.00
☐ 1947, Straight 7 With Leaf Reverse	—	50.00
☐ 1947, Curved 7 With Leaf Reverse	—	1800.00
☐ 1948	—	90.00
☐ 1949	—	10.00
☐ 1950	—	4.50
☐ 1951	—	4.50
☐ 1952	—	4.50

	ABP FINE	AVERAGE FINE
Fifty Cents, Elizabeth, Silver, 1953–1967		
☐ 1953, Small Date	—	$2.50
☐ 1953, Large Date	—	8.50
☐ 1953, Large Date with Shoulder Line Reverse	—	6.00
☐ 1954	—	5.50
☐ 1955	—	5.00
☐ 1956	—	3.50
☐ 1957	—	3.00
☐ 1958	—	3.00
☐ 1959	—	3.00
☐ 1960	—	2.00
☐ 1961	—	2.00
☐ 1962	—	2.00
☐ 1963	—	2.00
☐ 1964	—	2.00
☐ 1965	—	2.00
☐ 1966	—	2.00
☐ 1967	—	2.00

	ABP FINE	AVERAGE FINE
Fifty Cents, Elizabeth II, Nickel, 1968 to Date		
☐ 1968	$1.20	2.00
☐ 1969	1.20	2.00
☐ 1970–1979	.80	1.50
☐ 1980–1989	.60	1.00
☐ 1990 to Date	—	.75

	ABP FINE	AVERAGE FINE
Dollars, George V, Silver, 1935–1936		
☐ 1935	—	$24.00
☐ 1936	—	20.00

	ABP FINE	AVERAGE FINE
Dollars, George VI, Silver, 1937–1952		
☐ 1937	—	14.00
☐ 1938	—	42.00
☐ 1939	—	10.00
☐ 1945	—	140.00
☐ 1946	—	28.00
☐ 1947, 7 Without Tail Reverse	—	110.00
☐ 1947, 7 With Tail Reverse	—	65.00
☐ 1948	—	710.00
☐ 1949, Ship Reverse	—	14.00
☐ 1950	—	9.00
☐ 1950, Water Line Reverse	—	18.00
☐ 1951	—	6.50
☐ 1951, Water Line Reverse	—	40.00
☐ 1952	—	6.00
☐ 1952, Water Line Reverse	—	10.00

	ABP FINE	AVERAGE FINE
Dollars, Elizabeth II, Silver, 1953–1967		
☐ 1953	—	7.50
☐ 1953, Line On Shoulder Obverse	—	7.50
☐ 1954	—	8.50
☐ 1955	—	10.00
☐ 1955, No Water Lines Reverse	—	100.00

	ABP FINE	AVERAGE FINE
□ 1956	—	$11.50
□ 1957	—	7.00
□ 1957, No Water Lines Reverse	—	10.50
□ 1958, Commemorative Reverse	—	8.50
□ 1959	—	5.50
□ 1960	—	3.50
□ 1961	—	3.50
□ 1962	—	3.50
□ 1963	—	3.50
□ 1964, Commemorative Reverse	—	4.00
□ 1965, Small Dot Obverse, 5 With Tail Reverse	—	3.50
□ 1965, Small Dot Obverse, 5 Without Tail Reverse	—	3.50
□ 1965, Large Dot Obverse, 5 With Tail Reverse	—	4.50
□ 1965, Large Dot Obverse, 5 Without Tail Reverse	—	4.50
□ 1966, Small Dot Obverse	—	1000.00
□ 1966, Large Dot Obverse	—	5.00
□ 1967, Commemorative Reverse	—	6.50

Dollars, Elizabeth II, Nickel, 1968–1987

	ABP FINE	AVERAGE FINE
□ 1968	$1.10	1.75
□ 1969	1.10	1.75
□ 1970, Commemorative Manitoba Reverse	1.85	3.00
□ 1971, Commemorative British Columbia Reverse	1.85	3.00
□ 1972	1.10	1.75
□ 1973, Commemorative Prince Edward Reverse	1.85	3.00
□ 1974, Commemorative Winnipeg Reverse	2.25	4.00
□ 1975	1.10	1.75
□ 1976	1.10	1.75
□ 1977, Short Line Reverse	1.25	1.75
□ 1977, Long Line Reverse	1.25	1.75
□ 1978	1.10	1.75
□ 1979	1.10	1.75
□ 1980	1.10	1.75

	ABP FINE	AVERAGE FINE
☐ 1981	$1.10	$1.75
☐ 1982	1.10	1.75
☐ 1983, Commemorative Constitution Reverse	1.85	3.00
☐ 1984	1.10	1.75
☐ 1984, Commemorative Jaques Carter Reverse	1.85	3.00
☐ 1985	1.10	1.75
☐ 1986	1.50	2.50
☐ 1987, Commemorative Voyager Reverse—Sets Only	—	1.75

Dollars, Elizabeth II, Nickel-Bronze, 1987 to Date

	ABP FINE	AVERAGE FINE
☐ 1987, Loon Reverse	1.20	2.00
☐ 1988, Loon Reverse	—	1.75
☐ 1989, Loon Reverse	—	1.75
☐ 1990, Loon Reverse	—	1.75
☐ 1991, Loon Reverse	—	1.75
☐ 1992, Loon Reverse	1.50	2.75
☐ 1992, Commemorative Canada's 125th Birthday Reverse	1.50	2.75
☐ 1993, Loon Reverse	1.50	2.50
☐ 1994, Loon Reverse	1.50	2.50
☐ 1994, Commemorative War Memorial everse	1.50	2.50
☐ 1995, Commemorative Peace Reverse	1.50	2.50
☐ 1995, Loon Reverse	1.20	2.00
☐ 1996, Loon Reverse	—	2.00
☐ 1997, Loon Reverse	—	2.00

Two Dollar, Elizabeth II, Nickel-Aluminum-Bronze, 1996

	ABP FINE	AVERAGE FINE
☐ 1996	$2.00	$3.75

	ABP FINE	AVERAGE FINE
Five Dollar, George V, Gold, 1912–1914		
☐ 1912	—	175.00
☐ 1913	—	175.00
☐ 1914	—	375.00

Gold Coinage of Canada

Courtesy of Q. David Bowers, Bowers and Merena Galleries, Inc.

Gold sovereigns (equivalent to one pound sterling in British funds) were made at the Ottawa Mint from 1908 to 1916. The designs were the same as sovereigns made elsewhere in the British Empire and were identified as being of Canadian origin only by their C mint mark. The Canadian and other British Empire pieces bore no mark of denominations, and were mainly used as international trade coins. Some numismatists have suggested that these are British, not Canadian, coins but as they were struck at the Ottawa Mint and bear C mint marks, virtually every Canadian specialist we have encountered desires examples as part of an advanced cabinet.

In 1908 gold coins of the United States were readily available at Canadian banks in medium- and large-size cities, as they had been for many years. The $2 gold issues of Newfoundland 1865–1888 had been popular at one time, but were mostly withdrawn beginning about 1894, due to a financial crisis on that island. When plans were laid in 1901 for the Ottawa Mint, gold from the Klondike and British Columbia was plentiful, and a generous annual production of Canadian gold coins was anticipated, perhaps up to two million a year. However, by 1908 when the Ottawa Mint opened, newly refined gold supplies had diminished sharply. Thus, given the American gold coins already in circulation and the smaller incoming quantities of raw metal, the need for domestically minted gold coins lessened.

Fewer than a thousand gold sovereigns were struck in Ottawa in 1908, these all being matte Specimens intended for souvenirs and numismatic purposes, after which production quantities increased, but never even remotely challenged the two-million capacity. These gold sovereigns did not replace the United States issues, but were primarily used in export transactions or acquired by travelers desiring to go to other countries in the British Empire, throughout which sovereigns were ubiquitous. Most Canadian sovereigns of the 1908–1919 years thus found their way to foreign banks. The writer recalls that in the late 1960s and early 1970s cloth bags of unsorted British Empire sovereigns were a popular investment with "hard money" advocates. Most such quantities came from Swiss banks. Among the pieces, which were mostly made in England, would be found a few coins with worldwide mint marks including C for Ottawa. The typical grade of such coins was EF to AU with lustre.

The Coinage Act of 1910 authorized Canadian denominations of $2.50, $5, $10, and $20 in 90% gold and of weights of 64.5, 129, 258, and 516 grains. However, only the $5 and $10 values were ever struck. Under this legislation Canadian $5 gold coins of slightly heavier weight and of different design were made from 1912 through 1914, were denominated as FIVE DOLLARS, and were used within Canada (and also in the export trade). Canadian coins denominated TEN DOLLARS were made from 1912 through 1914 inclusive. The reverse design of the $5 and $10 gold coins, by W. H. J. Blakemore, displays a Canadian coat of arms depicting the four founding provinces (clockwise from upper left): Ontario, Quebec, New Brunswick, and Nova Scotia. Both of these denominations differed from the "generic" gold sovereigns in that the $5 and $10 pieces had inscriptions specifically relating to Canada. An effort was made to call these coins "Georges" and "Double Georges," but the cognomens never took hold.

In 1928 strong consideration was given to the revival of Canadian gold coin production, and patterns were struck in bronze. However, no circulating coinage materialized. After 1933, when the United States discontinued striking gold coins, the thought of Canadian gold issues became even more distant. In 1967 gold commemoratives were issued and sold at a premium, but by this time no world country had a circulating coinage in this metal. Later, additional gold commemoratives were produced. To cater to demand for bullion gold, Canada has issued "Maple Leaf" gold discs from 1979 to the present.

	ABP FINE	AVERAGE FINE
Five Dollar, George V, 1912–1914		
□ 1912	—	$175.00
□ 1913	—	175.00
□ 1914	—	375.00

Ten Dollar, George V, Gold, 1912–1914		
□ 1912	—	400.00
□ 1913	—	425.00
□ 1914	—	475.00

Sovereigns, Edward VII, Gold, 1908–1910		
□ 1908C	—	3500.00
□ 1909C	—	475.00
□ 1910C	—	475.00

Sovereigns, George V, Gold, 1911–1919		
□ 1911C	—	150.00
□ 1913C	—	1450.00
□ 1914C	—	650.00
□ 1916C	—	20,000.00
□ 1917C	—	175.00
□ 1918C	—	175.00
□ 1919C	—	175.00

Canada—Coinage of New Brunswick

Courtesy of Q. David Bowers, Bowers and Merena Galleries, Inc..

As is the case with other districts of British North America, coins in circulation in New Brunswick in the early days were a curious admixture of United States, British, and other foreign issues to which were added examples from a New Brunswick halfpenny and penny coinage of 1843 and 1854 struck for the province by private firms in England (Soho Mint and Heaton Mint respectively).

In 1850 and 1851, discussions were held concerning the adoption of a decimal system, culminating in a meeting of various agents of British North America districts held in Toronto on June 1 of the latter year. At the time the American dollar was in the widest use in local trade, but England preferred that its scheme of pounds, shillings, and pence take precedence. The ideas of residents of New Brunswick were often at odds with those of the English authorities to whom they reported. Moreover, what was happening in distant New Brunswick and the needs of that province seemed to be of minor importance in England.

Among proposals made in the 1850s and 1860s was for a gold coin to be smaller than a British gold sovereign, equal to $2 or 100 pence, and to be called a ducat or royal. Another suggestion was for a North American gold "pound" to contain 92.877 grains of pure gold. By mathematics it was determined that as a British gold sovereign had 113 grains of gold and was worth close to $4.87 in United States funds, this North American pound would be worth $4 U.S., and the half pound would be worth $2. The coinage of a gold dollar was also considered, but confreres believed that the United States had found this denomination too small for convenience, and the thought was dropped. Although New Brunswick never had its own gold coins of any denomination, the Newfoundland $2 issue of 1865 was a direct result of these monetary discussions.

In 1858 the Province of Canada placed an order for decimal-based coins with England, prompting New Brunswick to consider similar action. On April 9, 1860, the lieutenant-governor of New Brunswick approved a request that $10,000 worth of bronze cents, $5,000 in silver 5-cent coins, $15,000 in 10-cent pieces, and $30,000 face value of 20-cent pieces be struck in England. The designs were to be similar to the Canadian issues of 1858, except for the marking NEW BRUNSWICK instead of CANADA.

Across the Atlantic Ocean, the British Colonial Office felt that it would be a mistake for New Brunswick to have 10- and 20-cent coins made, as they had heard via Inspector General A.T. Gault that Canada was experiencing difficulty distributing its similarly denominated issues of 1858. The office suggested that values of 12½ cents and 25 cents be coined instead. No matter, the Executive

Council in New Brunswick wanted the coins it had originally ordered, and reiterated the request. Meanwhile, there was a coin shortage in New Brunswick, and between October 29, 1860, and October 31, 1861, $8,000 face value of Canadian bronze cents—presumably mostly dated 1859—were brought in. Apparently, others were brought in as well, as a number of Canadian numismatic texts place the number of coins at 100,000 (or $10,000 face).

On November 22, 1861, 12 reverse dies for New Brunswick were made at the Royal Mint, London. Two major errors were made in the process. Instead of following the instructions to adapt Province of Canada designs by changing the wording to NEW BRUNSWICK, someone at the Royal Mint decided to use *Nova Scotia* designs instead, the latter province having ordered copper coins at around the same time. The reverse motif of the Nova Scotia pieces, designed by C. Hill and cut by Leonard Charles Wyon, was of Nova Scotia flavor and depicted a wreath of roses and mayflowers well known in that district, but not relative at all to New Brunswick. Apparently, Wyon thought that one British North America province was about the same as another. On a later occasion in 1862, the Province of Canada maple leaf design was arbitrarily assigned to the reverse of the New Brunswick silver 20-cent piece.

In another misjudgment, 12 reverse dies were made at the Royal Mint for a New Brunswick *half cent*, although that province had placed no such order (but Nova Scotia had). Once again, the coinage interests of New Brunswick were of little importance to the British authorities, and certain of the resulting issues differed from what had been requested.

While Canadian cents of 1858 and 1859 had been struck to the ratio of 100 coins per one pound weight avoirdupois, the cents of New Brunswick and Nova Scotia were made at the weight of 80 to the pound, concurrent with the new British halfpenny standard adopted in 1860. The diameter of one inch was the same as the Canadian cent, however.

The first New Brunswick silver coins were received from the Royal Mint on August 18, 1862. Silver issues with a face value of $50,206.65 cost the province $48,165.62, thus the seignorage was negligible, unlike the bronze issues which yielded a large profit.

As it turned out, coinage for New Brunswick was ephemeral and lasted only through 1864. In that year the province joined with Quebec, Ontario, and Nova Scotia to form the Dominion of Canada, thus ending the need for a local coinage. Further historical details are given under the individual descriptions below.

One of the finest books ever to be published on a Canadian specialty, Richard W. Bird's *Coins of New Brunswick*, is recommended for readers interested in the fascinating historical details and other aspects of the coinage. Certain of the coins illustrated are from our past auction sales.

	ABP FINE	AVERAGE FINE
Half Cent, Victoria, Copper, 1861		
☐ 1861	$180.00	$200.00

	ABP FINE	AVERAGE FINE
Large Cents, Victoria, Copper, 1861–1864		
☐ 1861	5.00	8.50
☐ 1864	5.00	8.50

	ABP FINE	AVERAGE FINE
Five Cents, Victoria, Silver, 1862–1864		
☐ 1862	—	200.00
☐ 1864	—	200.00

	ABP FINE	AVERAGE FINE
Ten Cents, Victoria, Silver, 1862–1864		
☐ 1862	—	$175.00
☐ 1862, Double 2 Reverse	—	275.00
☐ 1864	—	175.00

Twenty Cents, Victoria, Gold, 1862–1864		
☐ 1862	—	75.00
☐ 1864	—	85.00

Canada—Newfoundland

Small Cents, Victoria, Copper, 1865–1896		
☐ 1865	$5.00	8.50
☐ 1872H	4.50	7.50
☐ 1873	4.50	7.50
☐ 1876H, 0 In Date	4.50	7.50
☐ 1880, Condensed 0, Reverse	4.50	7.50
☐ 1880, Wide 0 In Date Reverse	170.00	275.00
☐ 1885	36.00	60.00
☐ 1888	27.00	45.00
☐ 1890	5.00	8.50
☐ 1894	5.00	8.50
☐ 1896	3.50	6.00

	ABP FINE	AVERAGE FINE
Small Cents, Edward VII, Copper, 1904–1909		
☐ 1904H	$17.00	$28.00
☐ 1907	4.75	8.00
☐ 1909	4.75	8.00
Small Cents, George V, Copper, 1913–1936		
☐ 1913	2.10	3.50
☐ 1917C	2.10	3.50
☐ 1919C	2.10	3.50
☐ 1920C	3.25	5.50
☐ 1929	2.10	3.50
☐ 1936	1.80	3.00
Small Cents, George VI, Copper, 1938–1947		
☐ 1938	1.50	2.50
☐ 1940	2.75	4.50
☐ 1941C	.90	1.50
☐ 1942	.90	1.50
☐ 1943C	.90	1.50
☐ 1944C	2.25	3.75
☐ 1947C	2.00	3.50

	ABP FINE	AVERAGE FINE
Five Cents, Victoria, Silver, 1865–1896		
☐ 1865	—	$80.00
☐ 1870	—	110.00
☐ 1872H	—	90.00
☐ 1873	—	210.00
☐ 1873H	—	2400.00
☐ 1876H	—	250.00
☐ 1880	—	125.00
☐ 1881	—	75.00
☐ 1882H	—	65.00
☐ 1885	—	325.00
☐ 1888	—	85.00
☐ 1890	—	50.00
☐ 1894	—	45.00
☐ 1896	—	28.00

	ABP FINE	AVERAGE FINE
Five Cents, Edward VII, Silver, 1903–1908		
☐ 1903	—	28.00
☐ 1904H	—	20.00
☐ 1908	—	16.00

	ABP FINE	AVERAGE FINE
Five Cents, George V, Silver, 1912–1929		
□ 1912	—	$6.25
□ 1917C	—	6.25
□ 1919C	—	11.50
□ 1929	—	5.75

	ABP FINE	AVERAGE FINE
Five Cents, George VI, Silver, 1938–1947		
□ 1938	—	2.75
□ 1940C	—	2.75
□ 1941C	—	1.50
□ 1942C	—	1.75
□ 1943C	—	1.75
□ 1944C	—	2.75
□ 1945C	—	1.75
□ 1946C	—	4.25
□ 1947C	—	8.75

	ABP FINE	AVERAGE FINE
Ten Cents, Victoria, Silver, 1865–1896		
☐ 1865	—	$85.00
☐ 1870	—	550.00
☐ 1872H	—	72.00
☐ 1873	—	150.00
☐ 1876H	—	125.00
☐ 1880	—	175.00
☐ 1882H	—	140.00
☐ 1885	—	350.00
☐ 1888	—	120.00
☐ 1890	—	38.00
☐ 1894	—	34.00
☐ 1896	—	35.00

Ten Cents, Edward VII, Silver, 1903–1904

	ABP FINE	AVERAGE FINE
☐ 1903	—	45.00
☐ 1904H	—	30.00

Ten Cents, George V, Silver, 1912–1919

	ABP FINE	AVERAGE FINE
☐ 1912	—	9.00
☐ 1917C	—	8.00
☐ 1919C	—	8.50

	ABP FINE	AVERAGE FINE
Ten Cents, George VI, Silver, 1938–1947		
☐ 1938	—	$4.10
☐ 1940	—	3.20
☐ 1941C	—	3.20
☐ 1942C	—	3.20
☐ 1943C	—	3.20
☐ 1944C	—	4.10
☐ 1945C	—	2.25
☐ 1946C	—	12.00
☐ 1947C	—	5.25

	ABP FINE	AVERAGE FINE
Twenty Cents, Victoria, Silver, 1865–1900		
☐ 1865	—	60.00
☐ 1870	—	100.00
☐ 1872H	—	50.00
☐ 1873	—	100.00
☐ 1876H	—	90.00
☐ 1880	—	100.00
☐ 1881	—	50.00
☐ 1882H	—	38.00
☐ 1885	—	55.00
☐ 1888	—	45.00
☐ 1890	—	38.00
☐ 1894	—	28.00
☐ 1896, Small Date	—	28.00
☐ 1896, Large Date	—	35.00
☐ 1899, Small Date	—	65.00

	ABP FINE	AVERAGE FINE
□ 1899, Large Date	—	$28.00
□ 1900	—	28.00

Twenty Cents, Edward VII, Silver, 1904

□ 1904H	—	75.00

Twenty Cents, George V, Silver, 1912

□ 1912	—	14.00

Twenty-five Cents, George V, Silver, 1917–1919

□ 1917C	—	5.50
□ 1919C	—	6.50

Fifty Cents, Victoria, Silver, 1870–1900

	ABP FINE	AVERAGE FINE
☐ 1870	—	$80.00
☐ 1872H	—	75.00
☐ 1873	—	250.00
☐ 1874	—	175.00
☐ 1876H	—	150.00
☐ 1880	—	160.00
☐ 1881	—	65.00
☐ 1882H	—	75.00
☐ 1885	—	140.00
☐ 1888	—	160.00
☐ 1894	—	75.00
☐ 1896	—	55.00
☐ 1898	—	55.00
☐ 1899, Small Date	—	45.00
☐ 1899, Large Date	—	60.00
☐ 1900	—	45.00

Fifty Cents, Edward VII, Silver, 1904–1909

	ABP FINE	AVERAGE FINE
☐ 1904H	—	24.00
☐ 1907	—	26.00
☐ 1908	—	20.00
☐ 1909	—	20.00

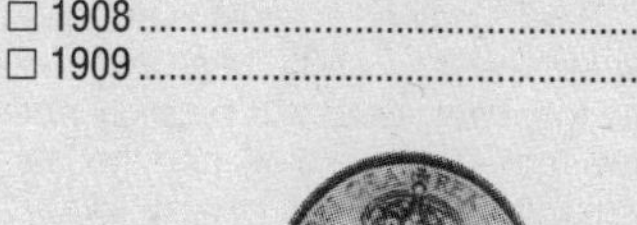

Fifty Cents, George V, Silver, 1911–1919

	ABP FINE	AVERAGE FINE
☐ 1911	—	11.00
☐ 1917C	—	10.00

	ABP FINE	AVERAGE FINE
□ 1918C	—	$10.00
□ 1919C	—	10.00

$2 GOLD COINAGE

Courtesy of Q. David Bowers, Bowers and Merena Galleries, Inc.

The Newfoundland $2 gold coins, minted from 1865 to 1888, stand today as one of the most popular specialties within the Canadian series. The expanse of date and mint mark (just one from the Heaton Mint) varieties exceeds that of the Dominion of Canada $5 and $10 pieces combined. In addition, three different obverse varieties lend interest and collecting possibilities. In some instances the same obverse die was used to strike Newfoundland 10¢ pieces and $2 gold coins, both being of like diameter. The study of die characteristics of a significant number of pieces would help identify specific linkages.

The obverse pictures Queen Victoria and, as noted, is similar to that used on the Newfoundland 10-cent piece. On the reverse these coins were denominated three different ways: TWO HUNDRED CENTS, 2 DOLLARS, and TWO HUNDRED PENCE. These were sometimes called "double dollars."

They served excellent duty not only on the island of Newfoundland, but throughout the eastern section of Canada, where they were readily accepted in commerce. In 1894 the Newfoundland banks "crashed," and the island's monetary system was taken over by outside banks that came in to stabilize the currency. Around this time, the supply of $2 coins virtually disappeared, as they were ideal "hard money" in comparison to paper notes which were widely distrusted. Similarly, large-denomination Newfoundland 25¢ and 50¢ pieces were hoarded.

Today the typically encountered Newfoundland $2 coin is apt to be in EF or AU grade, reflective of their one-time utility. Mint State examples are in all instances rare and for some issues exceedingly rare. A few Specimen strikings are known from polished dies, and the Norweb cabinet is remarkable in its selection of these. Typically, even a single Specimen issue is not found even in an advanced collection.

Two Dollar, Victoria, Gold, 1865–1888

☐ 1865	—	190.00
☐ 1870	—	250.00
☐ 1872	—	300.00
☐ 1880	—	1400.00
☐ 1881	—	175.00
☐ 1882H	—	175.00
☐ 1885	—	175.00
☐ 1888	—	175.00

Canada—Coinage of Nova Scotia

Courtesy of Q. David Bowers, Bowers and Merena Galleries, Inc.

The history of the coinage of Nova Scotia is short, sweet, and interesting.

Nova Scotia adopted a decimal system in 1859 based upon the pound sterling rated at an exact $5. Under this system, British sixpence passed for 12½¢, shillings for 25¢, and florins for 50¢. While plentiful British coins could serve handily for larger denominations, there arose a need for cents and half cents, the latter being needed to make change when sixpence pieces were tendered.

Half cents were struck with the dates 1861 and 1864, the obverse being the die used for regular British farthings (¼ penny) and the reverse showing a wreath enclosing a crown and the date. Cents were similar, were dated 1861, 1862, and 1864, and utilized obverse dies for contemporary British halfpennies. Thus, for the circulating copper coinage of Nova Scotia there is a direct die linkage with British issues.

Nova Scotia could have used British farthings and halfpennies by fiat, but did not, presumably because the inscription on the reverse of the British halfpenny, identifying it as such, might be confused with its Nova Scotia valuation of one cent. As it turned out, the Nova Scotia half cent was not a popular denomination, and commercial circulation was limited. Presumably, they did not fit well into trade outside of Nova Scotia in a milieu in which the popular private issues, Bank of Montreal issues, and the like, passed as cents, and no small half cent coin was needed.

The Nova Scotia coinage is a compact and interesting numismatic series. The half cent has an interesting connection with the 1861 coin of the same denomination made for New Brunswick.

	ABP FINE	AVERAGE FINE
Half Cents, Victoria, Copper, 1861–1864		
□ 1861	$7.25	$12.00
□ 1864	7.25	12.00

	ABP FINE	AVERAGE FINE
Large Cents, Victoria, Copper, 1861–1864		
□ 1861	5.00	8.50
□ 1862	42.50	70.00
□ 1864	5.25	8.75

Canada—Coinage of Prince Edward Island

Courtesy of Q. David Bowers, Bowers and Merena Galleries, Inc.

Through the Act of April 17, 1871, the island adopted a decimal coinage with one dollar composed of 100 cents, although legislation in this regard had been introduced in the House of Assembly as early as February 23, 1860. By that time the island, called Saint John (earlier Ile St. Jean) until 1798, was home to numerous varieties of private tokens (the best known being the SHIPS, COLONIES & COMMERCE issues) and used British, United States, and other coins in commerce, but had no government issues.

On September 13, 1871, the Royal Mint sought bids for two million cents for Prince Edward Island, these to be made to the same standard as British bronze issues. On December 25, 1871, Christmas Day, Ralph Heaton & Sons, Birmingham, was given the nod over the other bidder, James Watt & Co. (with some slight historical connections to the old Boulton & Watt firm), which was asserting itself as an up-and-coming rival, but which would cease coining in the 1890s. No other denominations were ever struck. Dies were cut at the Royal Mint, London, as per usual practice for British colonial coins, and shipped to Heaton.

In due course Heaton struck the coins and arranged with the Union Bank of London to receive the funds for them, with the pieces to be picked up by the Birmingham and Midland Bank and shipped in boxes to the Bank of Prince Edward Island, Charlotte Town, Prince Edward Island. The newly minted pieces were rolled in paper wrappers of 50 coins each and packed in 200 boxes, each with 10,000 cents. On November 25 they left the Heaton Mint, and in December they arrived at their intended destination across the Atlantic.

The quantity of two million was staggering, to say the least, inasmuch as there were only about 75,000 people in the district at the time. This amounted to about 27 coins per person! No wonder that quantities of these pieces remained in the vaults of the Bank of Prince Edward Island, Charlottetown, undistributed for eight years. Following an authorization dated December 11, 1878, the dregs were parceled out at a 10% discount (shades of the Randall Hoard of American large cents!). This offer was eagerly received, and 10,000 were shipped to Halifax, 70,000 were sold to A. J. Tait of Montreal, and 130,000 went to various towns in New Brunswick. By that time the island was a part of the Dominion of Canada, having joined in 1873, although it did not fully adopt the Dominion Uniform Currency Act until eight years later.

In 1894 P. N. Breton commented: "There was a very large issue of this coin, over 2,000,000. It is thus found plentifully in circulation, and will be considered very common for some time to come." Breton was right, and these cents circulated in the eastern part of Canada until well into the present century.

	ABP FINE	AVERAGE FINE
Large Cent, Victoria, Copper, 1871		
□ 1871	4.75	8.00

CHINA

The first coins, cast in molds, were used in 6th century B.C. Imitation coins were made of cast bronze. Hoe-shaped coins were produced in the mid-3rd century B.C. Round coins with holes were made at a few mints. The round coins and the tool coins were issued in different denominations, based on the weight of the metal in each coin. The bronze 5-grain coin was introduced in 118 B.C. and was the standard until the early 7th century A.D. Bronze coins with square holes remained through the 13th century. The silver dirhem was in evidence in the 13th century, followed by the brass coin and the silver dollar in the 18th and 19th centuries. Decimal coins appeared in the 1st century A.D. The currency today is the yuan.

China—People's Republic

DATE	COIN TYPE/VARIETY/METAL	ABP FINE	AVERAGE FINE
□ 1955–1987	1 Fen, People's Republic, Aluminum	—	$ .20

DATE	COIN TYPE/VARIETY/METAL	ABP FINE	AVERAGE FINE
☐ 1955–1990	2 Fen, People's Republic, Aluminum	—	$ .15
☐ 1955–1990	5 Fen, People's Republic, Aluminum	—	.20
☐ 1980 to Date	Jiao, People's Republic, opper-Zinc	$ .20	.40
☐ 1987	Jiao, People's Republic, 6th National Games—Soccer, Brass	.25	.70
☐ 1987	Jiao, People's Republic, 6th National Games—Volleyball, Brass	.25	.70

☐ 1987	Jiao, People's Republic, 6th National Games—Gymnast, Brass	.25	.70
☐ 1980–1986	2 Jiao, People's Republic, Copper-Zinc	.15	.40
☐ 1980–1986	5 Jiao, People's Republic, Copper-Zinc	.15	.40
☐ 1983	5 Jiao, People's Republic, Marco Polo, Silver	—	10.00
☐ 1991	5 Jiao, People's Republic, Brass	.20	.45
☐ 1980	Yuan, People's Republic, 1980 Olympics—Alpine Skiing, Copper	1.75	4.00
☐ 1980	Yuan, People's Republic, 1980 Olympics—Equestrian, Copper	1.75	4.00
☐ 1980	Yuan, People's Republic, 1980 Olympics—Wrestling, Copper	1.75	4.00
☐ 1980	Yuan, People's Republic, 1980 Olympics—Archery, Copper	1.75	4.00
☐ 1980	Yuan, People's Republic, 1980 Olympics—Biathlon, Copper	1.75	4.00
☐ 1980	Yuan, People's Republic, 1980 Olympics—Figure Skating, Copper	1.75	4.00

DATE	COIN TYPE/VARIETY/METAL	ABP FINE	AVERAGE FINE
☐ 1980	Yuan, People's Republic, 1980 Olympics—Soccer, Copper	$1.75	$4.00
☐ 1980	Yuan, People's Republic, 1980 Olympics—Speed Skating, Copper	1.75	4.00
☐ 1980–1986	Yuan, People's Republic, Cupro-Nickel	1.40	3.50
☐ 1982	Yuan, People's Republic, World Cup Soccer, Copper	.50	1.40
☐ 1983	Yuan, People's Republic, Panda, Copper	.50	1.40
☐ 1984	Yuan, People's Republic, Panda, Copper	.50	1.40
☐ 1984	Yuan, People's Republic, 35th Anniversary, Cupro-Nickel	.75	2.50
☐ 1985	Yuan, People's Republic, Tibet 20th Anniversary, Cupro-Nickel	.50	1.50

DATE	COIN TYPE/VARIETY/METAL	ABP FINE	AVERAGE FINE
☐ 1985	Yuan, People's Republic, Sinkiang 30th Anniversary, Cupro-Nickel	.50	1.50
☐ 1986	Yuan, People's Republic, Year of Peace, Cupro-Nickel	.50	1.00
☐ 1987	Yuan, People's Republic, Mongolian 40th Anniversary, Cupro-Nickel	.40	1.70
☐ 1988	Yuan, People's Republic, Ninghsia 30th Anniversary, Cupro-Nickel	.60	1.10
☐ 1988	Yuan, People's Republic, People's Bank 40th Anniversary, Cupro-Nickel	.60	1.10
☐ 1988	Yuan, People's Republic, Kwangsi 30th Anniversary, Cupro-Nickel	.60	1.10
☐ 1989	Yuan, People's Republic, 40th Anniversary, Nickel-clad Steel	.50	2.00
☐ 1990	Yuan, People's Republic, XI Asian Games—Female Archer, Nickel-clad Steel	2.50	5.50
☐ 1990	Yuan, People's Republic, XI Asian Games—Sword Dancer, Nickel-clad Steel	2.50	5.50
☐ 1991	Yuan, People's Republic, 1978 Party Conference, Nickel-plated Steel	2.50	5.50

DATE	COIN TYPE/VARIETY/METAL	ABP FINE	AVERAGE FINE
☐ 1991	Yuan, People's Republic, Women's Soccer Championship—Player, Nickel-plated Steel	$1.40	$3.00
☐ 1991	Yuan, People's Republic, Planting Trees Festival—Seedling, Cupro-Nickel	1.40	3.00
☐ 1991	Yuan, People's Republic, Chinese Communist Party 1st Meeting, Nickel-plated Steel	1.40	3.00
☐ 1991	Yuan, People's Republic, Planting Trees Festival—Globe, Cupro-Nickel	1.40	3.00
☐ 1991	Yuan, People's Republic, Women's Soccer Championship—Goalie, Nickel-plated Steel	1.40	3.00
☐ 1991	Yuan, People's Republic, Planting Trees Festival—Portrait, Cupro-Nickel	1.40	3.00
☐ 1991	Yuan, People's Republic, Party Meeting, Nickel-plated Steel	1.40	3.00
☐ 1983	5 Yuan, People's Republic, Marco Polo, Silver	—	75.00
☐ 1984	5 Yuan, People's Republic, Olympics—High Jumper, Silver	—	50.00
☐ 1984	5 Yuan, People's Republic, Soldier Statues, Silver	—	65.00
☐ 1985	5 Yuan, People's Republic, Founders of Chinese Culture—Lao-Tse, Silver	—	65.00
☐ 1985	5 Yuan, People's Republic, Founders of Chinese Culture—Wu Guang, Silver	—	65.00
☐ 1985	5 Yuan, People's Republic, Founders of Chinese Culture—Qu Yuan, Silver	—	65.00
☐ 1985	5 Yuan, People's Republic, Founders of Chinese Culture—Sun Wu, Silver	—	65.00
☐ 1986	5 Yuan, People's Republic, Chinese Culture—Chemist, Silver	—	45.00
☐ 1986	5 Yuan, People's Republic, Chinese Culture—Mathematician, Silver	—	45.00
☐ 1986	5 Yuan, People's Republic, Soccer—2 Players, Silver	—	45.00
☐ 1986	5 Yuan, People's Republic, Chinese Culture—Historian, Silver	—	65.00
☐ 1986	5 Yuan, People's Republic, Great Wall, Silver	—	20.00
☐ 1986	5 Yuan, People's Republic, Wildlife—Giant Panda, Silver	—	40.00
☐ 1986	5 Yuan, People's Republic, Year of Peace, Silver	—	140.00

DATE	COIN TYPE/VARIETY/METAL	ABP FINE	AVERAGE FINE
□ 1986	5 Yuan, People's Republic, Soccer, Silver	—	$40.00
□ 1986	5 Yuan, People's Republic, Chinese Culture—Paper Making, Silver	—	65.00
□ 1987	5 Yuan, People's Republic, Poet Du Fu, Silver	—	40.00
□ 1987	5 Yuan, People's Republic, Princess Cheng Wen & Song Zuan Gan Bu, Silver	—	40.00
□ 1987	5 Yuan, People's Republic, Poet Li Bal, Silver	—	65.00
□ 1987	5 Yuan, People's Republic, Bridge Builder Li Chun, Silver	—	65.00
□ 1988	5 Yuan, People's Republic, Olympics—Downhill Skier, Silver	—	40.00
□ 1988	5 Yuan, People's Republic, Olympics—Sailboat Racing, Silver	—	40.00
□ 1988	5 Yuan, People's Republic, Poetess Li Qing-zhao, Silver	—	50.00
□ 1988	5 Yuan, People's Republic, Yue Fei—Military Hero, Silver	—	50.00
□ 1988	5 Yuan, People's Republic, Olympics—Woman Hurdler, Silver	—	25.00
□ 1988	5 Yuan, People's Republic, Poet Su Shi, Silver	—	55.00
□ 1988	5 Yuan, People's Republic, Olympics—Fencing, Silver	—	55.00
□ 1988	5 Yuan, People's Republic, Bi Sheng Inventor of Movable Type Printing, Silver	—	35.00
□ 1989	5 Yuan, People's Republic, Soccer Players, Silver	—	45.00
□ 1989	5 Yuan, People's Republic, Playwright Guan Hanqing, Silver	—	55.00
□ 1989	5 Yuan, People's Republic, Kublai Khan, Silver	—	70.00
□ 1989	5 Yuan, People's Republic, Huang Daopo—Invented Water Wheel, Silver	—	40.00
□ 1989	5 Yuan, People's Republic, Save the Children Fund, Silver	—	60.00
□ 1989	5 Yuan, People's Republic, Scientist Guo Shousing, Silver	—	40.00
□ 1990	5 Yuan, People's Republic, Bronze Archaeological Finds—Elephant Pitcher, Silver	—	38.00
□ 1990	5 Yuan, People's Republic, Historian Luo Guan Zhong, Silver	—	38.00

DATE	COIN TYPE/VARIETY/METAL	ABP FINE	AVERAGE FINE
☐ 1990	5 Yuan, People's Republic, Soccer—Goalie, Silver	—	$38.00
☐ 1990	5 Yuan, People's Republic, Seafarer Zeng He, Silver	—	38.00
☐ 1990	5 Yuan, People's Republic, Bronze Archaeological Finds—Rhinocerus, Silver	—	38.00
☐ 1990	5 Yuan, People's Republic, Soccer Players, Silver	—	38.00
☐ 1990	5 Yuan, People's Republic, Revolutionary Li Zicheng, Silver	—	38.00
☐ 1990	5 Yuan, People's Republic, Bronze Archaeological Finds—Mythical Creature, Silver	—	38.00
☐ 1990	5 Yuan, People's Republic, Bronze Archaeological Finds—Leopard, Silver	—	38.00
☐ 1990	5 Yuan, People's Republic, Naturalist Li Shi Zhen, Silver	—	38.00
☐ 1991	5 Yuan, People's Republic, Scientist Song Ying Xing, Silver	—	BV*
☐ 1991	5 Yuan, People's Republic, Writer Cao Xue Qin, Silver	—	BV
☐ 1991	5 Yuan, People's Republic, Official—Lin Ze Xu, Silver	—	BV
☐ 1991	5 Yuan, People's Republic, Revolutionary Hong Xu Quan, Silver	—	BV
☐ 1992	5 Yuan, People's Republic, Ancient Kite Flying, Silver	—	BV
☐ 1992	5 Yuan, People's Republic, Metal Working Scene, Silver	—	BV
☐ 1992	5 Yuan, People's Republic, First Compass, Silver	—	BV
☐ 1992	5 Yuan, People's Republic, Great Wall, Silver	—	BV
☐ 1992	5 Yuan, People's Republic, First Seismograph, Silver	—	BV

***BV** = These coins are relatively current so their collector value is minimal. Since these coins were minted and sold primarily for their bullion value, their current value is determined by the current "spot" price of the precious metal indicated. For accurate prices, contact your local coin dealer.

CUBA

Cuba was never provided with its own coinage. Spanish coins were used, with the silver peso in 1915, the gold peso in 1916, the silver centavo in 1920, and the aluminum centavo in 1981. The decimal system was established in 1915. Today's currency is the peso.

Cuba—Type Coinage

DATE	COIN TYPE/VARIETY/METAL	ABP FINE	AVERAGE FINE
□ 1953	1 Centavo, Marti Centennial, Brass	—	$ .10
□ 1915–1938	1 Centavo, Cupro-Nickel	—	.10
□ 1943	1 Centavo, Brass	—	.10
□ 1946–1961	1 Centavo, Cupro-Nickel	—	.15

□ 1958	1 Centavo, Cupro-Nickel	—	.10

□ 1915–1916	2 Centavos, Cupro-Nickel	—	.30

DATE	COIN TYPE/VARIETY/METAL	ABP FINE	AVERAGE FINE
☐ 1915–1920	5 Centavos, Cupro-Nickel	—	$ .12
☐ 1943	5 Centavos, Brass	$ .50	1.20
☐ 1946–1961	5 Centavos, Cupro-Nickel	—	.12
☐ 1952	10 Centavos, Republic 50th Anniversary, Silver	—	.60

DATE	COIN TYPE/VARIETY/METAL	ABP FINE	AVERAGE FINE
☐ 1915–1949	10 Centavos, Silver	—	1.50

DATE	COIN TYPE/VARIETY/METAL	ABP FINE	AVERAGE FINE
☐ 1952	20 Centavos, Republic 50th Anniversary, Silver	—	1.25
☐ 1915–1949	20 Centavos, Silver	—	150.00
☐ 1953	25 Centavos, Marti Centennial, Silver	—	2.00

DATE	COIN TYPE/VARIETY/METAL	ABP FINE	AVERAGE FINE
□ 1952	40 Centavos, Republic 50th Anniversary, Silver	—	$3.00
□ 1915–1920	40 Centavos, Silver	—	4.00
□ 1953	50 Centavos, Marti Centennial, Silver	—	2.00
□ 1898	1 Peso, Silver	—	125.00
□ 1953	1 Peso, Marti Centennial, Silver	—	5.00
□ 1915–1934	1 Peso, Silver	—	8.00
□ 1915–1916	1 Peso, Gold	—	60.00
□ 1934–1939	1 Peso, Silver	—	15.00
□ 1915–1916	2 Pesos, Gold	—	75.00
□ 1915–1916	4 Pesos, Gold	—	130.00
□ 1915–1916	10 Pesos, Gold	—	250.00
□ 1915–1916	20 Pesos, Gold	—	450.00

EGYPT

The first coins were used in the 4th century B.C. The earliest coins were silver pieces and gold coins. The silver "owl" drachmas appeared in the 5th century B.C., followed by bronze coins, gold drachmas, and gold solidus. The copper fals was in evidence in the 760s, then the gold dinar, silver qirsh, the cupro-nickel, gold piastres, and bronze milliemes. The decimal system was established in 1916. Today's currency is the Egyptian pound.

Egypt—Type Coinage

DATE	COIN TYPE/VARIETY/METAL	ABP FINE	AVERAGE FINE
□ 1917	½ Millieme, Hussein Kamil, Bronze	$1.00	$2.50
□ 1924	½ Millieme, Fuad I, Bronze	1.60	4.00
□ 1929–1932	½ Millieme, Fuad I, Bronze	4.50	10.00
□ 1938	½ Millieme, Farouk I, Bronze	1.40	3.00
□ 1917	1 Millieme, Hussein Kamil, Cupro-Nickel	1.00	2.50
□ 1924	1 Millieme, Fuad I, Bronze	1.00	2.50
□ 1929–1935	1 Millieme, Fuad I, Bronze	.30	.75
□ 1938–1950	1 Millieme, Farouk I, Bronze	.40	1.00

DATE	COIN TYPE/VARIETY/METAL	ABP FINE	AVERAGE FINE
□ 1954–1958	1 Millieme, Republic, Aluminum-Bronze	.40	1.00

DATE	COIN TYPE/VARIETY/METAL	ABP FINE	AVERAGE FINE
□ 1916–1917	2 Milliemes, Hussein Kamil, Cupro-Nickel	1.00	2.00
□ 1924	2 Milliemes, Fuad I, Cupro-Nickel	1.00	2.00

DATE	COIN TYPE/VARIETY/METAL	ABP FINE	AVERAGE FINE
□ 1929	2 Milliemes, Fuad I, Cupro-Nickel	.30	.75
□ 1938	2 Milliemes, Farouk I, Cupro-Nickel	1.40	3.00
□ 1933	2½ Milliemes, Fuad I, Cupro-Nickel	1.00	2.50

DATE	COIN TYPE/VARIETY/METAL	ABP FINE	AVERAGE FINE
□ 1916–1917	5 Milliemes, Hussein Kamil, Cupro-Nickel	$1.00	$2.00
□ 1924	5 Milliemes, Fuad I, Cupro-Nickel	1.00	2.00
□ 1929–1935	5 Milliemes, Fuad I, Cupro-Nickel	.60	1.50

DATE	COIN TYPE/VARIETY/METAL	ABP FINE	AVERAGE FINE
□ 1938–1941	5 Milliemes, Farouk I, Cupro-Nickel	.30	.75
□ 1938–1943	5 Milliemes, Farouk I, Bronze	.30	.75
□ 1954–1958	5 Milliemes, Republic, Aluminum-Bronze	1.40	3.00
□ 1916–1917	10 Milliemes, Hussein Kamil, Cupro-Nickel	1.40	3.00
□ 1924	10 Milliemes, Fuad I, Cupro-Nickel	1.75	4.00
□ 1929–1935	10 Milliemes, Fuad I, Cupro-Nickel	1.40	3.00

DATE	COIN TYPE/VARIETY/METAL	ABP FINE	AVERAGE FINE
□ 1938–1941	10 Milliemes, Farouk I, Cupro-Nickel	.30	.75
□ 1938–1943	10 Milliemes, Farouk I, Bronze	.30	.75
□ 1954–1958	10 Milliemes, Republic, Aluminum-Bronze	1.40	3.00
□ 1916–1917	2 Piastres, Hussein Kamil, Silver	—	3.00
□ 1920	2 Piastres, Fuad, Silver	—	50.00

DATE	COIN TYPE/VARIETY/METAL	ABP FINE	AVERAGE FINE
☐ 1885–1910	1/40 Ghirsh, Abdul Hamid II, Minted in Europe, Bronze	$ .40	$1.00
☐ 1910–1914	1/40 Ghirsh, Mohammed V, Bronze	.80	2.00
☐ 1885–1910	1/20 Ghirsh, Abdul Hamid II, Minted in Europe, Bronze	.40	1.00
☐ 1910–1914	1/20 Ghirsh, Mohammed V, Bronze	.60	1.50

DATE	COIN TYPE/VARIETY/METAL	ABP FINE	AVERAGE FINE
☐ 1916–1917	5 Piastres, Hussein Kamil, Silver	—	3.00
☐ 1920	5 Piastres, Fuad, Silver	—	40.00
☐ 1864	4 Para, Abdul Aziz, Minted in Europe, Bronze	1.40	3.00
☐ 1885–1910	1/10 Ghirsh, Abdul Hamid II, Minted in Europe, Cupro-Nickel	.30	.75
☐ 1910–1914	1/10 Ghirsh, Mohammed V, Cupro-Nickel	.40	1.00

DATE	COIN TYPE/VARIETY/METAL	ABP FINE	AVERAGE FINE
☐ 1916–1917	10 Piastres, Hussein Kamil, Silver	—	7.50
☐ 1920	10 Piastres, Fuad, Silver	—	30.00
☐ 1885–1910	2/10 Ghirsh, Abdul Hamid II, Minted in Europe, Cupro-Nickel	.50	1.20

DATE	COIN TYPE/VARIETY/METAL	ABP FINE	AVERAGE FINE
□ 1910–1914	2/10 Ghirsh, Mohammed V, Cupro-Nickel	$ .60	$ 1.50
□ 1916–1917	20 Piastres, Hussein Kamil, Silver	—	20.00
□ 1862–1876	10 Para, Abdul Aziz, Silver	—	22.00
□ 1864–1870	10 Para, Abdul Aziz, Minted in Europe, Bronze	.80	1.50
□ 1868–1871	10 Para, Abdul Aziz, Copper	—	300.00
□ 1876–1878	10 Para, Abdul Hamid II, Silver	—	90.00
□ 1861–1875	20 Para, Abdul Aziz, Silver	—	15.00

DATE	COIN TYPE/VARIETY/METAL	ABP FINE	AVERAGE FINE
□ 1863–1870	20 Para, Abdul Aziz, Minted in Europe, Bronze	1.10	2.50
□ 1868–1871	20 Para, Abdul Aziz, Copper	5.00	12.00
□ 1876–1878	20 Para, Abdul Hamid II, Silver	—	80.00

DATE	COIN TYPE/VARIETY/METAL	ABP FINE	AVERAGE FINE
□ 1885–1910	5/10 Ghirsh, Abdul Hamid II, Minted in Europe, Cupro-Nickel	.40	1.00
□ 1910–1914	5/10 Ghirsh, Mohammed V, Cupro-Nickel	.80	2.00
□ 1868–1871	40 Para, Abdul Aziz, Copper	200.00	400.00
□ 1870	40 Para, Abdul Aziz, Minted in Europe, Bronze	1.50	3.50
□ 1861–1876	1 Ghirsh, Abdul Aziz, Silver	—	8.00
□ 1876	1 Ghirsh, Mohammed V, Minted in Europe, Silver	—	2.50
□ 1876–1880	1 Ghirsh, Abdul Hamid II, Silver	—	3.50
□ 1885–1908	1 Ghirsh, Abdul Hamid II, Minted in Europe, Silver	—	1.50
□ 1897–1908	1 Ghirsh, Abdul Hamid II, Minted in Europe, Cupro-Nickel	1.25	3.00

DATE	COIN TYPE/VARIETY/METAL	ABP FINE	AVERAGE FINE
☐ 1910–1911	1 Ghirsh, Mohammed V, Silver	—	$2.50
☐ 1910–1914	1 Ghirsh, Mohammed V, Cupro-Nickel	$1.40	3.00
☐ 1916	100 Piastres, Hussein Kamil, Gold	—	80.00
☐ 1885–1908	2 Ghirsh, Abdul Hamid II, Minted in Europe, Silver	—	2.50
☐ 1910–1911	2 Ghirsh, Mohammed V, Silver	—	8.00
☐ 1864	2½ Ghirsh, Abdul Aziz, Minted in Europe, Silver	—	45.00
☐ 1868–1875	2½ Ghirsh, Abdul Aziz, Silver	—	200.00
☐ 1861–1870	5 Ghirsh, Abdul Aziz, Silver	—	175.00
☐ 1862–1876	5 Ghirsh, Abdul Aziz, Gold	—	25.00
☐ 1864	5 Ghirsh, Abdul Aziz, Minted in Europe, Silver	—	50.00

DATE	COIN TYPE/VARIETY/METAL	ABP FINE	AVERAGE FINE
☐ 1877–1882	5 Ghirsh, Abdul Hamid II, Gold	—	120.00
☐ 1885–1908	5 Ghirsh, Abdul Hamid II, Minted in Europe, Silver	—	8.00
☐ 1891–1909	5 Ghirsh, Abdul Hamid II, Gold	—	80.00
☐ 1910–1914	5 Ghirsh, Mohammed V, Silver	—	6.00
☐ 1862–1871	10 Ghirsh, Abdul Aziz, Silver	—	220.00
☐ 1864	10 Ghirsh, Abdul Aziz, Minted in Europe, Silver	—	65.00
☐ 1870–1874	10 Ghirsh, Abdul Aziz, Gold	—	65.00
☐ 1885–1908	10 Ghirsh, Abdul Hamid II, Minted in Europe, Silver	—	15.00
☐ 1892–1909	10 Ghirsh, Abdul Hamid II, Gold	—	35.00
☐ 1910–1914	10 Ghirsh, Mohammed V, Silver	—	10.00
☐ 1861–1862	20 Ghirsh, Abdul Aziz, Silver	—	250.00
☐ 1876–1880	20 Ghirsh, Abdul Hamid II, Silver	—	800.00
☐ 1885–1908	20 Ghirsh, Abdul Hamid II, Minted in Europe, Silver	—	20.00
☐ 1910–1914	20 Ghirsh, Mohammed V, Silver	—	30.00
☐ 1868–1875	25 Ghirsh, Abdul Aziz, Gold	—	40.00
☐ 1871–1876	50 Ghirsh, Abdul Aziz, Gold	—	100.00
☐ 1861–1876	100 Ghirsh, Abdul Aziz, Gold	—	150.00
☐ 1864	100 Ghirsh, Abdul Aziz, Minted in Europe, Gold	—	200.00

DATE	COIN TYPE/VARIETY/METAL	ABP FINE	AVERAGE FINE
☐ 1876–1883	100 Ghirsh, Abdul Hamid II, Gold	—	$600.00
☐ 1887	100 Ghirsh, Abdul Hamid II, Minted in Europe, Gold	—	140.00
☐ 1868–1875	500 Ghirsh, Abdul Aziz, Gold	—	—
☐ 1876–1881	500 Ghirsh, Abdul Hamid II, Gold	—	—
☐ 1955	1 Pound, Republic, Revolution 3rd & 5th Anniversaries, Gold,	—	120.00
☐ 1955	5 Pounds, Republic, Revolution 3rd & 5th Anniversaries, Gold	—	400.00

Egypt—United Arab Republic

☐ 1960–1966	Millieme, UAR, Aluminum-Bronze	—	.15

☐ 1962–1966	2 Milliemes, UAR, Aluminum-Bronze	—	.50

☐ 1960–1966	5 Milliemes, UAR, Aluminum-Bronze	—	.40

DATE	COIN TYPE/VARIETY/METAL	ABP FINE	AVERAGE FINE
□ 1960–1966	10 Milliemes, UAR, Aluminum-Bronze	—	$.40
□ 1958	20 Milliemes, UAR, Agriculture & Industry Fair, Aluminum-Bronze	—	.50
□ 1958	1/2 Pound, UAR, Founding of the United Arab Republic, Gold	—	200.00
□ 1960	Pound, UAR, Aswan Dam, Gold	—	160.00
□ 1960	5 Pounds, UAR, Aswan Dam, Gold	—	700.00

FINLAND

Evidence of coinage became common late in the Middle Ages. The first coins were used around 1410. Most were silver ortugs, and nearly all bore the king's name. In the 1800s, the ruble was declared Finland's monetary unit, then the pennia and the markka. In 1963, the new 1 penni equaled the old 1 markka.

Finland—Type Coinage

DATE	COIN TYPE/VARIETY/METAL	ABP FINE	AVERAGE FINE
☐ 1864–1917	1 Penni, Copper	$ .18	$ .30
☐ 1919–1924	1 Penni, Copper	.22	.35
☐ 1963–1969	1 Penni, Copper	—	.12
☐ 1969–1979	1 Penni, Aluminum	—	.12
☐ 1865–1917	5 Pennia, Copper	.22	.40
☐ 1918–1940	5 Pennia, Copper	—	.15
☐ 1941–1943	5 Pennia, Copper	—	.15
☐ 1963–1977	5 Pennia, Copper	—	.12
☐ 1977–1990	5 Pennia, Aluminum	—	.20

DATE	COIN TYPE/VARIETY/METAL	ABP FINE	AVERAGE FINE
☐ 1865–1917	10 Pennia, Copper	$ .60	$ .75
☐ 1919–1940	10 Pennia, Copper	—	.20
☐ 1941–1943	10 Pennia, Copper	.22	.50
☐ 1943–1945	10 Pennia, Iron	.22	.50
☐ 1865–1917	25 Pennia, Silver	—	1.50
☐ 1921–1940	25 Pennia, Cupro-Nickel	.28	.50
☐ 1940–1943	25 Pennia, Copper	—	.20
☐ 1943–1945	25 Pennia, Iron	.18	.30

DATE	COIN TYPE/VARIETY/METAL	ABP FINE	AVERAGE FINE
☐ 1864–1917	50 Pennia, Silver	—	2.00
☐ 1921–1940	50 Pennia, Cupro-Nickel	—	.20
☐ 1940–1943	50 Pennia, Copper	.18	.30
☐ 1943–1948	50 Pennia, Iron	.32	.50
☐ 1864–1915	1 Markkaa, Silver	—	5.00
☐ 1921–1924	1 Markkaa, Cupro-Nickel	2.00	4.00
☐ 1928–1940	1 Markkaa, Cupro-Nickel	—	.20
☐ 1940–1951	1 Markkaa, Copper	.16	.25
☐ 1943–1952	1 Markkaa, Iron	—	.20
☐ 1952–1962	1 Markkaa, Iron	—	.15

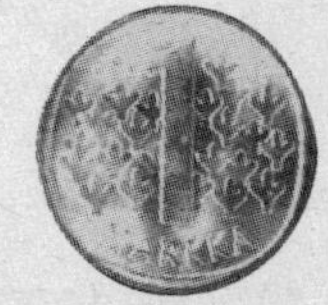

DATE	COIN TYPE/VARIETY/METAL	ABP FINE	AVERAGE FINE
□ 1964–1968	1 Markkaa, Silver	—	$1.50
□ 1969–1993	1 Markkaa, Cupro-Nickel	$ .22	.40
□ 1993 to Date	1 Markkaa, Aluminum-Bronze	—	.12
□ 1865–1908	2 Markkaa, Silver	—	10.00
□ 1928–1946	5 Markkaa, Aluminum-Bronze	1.00	2.00

DATE	COIN TYPE/VARIETY/METAL	ABP FINE	AVERAGE FINE
□ 1946–1952	5 Markkaa, Brass	.22	.35
□ 1952–1962	5 Markkaa, Iron	.18	.30
□ 1972–1978	5 Markkaa, Aluminum-Bronze	1.00	2.00
□ 1979–1993	5 Markkaa, Aluminum-Bronze	.60	1.50
□ 1992	5 Markkaa, Aluminum-Bronze	1.75	4.00
□ 1963–1982	10 Pennia, Aluminum-Bronze	—	.12
□ 1983–1990	10 Pennia, Aluminum	—	.12
□ 1990 to Date	10 Pennia, Cupro-Nickel	—	.10

DATE	COIN TYPE/VARIETY/METAL	ABP FINE	AVERAGE FINE
□ 1878–1913	10 Markkaa, Gold	—	150.00
□ 1928–1939	10 Markkaa, Aluminum-Bronze	1.75	3.00
□ 1952–1962	10 Markkaa, Aluminum-Bronze	.22	.40

DATE	COIN TYPE/VARIETY/METAL	ABP FINE	AVERAGE FINE
□ 1967–1977	10 Markkaa, Commemorative, Silver	—	4.00
□ 1963–1990	20 Pennia, Aluminum-Bronze	—	.12

DATE	COIN TYPE/VARIETY/METAL	ABP FINE	AVERAGE FINE
☐ 1878–1913	20 Markkaa, Gold	—	$200.00
☐ 1931–1939	20 Markkaa, Aluminum-Bronze	$2.00	3.50
☐ 1952–1962	20 Markkaa, Aluminum-Bronze	.22	.40

☐ 1978–1979	25 Markkaa, Commemorative, Silver	—	8.00
☐ 1963–1990	50 Pennia, Aluminum-Bronze	.18	.30
☐ 1990 to Date	50 Pennia, Cupro-Nickel	—	.20

☐ 1952–1962	50 Markkaa, Aluminum-Bronze	1.75	3.00

☐ 1981–1985	50 Markkaa, Commemorative, Silver	—	20.00
☐ 1926	100 Markkaa, Gold	—	500.00

DATE	COIN TYPE/VARIETY/METAL	ABP FINE	AVERAGE FINE
☐ 1956–1960	100 Markkaa, Silver	—	$4.00
☐ 1989–1992	100 Markkaa, Commemorative, Silver	—	50.00
☐ 1926	200 Markkaa, Gold	—	600.00
☐ 1956–1959	200 Markkaa, Silver	—	5.00

☐ 1951–1952	500 Markkaa, Commemorative Coin Issued on the Occasion of the Olympic Games in Helsinki, Silver	—	30.00
☐ 1960	1000 Markkaa, Commemorative Coin Issued on the Occasion of the Centenary of the Finnish Mint, Silver	—	10.00

FRANCE

The earliest coins date from about 500 B.C. The silver drachma was the typical coin from the 4th century B.C., with the gold stater prominent in the 2nd century B.C. The silver denier became popular around 600 A.D. The Middle Ages saw a great amount of feudal coinage, followed by coins influenced by the French Revolution. By the First World War, paper money was substituted for gold. In 1961, the range of coins still used today was introduced.

France—Type Coinage

DATE	COIN TYPE/VARIETY/METAL	ABP FINE	AVERAGE FINE
☐ 1848–1852A	Un Centime, Second Republic, Copper	$2.00	$4.00
☐ 1853–1862	Un Centime, Second Empire, Bronze	1.70	3.50
☐ 1872–1920	Un Centime, Third Republic, Bronze	.90	2.00
☐ 1962–1993	Un Centime, Fifth Republic, Chrome-Steel	—	.12
☐ 1853–1862	Deux Centimes, Second Empire, Bronze	.85	2.00
☐ 1877–1920	Deux Centimes, Third Republic, Bronze	1.30	2.75
☐ 1808BB	Cinq Centimes, Copper	60.00	100.00

DATE	COIN TYPE/VARIETY/METAL	ABP FINE	AVERAGE FINE
☐ 1853–1864	Cinq Centimes, Second Empire, Bronze	2.65	5.00
☐ 1871–1921	Cinq Centimes, Third Republic, Bronze	1.25	3.00
☐ 1914–1938	Cinq Centimes, Third Republic, Copper-Nickel	.18	.40
☐ 1938–1939	Cinq Centimes, Third Republic, Nickel-Bronze	.16	.25
☐ 1961–1964	Cinq Centimes, Fifth Republic, Chrome-Steel	—	.12
☐ 1966–1993	Cinq Centimes, Fifth Republic, Aluminum-Bronze	—	.12
☐ 1814–1815BB	Decime, Strasbourg Provisional Issue, Bronze	18.00	25.00
☐ 1807–1809	Dix Centimes, Billon	5.00	8.00

DATE	COIN TYPE/VARIETY/METAL	ABP FINE	AVERAGE FINE
□ 1852–1864	Dix Centimes, Bronze	$2.00	$4.00
□ 1870–1921	Dix Centimes, Third Republic, Bronze	1.00	2.25
□ 1914	Dix Centimes, Third Republic, Nickel	300.00	500.00
□ 1917–1938	Dix Centimes, Third Republic, Copper-Nickel	.20	.35
□ 1938–1939	Dix Centimes, Third Republic, Nickel-Bronze	.18	.30
□ 1941–1945	Dix Centimes, Third Republic, Zinc	1.00	2.00
□ 1962–1993	Dix Centimes, Fifth Republic, Aluminum-Bronze	—	.12

DATE	COIN TYPE/VARIETY/METAL	ABP FINE	AVERAGE FINE
□ 1849–1850	Vingt Centimes, Second Republic, Silver	—	10.00
□ 1853–1889	Vingt Centimes, Second Empire, Silver	—	10.00
□ 1941–1945	Vingt Centimes, Second Empire, Zinc	1.00	2.00
□ 1962–1993	Vingt Centimes, Fifth Republic, Aluminum-Bronze	—	.12
□ 1806–1807	Quart Franc, Silver	—	65.00
□ 1807	Quart Franc, Negro Head, Silver	—	50.00
□ 1807–1845	Quart Franc, Laureate Head, Silver	—	50.00
□ 1845–1846	25 Centimes, Silver	—	8.00

DATE	COIN TYPE/VARIETY/METAL	ABP FINE	AVERAGE FINE
☐ 1903–1917	25 Centimes, Third Republic, Nickel	$2.00	$4.00
☐ 1917–1937	25 Centimes, Third Republic, Copper-Nickel	—	.20
☐ 1938–1940	25 Centimes, Third Republic, Nickel-Bronze	.20	.35
☐ 1807	Demi Franc, Negro Head, Silver	—	10.00
☐ 1807–1845	Demi Franc, Laureate Head, Silver	—	20.00
☐ 1845–1846	50 Centimes, Silver	—	30.00
☐ 1849–1850	50 Centimes, Second Republic, Silver	—	30.00
☐ 1852–1852	50 Centimes, Second Republic, President Louis Napoleon, Silver	—	30.00
☐ 1853–1867	50 Centimes, Second Empire, Silver	—	8.00

DATE	COIN TYPE/VARIETY/METAL	ABP FINE	AVERAGE FINE
☐ 1871–1920	50 Centimes, Third Republic, Silver	—	2.00
☐ 1921–1939	50 Centimes, Third Republic, Aluminum-Bronze	.16	.25
☐ 1941–1945	50 Centimes, Third Republic, Aluminum	.20	.50
☐ 1962–1963	50 Centimes, Third Republic, Aluminum-Bronze	.18	.40

DATE	COIN TYPE/VARIETY/METAL	ABP FINE	AVERAGE FINE
☐ 1965–1993	1/2 Franc, Nickel	—	.18
☐ 1807	1 Franc, Negro Head, Silver	—	20.00
☐ 1807–1848	1 Franc, Laureate Head, Silver	—	22.00
☐ 1849–1868	1 Franc, Second Republic, Silver	—	35.00

DATE	COIN TYPE/VARIETY/METAL	ABP FINE	AVERAGE FINE
□ 1871–1920	1 Franc, Third Republic, Silver	—	$15.00
□ 1920–1941	1 Franc, Third Republic, Chamber of Commerce, Aluminum-Bronze	$ .18	.30
□ 1941–1959	1 Franc, Third Republic, Chamber of Commerce, Aluminum	—	.25
□ 1943	1 Franc, Third Republic, Chamber of Commerce, Zinc	100.00	175.00
□ 1960–1993	1 Franc, Fifth Republic, Nickel	—	.25
□ 1807	2 Francs, Negro Head, Silver	—	600.00
□ 1807–1846	2 Francs, Laureate Head, Silver	—	45.00
□ 1849–1850	2 Francs, Second Republic, Silver	—	175.00
□ 1853–1868	2 Francs, Second Empire, Silver	—	400.00

DATE	COIN TYPE/VARIETY/METAL	ABP FINE	AVERAGE FINE
□ 1870–1920	2 Francs, Third Republic, Silver	—	12.00
□ 1920–1941	2 Francs, Third Republic, Chamber of Commerce, Aluminum-Bronze	—	5.00
□ 1941–1946	2 Francs, Third Republic, Chamber of Commerce, Aluminum	—	.25
□ 1814–1815	5 Francs, First Restoration, Silver	—	25.00
□ 1815	5 Francs, The Hundred Days, Silver	—	85.00
□ 1816–1830	5 Francs, Second Restoration, Silver	—	60.00
□ 1830–1846	5 Francs, Second Restoration, Louis Phillipe, Silver	—	35.00
□ 1848–1852	5 Francs, Second Republic, Silver	—	35.00
□ 1854–1860	5 Francs, Second Empire, Gold	—	50.00
□ 1861–1870	5 Francs, Second Empire, Silver	—	35.00
□ 1862–1869	5 Francs, Second Empire, Gold	—	28.00

DATE	COIN TYPE/VARIETY/METAL	ABP FINE	AVERAGE FINE
☐ 1870–1878	5 Francs, Third Republic, Silver	—	$35.00
☐ 1871	5 Francs, Third Republic, Trident, Silver	—	100.00
☐ 1933–1939	5 Francs, Third Republic, Nickel	$ .30	.75
☐ 1933–1939	5 Francs, Third Republic, Nickel	.30	.75
☐ 1938–1946	5 Francs, Third Republic, Aluminum-Bronze	.50	1.20
☐ 1945–1946	5 Francs, Third Republic, Aluminum	—	.25
☐ 1960–1969	5 Francs, Fifth Republic, Silver	—	3.00
☐ 1970–1993	5 Francs, Fifth Republic, Copper-Nickel	1.00	2.00
☐ 1989	5 Francs, Fifth Republic, Eiffel Tower Centennial, Platinum	—	500.00
☐ 1989	5 Francs, Fifth Republic, Eiffel Tower Centennial, Gold	—	410.00
☐ 1989	5 Francs, Fifth Republic, Eiffel Tower Centennial, Copper-Nickel	2.25	5.00
☐ 1989	5 Francs, Fifth Republic, Eiffel Tower Centennial, Silver	—	48.00
☐ 1850–1914	10 Francs, Gold	—	125.00
☐ 1929–1939	10 Francs, Silver	—	4.00
☐ 1945–1949	10 Francs, Copper-Nickel	.20	.45
☐ 1950–1958	10 Francs, Aluminum-Bronze	.16	.30

DATE	COIN TYPE/VARIETY/METAL	ABP FINE	AVERAGE FINE
☐ 1965–1973	10 Francs, Fifth Republic, Silver	—	8.00
☐ 1974–1987	10 Francs, Fifth Republic, Nickel-Brass	.95	2.25
☐ 1982	10 Francs, Fifth Republic, Leon Gambetta—100th Anniversary, Copper-Nickel	.80	2.00

DATE	COIN TYPE/VARIETY/METAL	ABP FINE	AVERAGE FINE
☐ 1983	10 Francs, Fifth Republic, Montgolfier Balloon—200th Anniversary, Nickel Bronze	$ .80	$2.00
☐ 1983	10 Francs, Fifth Republic, Birth of Stendhal—200th Anniversary, Nickel Bronze	.80	2.00
☐ 1984	10 Francs, Fifth Republic, Birth of Francois Rudei—200th Anniversary, Nickel Bronze	.80	2.00
☐ 1985	10 Francs, Fifth Republic, Victor Hugo Centennial, Silver	—	30.00
☐ 1986	10 Francs, Fifth Republic, Robert Schumann—100th Anniversary, Gold	—	350.00
☐ 1986	10 Francs, Fifth Republic, Robert Schumann—100th Anniversary, Silver	—	100.00
☐ 1986	10 Francs, Fifth Republic, Robert Schumann—100th Anniversary, Nickel-Bronze	.80	2.00
☐ 1987	10 Francs, Fifth Republic, French Millenium, Silver	—	24.00
☐ 1987	10 Francs, Fifth Republic, French Millenium, Platinum	—	675.00
☐ 1987	10 Francs, Fifth Republic, French Millenium, Nickel-Bronze	.80	2.00
☐ 1987	10 Francs, Fifth Republic, French Millenium, Gold	—	340.00
☐ 1988	10 Francs, Fifth Republic, Rolland Garros—100th Anniversary, Aluminum-Bronze	.80	2.00
☐ 1988	10 Francs, Fifth Republic, Bastille, Dual Metal	.80	2.00
☐ 1988	10 Francs, Fifth Republic, Rolland Garros—100th Anniversary, Silver	—	60.00
☐ 1988	10 Francs, Fifth Republic, Rolland Garros—100th Anniversary, Gold	—	450.00
☐ 1989	10 Francs, Fifth Republic, Montesquieu—300th Anniversary, Dual Metal	1.30	3.00
☐ 1990–1990	European Currency Units, Charlemagne, Silver	—	110.00
☐ 1991–1991	European Currency Units, Descartes, Silver	—	100.00
☐ 1992–1992	European Currency Units, Monet, Silver	—	80.00
☐ 1814	20 Francs, Gold	—	85.00

DATE	COIN TYPE/VARIETY/METAL	ABP FINE	AVERAGE FINE
☐ 1929–1939	20 Francs, Silver	—	$ 7.00
☐ 1950–1954	20 Francs, Aluminum-Bronze	$ .26	.60
☐ 1992	20 Francs, Mont St. Michel, Dual Metal	4.50	10.00
☐ 1855–1904	50 Francs, Gold	—	300.00
☐ 1950–1954	50 Francs, Aluminum-Bronze	.30	.75
☐ 1974–1980	50 Francs, Silver	—	14.00
☐ 1990	European Currency Units, Charlemagne, Gold	—	600.00
☐ 1990	European Currency Units, Charlemagne, Platinum	—	800.00
☐ 1991	European Currency Units, Descartes, Gold	—	600.00
☐ 1991	European Currency Units, Descartes, Platinum	—	800.00
☐ 1992	European Currency Units, Monet, Platinum	—	550.00

DATE	COIN TYPE/VARIETY/METAL	ABP FINE	AVERAGE FINE
☐ 1992	European Currency Units, Monet, Gold	—	$750.00
☐ 1855–1936	100 Francs, Gold	—	500.00

DATE	COIN TYPE/VARIETY/METAL	ABP FINE	AVERAGE FINE
☐ 1954–1958	100 Francs, Copper-Nickel	$ .80	2.00
☐ 1982–1993	100 Francs, Pantheon, Silver	—	25.00
☐ 1984	100 Francs, Marie Curie—50th Anniversary, Silver	—	275.00
☐ 1984	100 Francs, Marie Curie—50th Anniversary, Gold	—	500.00
☐ 1985	100 Francs, Germinal Centennial, Gold	—	500.00
☐ 1985	100 Francs, Germinal Centennial, Silver	—	150.00
☐ 1986	100 Francs, Statue of Liberty Centennial, Platinum	—	650.00
☐ 1986	100 Francs, Statue of Liberty Centennial, Gold	—	300.00
☐ 1986	100 Francs, Statue of Liberty Centennial, Silver	—	30.00
☐ 1986	100 Francs, Statue of Liberty Centennial, Palladium	—	300.00
☐ 1987	100 Francs, Lafayette—230th Anniversary, Platinum	—	700.00
☐ 1987	100 Francs, Lafayette—230th Anniversary, Gold	—	400.00
☐ 1987	100 Francs, Lafayette—230th Anniversary, Palladium	—	275.00
☐ 1987	100 Francs, Lafayette—230th Anniversary, Silver	—	85.00
☐ 1988	100 Francs, Fraternity, Gold	—	400.00
☐ 1988	100 Francs, Fraternity, Platinum	—	675.00
☐ 1988	100 Francs, Fraternity, Silver	—	40.00
☐ 1988	100 Francs, Fraternity, Palladium	—	260.00
☐ 1989	100 Francs, Olympics—Ice Skating, Silver	—	50.00
☐ 1989	100 Francs, Olympics—Alpine Skating, Silver	—	50.00
☐ 1989	100 Francs, Human Rights, Palladium	—	300.00
☐ 1989	100 Francs, Human Rights, Gold	—	450.00

DATE	COIN TYPE/VARIETY/METAL	ABP FINE	AVERAGE FINE
☐ 1989	100 Francs, Human Rights, Platinum	—	$1000.00
☐ 1990	100 Francs, Olympics—Speed Skating, Silver	—	50.00
☐ 1990	100 Francs, Charlemagne, Silver	—	30.00
☐ 1990	100 Francs, Olympics—Bobsledding, Silver	—	50.00
☐ 1990	100 Francs, Olympic—Slalom Skier, Silver	—	50.00
☐ 1990	100 Francs, Olympic—Freestyle, Silver	—	50.00
☐ 1991	100 Francs, Olympic—Hockey Player, Silver	—	BV*
☐ 1991	100 Francs, Olympic—Ski Jumper, Silver	—	BV
☐ 1991	100 Francs, Basketball—100th Anniversary, Silver	—	BV
☐ 1991	100 Francs, Descartes, Silver	—	BV
☐ 1991	100 Francs, Olympic—Cross Country Skier, Silver	—	BV
☐ 1992	100 Francs, Paralympics, Silver	—	BV
☐ 1993	100 Francs, Louvre Bicentennial—Victory, Silver	—	BV
☐ 1993	100 Francs, Louvre Bicentennial—Mona Lisa, Silver	—	BV
☐ 1993	100 Francs, Louvre Bicentennial—Victory, Gold	—	BV
☐ 1993	100 Francs, Louvre Bicentennial—Liberty, Silver	—	BV
☐ 1993	100 Francs, Louvre Bicentennial—Liberty, Gold	—	BV
☐ 1989	500 Francs, Olympic—Alpine Skiing, Gold	—	600.00
☐ 1989	500 Francs, Olympic—Ice Skating, Gold	—	600.00
☐ 1990	500 Francs, Olympic—Freestyle Skier, Gold	—	BV
☐ 1990	500 Francs, Olympic—Bobsledding, Gold	—	BV
☐ 1990	500 Francs, Olympic—Slalom Skier, Gold	—	BV
☐ 1990	500 Francs, Olympic—Speed Skating, Gold	—	BV
☐ 1991	500 Francs, Olympic—Coubertin, Gold	—	BV
☐ 1991	500 Francs, Olympic—Hockey Player, Gold	—	BV
☐ 1991	500 Francs, Olympic—Cross Country Skier, Gold	—	BV
☐ 1991	500 Francs, Basketball—100th Anniversary, Gold	—	BV

DATE	COIN TYPE/VARIETY/METAL	ABP FINE	AVERAGE FINE
□ 1991	500 Francs, Olympic—Ski Jumpers, Gold	—	BV
□ 1993	500 Francs, Louvre—Mona Lisa, Gold	—	BV

*BV—These coins are relatively current so their collector value is minimal. Since these coins were minted and sold primarily for their bullion value, their current value is determined by the current "spot" price of the precious metal indicated. For accurate prices, contact your local coin dealer.

GERMANY (FED. REP.)

The first coins were used in the 3rd century B.C. as gold staters. In the 1st century B.C., small silver coins were produced. A local gold coin, known as a rainbow-cup, came to an end in the mid-1st century B.C. The silver denar was produced in the 800s. The bracteates became popular in the 1100s, as did pfennigs. A larger silver piece was used in the 14th century, along with other gold coinage. In the 1600s, good coinage had to be restored, with medallic taler being produced. The first decimal coins were used in 1871. Today's currency is the mark.

GERMANY (DEM. REP.)

The first coins were used in 1949 when the German Democratic Republic was formed. Its coinage was based on 100 pfennigs to the mark, some in aluminum and some in brass. The mark was cupronickel or silver.

Germany—German Empire Coinage

DATE	COIN TYPE/VARIETY/METAL	ABP FINE	AVERAGE FINE
☐ 1873–1889	1 Pfennig (1st Coinage), Rev: Small Eagle, Copper	$2.75	$5.00
☐ 1890–1916	1 Pfennig (2nd Coinage), Rev: Large Eagle, Copper	—	.20
☐ 1873–1877	2 Pfennig (1st Coinage), Rev: Small Eagle, Copper	.28	.50
☐ 1904–1916	2 Pfennig (2nd Coinage), Rev: Large Eagle, Copper	—	.20
☐ 1874–1889	5 Pfennig (1st Coinage), Rev: Small Eagle, Cupro-Nickel	.32	.60
☐ 1890–1915	5 Pfennig (2nd Coinage), Rev: Large Eagle, Cupro-Nickel	—	.12

DATE	COIN TYPE/VARIETY/METAL	ABP FINE	AVERAGE FINE
☐ 1873–1889	10 Pfennig (1st Coinage), Rev: Small Eagle, Cupro-Nickel	$ .60	$1.50
☐ 1890–1915	10 Pfennig (2nd Coinage), Rev: Large Eagle, Cupro-Nickel	—	.12
☐ 1873–1877	20 Pfennig (1st Coinage), Rev: Small Eagle, Silver	—	8.00
☐ 1887–1888	20 Pfennig (1st Coinage), Rev: Small Eagle, Cupro-Nickel	5.00	12.00
☐ 1890–1892	20 Pfennig (2nd Coinage), Rev: Large Eagle, Cupro-Nickel	8.00	20.00
☐ 1909–1912	25 Pfennig (2nd Coinage), Rev: Large Eagle, Nickel	2.75	4.50
☐ 1877–1878	50 Pfennig (1st Coinage), Rev: Small Eagle, Silver	—	25.00
☐ 1875–1877	50 Pfennig (1st Coinage), Rev: Small Eagle, Silver	—	10.00
☐ 1896–1901	50 Pfennig (2nd Coinage), Rev: Large Eagle, Silver	—	110.00

DATE	COIN TYPE/VARIETY/METAL	ABP FINE	AVERAGE FINE
☐ 1905–1919	1/2 Mark (2nd Coinage), Rev: Large Eagle, Silver	—	1.00

DATE	COIN TYPE/VARIETY/METAL	ABP FINE	AVERAGE FINE
□ 1873–1887	1 Mark (1st Coinage), Rev: Small Eagle, Silver	—	$3.00

DATE	COIN TYPE/VARIETY/METAL	ABP FINE	AVERAGE FINE
□ 1891–1916	1 Mark (2nd Coinage), Rev: Large Eagle, Silver	—	3.50

Germany—World War I Coinage

DATE	COIN TYPE/VARIETY/METAL	ABP FINE	AVERAGE FINE
□ 1916–1918	1 Pfennig, WWI, Rev: Large Eagle, Aluminum	$ .18	.30
□ 1915–1922	5 Pfennig, WWI, Rev: Large Eagle, Iron	—	.15
□ 1915–1922	10 Pfennig, WWI, Rev: Small Eagle, Iron	—	.20
□ 1916–1917	10 Pfennig, WWI, Rev: Small Eagle, Zinc	30.00	75.00
□ 1916	1 Kopek, WWI, Aluminum	1.40	3.00
□ 1916	2 Kopeks, WWI, Aluminum	1.40	3.00
□ 1916	3 Kopeks, WWI, Aluminum	1.40	3.00

Germany—Weimar Republic Coinage

DATE	COIN TYPE/VARIETY/METAL	ABP FINE	AVERAGE FINE
□ 1923–1929	1 Rentenpfennig, Weimar Republic, Bronze	.18	.25
□ 1924–1936	1 Reichspfennig, Weimar Republic, Bronze	—	.15
□ 1923–1924	2 Rentenpfennig, Weimar Republic, Bronze	—	.15
□ 1924–1936	2 Reichspfennig, Weimar Republic, Bronze	—	.15
□ 1932–1932	4 Reichspfennig, Weimar Republic, Rev: Large Eagle, Bronze	1.35	3.00

DATE	COIN TYPE/VARIETY/METAL	ABP FINE	AVERAGE FINE
□ 1923–1925	5 Rentenpfennig, Weimar Republic, Aluminum-Bronze	$ .18	$ .25
□ 1924–1936	5 Reichspfennig, Weimar Republic, Rev: Large Eagle, Aluminum-Bronze	.20	.30

DATE	COIN TYPE/VARIETY/METAL	ABP FINE	AVERAGE FINE
□ 1923–1925	10 Rentenpfennig, Weimar Republic, Aluminum-Bronze	.18	.30
□ 1924–1936	10 Reichspfennig, Weimar Republic, Rev: Large Eagle, Aluminum-Bronze	.14	.28

DATE	COIN TYPE/VARIETY/METAL	ABP FINE	AVERAGE FINE
□ 1919–1922	50 Pfennig, Weimar Republic, Aluminum	.18	.30

DATE	COIN TYPE/VARIETY/METAL	ABP FINE	AVERAGE FINE
☐ 1923–1924	50 Rentenpfennig, Weimar Republic, Aluminum-Bronze	$3.75	$8.00
☐ 1924–1925	50 Reichspfennig, Weimar Republic, Aluminum-Bronze	275.00	500.00
☐ 1924–1925	Mark, Weimar Republic, Rev: Large Eagle, Silver	—	8.00
☐ 1925–1927	1 Reichsmark, Weimar Republic, Rev: Large Eagle, Silver	—	10.00
☐ 1925–1931	2 Reichsmark, Weimar Republic, Rev: Large Eagle, Silver	—	12.00
☐ 1922–1923	3 Mark, Weimar Republic, 3rd Anniversary—Weimar Constitution, Aluminum	.60	1.00
☐ 1925	3 Reichsmark, Weimar Republic, Commemorative—Millenium Unification of Rhineland, Silver	—	25.00
☐ 1926	3 Reichsmark, Weimar Republic, Commemorative—700th Anniversary of the Freedom of Lubeck, Silver	—	60.00
☐ 1927	3 Reichsmark, Weimar Republic, Commemorative—Bremhaven Centennial, Silver	—	65.00
☐ 1927	3 Reichsmark, Weimar Republic, Commemorative—University of Marburg 400th Anniversary, Silver	—	65.00
☐ 1927	3 Reichsmark, Weimar Republic, Commemorative—University of Tubingen 450th Anniversary, Silver	—	165.00
☐ 1927	3 Reichsmark, Weimar Republic, Commemorative—Nordhausen Millenium, Silver	—	65.00
☐ 1928	3 Reichsmark, Weimar Republic, Commemorative—City of Naumburg—900th Anniversary, Silver	—	65.00
☐ 1928	3 Reichsmark, Weimar Republic, Commemorative—City of Dinkelsbuhl Millenium, Silver	—	275.00
☐ 1928	3 Reichsmark, Weimar Republic, Commemorative—Death of Durer—400th Anniversary, Silver	—	175.00
☐ 1929	3 Reichsmark, Weimar Republic, Commemorative—Birth of Lessing Bicentennial, Silver	—	25.00
☐ 1929	3 Reichsmark, Weimar Republic, Commemorative—Waldeck-Prussia Union, Silver	—	65.00

DATE	COIN TYPE/VARIETY/METAL	ABP FINE	AVERAGE FINE
□ 1929	3 Reichsmark, Weimar Republic, Commemorative—City of Meissen Millenium, Silver	—	$28.00
□ 1929	3 Reichsmark, Weimar Republic, Commemorative—Constitution 10th Anniversary, Silver	—	25.00
□ 1930	3 Reichsmark, Weimar Republic, Commemorative—End of Rhineland Occupation, Silver	—	25.00
□ 1930	3 Reichsmark, Weimar Republic, Commemorative—Flight of Graf Zeppelin, Silver	—	50.00
□ 1930	3 Reichsmark, Weimar Republic, Commemorative—Death of Vogelweide 700th Anniversary, Silver	—	50.00
□ 1931	3 Reichsmark, Weimar Republic, Commemorative—Death of von Stein Centennial, Silver	—	65.00
□ 1931	3 Reichsmark, Weimar Republic, Commemorative—Magdeburg Rebuilding 300th Anniversary, Silver	—	120.00
□ 1931–1933	3 Reichsmark, Weimar Republic, Rev: Large Eagle, Silver	—	150.00
□ 1932	3 Reichsmark, Weimar Republic, Commemorative—Death of Goethe, Silver	—	50.00

DATE	COIN TYPE/VARIETY/METAL	ABP FINE	AVERAGE FINE
□ 1922	3 Mark, Weimar Republic, Obv: Large Eagle, Aluminum	$ .20	.50
□ 1924–1925	3 Mark, Weimar Republic, Rev: Large Eagle, Silver	—	25.00
□ 1925	5 Reichsmark, Weimar Republic, Commemorative—Millenium Unification of Rhineland, Silver	—	60.00
□ 1927–1933	5 Reichsmark, Weimar Republic, Rev: Large Eagle, Silver	—	45.00

DATE	COIN TYPE/VARIETY/METAL	ABP FINE	AVERAGE FINE
□ 1927	5 Reichsmark, Weimar Republic, Commemorative—University of Tubingen 450th Anniversary, Silver	—	$200.00
□ 1929	5 Reichsmark, Weimar Republic, Commemorative—Birth of Lessing Bicentennial, Silver	—	70.00
□ 1929	5 Reichsmark, Weimar Republic, Commemorative—Constitution 10th Anniversary, Silver	—	70.00
□ 1929	5 Reichsmark, Weimar Republic, Commemorative—City of Meissen Millenium, Silver	—	160.00
□ 1930	5 Reichsmark, Weimar Republic, Commemorative—End of Rhineland Occupation, Silver	—	90.00
□ 1930	5 Reichsmark, Weimar Republic, Commemorative—Flight of Graf Zeppelin, Silver	—	90.00
□ 1932	5 Reichsmark, Weimar Republic, Commemorative—Death of Goethe, Silver	—	800.00

DATE	COIN TYPE/VARIETY/METAL	ABP FINE	AVERAGE FINE
□ 1923	200 Mark, Weimar Republic, Obv: Large Eagle, Aluminum	$ .18	.30

DATE	COIN TYPE/VARIETY/METAL	ABP FINE	AVERAGE FINE
□ 1923	500 Mark, Weimar Republic, Obv: Large Eagle, Aluminum	.18	.30

Germany—Third Reich Coinage

DATE	COIN TYPE/VARIETY/METAL	ABP FINE	AVERAGE FINE
□ 1936–1940	1 Reischspfennig, Third Reich, Obv: Hindenburg, Bronze	—	$ .12
□ 1940–1945	1 Reischspfennig, Third Reich, Zinc	—	.12

DATE	COIN TYPE/VARIETY/METAL	ABP FINE	AVERAGE FINE
□ 1936–1940	2 Reischspfennig, Third Reich, Obv: Hindenburg, Bronze	—	.12

DATE	COIN TYPE/VARIETY/METAL	ABP FINE	AVERAGE FINE
□ 1936–1939	5 Reischspfennig, Third Reich, Obv: Hindenburg, Aluminum-Bronze	—	.15
□ 1940–1941	5 Reischspfennig, Third Reich, German Army, Zinc	$30.00	60.00
□ 1940–1944	5 Reischspfennig, Third Reich, Zinc	.10	.25

DATE	COIN TYPE/VARIETY/METAL	ABP FINE	AVERAGE FINE
□ 1936–1939	10 Reischspfennig, Third Reich, Obv: Hindenburg, Aluminum-Bronze	$ .28	$ .50
□ 1940–1941	10 Reischspfennig, Third Reich, German Army, Zinc	35.00	50.00
□ 1940–1945	10 Reischspfennig, Third Reich, Zinc	.10	.25

DATE	COIN TYPE/VARIETY/METAL	ABP FINE	AVERAGE FINE
□ 1935	50 Reischspfennig, Third Reich, Aluminum	.18	.30
□ 1938–1939	50 Reischspfennig, Third Reich, Nickel	7.00	15.00
□ 1939–1944	50 Reischspfennig, Third Reich, Aluminum	1.60	3.00
□ 1933–1939	1 Reischsmark, Third Reich, Nickel	4.50	10.00
□ 1933	2 Reischsmark, Third Reich, Commemorative—Birth of Martin Luther 450th Anniversary, Silver	—	15.00
□ 1934	2 Reischsmark, Third Reich, Commemorative—Anniversary of Nazi Rule, Silver	—	8.00
□ 1934	2 Reischsmark, Third Reich, Commemorative—Birth of Schiller 175th Anniversary, Silver	—	30.00
□ 1936–1939	2 Reichsmark, Third Reich, Obv: Hindenburg, Silver	—	3.00
□ 1933	5 Reischsmark, Third Reich, Commemorative—Birth of Martin Luther 450th Anniversary, Silver	—	80.00

DATE	COIN TYPE/VARIETY/METAL	ABP FINE	AVERAGE FINE
□ 1934	5 Reischsmark, Third Reich, Commemorative—Anniversary of Nazi Rule, Silver	—	$10.00
□ 1934	5 Reischsmark, Third Reich, Commemorative—Birth of Schiller 175th Anniversary, Silver	—	6.00
□ 1934–1935	5 Reischsmark, Third Reich, Silver	—	6.00
□ 1935–1936	5 Reischsmark, Third Reich, Obv: Hindenburg, Silver	—	5.00
□ 1936–1939	5 Reichsmark, Third Reich, Obv: Hindenburg, Silver	—	6.00

Germany—Allied Occupation Coinage

DATE	COIN TYPE/VARIETY/METAL	ABP FINE	AVERAGE FINE
□ 1944–1946	1 Reichspfennig, Allied Occ, Zinc	$6.00	10.00

DATE	COIN TYPE/VARIETY/METAL	ABP FINE	AVERAGE FINE
□ 1948–1949	1 Pfennig, Allied Occ, Bank Deutscher, Lander, Bronze-Steel	.35	.65
□ 1944–1946	5 Reichspfennig, Allied Occ, Zinc	9.00	20.00

DATE	COIN TYPE/VARIETY/METAL	ABP FINE	AVERAGE FINE
□ 1949	5 Pfennig, Allied Occ, Bank Deutscher Lander, Brass-Steel	1.60	3.00
□ 1945–1948	10 Reichspfennig, Allied Occ, Zinc	4.00	10.00

DATE	COIN TYPE/VARIETY/METAL	ABP FINE	AVERAGE FINE
□ 1949	10 Pfennig, Allied Occ, Bank Deutscher Lander, Brass-Steel	$ .28	$ .60

DATE	COIN TYPE/VARIETY/METAL	ABP FINE	AVERAGE FINE
□ 1949–1950	50 Pfennig, Allied Occ, Bank Deutscher Lander, Cupro-Nickel	.55	1.00

Germany—German Federal Republic Coinage

DATE	COIN TYPE/VARIETY/METAL	ABP FINE	AVERAGE FINE
□ 1950 to Date	1 Pfennig, Federal Republic, Bundesrepublik Deutschland, Bronze-Steel	—	.12

DATE	COIN TYPE/VARIETY/METAL	ABP FINE	AVERAGE FINE
□ 1950–1968	2 Pfennig, Federal Republic, Bundesrepublik Deutschland, Bronze	—	$ .12
□ 1969 to Date	2 Pfennig, Federal Republic, Bundesrepublik Deutschland, Bronze-Steel	—	.12
□ 1950 to Date	5 Pfennig, Federal Republic, Bundesrepublik Deutschland, Brass-Steel	—	.12
□ 1950 to Date	10 Pfennig, Federal Republic, Bundesrepublik Deutschland, Brass-Steel	$ .10	.25
□ 1950–1971	50 Pfennig, Federal Republic, Bundesrepublik Deutschland, Cupro-Nickel	.28	.50
□ 1972 to Date	50 Pfennig, Federal Republic, Bundesrepublik Deutschland, Cupro-Nickel	.25	.40

DATE	COIN TYPE/VARIETY/METAL	ABP FINE	AVERAGE FINE
☐ 1950 to Date	1 Deutsche Mark, Federal Republic, Bundesrepublik Deutschland, Cupro-Nickel	$ .35	$ .80
☐ 1951	2 Deutsche Mark, Federal Republic, Bundesrepublik Deutschland, Cupro-Nickel	5.00	12.00
☐ 1957–1971	2 Deutsche Mark, Federal Republic, Bundesrepublik Deutschland, Cupro-Nickel	1.00	2.00
☐ 1957–1971	2 Deutsche Mark, Federal Republic, Bundesrepublik Deutschland, Rev: Max Planck, Cupro-Nickel	1.00	2.00
☐ 1968–1991	2 Deutsche Mark, Federal Republic, Bundesrepublik Deutschland, Rev: Ludwig Erhard, Cupro-Nickel	.80	1.75
☐ 1969–1987	2 Deutsche Mark, Federal Republic, Bundesrepublik Deutschland, Rev: Konrad Adenauer, Cupro-Nickel	.80	1.75
☐ 1970–1987	2 Deutsche Mark, Federal Republic, Bundesrepublik Deutschland, Rev: Theodor Heuss, Cupro-Nickel	.80	1.75
☐ 1979–1991	2 Deutsche Mark, Federal Republic, Bundesrepublik Deutschland, Rev: Kurt Schumacher, Cupro-Nickel	.70	1.50
☐ 1990–1991	2 Deutsche Mark, Federal Republic, Bundesrepublik Deutschland, Rev: Franz Strauss, Cupro-Nickel	.70	1.50

DATE	COIN TYPE/VARIETY/METAL	ABP FINE	AVERAGE FINE
☐ 1951–1974	5 Deutsche Mark, Federal Republic, Bundesrepublik Deutschland, Silver	—	$3.00
☐ 1975 to Date	5 Deutsche Mark, Federal Republic, Rev: Large Eagle, Cupro-Nickel	$2.00	4.00
☐ 1952	5 Deutsche Mark, Federal Republic, Commemorative—Nurnberg Museum Centennial, Silver	—	500.00
☐ 1955	5 Deutsche Mark, Federal Republic, Commemorative—von Schiller 150th Anniversary of Death, Silver	—	350.00
☐ 1955	5 Deutsche Mark, Federal Republic, Commemorative—Birth of Ludwig von Baden 300th Anniversary, Silver	—	275.00
☐ 1957	5 Deutsche Mark, Federal Republic, Commemorative—Death of von Eichendorff Centennial, Silver	—	275.00
☐ 1964	5 Deutsche Mark, Federal Republic, Commemorative—Death of Fichte 150th Anniversary, Silver	—	140.00
☐ 1966	5 Deutsche Mark, Federal Republic, Commemorative—Death of Leibniz 250th Anniversary, Silver	—	30.00
☐ 1967	5 Deutsche Mark, Federal Republic, Commemorative—Wilhelm & Alexander von Humboldt, Silver	—	30.00
☐ 1968	5 Deutsche Mark, Federal Republic, Commemorative—Birth of Ralfellsen 150th Anniversary, Silver	—	4.00
☐ 1968	5 Deutsche Mark, Federal Republic, Commemorative—Death of von Pettenkoffer 150th Anniversary, Silver	—	4.00
☐ 1969	5 Deutsche Mark, Federal Republic, Commemorative—Birth of Fontana 150th Anniversary, Silver	—	10.00
☐ 1969	5 Deutsche Mark, Federal Republic, Commemorative—Death of Mercator 375th Anniversary, Silver	—	4.00
☐ 1970	5 Deutsche Mark, Federal Republic, Commemorative—Birth of Beethoven 200th Anniversary, Silver	—	4.00
☐ 1971	5 Deutsche Mark, Federal Republic, Commemorative—Birth of Durer 500th Anniversary, Silver	—	4.00
☐ 1971	5 Deutsche Mark, Federal Republic, Commemorative—German Unification, Silver	—	6.00

DATE	COIN TYPE/VARIETY/METAL	ABP FINE	AVERAGE FINE
☐ 1973	5 Deutsche Mark, Federal Republic, Commemorative—Birth of Copernicus 500th Anniversary, Silver	—	$4.00
☐ 1973	5 Deutsche Mark, Federal Republic, Commemorative—Frankfurt Parliament 125th Anniversary, Silver	—	4.00
☐ 1974	5 Deutsche Mark, Federal Republic, Commemorative—Birth of Kant 250th Anniversary, Silver	—	4.00
☐ 1974	5 Deutsche Mark, Federal Republic, Commemorative—Constitutional Law 25th Anniversary, Silver	—	4.00
☐ 1975	5 Deutsche Mark, Federal Republic, Commemorative—Birth of Schweitzer Centenary, Silver	—	4.00
☐ 1975	5 Deutsche Mark, Federal Republic, Commemorative—Death of Ebert 250th Anniversary, Silver	—	4.00
☐ 1975	5 Deutsche Mark, Federal Republic, Commemorative—European Monument Protection, Silver	—	4.00
☐ 1976	5 Deutsche Mark, Federal Republic, Commemorative—Death of von Grimmelshausen 300th Anniversary, Silver	—	4.00
☐ 1977	5 Deutsche Mark, Federal Republic, Commemorative—Birth of Stresemann 100th Anniversary, Silver	—	4.00
☐ 1977	5 Deutsche Mark, Federal Republic, Commemorative—Birth of von Kleist 200th Anniversary, Silver	—	4.00
☐ 1977	5 Deutsche Mark, Federal Republic, Commemorative—Birth of Gauss 200th Anniversary, Silver	—	4.00
☐ 1978	5 Deutsche Mark, Federal Republic, Commemorative—Death of Neumann 275th Anniversary, Silver	—	4.00
☐ 1979	5 Deutsche Mark, Federal Republic, Commemorative—Birth of Hahn 100th Anniversary, Cupro-Nickel	$2.00	4.00
☐ 1979	5 Deutsche Mark, Federal Republic, Commemorative—Birth of Hahn 100th Anniversary, Silver	—	20,000.00
☐ 1979	5 Deutsche Mark, Federal Republic, Commemorative—German Archaeological Institute Anniversary, Silver	—	4.00

DATE	COIN TYPE/VARIETY/METAL	ABP FINE	AVERAGE FINE
□ 1980	5 Deutsche Mark, Federal Republic, Commemorative—Cologne Cathedral 100th Anniversary, Cupro-Nickel	$2.00	$4.00
□ 1980	5 Deutsche Mark, Federal Republic, Commemorative—Death of Vogelwelde 750th Anniversary, Cupro-Nickel	2.00	4.00
□ 1981	5 Deutsche Mark, Federal Republic, Commemorative, Death of von Stein 150th Anniversary, Cupro-Nickel	2.00	4.00
□ 1981	5 Deutsche Mark, Federal Republic, Commemorative—Death of Lessing 200th Anniversary, Cupro-Nickel	2.00	4.00
□ 1982	5 Deutsche Mark, Federal Republic, Commemorative—Death of von Goethe 150th Anniversary, Cupro-Nickel	2.00	4.00
□ 1982	5 Deutsche Mark, Federal Republic, Commemorative, U.N. Environmental Conference 10th Anniversary, Cupro-Nickel	2.00	4.00
□ 1983	5 Deutsche Mark, Federal Republic, Commemorative—Death of Carl Marx 100th Anniversary, Cupro-Nickel	2.00	4.00
□ 1983	5 Deutsche, Mark, Federal Republic, Commemorative—Birth of Martin Luther 500th Anniversary, Cupro-Nickel	2.00	4.00
□ 1984	5 Deutsche Mark, Federal Republic, Commemorative—Birth of Bartholdy 175th Anniversary, Cupro-Nickel	2.00	4.00
□ 1984	5 Deutsche Mark, Federal Republic, Commemorative—German Customs Union 150th Anniversary, Cupro-Nickel	2.00	4.00
□ 1985	5 Deutsche Mark, Federal Republic, Commemorative—German Railroad 150th Anniversary, Cupro-Nickel	2.00	4.00
□ 1985	5 Deutsche Mark, Federal Republic, Commemorative—European Year of Music, Cupro-Nickel	2.00	4.00
□ 1986	5 Deutsche Mark, Federal Republic, Commemorative—Death of Frederick the Great 200th Anniversary, Cupro-Nickel	2.00	4.00

DATE	COIN TYPE/VARIETY/METAL	ABP FINE	AVERAGE FINE
☐ 1986	5 Deutsche Mark, Federal Republic, Commemorative—Heidenberg University 600th Anniversary, Cupro-Nickel	$2.00	$4.00
☐ 1972	10 Deutsche Mark, Federal Republic, Commemorative—Munich Olympics—Stadium, Silver	—	6.00
☐ 1972	10 Deutsche Mark, Federal Republic, Commemorative—Munich Olympics—Munchen, Silver	—	6.00
☐ 1972	10 Deutsche Mark, Federal Republic, Commemorative—Munich Olympics—Deutschland, Silver	—	6.00
☐ 1972	10 Deutsche Mark, Federal Republic, Commemorative—Munich Olympics—Athletes, Silver	—	6.00
☐ 1972	10 Deutsche Mark, Federal Republic, Commemorative—Munich Olympics—Flame, Silver	—	6.00
☐ 1972	10 Deutsche Mark, Federal Republic, Commemorative—Munich Olympics—Knot, Silver	—	6.00
☐ 1987	10 Deutsche Mark, Federal Republic, Commemorative—Berlin 750 Anniversary, Silver	—	15.00
☐ 1987	10 Deutsche Mark, Commemorative—European Unity, Silver	—	15.00
☐ 1988	10 Deutsche Mark, Commemorative—Death of Zeiss 100th Anniversary, Silver	—	15.00
☐ 1988	10 Deutsche Mark, Federal Republic, Commemorative—Birth of Schopenhauer, Silver	—	15.00
☐ 1989	10 Deutsche Mark, Federal Republic, Commemorative—Port of Hamburg 800th Anniversary, Silver	—	15.00
☐ 1989	10 Deutsche Mark, Federal Republic, Commemorative—Republic 40th Anniversary, Silver	—	15.00
☐ 1989	10 Deutsche Mark, Federal Republic, Commemorative—City of Bonn 200th Anniversary, Silver	—	15.00
☐ 1990	10 Deutsche Mark, Federal Republic, Commemorative—Teutonic Order 800th Anniversary, Silver	—	15.00

DATE	COIN TYPE/VARIETY/METAL	ABP FINE	AVERAGE FINE
☐ 1989	10 Deutsche Mark, Federal Republic, Commemorative—Port of Hamburg 800th Anniversary, Silver	—	$12.00
☐ 1989	10 Deutsche Mark, Federal Republic, Commemorative—Republic 40th Anniversary, Silver	—	12.00
☐ 1989	10 Deutsche Mark, Federal Republic, Commemorative—City of Bonn 2000th Anniversary, Silver	—	12.00
☐ 1990	10 Deutsche Mark, Federal Republic, Commemorative—Teutonic Order 800th Anniversary, Silver	—	12.00
☐ 1990	10 Deutsche Mark, Federal Republic, Commemorative—Death of Barbarossa, Silver	—	12.00
☐ 1991	10 Deutsche Mark, Federal Republic, Commemorative—Brandenburg Gate, Silver	—	12.00
☐ 1992	10 Deutsche Mark, Federal Republic, Commemorative—Civil Pour le Merite Order, Silver	—	12.00
☐ 1992	10 Deutsche Mark, Federal Republic, Commemorative—Kathe Kollwitz Artist, Silver	—	12.00

Germany—Democratic Republic Coinage

DATE	COIN TYPE/VARIETY/METAL	ABP FINE	AVERAGE FINE
☐ 1948–1950	1 Pfennig, Democratic Republic, Aluminum	$ .10	.25
☐ 1952–1953	1 Pfennig, Democratic Republic, Aluminum	.18	.40

DATE	COIN TYPE/VARIETY/METAL	ABP FINE	AVERAGE FINE
☐ 1948–1950	5 Pfennig, Democratic Republic, Aluminum	.28	.60
☐ 1952–1953	5 Pfennig, Democratic Republic, Aluminum	.18	.40

DATE	COIN TYPE/VARIETY/METAL	ABP FINE	AVERAGE FINE
☐ 1948–1950	10 Pfennig, Democratic Republic, Aluminum	$ .28	$ .60
☐ 1952–1953	10 Pfennig, Democratic Republic, Aluminum	.28	.60

DATE	COIN TYPE/VARIETY/METAL	ABP FINE	AVERAGE FINE
☐ 1949–1950	50 Pfennig, Democratic Republic, Aluminum-Bronze	1.00	2.25

GREECE

The first coins were used in mid-6th century B.C. Except for a few white-gold coins, early Greek coins were silver. The first gold coins were produced toward the end of the Peloponnesian War. The first bronze coins appeared in the late 5th century B.C. Roman coins were introduced in Greece around the mid-1st century B.C. Bronze coins became more popular, though all coins varied from period to period. Independent coinage was begun in 1827, and the first Greek coinage was struck in Aegina, including copper and silver coins. All had a phoenix rising from the ashes to symbolize the rebirth of the nation and the date of the Greek Revolt (1821). The first decimal coins were used in 1831. The currency today is the drachma.

Greece—Type and Democratic Republic Coinage

DATE	COIN TYPE/VARIETY/METAL	ABP FINE	AVERAGE FINE
☐ 1869–1870	1 Lepton, Georgios I, Young Head, Copper	$2.00	$5.00
☐ 1878–1879	1 Lepton, Georgios I, Older Head—Second Coinage, Copper	1.75	3.00
☐ 1869	2 Lepta, Georgios I, Young Head, Copper	1.00	2.50
☐ 1878	2 Lepta, Georgios I, Older Head—Second Coinage, Copper	.60	1.50
☐ 1869–1870	5 Lepta, Georgios I, Young Head, Copper	2.00	5.00
☐ 1878–1882	5 Lepta, Georgios I, Older Head—Second Coinage, Copper	4.00	10.00
☐ 1894–1895	5 Lepta, Georgios I, Third Coinage, Cupro-Nickel	.60	1.50
☐ 1912	5 Lepta, Georgios I, Third Coinage, Nickel	.28	.60

DATE	COIN TYPE/VARIETY/METAL	ABP FINE	AVERAGE FINE
☐ 1954–1971	5 Lepta, Aluminum	.10	.25
☐ 1869–1870	10 Lepta, Georgios I, Young Head, Copper	3.00	6.00
☐ 1878-1882	10 Lepta, Georgios I, Older Head—Second Coinage, Copper	4.50	10.00
☐ 1894–1895	10 Lepta, Georgios I, Third Coinage, Cupro-Nickel	.60	1.50

DATE	COIN TYPE/VARIETY/METAL	ABP FINE	AVERAGE FINE
□ 1912	10 Lepta, Georgios I, Third Coinage, Nickel	$ .18	$ .30
□ 1922	10 Lepta, Konstantinos I, Second Reign, Aluminum	.60	1.50
□ 1954–1971	10 Lepta, Aluminum	—	.12
□ 1973–1978	10 Lepta, Aluminum	—	.12
□ 1869–1883	20 Lepta, Georgios I, Young Head, Silver	—	4.00
□ 1893–1895	20 Lepta, Georgios I, Older Head—Third Coinage, Cupro-Nickel	1.00	2.00

DATE	COIN TYPE/VARIETY/METAL	ABP FINE	AVERAGE FINE
□ 1912	20 Lepta, Georgios I, Third Coinage, Nickel	.28	.60
□ 1926	20 Lepta, Republic, Cupro-Nickel	.28	.60
□ 1954–1971	20 Lepta, Aluminum	—	.12
□ 1973–1978	20 Lepta, Aluminum	.10	.25
□ 1868–1883	50 Lepta, Georgios I, Young Head, Silver	—	18.00
□ 1921	50 Lepta, Konstantinos I, Second Reign, Cupro-Nickel	.10	.25
□ 1926	50 Lepta, Republic, Cupro-Nickel	.10	.25

DATE	COIN TYPE/VARIETY/METAL	ABP FINE	AVERAGE FINE
□ 1954–1965	50 Lepta, Paulos I, Cupro-Nickel	—	.18
□ 1973–1986	50 Lepta, Brass	—	.12
□ 1868–1883	1 Drachma, Georgios I, Young Head, Silver	—	35.00
□ 1910–1911	1 Drachma-Georgios I, Third Coinage, Silver	—	6.00
□ 1926	1 Drachma, Republic, Cupro-Nickel	—	.25

DATE	COIN TYPE/VARIETY/METAL	ABP FINE	AVERAGE FINE
□ 1954–1965	1 Drachma, Paulos 1, Cupro-Nickel	—	$ .18
□ 1973–1986	1 Drachma, Brass	—	.12
□ 1988–1990	Drachma, Copper	—	.10
□ 1868–1883	2 Drachmai, Georgios I, Young Head, Silver	—	40.00
□ 1911	2 Drachmai, Georgios I, Third Coinage, Silver	—	6.00

DATE	COIN TYPE/VARIETY/METAL	ABP FINE	AVERAGE FINE
□ 1926	2 Drachmai, Republic, Cupro-Nickel	—	.25
□ 1954–1965	2 Drachmai, Paulos I, Cupro-Nickel	$ .28	.60
□ 1973–1980	2 Drachmai, Brass	—	.20
□ 1982–1986	2 Drachmes, Brass	—	.12
□ 1988–1990	2 Drachmes, Copper	—	.12
□ 1875–1876	5 Drachmai, Georgios I, Older Head—Second Coinage, Silver	—	30.00
□ 1876	5 Drachmai, Georgios I, Young Head, Gold	—	300.00

DATE	COIN TYPE/VARIETY/METAL	ABP FINE	AVERAGE FINE
☐ 1930	5 Drachmai, Republic, Nickel	$ .65	$1.50
☐ 1954–1965	5 Drachmai, Paulos I, Cupro-Nickel	.18	.30
☐ 1973–1980	5 Drachmai, Cupro-Nickel	—	.15
☐ 1982–1990	5 Drachmes, Cupro-Nickel	—	.12
☐ 1876	10 Drachmai, Georgios I, Young Head, Gold	—	225.00
☐ 1930	10 Drachmai, Republic, Silver	—	3.00

DATE	COIN TYPE/VARIETY/METAL	ABP FINE	AVERAGE FINE
☐ 1959–1965	10 Drachmai, Paulos I, Nickel	.16	.40
☐ 1973–1980	10 Drachmai, Cupro-Nickel	.12	.25
☐ 1982–1990	10 Drachmes, Cupro-Nickel	—	.18
☐ 1876	20 Drachmai, Georgios I, Young Head, Gold	—	135.00
☐ 1884	20 Drachmai, Georgios I, Older Head—Second Coinage, Gold	—	100.00
☐ 1930	20 Drachmai, Republic, Silver	—	5.00
☐ 1935	20 Drachmai, Georgios II, Restoration Commemorative, Gold	—	4500.00

DATE	COIN TYPE/VARIETY/METAL	ABP FINE	AVERAGE FINE
☐ 1960–1965	20 Drachmai, Paulos I, Silver	—	6.00
☐ 1973–1980	20 Drachmai, Cupro-Nickel	—	.25
☐ 1982–1988	20 Drachmes, Cupro-Nickel	—	.25
☐ 1963	30 Drachmai, Paulos I, Centennial of Royal Greek Dynasty, Silver	—	5.00
☐ 1876	50 Drachmai, Georgios I, Older Head—Second Coinage, Gold	—	130.00
☐ 1980	50 Drachmai, Cupro-Nickel	.22	.50
☐ 1982	50 Drachmes, Cupro-Nickel	.22	.50
☐ 1986–1990	50 Drachmes, Brass	.22	.50

DATE	COIN TYPE/VARIETY/METAL	ABP FINE	AVERAGE FINE
☐ 1876	100 Drachmai, Georgios I, Older Head—Second Coinage, Gold	—	$6000.00
☐ 1935	100 Drachmai, Georgios II, Restoration Commemorative, Gold	—	10,000.00
☐ 1935	100 Drachmai, Georgios II, Restoration Commemorative, Silver	—	1000.00
☐ 1978–1982	100 Drachmai, Silver	—	12.00
☐ 1988	100 Drachmes, 28th Chess Olympics, Cupro-Nickel	$3.00	6.00
☐ 1990–1991	100 Drachmes, Alexander the Great, Brass	.75	2.00
☐ 1981–1982	250 Drachmai, Pan-European Games, Silver	—	18.00
☐ 1979	500 Drachmes, Common Market Membership, Silver	—	140.00
☐ 1981–1982	500 Drachmai, Pan European Games, Silver	—	25.00
☐ 1984	500 Drachmes, Olympics—Torch, Silver	—	30.00
☐ 1988	500 Drachmes, 28th Chess Olympics, Silver	—	120.00
☐ 1991	500 Drachmes, XI Mediterranean Games, Silver	—	28.00
☐ 1985	1000 Drachmes, Decade for Women, Silver	—	50.00
☐ 1990	1000 Drachmes, Italian Invasion of Greece—50th Anniversary, Silver	—	60.00
☐ 1981–1982	2500 Drachmes, Pan-European Games, Gold	—	150.00
☐ 1981–1982	5000 Drachmai, Pan-European Games, Gold	—	250.00
☐ 1984	5000 Drachmes, Olympics—Apollo, Gold	—	500.00
☐ 1979	10000 Drachmes, Common Market Membership, Gold	—	575.00
☐ 1985	10000 Drachmes, Decade for Women, Gold	—	325.00
☐ 1991	10000 Drachmes, XI Mediterranean Games, Gold	—	350.00
☐ 1990	20000 Drachmes, Italian Invasion of Greece—50th Anniversary, Gold	—	350.00

HUNGARY

The first coins were used in the 3rd century B.C. and were of silver. In the 2nd century B.C., bronze coins were produced. The silver denar appeared in the 11th century, followed by copper denars, gold ducats, and silver talers. The decimal system was established in 1857. Today's currency is the forint.

Hungary—Type Coinage

DATE	COIN TYPE/VARIETY/METAL	ABP FINE	AVERAGE FINE
☐ 1882	5/10 Kreuzer, Franz Joseph, Rev: Shield, Copper	$1.40	$3.00
☐ 1868–1892	1 Kreuzer, Franz Joseph, Rev: Shield, Copper	2.00	4.00
☐ 1892–1906	1 Filler, Franz Joseph, Rev: Crown, Bronze	1.50	3.00

DATE	COIN TYPE/VARIETY/METAL	ABP FINE	AVERAGE FINE
☐ 1926–1938	1 Filler, Horthy Regency, Crown, Bronze	—	.12

DATE	COIN TYPE/VARIETY/METAL	ABP FINE	AVERAGE FINE
□ 1892–1915	2 Filler, Franz Joseph, Rev: Crown, Bronze	$ .28	$ .50
□ 1926–1938	2 Filler, Horthy Regency, Crown, Bronze	—	.12
□ 1940–1944	2 Filler, Horthy Regency, Stainless Steel	—	.20
□ 1946–1947	2 Filler, Republic, Hungarian Arms, Bronze	—	.12
□ 1950	2 Filler, Republic, Rev: Spray, Aluminum	—	.15
□ 1948–1951	5 Filler, Republic, Rev: Spray, Aluminum	—	.12

DATE	COIN TYPE/VARIETY/METAL	ABP FINE	AVERAGE FINE
□ 1868–1889	10 Kreuzer, Franz Joseph, Rev: Shield, Silver	—	18.00
□ 1892–1896	10 Filler, Franz Joseph, Rev: Crown, Cupro-Nickel	.18	.30
□ 1906–1916	10 Filler, Franz Joseph, Rev: Crown, Nickel	.22	.40
□ 1926–1938	10 Filler, Horthy Regency, Crown, Cupro-Nickel	.28	.60
□ 1940–1944	10 Filler, Horthy Regency, Stainless Steel	—	.12

DATE	COIN TYPE/VARIETY/METAL	ABP FINE	AVERAGE FINE
□ 1946–1947	10 Filler, Republic, Dove, Copper-Aluminum	—	.12
□ 1948–1951	10 Filler, Republic, Rev: Spray, Aluminum	—	.20
□ 1868–1872	20 Kreuzer, Franz Joseph, Rev: Shield, Silver	—	10.00
□ 1892–1894	20 Filler, Franz Joseph, Rev: crown, Cupro-Nickel	.40	1.00

DATE	COIN TYPE/VARIETY/METAL	ABP FINE	AVERAGE FINE
☐ 1906–1914	20 Filler, Franz Joseph, Rev: Crown, Nickel	$ .40	$1.00
☐ 1926–1938	20 Filler, Horthy Regency, Crown, Cupro-Nickel	2.00	4.00
☐ 1940–1944	20 Filler, Horthy Regency, Center Hole, Stainless Steel	.75	2.00
☐ 1946–1947	20 Filler, Republic, Ears of Wheat, Copper-Aluminum	—	.12
☐ 1948–1950	20 Filler, Republic, Rev: Spray, Aluminum	—	.18
☐ 1926–1938	50 Filler, Horthy Regency, Crown, Cupro-Nickel	.16	.40
☐ 1948–1950	50 Filler, Republic, Rev: Spray, Aluminum	.40	1.00

DATE	COIN TYPE/VARIETY/METAL	ABP FINE	AVERAGE FINE
☐ 1926–1938	1 Pengo, Horthy Regency, Arms, Silver	1.00	2.00
☐ 1941	1 Pengo, Horthy Regency, Hungarian Arms, Aluminum	—	.12
☐ 1892–1916	1 Korona, Franz Joseph, Rev: Crown, Silver	—	5.00
☐ 1946–1947	1 Forint, Republic, Hungarian Arms, Aluminum	—	2.00
☐ 1949–1951	1 Forint, Republic, Rev: Spray, Aluminum	.80	2.00
☐ 1929–1938	2 Pengo, Horthy Regency, Madonna, Silver	.32	.60
☐ 1935	2 Pengo, Horthy Regency, Rakoczi, Silver	—	3.00
☐ 1935	2 Pengo, Horthy Regency, University of Budapest, Silver	—	3.00
☐ 1936	2 Pengo, Horthy Regency, Liszt, Silver	—	2.00
☐ 1941	2 Pengo, Horthy Regency, Hungarian Arms, Aluminum	—	.20
☐ 1912–1914	2 Korona, Franz Joseph, Silver	—	5.00
☐ 1946–1947	2 Forint, Republic, Hungarian Arms, Aluminum	—	2.00

DATE	COIN TYPE/VARIETY/METAL	ABP FINE	AVERAGE FINE
□ 1950–1951	2 Forint, Republic, Star With Rays, Hammer and Wheat, Rev: Wreath, Cupro-Nickel	$1.00	$2.50
□ 1938	5 Pengo, Horthy Regency, Death of St. Stephen 900th Anniversary, Silver	.35	.75
□ 1943	5 Pengo, Horthy Regency, 75th Birthday of Admiral Horthy, Aluminum	—	5.00
□ 1939	5 Pengo, Horthy Regency, Bust of Admiral Horthy, Silver	—	5.00
□ 1945	5 Pengo, Horthy Regency, Parliament Building, Aluminum	.60	1.00
□ 1948	5 Forint, Republic, Revolution Commemorative, Silver	—	3.00
□ 1900–1909	5 Korona, Franz Joseph, Rev: Angels Holding Crown, Silver	—	14.00
□ 1907	5 Korona, Franz Joseph, Jubilee Coronation Scene, Silver	—	18.00
□ 1930	5 Pengo, Horthy Regency, Bust, Silver	—	5.00
□ 1946–1947	5 Forint, Republic, Head of Kossuth, Silver	—	4.00
□ 1948	10 Forint, Republic, Revolution Commemorative, Silver	—	3.00
□ 1948	20 Forint, Republic, Revolution Commemorative, Silver	—	7.00

ICELAND

Iceland's coinage was originally that of its neighbors, Norway and Denmark. Although an independent republic, Iceland did not have its own currency, the krona, until 1922. In 1944, new denominations were added. In 1981, a new krona was introduced that was equal to 100 old kronur.

Iceland—Type Coinage

DATE	COIN TYPE/VARIETY/METAL	ABP FINE	AVERAGE FINE
□ 1926–1942	1 Eyrir, Kingdom, Bronze	$ .75	$1.25
□ 1946–1966	1 Eyrir, Republic, Bronze	—	.05

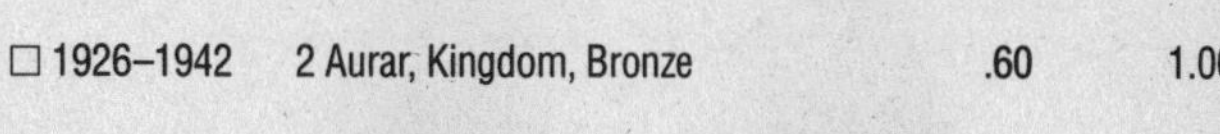

DATE	COIN TYPE/VARIETY/METAL	ABP FINE	AVERAGE FINE
□ 1926–1942	2 Aurar, Kingdom, Bronze	.60	1.00

DATE	COIN TYPE/VARIETY/METAL	ABP FINE	AVERAGE FINE
☐ 1926–1942	5 Aurar, Kingdom, Bronze	$1.50	$3.00
☐ 1946–1966	5 Aurar, Republic, Bronze	—	.05
☐ 1981	5 Aurar, Sting Ray, Bronze	—	.05

DATE	COIN TYPE/VARIETY/METAL	ABP FINE	AVERAGE FINE
☐ 1922–1942	10 Aurar, Kingdom, Cupro-Nickel	1.40	2.50
☐ 1946–1969	10 Aurar, Republic, Cupro-Nickel	—	.20
☐ 1970–1974	10 Aurar, Republic, Aluminum	—	.05
☐ 1981	10 Aurar, Cuttlefish, Bronze	—	.05

DATE	COIN TYPE/VARIETY/METAL	ABP FINE	AVERAGE FINE
☐ 1926–1942	25 Aurar, Kingdom, Cupro-Nickel	.50	.90
☐ 1948–1967	25 Aurar, Republic, Cupro-Nickel	—	.08
☐ 1969–1974	50 Aurar, Republic, Brass	—	.05
☐ 1981	50 Aurar, Lobster, Bronze	—	—

DATE	COIN TYPE/VARIETY/METAL	ABP FINE	AVERAGE FINE
☐ 1926–1942	1 Kronur, Kingdom, Cupro-Nickel	—	.05
☐ 1946	1 Kronur, Republic, Aluminum-Bronze	—	.05
☐ 1957–1975	1 Kronur, Republic, Brass	—	.05
☐ 1976–1980	1 Kronur, Republic, Aluminum	—	.05
☐ 1981–1987	1 Kronur, Cod, Cupro-Nickel	—	.05
☐ 1990	1 Kronur, Cod, Stainless Steel	—	.05

DATE	COIN TYPE/VARIETY/METAL	ABP FINE	AVERAGE FINE
□ 1925–1940	2 Kronur, Kingdom, Cupro-Nickel	$1.00	$1.75
□ 1946	2 Kronur, Republic, Aluminum-Bronze	—	.15
□ 1958–1966	2 Kronur, Republic, Brass	—	.15
□ 1969–1980	5 Kronur, Republic, Cupro-Nickel	—	.10
□ 1981–1987	5 Kronur, Dolphins, Cupro-Nickel	—	.10
□ 1967–1980	10 Kronur, Republic, Cupro-Nickel	—	.05
□ 1984–1987	10 Kronur, Capelins, Cupro-Nickel	—	.10
□ 1968	50 Kronur, Sovereignty—50th Anniversary, Nickel	.60	1.25
□ 1970–1980	50 Kronur, Parliament, Cupro-Nickel	—	.20
□ 1987	50 Kronur, Crab, Brass	—	.05
□ 1961	500 Kronur, Sesquicentennial—Sigurdsson, Gold	—	125.00
□ 1974	500 Kronur, 1st Settlement—1100th Anniversary, Silver	—	6.00
□ 1986	500 Kronur, Icelandic Bank Notes—100th Anniversary, Silver	—	30.00
□ 1974	1000 Kronur, 1st Settlement—1100th Anniversary, Silver	—	4.00
□ 1974	10000 Kronur, 1st Settlement—1100th Anniversary, Gold	—	175.00

INDIA

The first coins were used in the early 4th century B.C., as seen in silver punchmarked coins. Copper-cast coins appeared in 200 B.C., with lead coins in 100 A.D. The silver dramma was in evidence in 190 A.D., and the copper drachmas and gold denara in 350. The gold mohur appeared in the 1500s, and the silver rupees in the 1600s. The copper paisas were in use in the 1800s and the cupronickel rupees in 1974. Decimal coins were used in 1957. The currency today is the rupee.

India—Decimal and Non-Decimal Coinage

DATE	COIN TYPE/VARIETY/METAL	ABP FINE	AVERAGE FINE
□ 1957–1962	1 Naye Paisa, Bronze	—	$ .10
□ 1962–1963	1 Naye Paisa, Brass	—	.10
□ 1964	1 Paisa, Bronze	—	.10
□ 1964	1 Paisa, Brass	—	.10

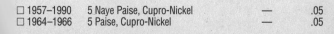

DATE	COIN TYPE/VARIETY/METAL	ABP FINE	AVERAGE FINE
□ 1965–1970	1 Paisa, Aluminum	—	$ .10
□ 1950–1955	1 Pice, Bronze	—	.15
□ 1957–1963	2 Naye Paise, Cupro-Nickel	—	.10
□ 1964	2 Paise, Cupro-Nickel	—	.10
□ 1965–1981	2 Paise, Aluminum	—	.10
□ 1964–1981	3 Paise, Aluminum	—	.05
□ 1950–1955	½ Anna, Cupro-Nickel	—	.10
□ 1957–1990	5 Naye Paise, Cupro-Nickel	—	.05
□ 1964–1966	5 Paise, Cupro-Nickel	—	.05

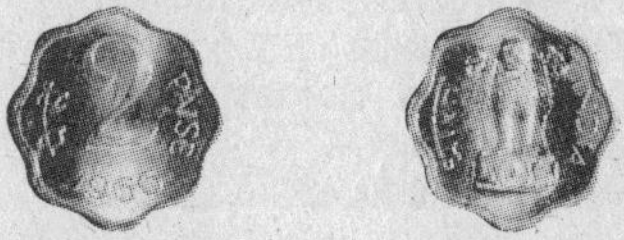

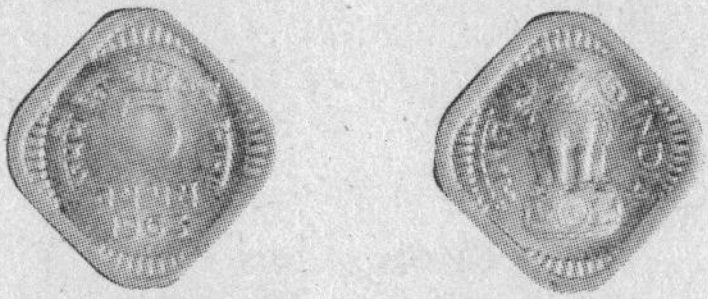

DATE	COIN TYPE/VARIETY/METAL	ABP FINE	AVERAGE FINE
☐ 1967–1984	5 Paise, Aluminum	—	$ .05
☐ 1976	5 Paise, FAO Issues: Food & Work For All, Aluminum	—	.05
☐ 1977	5 Paise, FAO Issues: Save For Development, Aluminum	—	.05
☐ 1978	5 Paise, FAO Issues: Food & Shelter For All, Aluminum	—	.05
☐ 1979	5 Paise, International Year of the Child, Aluminum	—	.05
☐ 1950–1955	1 Anna, Cupro-Nickel	$ .15	.30

DATE	COIN TYPE/VARIETY/METAL	ABP FINE	AVERAGE FINE
☐ 1957–1963	10 Naye Paise, Cupro-Nickel	—	.15
☐ 1964–1967	10 Paise, Cupro-Nickel	—	.15
☐ 1968–1982	10 Paise, Brass	—	.15

DATE	COIN TYPE/VARIETY/METAL	ABP FINE	AVERAGE FINE
☐ 1974	10 Paise, FAO Issue, Brass	—	.10
☐ 1975	10 Paise, FAO Issue—Woman's Year, Brass	—	.05
☐ 1976	10 Paise, FAO Issue—Food & Work For All, Brass	—	.05

DATE	COIN TYPE/VARIETY/METAL	ABP FINE	AVERAGE FINE
☐ 1977	10 Paise, FAO Issue—Save For Development, Brass	—	$ .05
☐ 1978	10 Paise, FAO Issue—Food & Shelter For All, Brass	—	.05
☐ 1979	10 Paise, International Year of the Child, Brass	—	.05
☐ 1980	10 Paise, Rural Women's Advancement, Brass	—	.05
☐ 1981	10 Paise, World Food Day, Brass	—	.05
☐ 1982	10 Paise, IX Asian Games, Brass	—	.05
☐ 1983–1990	10 Paise, Aluminum	—	.05
☐ 1950–1955	2 Annas, Cupro-Nickel	—	.20

DATE	COIN TYPE/VARIETY/METAL	ABP FINE	AVERAGE FINE
☐ 1968–1971	20 Paise, Brass	—	.05
☐ 1969	20 Paise, Aluminum-Bronze	—	.05
☐ 1970–1971	20 Paise, FAO Issue, Aluminum-Bronze	—	.05
☐ 1982–1991	20 Paise, Aluminum	—	.05
☐ 1982	20 Paise, World Food Day, Aluminum	—	.05
☐ 1983	20 Paise, FAO Issue—Fisheries, Aluminum	—	.05

DATE	COIN TYPE/VARIETY/METAL	ABP FINE	AVERAGE FINE
☐ 1950–1956	1/4 Rupee, Nickel	—	.30

DATE	COIN TYPE/VARIETY/METAL	ABP FINE	AVERAGE FINE
☐ 1957–1968	25 Paise, Nickel	—	$ .05
☐ 1957–1963	25 Paise, Nickel	—	.10
☐ 1972–1990	25 Paise, Cupro-Nickel	—	.05
☐ 1980	25 Paise, Rural Women's Advancement, Cupro-Nickel	—	.05
☐ 1981	25 Paise, World Food Day, Cupro-Nickel	—	.05
☐ 1982	25 Paise, IX Asian Games, Cupro-Nickel	—	.05
☐ 1985	25 Paise, Forestry, Cupro-Nickel	—	.05
☐ 1988–1991	25 Paise, Rhinoceros, Stainless Steel	—	.05

DATE	COIN TYPE/VARIETY/METAL	ABP FINE	AVERAGE FINE
☐ 1950–1956	½ Rupee, Nickel	—	.40
☐ 1964–1983	50 Paise, Nickel	—	.10
☐ 1964	50 Paise, Nehru Death, Nickel	—	.20
☐ 1969	50 Paise, Centennial—Mahatma Ghandi, Nickel	—	.10
☐ 1972–1973	50 Paise, Independence—25th Anniversary, Cupro-Nickel	—	.10

DATE	COIN TYPE/VARIETY/METAL	ABP FINE	AVERAGE FINE
☐ 1973	50 Paise, FAO Issue—Grow More Food, Cupro-Nickel	—	.10
☐ 1982	50 Paise, National Integration, Cupro-Nickel	—	.10
☐ 1984–1990	50 Paise, Cupro-Nickel	—	.05
☐ 1985	50 Paise, Indira Ghandi—Death, Cupro-Nickel	—	.15
☐ 1985	50 Paise, Reserve Bank of India—Golden Jubilee, Cupro-Nickel	—	.15
☐ 1986	50 Paise, FAO—Fisheries, Cupro-Nickel	—	.20

DATE	COIN TYPE/VARIETY/METAL	ABP FINE	AVERAGE FINE
□ 1988–1991	50 Paise, Parliament Building, Stainless Steel	—	$ .05
□ 1950–1954	1 Rupee, Nickel	$ .30	.90
□ 1962–1974	1 Rupee, Nickel	—	.30

DATE	COIN TYPE/VARIETY/METAL	ABP FINE	AVERAGE FINE
□ 1964	1 Rupee, Nehru Death, Nickel	—	.40
□ 1969	1 Rupee, Mahatma Ghandi Centennial, Nickel	—	.15
□ 1975–1991	1 Rupee, Cupro-Nickel	—	.10
□ 1985	1 Rupee, Youth Year, Cupro-Nickel	—	.15
□ 1987	1 Rupee, FAO—Small Farmers, Cupro-Nickel	—	.15
□ 1989	1 Rupee, FAO—Food & Environment, Cupro-Nickel	—	.05
□ 1989	1 Rupee, Nehru's Birth—100th Anniversary, Cupro-Nickel	—	.05
□ 1990	1 Rupee, SAARC Year—Care For the Girl Child, Cupro-Nickel	—	.05
□ 1990	1 Rupee, ICDS—15th Anniversary, Cupro-Nickel	—	.05
□ 1990	1 Rupee, FAO Farming Scene, Cupro-Nickel	—	.05
□ 1990	1 Rupee, Dr. Ambedker, Cupro-Nickel	—	.05
□ 1991	1 Rupee, Rajiv Ghandi, Cupro-Nickel	—	.05
□ 1991	1 Rupee, Parliamentary Conference, Cupro-Nickel	—	.05
□ 1982	2 Rupees, IX Asian Games, Cupro-Nickel	—	.20
□ 1982–1992	2 Rupees, National Integration, Cupro-Nickel	—	.20
□ 1985	2 Rupees, Reserve Bank of India—Golden Jubilee, Cupro-Nickel	12.00	20.00 Proof
□ 1985	5 Rupees, Indira Ghandi Death, Cupro-Nickel	—	.35
□ 1989	5 Rupees, Nehru's Birth—100th Anniversary, Cupro-Nickel	.50	1.00

DATE	COIN TYPE/VARIETY/METAL	ABP FINE	AVERAGE FINE
□ 1969	10 Rupees, Centennial Birth of Mahatma Ghandi, Silver	—	$1.50
□ 1970	10 Rupees, FAO Issue, Silver	—	2.50
□ 1972	10 Rupees, Independence—25th Anniversary, Silver	—	2.50
□ 1973	10 Rupees, FAO Issue, Silver	—	2.50
□ 1974	10 Rupees, FAO Issue, Cupro-Nickel	$ .50	1.00
□ 1975	10 Rupees, FAO—Women's Year, Cupro-Nickel	.50	1.00
□ 1976	10 Rupees, FAO—Food & Work For All, Cupro-Nickel	.50	1.00
□ 1977	10 Rupees, FAO—Save For Development, Cupro-Nickel	.50	1.00
□ 1978	10 Rupees, FAO—Food & Shelter For All, Cupro-Nickel	.50	1.00
□ 1979	10 Rupees, International Year of the Child, Cupro-Nickel	.50	1.00
□ 1980	10 Rupees, Rural Women's Advancement, Cupro-Nickel	.70	1.50
□ 1981	10 Rupees, World Food Day, Cupro-Nickel	.70	1.50
□ 1982	10 Rupees, IX Asian Games, Cupro-Nickel	.70	1.50
□ 1982	10 Rupees, National Integration, Cupro-Nickel	.70	1.50
□ 1985	10 Rupees, Youth Year, Cupro-Nickel	8.00	15.00
□ 1985	10 Rupees, Reserve Bank of India—Golden Jubilee, Cupro-Nickel	8.00	15.00

DATE	COIN TYPE/VARIETY/METAL	ABP FINE	AVERAGE FINE
☐ 1973	20 Rupees, FAO Issue, Silver	—	$ 3.00
☐ 1985	20 Rupees, Death of Indira Ghandi, Cupro-Nickel	$ 5.00	8.00
☐ 1986	20 Rupees, FAO Fisheries, Cupro-Nickel	1.50	3.00
☐ 1987	20 Rupees, FAO—Small Farmers, Cupro-Nickel	1.50	3.00
☐ 1989	20 Rupees, Nehru's Birth—100th Anniversary, Cupro-Nickel	1.50	3.00
☐ 1974	50 Rupees, FAO Issue, Silver	—	3.00
☐ 1975	50 Rupees, FAO—Women's Year, Silver	—	3.00
☐ 1976	50 Rupees, FAO—Food & Work For All, Silver	—	3.00
☐ 1977	50 Rupees, FAO—Save For Development, Silver	—	3.00
☐ 1978	50 Rupees, FAO—Food & Shelter For All, Silver	—	3.00
☐ 1979	50 Rupees, International Year of the Child, Silver	—	3.00
☐ 1980	100 Rupees, Rural Women's Advancement, Silver	—	8.00
☐ 1981	100 Rupees, International Year of the Child, Silver	—	8.00
☐ 1981	100 Rupees, World Food Day, Silver	—	8.00
☐ 1982	100 Rupees, National Integration, Silver	—	8.00
☐ 1982	100 Rupees, IX Asian Games, Silver	—	8.00
☐ 1985	100 Rupees, Youth Year, Silver	—	8.00
☐ 1985	100 Rupees, Death of Indira Ghandi, Silver	—	18.00
☐ 1985	100 Rupees, Reserve Bank of India—Golden Jubilee, Silver	—	21.00
☐ 1986	100 Rupees, FAO—Fisheries, Silver	—	21.00
☐ 1987	100 Rupees, FAO—Small Farmers, Silver	—	21.00
☐ 1989	100 Rupees, Nehru's Birth—100th Anniversary, Silver	—	21.00

IRELAND

The first coins—pennies—appeared in the late 10th century, followed by farthings and halfpennies around 1190. In the mid-1400s, groats were issued, and shillings in the mid-1500s. In the mid-17th century, the Inchiquin was formed. In 1649, halfcrowns and crowns were issued. Cupro-nickel replaced silver in 1951, and a decimal currency system was set up in 1971.

Ireland—Type Coinage

DATE	COIN TYPE/VARIETY/METAL	ABP FINE	AVERAGE FINE
☐ 1928–1938	1/2 Penny, Saorstat Eirean, Bronze	—	$ .50
☐ 1939–1969	1/2 Penny, Eire, Bronze	—	.50

☐ 1969–1989	1/2 Penny, Irish Decimal, Bronze	—	.05

DATE	COIN TYPE/VARIETY/METAL	ABP FINE	AVERAGE FINE
☐ 1928–1938	1 Penny, Saorstat Eireann, Bronze	$ .30	$ .70
☐ 1939–1969	1 Penny, Eire, Bronze	—	.20
☐ 1969–1989	1 Penny, Irish Decimal, Bronze	—	.05
☐ 1990–1993	1 Penny, Irish Decimal, Copper-plated Steel	—	.05
☐ 1969–1989	2 Pence, Irish Decimal, Bronze	—	.05
☐ 1990–1993	2 Pence, Irish Decimal, Copper Plated Steel	—	.05

☐ 1969–1993	5 Pence, Irish Decimal, Cupro-Nickel	—	.05

DATE	COIN TYPE/VARIETY/METAL	ABP FINE	AVERAGE FINE
□ 1969–1993	10 Pence, Irish Decimal, Cupro-Nickel	—	$ .05
□ 1969–1993	20 Pence, Irish Decimal, Nickel-Brass	—	.20

DATE	COIN TYPE/VARIETY/METAL	ABP FINE	AVERAGE FINE
□ 1969–1993	50 Pence, Irish Decimal, Cupro-Nickel	$ .15	.50

DATE	COIN TYPE/VARIETY/METAL	ABP FINE	AVERAGE FINE
□ 1928–1938	1 Farthing, Soarstat Eireann, Bronze	.25	.50
□ 1939–1969	1 Farthing, Eire, Bronze	.25	.50
□ 1928–1938	1 Shilling, Saorstat Eireann, Silver	—	1.50

DATE	COIN TYPE/VARIETY/METAL	ABP FINE	AVERAGE FINE
□ 1939–1942	1 Shilling, Eire, Silver	—	2.00
□ 1942–1969	1 Shilling, Eire, Cupro-Nickel	—	.20
□ 1969–1993	1 Pound, Irish Decimal, Cupro-Nickel	2.00	3.00

DATE	COIN TYPE/VARIETY/METAL	ABP FINE	AVERAGE FINE
□ 1928–1938	1 Florin, Saorstat Eireann, Silver	—	$2.50
□ 1939–1942	1 Florin, Eire, Silver	—	2.50
□ 1942–1969	1 Florin, Eire, Cupro-Nickel	$ .25	.90

□ 1928–1938	Threepence, Saorstat Eirea, Nickel	.10	.40
□ 1939–1942	Threepence, Eire, Nickel	.50	1.25
□ 1942–1969	Threepence, Eire, Cupro-Nickel	.50	1.25

□ 1928–1938	Sixpence, Saorstat Eireann, Nickel	.40	.75
□ 1939–1942	Sixpence, Eire, Nickel	.25	.60
□ 1942–1969	Sixpence, Eire, Cupro-Nickel	—	.25

ISRAEL

The first coins were used in the 5th century B.C. In 300 B.C. silver tetradrachms and gold staters were produced. Bronze coins appeared in 26 A.D. The copper fals was in evidence in the 600s and 700s, followed by the gold bezant and the base-silver denier. Bronze mils, cupro-nickel prutots, and the silver lira became popular in the 20th century. Today's currency is the livre.

Israel—Type Commemorative and Monetary Reform Coinage

DATE	COIN TYPE/VARIETY/METAL	ABP FINE	AVERAGE FINE
□ 1948–1949	1 Prutah, Hebrew Date 5709 Anchor, Aluminum	—	$ .25

DATE	COIN TYPE/VARIETY/METAL	ABP FINE	AVERAGE FINE
☐ 1949	5 Prutah, Hebrew Date 5709 Harp, Bronze	—	$ .25
☐ 1949	10 Prutah, Hebrew Date 5709 Amphora, Bronze	—	.25
☐ 1952	10 Prutah, Hebrew Date 5712, Aluminum	—	.30
☐ 1960–1979	1 Agora, Aluminum	$1.50	2.50
☐ 1973	1 Agora, 25th Anniversary of Bank of Israel, Nickel	—	.30
☐ 1973	1 Agora, 25th Anniversary of Independence, Aluminum	—	.30

DATE	COIN TYPE/VARIETY/METAL	ABP FINE	AVERAGE FINE
☐ 1948–1949	25 Mils, Hebrew Date 5708–09 Grape Clusters, Aluminum	15.00	25.00

DATE	COIN TYPE/VARIETY/METAL	ABP FINE	AVERAGE FINE
□ 1949	25 Pruta, Hebrew Date 5709 Grape Clusters, Cupro-Nickel	—	$ .30
□ 1954	25 Pruta, Hebrew Date 5714, Nickel-clad Steel	—	.30

DATE	COIN TYPE/VARIETY/METAL	ABP FINE	AVERAGE FINE
□ 1949–1954	50 Pruta, Hebrew Date 5709–14 Fig Leaves, Cupro-Nickel	—	.35
□ 1954	50 Pruta, Hebrew Date 5714, Nickel-clad Steel	—	.35
□ 1960–1972	5 Agorot, Aluminum-Bronze	$1.50	2.50
□ 1973	5 Agorot, 25th Anniversary of Independence, Cupro-Nickel	.50	1.00
□ 1973	5 Agorot, 25th Anniversary of Bank of Israel, Nickel	.50	1.00
□ 1974–1979	5 Agorot, Cupro-Nickel	.50	1.00
□ 1976–1979	5 Agorot, Aluminum	—	.15

DATE	COIN TYPE/VARIETY/METAL	ABP FINE	AVERAGE FINE
☐ 1949	100 Pruta, Hebrew Date 5709 Palm Tree, Cupro-Nickel	$ .10	$ .50
☐ 1954	100 Pruta, Hebrew Date 5714, Nickel-clad Steel	.10	.50

DATE	COIN TYPE/VARIETY/METAL	ABP FINE	AVERAGE FINE
☐ 1960–1972	10 Agorot, Aluminum-Bronze	—	.35
☐ 1973	10 Agorot, 25th Anniversary of Independence, Cupro-Nickel	.20	.75
☐ 1973	10 Agorot, 25th Anniversary of Bank of Israel, Nickel	.20	.75
☐ 1974–1979	10 Agorot, Cupro-Nickel	.20	.70
☐ 1977–1980	10 Agorot, Aluminum	—	.05

DATE	COIN TYPE/VARIETY/METAL	ABP FINE	AVERAGE FINE
☐ 1949	250 Pruta, Hebrew Date 5709 Ears of Wheat, Silver	.50	1.00
☐ 1949	250 Pruta, Hebrew Date 5709 Ears of Wheat, Cupro-Nickel	.50	1.00

DATE	COIN TYPE/VARIETY/METAL	ABP FINE	AVERAGE FINE
□ 1960–1979	25 Agorot, Aluminum-Bronze	—	$ .05
□ 1974–1979	25 Agorot, Cupro-Nickel	—	.05
□ 1974–1979	25 Agorot, 25th Anniversary of Bank of Israel, Nickel	$ .50	1.00

DATE	COIN TYPE/VARIETY/METAL	ABP FINE	AVERAGE FINE
□ 1949	500 Pruta, Hebrew Date 5709 Pomegranates, Silver	1.50	3.00
□ 1961–1962	½ Pound, Feast of Purim, Cupro-Nickel	3.00	7.00

DATE	COIN TYPE/VARIETY/METAL	ABP FINE	AVERAGE FINE
□ 1963–1979	½ Lira, 25th Anniversary of Bank of Israel, Nickel	.50	1.00
□ 1963–1979	½ Lira, 25th Anniversary of Independence, Cupro-Nickel	.50	1.00
□ 1963–1979	½ Lira, Cupro-Nickel	—	.05
□ 1958	1 Pound, Law Is Light, Cupro-Nickel	—	—
□ 1960	1 Pound, Henrietta Szold—Hadassa Medical Center, Cupro-Nickel	12.00	22.00
□ 1960	1 Pound, Deganya, Cupro-Nickel	1.00	2.00

DATE	COIN TYPE/VARIETY/METAL	ABP FINE	AVERAGE FINE
□ 1961	1 Pound, Heroism & Sacrifice, Cupro-Nickel, can't find	—	—
□ 1962	1 Pound, Chanuka—Italian Lamp, Cupro-Nickel	$12.00	$20.00
□ 1963	1 Pound, Chanuka—North African Lamp, Cupro-Nickel	12.00	20.00

DATE	COIN TYPE/VARIETY/METAL	ABP FINE	AVERAGE FINE
□ 1963–1980	1 Lira, Cupro-Nickel	—	—

DATE	COIN TYPE/VARIETY/METAL	ABP FINE	AVERAGE FINE
□ 1958	5 Pounds, Tenth Anniversary of Republic, Silver	—	15.00
□ 1959	5 Pounds, Ingathering of Exiles, Silver	—	20.00
□ 1960	5 Pounds, Dr. Theodore Herzl, Silver	—	20.00
□ 1961	5 Pounds, Bar Mitzvahr, Silver	—	40.00
□ 1962	5 Pounds, 10th Anniversary—Death of Chaim Weizman, Gold	—	200.00
□ 1962	5 Pounds, Industrialization of the Negev, Silver	—	40.00
□ 1963	5 Pounds, Seafaring, Silver	—	200.00
□ 1964	5 Pounds, Israel Museum, Silver	—	35.00

DATE	COIN TYPE/VARIETY/METAL	ABP FINE	AVERAGE FINE
☐ 1978–1979	5 Lirot, Cupro-Nickel	—	—
☐ 1960	20 Pounds, Dr. Theodore Herzl, Gold	—	$200.00
☐ 1964	50 Pounds, 10th Anniversary—Bank of Israel, Gold	—	300.00
☐ 1962	100 Pounds, 10th Anniversary—Death of Chaim Weizman, Gold	—	400.00

ITALY

The first coins were used in the 6th century B.C., with an unusual technique called incuse, involving the use of similar designs on both sides of the coin. The early coins were silver, but from about 440 B.C. bronze coins came into evidence, then gold coins appeared toward the end of the 5th century. Julius Caesar's head appeared on coins in 44 B.C., right before his assassination. Around 31 B.C. the Roman coinage system had denominations in gold, silver, and bronze that survived for the next 200 years. The decimal system was set up in 1804, and today's currency is the lira.

Italy—Type and Republic Coinage

DATE	COIN TYPE/VARIETY/METAL	ABP FINE	AVERAGE FINE
☐ 1861–1867	1 Centesimo, Vittorio Emanuel, Copper	$ .30	.70
☐ 1895–1900	1 Centesimo, Umberto I, Copper	.35	1.00
☐ 1902–1908	1 Centesimo, Vittorio III, Bronze	.30	.90
☐ 1908–1918	1 Centesimo, Vittorio III, Bronze	.30	.90

DATE	COIN TYPE/VARIETY/METAL	ABP FINE	AVERAGE FINE
□ 1861–1867	2 Centesimi, Vittorio Emanuel, Copper	—	$ .45
□ 1895–1900	2 Centesimi, Umberto I, Copper	$ .10	.50
□ 1903–1908	2 Centesimi, Vittorio III, Bronze	.10	.50
□ 1908–1917	2 Centesimi, Vittorio III, Bronze	.10	.50
□ 1861–1867	5 Centesimi, Vittorio Emanuel, Copper	.15	.55
□ 1895–1896	5 Centesimi, Umberto I, Copper	4.00	10.00
□ 1908–1918	5 Centesimi, Vittorio III, Bronze	.40	1.00

DATE	COIN TYPE/VARIETY/METAL	ABP FINE	AVERAGE FINE
□ 1919–1937	5 Centesimi, Vittorio III, Bronze	—	.24
□ 1936–1939	5 Centesimi, Vittorio III, Bronze	—	.24
□ 1939–1943	5 Centesimi, Vittorio III, Aluminum-Bronze	—	.24

DATE	COIN TYPE/VARIETY/METAL	ABP FINE	AVERAGE FINE
□ 1862–1867	10 Centesimi, Vittorio Emanuel, Copper	.65	1.25
□ 1893–1894	10 Centesimi, Umberto I, Copper	.65	1.25
□ 1908	10 Centesimi, Vittorio III, Bronze	3.75	9.00
□ 1911	10 Centesimi, Vittorio III, 50th Anniversary of Kingdom, Bronze	1.00	2.00
□ 1919–1937	10 Centesimi, Vittorio III, Bronze	—	.40
□ 1939–1943	10 Centesimi, Vittorio III, Aluminum-Bronze	—	.20
□ 1863–1867	20 Centesimi, Vittorio Eman, Silver	—	2.50

DATE	COIN TYPE/VARIETY/METAL	ABP FINE	AVERAGE FINE
☐ 1894–1895	20 Centesimi, Umberto I, Cupro-Nickel	—	—
☐ 1908–1935	20 Centesimi, Vittorio III, Nickel	$ .20	$ .50
☐ 1918–1920	20 Centesimi, Vittorio III, Cupro-Nickel	.20	.45
☐ 1936–1938	20 Centesimi, Vittorio III, Nickel	4.00	12.00
☐ 1939–1943	20 Centesimi, Vittorio III, Stainless Steel	—	.30
☐ 1902–1903	25 Centesimi, Vittorio III, Nickel	8.00	14.00

DATE	COIN TYPE/VARIETY/METAL	ABP FINE	AVERAGE FINE
☐ 1861–1863	50 Centesimi, Vittorio Eman., Silver	—	4.00
☐ 1863–1867	50 Centesimi, Vittorio Eman., Silver	—	4.00
☐ 1889–1892	50 Centesimi, Umberto I, Silver	—	20.00
☐ 1919–1935	50 Centesimi, Vittorio III, Nickel	.90	2.00
☐ 1936–1938	50 Centesimi, Vittorio III, Nickel	8.00	12.00
☐ 1939–1943	50 Centesimi, Vittorio III, Stainless Steel	—	.30
☐ 1861–1867	1 Lira, Vittorio Emanuele II, Silver	—	20.00
☐ 1863	1 Lira, Vittorio Emanuele, Silver	—	40.00
☐ 1883–1900	1 Lira, Umberto I, Silver	—	3.50
☐ 1901–1907	1 Lira, Vittorio III, Silver	—	4.50
☐ 1908–1913	1 Lira, Vittorio III, Silver	—	4.00
☐ 1915–1917	1 Lira, Vittorio III, Silver	—	3.00

DATE	COIN TYPE/VARIETY/METAL	ABP FINE	AVERAGE FINE
☐ 1922–1935	1 Lira, Vittorio III, Nickel	.35	.50
☐ 1936–1938	1 Lira, Vittorio III, Nickel	7.00	12.00
☐ 1939–1943	1 Lira, Vittorio III, Stainless Steel	—	.30
☐ 1946–1950	1 Lira, Republic, Aluminum	2.00	4.00
☐ 1951–1989	1 Lira, Republic, Aluminum	—	.20
☐ 1861–1863	2 Lire, Vittorio Emanuele I, Silver	—	6.00
☐ 1863	2 Lire, Vittorio Emanuele, Silver	—	7.00

DATE	COIN TYPE/VARIETY/METAL	ABP FINE	AVERAGE FINE
□ 1881–1899	2 Lire, Umberto I, Silver	—	$4.50
□ 1901–1907	2 Lire, Vittorio III, Silver	—	11.00
□ 1908–1912	2 Lire, Vittorio III, Silver	—	5.00
□ 1911	2 Lire, Vittorio III, 50th Anniversary of Kingdom, Silver	—	10.00
□ 1914–1917	2 Lire, Vittorio III, Silver	—	3.50

DATE	COIN TYPE/VARIETY/METAL	ABP FINE	AVERAGE FINE
□ 1922–1935	2 Lire, Vittorio III, Nickel	$ .25	1.00
□ 1936–1938	2 Lire, Vittorio III, Nickel	7.00	15.00
□ 1939–1943	2 Lire, Vittorio III, Stainless Steel	.30	.50
□ 1946–1950	2 Lire, Republic, Aluminum	3.00	6.00
□ 1953–1989	2 Lire, Republic, Aluminum	—	.20
□ 1861	5 Lire, Vittorio Emanuele I, Italian Unification, Silver	—	300.00
□ 1861–1878	5 Lire, Vittorio Emanuele I, Silver	—	12.00
□ 1863–1865	5 Lire, Vittorio Emanuele, Gold	—	65.00
□ 1878–1879	5 Lire, Umberto I, Silver	—	20.00
□ 1901	5 Lire, Vittorio III, Silver	—	1000.00
□ 1911	5 Lire, Vittorio III, 50th Anniversary of Kingdom, Silver	—	125.00
□ 1914	5 Lire, Vittorio III, Silver	—	400.00

DATE	COIN TYPE/VARIETY/METAL	ABP FINE	AVERAGE FINE
□ 1926–1935	5 Lire, Vittorio III, Silver	—	6.00
□ 1936–1941	5 Lire, Vittorio III, Silver	—	10.00
□ 1946–1950	5 Lire, Republic, Aluminum	—	.40
□ 1951–1990	5 Lire, Republic, Aluminum	—	.40
□ 1861–1865	10 Lire, Vittorio Emanuele, Gold	—	1200.00
□ 1910–1927	10 Lire, Vittorio III, Gold	—	600.00
□ 1926–1934	10 Lire, Vittorio III, Silver	—	30.00

DATE	COIN TYPE/VARIETY/METAL	ABP FINE	AVERAGE FINE
□ 1946–1950	10 Lire, Republic, Aluminum	—	$ .10

DATE	COIN TYPE/VARIETY/METAL	ABP FINE	AVERAGE FINE
□ 1951–1990	10 Lire, Republic, Aluminum	—	.10
□ 1923	20 Lire, Vittorio III, Anniversary of Fascist Government, Gold	—	140.00
□ 1928	20 Lire, Vittorio III, End of WWI 10th Anniversary, Gold	—	70.00
□ 1879–1897	20 Lire, Umberto I, Gold	—	40.00
□ 1902–1910	20 Lire, Vittorio III, Gold	—	300.00
□ 1910–1927	20 Lire, Vittorio III, Gold	—	200.00
□ 1927–1934	20 Lire, Vittorio III, Silver	—	40.00
□ 1936–1941	20 Lire, Vittorio III, Silver	—	200.00

DATE	COIN TYPE/VARIETY/METAL	ABP FINE	AVERAGE FINE
□ 1957–1959	20 Lire, Republic, Aluminum-Bronze	—	.15
□ 1864	50 Lire, Vittorio Emanuele, Gold	—	8000.00
□ 1884–1891	50 Lire, Umberto I, Gold	—	900.00
□ 1910–1927	50 Lire, Vittorio III, Gold	—	400.00
□ 1911	50 Lire, Vittorio III, 50th Anniversary of Kingdom, Gold	—	250.00

DATE	COIN TYPE/VARIETY/METAL	ABP FINE	AVERAGE FINE
□ 1931–1933	50 Lire, Vittorio III, Gold	—	$150.00
□ 1936	50 Lire, Vittorio III, Gold	—	800.00
□ 1954 to Date	50 Lire, Republic, Stainless Steel	—	15.00
□ 1864–1878	100 Lire, Vittorio Emanuele, Gold	—	2500.00
□ 1880–1891	100 Lire, Umberto I, Gold	—	850.00
□ 1903–1905	100 Lire, Vittorio III, Gold	—	1200.00
□ 1910–1927	100 Lire, Vittorio III, Gold	—	800.00
□ 1923	100 Lire, Vittorio III, Anniversary of Fascist Government, Gold	—	600.00
□ 1925	100 Lire, Vittorio III, 25th Anniversary of Reign & 10th Anniversary of WWI, Gold	—	
□ 1931–1933	100 Lire, Vittorio III, Gold	—	150.00
□ 1936	100 Lire, Vittorio III, Gold	—	800.00
□ 1937	100 Lire, Vittorio III, Gold	—	4000.00
□ 1974	100 Lire, Republic, Birth of Marconi 100th Anniversary, Stainless Steel	—	.10
□ 1979	100 Lire, Republic, F.A.O. Issue, Stainless Steel	—	.10
□ 1981	100 Lire, Republic, Livorno Naval Academy Centennial, Stainless Steel	—	.10

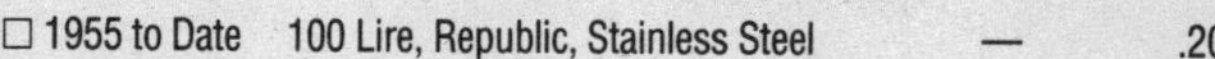

DATE	COIN TYPE/VARIETY/METAL	ABP FINE	AVERAGE FINE
□ 1955 to Date	100 Lire, Republic, Stainless Steel	—	.20

DATE	COIN TYPE/VARIETY/METAL	ABP FINE	AVERAGE FINE
□ 1977–1991	200 Lire, Republic, University of Bologna 900th Anniversary, Aluminum-Bronze	—	$ .15
□ 1980	200 Lire, Republic, World Food Day, Aluminum-Bronze	—	.15

DATE	COIN TYPE/VARIETY/METAL	ABP FINE	AVERAGE FINE
□ 1980	200 Lire, Republic, F.A.O. Issue & International Woman's Year, Aluminum-Bronze	—	.15
□ 1988	200 Lire, Republic, University of Bologna 900th Anniversary, Silver	—	2.00
□ 1989	200 Lire, Republic, Taranto Naval Yards, Silver	—	.20
□ 1989	200 Lire, Republic, Christopher Columbus, Silver	—	.50
□ 1989	200 Lire, Republic, Soccer, Silver	—	4.00
□ 1990	200 Lire, Republic, State Council Building, Silver	—	.50
□ 1991	200 Lire, Republic, Italian Flora & Fauna, Silver	—	4.00
□ 1992	200 Lire, Republic, Genoa Stamp Exposition, Silver	—	.30

DATE	COIN TYPE/VARIETY/METAL	ABP FINE	AVERAGE FINE
☐ 1958–1989	500 Lire, Republic, Silver	—	$8.00
☐ 1961	500 Lire, Republic, Italian Unification Centennial, Silver	—	1.50
☐ 1965	500 Lire, Republic, Birth of Alighieri, 700th Anniversary, Silver	—	1.50
☐ 1974	500 Lire, Republic, Birth of Marconi 100th Anniversary, Silver	—	1.50
☐ 1975	500 Lire, Republic, Birth of Michelangelo 500th Anniversary, Silver	—	15.00
☐ 1981	500 Lire, Republic, Birth of Virgil 2000th Anniversary, Silver	—	10.00
☐ 1982	500 Lire, Republic, Death of Garibaldi 100th Anniversary, Silver	—	15.00
☐ 1982–1991	500 Lire, Republic, Dual Metal	—	.30
☐ 1982	500 Lire, Republic, Galileo Galilei, Silver	—	8.00
☐ 1984	500 Lire, Republic, Common Market Presidency, Silver	—	20.00
☐ 1984	500 Lire, Republic, Los Angeles Olympics, Silver	—	20.00
☐ 1985	500 Lire, Republic, Etruscan Culture, Silver	—	20.00
☐ 1985	500 Lire, Republic, European Year of Music, Silver	—	20.00
☐ 1985	500 Lire, Republic, Birth of Manzoni, 200th Anniversary, Silver	—	35.00
☐ 1985	500 Lire, Republic, Duino College, Silver	—	18.00
☐ 1986	500 Lire, Republic, Birth of Donatello 600th Anniversary, Silver	—	32.00
☐ 1986	500 Lire, Republic, Soccer Championship, Silver	—	32.00
☐ 1986	500 Lire, Republic, Year of Peace, Silver	—	32.00
☐ 1987	500 Lire, Republic, World Athletic Championship, Silver	—	32.00
☐ 1987	500 Lire, Republic, Leopardi, Silver	—	35.00
☐ 1987	500 Lire, Republic, Year of the Family, Silver	—	35.00

DATE	COIN TYPE/VARIETY/METAL	ABP FINE	AVERAGE FINE
□ 1988	500 Lire, Republic, Constitution 40th Anniversary, Silver	—	$35.00
□ 1988	500 Lire, Republic, University of Bologna 900th Anniversary, Silver	—	35.00
□ 1988	500 Lire, Republic, Death of Bosco 100th Anniversary, Silver	—	45.00
□ 1988	500 Lire, Republic, Summer Olympics—Seoul, Silver	—	35.00
□ 1989	500 Lire, Republic, Soccer, Silver	—	30.00
□ 1989	500 Lire, Republic, Christopher Columbus, Silver	—	30.00
□ 1989	500 Lire, Republic, Fight Against Cancer, Silver	—	50.00
□ 1990	500 Lire, Republic, Birth of Tizian 500th Anniversary, Silver	—	40.00
□ 1990	500 Lire, Republic, Columbus—Discovery of America, Silver	—	35.00
□ 1990	500 Lire, Republic, Ponte Milvio 2100th Anniversary, Silver	—	45.00
□ 1990	500 Lire, Republic, EEC Council Presidency, Silver	—	35.00
□ 1991	500 Lire, Republic, Discovery of America, Silver	—	30.00
□ 1991	500 Lire, Republic, Flora & Fauna, Silver	—	30.00
□ 1992	500 Lire, Republic, Olympics Building & Track, Silver	—	30.00
□ 1992	500 Lire, Republic, Christopher Columbus, Silver	—	30.00
□ 1992	500 Lire, Republic, Rosini, Silver	—	30.00
□ 1992	500 Lire, Republic, Flora & Fauna, Silver	—	30.00
□ 1992	500 Lire, Republic, Lorenzo De'Medici, Silver	—	30.00
□ 1970	1000 Lire, Republic, Centennial of Rome, Silver	—	10.00

JAPAN

The first coins were used in 708 and were silver and copper imitations of Chinese cast-bronze coins. Copper coins were used for the next 250 years. After 958 no copper coins were issued, and by the end of the 10th century they were no longer in use. Imported Chinese bronze coins began circulating in the 13th century. Rectangular-shaped coins were in use in the 17th and 18th centuries. The first decimal coins were produced in 1870. Today's currency is the yen.

Japan—Type Coinage

DATE	COIN TYPE/VARIETY/METAL	ABP FINE	AVERAGE FINE
☐ 1873–1888	½ Sen, Obv: Sun With Rays, Rev: Value in Wreath, Bronze	$1.40	$3.00
☐ 1916–1919	5 Rin, Kiri Crest, Bronze	.28	.60
☐ 1873–1915	1 Sen, Obv: Sun With Rays, Rev: Value in Wreath, Bronze	.80	2.00

DATE	COIN TYPE/VARIETY/METAL	ABP FINE	AVERAGE FINE
☐ 1916–1937	1 Sen Kiri Crest, Bronze	$ .16	$ .25
☐ 1941–1943	1 Sen, Mt. Fuji Aluminum	—	.12
☐ 1873–1884	2 Sen, Obv: Sun With Rays, Rev: Value in Wreath, Bronze	.75	1.60
☐ 1870–1871	5 Sen, Obv: Coiled Dragon, Rev: Sun, Silver	—	175.00
☐ 1873–1880	5 Sen, Obv: Coiled Dragon, Rev: Value in Wreath, Silver	—	15.00
☐ 1897–1905	5 Sen, Obv: Sun With Rays, Rev: Value in Wreath, Cupro-Nickel	3.75	8.00

DATE	COIN TYPE/VARIETY/METAL	ABP FINE	AVERAGE FINE
☐ 1917–1932	5 Sen, Petaled Flower Around Hole, Cupro-Nickel	.75	2.00
☐ 1940–1942	5 Sen, Kite, Aluminum	.65	1.75
☐ 1870–1872	10 Sen, Obv: Coiled Dragon, Rev: Sun, Silver	—	15.00
☐ 1873–1906	10 Sen, Obv: Coiled Dragon, Rev: Value in Wreath, Silver	—	3.50
☐ 1907–1917	10 Sen, Obv: Sun With Rays, Rev: Value in Wreath, Silver	—	1.50
☐ 1920–1932	10 Sen, Petaled Flower Around Hole, Cupro-Nickel	.14	.30
☐ 1940–1943	10 Sen, Chrysanthemum, Aluminum	.18	.25
☐ 1946	10 Sen, Phoenix, Rev: Rice Plants, Aluminum	—	.20
☐ 1870–1872	20 Sen, Obv: Coiled Dragon, Rev: sun, Silver	—	15.00
☐ 1873–1905	20 Sen, Obv: Coiled Dragon, Rev: Value in Wreath, Silver	—	8.00
☐ 1906–1911	20 Sen, Obv: Sun With Rays, Rev: Value in Wreath, Silver	—	3.00
☐ 1870–1871	50 Sen, Obv: Coiled Dragon, Rev: Sun, Silver	—	35.00

DATE	COIN TYPE/VARIETY/METAL	ABP FINE	AVERAGE FINE
□ 1873–1905	50 Sen, Obv: Coiled Dragon, Rev: Value in Wreath, Silver	—	$10.00
□ 1906–1917	50 Sen, Obv: Sun With Rays, Rev: Value in Wreath, Silver	—	4.00
□ 1946	50 Sen, Phoenix, Rev: Rice Plants, Bronze	$.14	.30
□ 1947–1948	50 Sen, Chrysanthemum & Blossoms, Brass	—	.12
□ 1870–1872	Yen, Obv: Coiled Dragon, Rev: Sun, Silver	—	5.00

DATE	COIN TYPE/VARIETY/METAL	ABP FINE	AVERAGE FINE
□ 1874–1915	Yen, Obv: Coiled Dragon, Rev: Value in Wreath, Silver	—	5.00
□ 1948–1950	Yen, Blossoms, Brass	.12	.30
□ 1875–1878	Trade Dollar, Obv: Dragon, Rev: Wreath, Silver	—	325.00

LUXEMBOURG

The first coins were used in the late 10th century and were silver deniers. In the 1300s, silver sterlings were in evidence, followed by silver double gros and bronze centimes. The silver franc was popular in the mid-1900s, and the cupro-nickel franc in the latter 1900s. Decimal coins were used in 1854. The currency today is the franc.

Luxembourg—Type Coinage

DATE	COIN TYPE/VARIETY/METAL	ABP FINE	AVERAGE FINE
□ 1854–1908	2½ Centimes, Bronze	$ .80	$2.00
□ 1854–1870	5 Centimes, Bronze	.80	2.00
□ 1901	5 Centimes, Adolphe, Cupro-Nickel	.14	.30

DATE	COIN TYPE/VARIETY/METAL	ABP FINE	AVERAGE FINE
□ 1908	5 Centimes, Guillaume IV, Cupro-Nickel	.18	.40
□ 1915	5 Centimes, "Holed," Zinc	.60	1.50
□ 1918–1922	5 Centimes, Iron	.80	2.00
□ 1924	5 Centimes, Charlotte (1st), Cupro-Nickel	—	.20
□ 1930	5 Centimes, Charlotte (1st), Bronze	—	.12

DATE	COIN TYPE/VARIETY/METAL	ABP FINE	AVERAGE FINE
☐ 1854–1870	10 Centimes, Bronze	$ .80	$1.75
☐ 1901	10 Centimes, Adolphe, Cupro-Nickel	.16	.30
☐ 1915	10 Centimes, "Holed," Zinc	.50	1.40
☐ 1918–1923	10 Centimes, Iron	1.00	2.50
☐ 1924	10 Centimes, Charlotte (1st), Cupro-Nickel	.18	.30
☐ 1930	10 Centimes, Charlotte (1st), Bronze	—	.12
☐ 1918–1922	25 Centimes, Iron	1.40	3.00
☐ 1927	25 Centimes, Charlotte (1st), Cupro-Nickel	.18	.40

DATE	COIN TYPE/VARIETY/METAL	ABP FINE	AVERAGE FINE
☐ 1946–1947	25 Centimes, Charlotte (2nd) Letzeburg, Bronze	—	.18
☐ 1954–1972	25 Centimes, Charlotte (2nd) Letzeburg, Aluminum	—	.12
☐ 1980	25 Centimes, Charlotte (2nd), Silver	—	15.00
☐ 1924–1935	1 Franc, Charlotte (1st), Nickel	.14	.30

DATE	COIN TYPE/VARIETY/METAL	ABP FINE	AVERAGE FINE
□ 1939	1 Franc, Charlotte (1st), Letzeburg, Bronze	$.14	$.30
□ 1946–1947	1 Franc, Charlotte (2nd), Letzeburg, Cupro-Nickel	.10	.25
□ 1952	1 Franc, Charlotte (2nd), Letzeburg, Cupro-Nickel	—	.12
□ 1953–1964	1 Franc, Charlotte (2nd), Letzeburg, Cupro-Nickel	—	.12
□ 1965–1984	1 Franc, Charlotte (2nd), Millenium Commemorative, Cupro-Nickel	—	.12
□ 1980	1 Franc, Charlotte (2nd), Millenium Commemorative, Silver	—	.24
□ 1986–1987	1 Franc, Charlotte (2nd), Cupro-Nickel	—	.12
□ 1988 to Date	1 Franc, Charlotte (2nd), Nickel-Steel	—	.12
□ 1924	2 Francs, Charlotte (1st), Nickel	.50	1.25
□ 1929	5 Francs, Charlotte (1st), Nickel	1.25	3.00
□ 1949	5 Francs, Charlotte (2nd), Letzeburg, Cupro-Nickel	.18	.40
□ 1962	5 Francs, Charlotte (2nd), Cupro-Nickel	—	.12
□ 1971–1981	5 Francs, Charlotte (2nd), Cupro-Nickel	—	.10

DATE	COIN TYPE/VARIETY/METAL	ABP FINE	AVERAGE FINE
□ 1986 to Date	5 Francs, Charlotte (2nd), Brass	—	.15
□ 1929	10 Francs, Charlotte (1st), Nickel	2.75	5.00
□ 1971–1980	10 Francs, Charlotte (2nd), Nickel	.14	.30
□ 1946	20 Francs, Charlotte (2nd), 600th Anniversary Death of John the Blind, Silver	—	10.00
□ 1980	20 Francs, Charlotte (2nd), Silver	—	40.00

DATE	COIN TYPE/VARIETY/METAL	ABP FINE	AVERAGE FINE
□ 1980–1983	20 Francs, Charlotte (2nd), Bronze	$ .30	$ .75
□ 1989	20 Francs, Charlotte (2nd), 150th Anniversary of Grand Duchy, Gold	—	150.00
□ 1990–1991	20 Francs, Charlotte (2nd), Bronze	—	—
□ 1946	50 Francs, Charlotte (2nd), 600th Anniversary Death of John the Blind, Silver	—	2.50
□ 1987 to Date	50 Francs, Charlotte (2nd), Nickel	.75	1.65
□ 1946	100 Francs, Charlotte (2nd), 600th Anniversary Death of John the Blind, Silver	—	20.00
□ 1963	100 Francs, Charlotte (2nd), Silver	—	12.00
□ 1963	250 Francs, Charlotte (2nd), Millenium Commemorative, Silver	—	50.00

MALTA

The first coins, which were bronze, were used in the 3rd century B.C. The silver tari was in evidence in the 1500s, followed by the copper grano. In the early 1700s, the gold zecchini was in use, and the silver tari appeared in the mid-1700s. The bronze 10 cents was in use in the 1970s since decimal coins came into use in 1972. The currency today is the pound.

Malta—Type Coinage

DATE	COIN TYPE/VARIETY/METAL	ABP FINE	AVERAGE FINE
□ 1827	1/3 Farthing, Head of George IV, Copper	$ 5.00	$ 12.00
□ 1835	1/3 Farthing, Head of William IV, Copper	5.00	12.00
□ 1844	1/3 Farthing, Head of Victoria, Copper	12.00	25.00
□ 1866–1885	1/3 Farthing, Value in Wreath, Bronze	3.50	6.00
□ 1902	1/3 Farthing, Head of Edward VII, Bronze	1.75	4.00
□ 1913	1/3 Farthing, Head of George V, Bronze	1.75	4.00

MEXICO

The first coins—the silver Spanish reales—were used in 1536. At first coins were struck in silver, gold, and copper but copper was soon discontinued. The silver reales were popular in the 1800s, followed by the brass quartillas, gold pesos, bronze centavos, and silver pesos in the 1900s. The decimal system was established in 1863 and the currency today is the peso.

Mexico—Type and Republic Coinage

DATE	COIN TYPE/VARIETY/METAL	ABP FINE	AVERAGE FINE
□ 1863–1905	1 Centavo, Republic, Obv: Libertad, Copper	3.75	8.00
□ 1864	1 Centavo, Emperor Maximilian, Legend: Imperio Mexicano, Copper	16.00	42.00
□ 1869–1897	1 Centavo, Republic, Obv: Republica Mexicana, Copper	3.75	8.00
□ 1882–1883	1 Centavo, Republic, Reduced Size, Cupro-Nickel	3.75	8.00
□ 1898	1 Centavo, Republic, Obv: Restyled Eagle, Copper	2.00	4.50
□ 1899–1905	1 Centavo, Republic, Obv: Restyled Eagle, Copper	1.40	3.00

DATE	COIN TYPE/VARIETY/METAL	ABP FINE	AVERAGE FINE
□ 1905–1949	1 Centavo, Estados Unidos Mexicanos, Bronze	$ .28	$ .60
□ 1915	1 Centavo, Estados Unidos Mexicanos, Zapata, Bronze	5.50	12.00
□ 1950–1969	1 Centavo, Decree of December 29, 1949, Brass	—	.12
□ 1882–1883	2 Centavo, Republic, Cupro-Nickel	.80	2.00

DATE	COIN TYPE/VARIETY/METAL	ABP FINE	AVERAGE FINE
□ 1905–1941	2 Centavos, Estados Unidos Mexicanos, Bronze	.80	2.00
□ 1915	2 Centavos, Estados Unidos Mexicanos, Zapata, Bronze	2.25	5.00
□ 1863–1970	5 Centavos, Republic, Silver	—	30.00
□ 1864–1866	5 Centavos, Emperor Maximilian, Legend: Imperio Mexicano, Silver	—	25.00
□ 1867–1869	5 Centavos, Republic, Silver	—	25.00
□ 1869–1897	5 Centavos, Republic, Silver	—	3.00
□ 1882–1883	5 Centavos, Republic, Cupro-Nickel	.28	.60
□ 1898–1905	5 Centavos, Republic, Restyled Eagle, Silver	—	2.00

DATE	COIN TYPE/VARIETY/METAL	ABP FINE	AVERAGE FINE
☐ 1905–1914	5 Centavos, Estados Unidos Mexicanos, Zapata, Nickel	$ .75	$2.00
☐ 1914–1935	5 Centavos, Estados Unidos Mexicanos, Bronze	.75	2.00
☐ 1936–1942	5 Centavos, Cupro-Nickel	.40	1.00
☐ 1942–1955	5 Centavos, Rev: Josefa Dominguez, Bronze	.28	.50
☐ 1950	5 Centavos, Decree of December 29, 1949, Rev: Josefa Dominguez, Cupro-Nickel	.40	1.00
☐ 1954–1969	5 Centavos, Brass	—	.12
☐ 1992 to Date	5 Centavos, Stainless Steel	—	.10
☐ 1863–1870	10 Centavos, Republic, Silver	—	35.00
☐ 1864–1866	10 Centavos, Emperor Maximilian, Legend: Imperio Mexicano, Silver	—	35.00
☐ 1867–1869	10 Centavos, Republic, Silver	—	30.00
☐ 1869–1897	10 Centavos, Republic, Silver	—	5.00
☐ 1898–1905	10 Centavos, Republic, Restyled Eagle, Silver	—	2.00

DATE	COIN TYPE/VARIETY/METAL	ABP FINE	AVERAGE FINE
☐ 1905–1914	10 Centavos, Estados Unidos Mexicanos, Silver	—	10.00
☐ 1919–1921	10 Centavos, Estados Unidos Mexicanos, Bronze	8.00	20.00
☐ 1919	10 Centavos, Estados Unidos Mexicanos, .800 Silver	—	25.00
☐ 1925–1935	10 Centavos, Estados Unidos Mexicanos, Obv: "0.720," .720 Silver	—	3.00
☐ 1936–1946	10 Centavos, Cupro-Nickel	.14	.30
☐ 1955–1967	10 Centavos, Bronze	.12	.25
☐ 1974–1980	10 Centavos, Estados Unidos Mexicanos, Cupro-Nickel	.28	.60
☐ 1992 to Date	10 Centavos, Stainless Steel	—	.12
☐ 1898–1905	20 Centavos, Republic, Restyled Eagle, Silver	—	6.00

DATE	COIN TYPE/VARIETY/METAL	ABP FINE	AVERAGE FINE
□ 1905–1914	20 Centavos, Estados Unidos Mexicanos, Silver	—	$12.00
□ 1919	20 Centavos, Estados Unidos Mexicanos, .800 Silver	—	35.00
□ 1920–1935	20 Centavos, Estados Unidos Mexicanos, Bronze	$3.25	7.00
□ 1920–1943	20 Centavos, Estados Unidos Mexicanos, Obv: "0.720," .720 Silver	—	2.00
□ 1943–1955	20 Centavos, Bronze	.28	.60
□ 1955–1971	20 Centavos, Bronze	—	.20
□ 1974–1983	20 Centavos, Estados Unidos Mexicanos, Cupro-Nickel	—	.12
□ 1983–1984	20 Centavos, Estados Unidos Mexicanos, Olmec Culture, Bronze	—	.12
□ 1992 to Date	20 Centavos, Aluminum-Bronze	—	.12
□ 1829–1837	$^1/_4$ Real, Republica Mexicana, Copper	6.50	15.00
□ 1842–1863	$^1/_4$ Real, Silver	—	12.00
□ 1869–1892	25 Centavos, Republic, Silver	—	12.00
□ 1950–1953	25 Centavos, Decree of December 29, 1949, Billon	—	10.00
□ 1970–1983	25 Centavos, Estados Unidos Mexicanos, Stylized Eagle, Cupro-Nickel	.30	.75
□ 1824	$^1/_2$ Real, Obv: Hooked-neck Eagle, Silver	—	42.00
□ 1825–1869	$^1/_2$ Real, Obv: Upright Eagle, Silver	—	18.00
□ 1869–1895	50 Centavos, Republic, Silver	—	15.00

DATE	COIN TYPE/VARIETY/METAL	ABP FINE	AVERAGE FINE
□ 1905–1918	50 Centavos, Estados Unidos Mexicanos, Silver	—	$6.00
□ 1918–1919	50 Centavos, Estados Unidos Mexicanos, .800 Silver	—	12.00
□ 1919–1945	50 Centavos, Estados Unidos Mexicanos, Obv: "0.720," .720 Silver	—	4.00
□ 1935	50 Centavos, Estados Unidos Mexicanos, Billon	$ .80	2.00
□ 1950–1951	50 Centavos, Decree of December 29, 1949, Cuauhtemoc, Billon	.45	1.00
□ 1955–1959	50 Centavos, Bronze	.45	1.00
□ 1992 to Date	50 Centavos, Aluminum-Bronze	—	.12
□ 1824	1 Real, Obv: Hooked-neck Eagle, Silver	—	3000.00
□ 1825–1869	1 Real Obv: Upright Eagle, Silver	—	5.00
□ 1866–1867	1 Peso, Emperor Maximilian, Legend: Imperio Mexicano, Silver	—	325.00
□ 1869–1873	1 Peso, Republic, Silver	—	25.00
□ 1870–1905	1 Peso, Republic, Restyled Eagle, Gold	—	12.00
□ 1898–1909	1 Peso, Republic, Restyled Eagle, Silver	—	65.00
□ 1910–1914	1 Peso, Estados Unidos Mexicanos, Silver	—	45.00
□ 1918–1919	1 Peso, Estados Unidos Mexicanos, .800 Silver	—	25.00

DATE	COIN TYPE/VARIETY/METAL	ABP FINE	AVERAGE FINE
□ 1920–1945	1 Peso, Estados Unidos Mexicanos, Obv: "0.720," .720 Silver	—	4.00
□ 1947–1949	1 Peso, Rev: Jose Morelos, Silver	—	2.00
□ 1950	1 Peso, Decree of December 29, 1949, Rev: Jose Morelos, Billon	.80	2.00
□ 1955–1967	1 Peso, Silver Alloys	—	3.50
□ 1957	1 Peso, Constitution Centennial, 1.100 Fine., Silver Alloys	—	4.00
□ 1970–1983	1 Peso, Estados Unidos Mexicanos, Jose Morelos, Cupro-Nickel	—	.20
□ 1984–1987	1 Peso, Estados Unidos Mexicanos, Jose Morelos, Stainless Steel	—	.12

DATE	COIN TYPE/VARIETY/METAL	ABP FINE	AVERAGE FINE
☐ 1992	1 New Peso, Dual Metal	—	$ .10
☐ 1824	2 Reales, Obv: Hooked-neck Eagle, Silver	—	50.00
☐ 1825–1872	2 Reales, Obv: Upright Eagle, Silver	—	30.00
☐ 1919–1948	2 Pesos, Estados Unidos Mexicanos, Gold	—	30.00
☐ 1921	2 Pesos, Independence Centennial, Silver	—	40.00

☐ 1992 to Date	2 New Pesos, Dual Metal	—	.12

☐ 1870–1893	2½ Pesos, Republic, Restyled Eagle, Gold	—	200.00
☐ 1918–1948	2½ Pesos, Estados Unidos Mexicanos, Gold	—	35.00
☐ 1825–1869	4 Reales, Obv: Upright Eagle, Silver	—	30.00

DATE	COIN TYPE/VARIETY/METAL	ABP FINE	AVERAGE FINE
☐ 1870–1895	5 Pesos, Republic, Restyled Eagle, Gold	—	$250.00
☐ 1905–1955	5 Pesos, Estados Unidos Mexicanos, Gold	—	65.00
☐ 1947–1948	5 Peso, Rev: Cuahtemoc, Silver	—	7.00
☐ 1950	5 Pesos, Completion of Southeastern Railway, Silver	—	30.00
☐ 1951–1954	5 Pesos, Decree of December 29, 1949, Miguel Hidalgo, Silver	—	5.00
☐ 1953	5 Pesos, Bicentennial of Birth of Hidalgo, Silver	—	7.00
☐ 1955–1957	5 Pesos, .720 Fine, Silver Alloys	—	5.00
☐ 1957	5 Pesos, Constitution Centennial, .720 Fine, Silver Alloys	—	6.00
☐ 1959	5 Pesos, Centennial Birth of Carranza, Silver	—	5.00
☐ 1971–1978	5 Pesos, Estados Unidos Mexicanos, Vicente Guerrero, Cupro-Nickel	—	.12
☐ 1980–1985	5 Pesos, Estados Unidos Mexicanos, Quetzalcoatl, Cupro-Nickel	$ .18	.25
☐ 1985–1988	5 Pesos, Estados Unidos Mexicanos, Circulation Coinage, Brass	—	.12

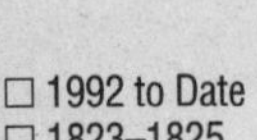

DATE	COIN TYPE/VARIETY/METAL	ABP FINE	AVERAGE FINE
☐ 1992 to Date	5 New Pesos, Dual Metal	—	.10
☐ 1823–1825	8 Reales, Obv: Hooked-neck Eagle, Silver	—	150.00

DATE	COIN TYPE/VARIETY/METAL	ABP FINE	AVERAGE FINE
☐ 1824–1869	8 Reales, Obv: Upright Eagle, Silver	—	50.00

DATE	COIN TYPE/VARIETY/METAL	ABP FINE	AVERAGE FINE
☐ 1869–1897	8 Reales, Republic. Restyled Eagle, Silver	—	$18.00
☐ 1870–1895	10 Pesos, Republic, Restyled Eagle, Gold	—	450.00
☐ 1905–1959	10 Pesos, Estados Unidos Mexicanos, Gold	—	150.00
☐ 1955–1956	10 Pesos, .900 Fine, Silver Alloys	—	12.00
☐ 1957	10 Pesos, Constitution Centennial, .900 Fine, Silver Alloys	—	12.00
☐ 1960	10 Pesos, Dual Commemorative—Revolutions of 1810 & 1910, Silver	—	7.00
☐ 1974–1985	Diez Pesos, Estados Unidos Mexicanos, Miguel Hidalgo, Cupro-Nickel	$ .28	.50
☐ 1985–1990	Diez Pesos, Estados Unidos Mexicanos, Miguel Hidalgo, Stainless Steel	—	.15
☐ 1992 to Date	10 New Pesos, Dual Metal	—	.10
☐ 1825–1870	1 Escudo, Obv: Upright Eagle, Gold	—	150.00
☐ 1866	20 Pesos, Emperor Maximilian, Legend: Imperio Mexicano, Gold	—	500.00

DATE	COIN TYPE/VARIETY/METAL	ABP FINE	AVERAGE FINE
☐ 1870–1895	20 Pesos, Republic, Restyled Eagle, Gold	—	$500.00
☐ 1917–1959	20 Pesos, Estados Unidos Mexicanos, Gold	—	250.00

DATE	COIN TYPE/VARIETY/METAL	ABP FINE	AVERAGE FINE
☐ 1980–1984	Viente Pesos, Estados Unidos Mexicanos, Cupro-Nickel	$ .18	.40
☐ 1985–1990	Viente Pesos, Estados Unidos Mexicanos, Guadelupe Victoria, Brass	—	.15

DATE	COIN TYPE/VARIETY/METAL	ABP FINE	AVERAGE FINE
☐ 1968	25 Pesos, Summer Olympics—Mexico City, Silver	—	4.00
☐ 1985–1986	25 Pesos, World Cup Soccer Games, Silver	—	10.00

DATE	COIN TYPE/VARIETY/METAL	ABP FINE	AVERAGE FINE
☐ 1992 to Date	25 Pesos, Eagle Warrior, Silver	—	$12.00
☐ 1825–1870	2 Escudos, Obv: Upright Eagle, Gold	—	150.00
☐ 1921–1947	50 Pesos, Independence Centennial, Gold	—	600.00

DATE	COIN TYPE/VARIETY/METAL	ABP FINE	AVERAGE FINE
☐ 1982–1984	50 Pesos, Coyolxauhqui, Cupro-Nickel	$ .80	2.00
☐ 1984–1988	50 Pesos, Benito Juarez, Cupro-Nickel	.18	.30
☐ 1985–1986	50 Pesos, World Cup Soccer Games, Silver	—	25.00
☐ 1988–1992	50 Pesos, Benito Juarez, Stainless Steel	—	.12
☐ 1992 to Date	50 Pesos, Eagle Warrior, Silver	—	25.00
☐ 1825–1869	4 Escudos, Obv: Upright Eagle, Gold	—	185.00

DATE	COIN TYPE/VARIETY/METAL	ABP FINE	AVERAGE FINE
☐ 1977–1979	Cien Pesos, Jose Morales, Silver	—	5.00
☐ 1984–1992	Cien Pesos, Carranza, Aluminum-Bronze	—	.25
☐ 1985–1986	Cien Pesos, World Cup Soccer Games, Silver	—	35.00
☐ 1987	Cien Pesos, World Wildlife Fund—Monarch Butterflies, Silver	—	50.00

DATE	COIN TYPE/VARIETY/METAL	ABP FINE	AVERAGE FINE
☐ 1988	Cien Pesos, Oil Industry Nationalization 50th Anniversary, Silver	—	$25.00
☐ 1991	Cien Pesos, Save the Children, Silver	—	30.00
☐ 1991	Cien Pesos, Ibero American Series—Pillars, Silver	—	50.00
☐ 1992 to Date	100 Pesos, Eagle Warrior, Silver	—	30.00
☐ 1823	8 Escudos, Obv: Hooked-neck Eagle, Gold	—	4000.00

DATE	COIN TYPE/VARIETY/METAL	ABP FINE	AVERAGE FINE
☐ 1825–1873	8 Escudos, Obv: Upright Eagle, Gold	—	375.00
☐ 1985	200 Pesos, Anniversary of 1910 Revolution, Cupro-Nickel	—	.25

DATE	COIN TYPE/VARIETY/METAL	ABP FINE	AVERAGE FINE
☐ 1985	200 Pesos, Anniversary of Independence, Cupro-Nickel	—	.25
☐ 1986	200 Pesos, World Cup Soccer Games, Cupro-Nickel	—	.25
☐ 1985	500 Pesos, Anniversary of 1910 Revolution, Silver	—	45.00
☐ 1985–1986	500 Pesos, World Cup Soccer Games, Gold	—	225.00

DATE	COIN TYPE/VARIETY/METAL	ABP FINE	AVERAGE FINE
□ 1986–1990	500 Pesos, Madero, Cupro-Nickel	$ .30	$ .75
□ 1988	500 Pesos, Oil Nationalization 50th Anniversary, Gold	—	250.00
□ 1985	1000 Pesos, Anniversary of Independence, Gold	—	300.00
□ 1986	1000 Pesos, World Cup Soccer Games, Gold	—	750.00
□ 1988	1000 Pesos, Oil Nationalization 50th Anniversary, Gold	—	600.00

DATE	COIN TYPE/VARIETY/METAL	ABP FINE	AVERAGE FINE
□ 1988–1992	1000 Pesos, Juana de Asbaje, Aluminum-Bronze	.40	1.00
□ 1986	2000 Pesos, World Cup Games, Gold	—	1500.00
□ 1988	5000 Pesos, Oil Industry Nationalization 50th Anniversary, Cupro-Nickel	1.40	3.00

MOROCCO

The first coins were used in the 2nd century B.C., with the silver denarius in 50 B.C., bronze coins in the 1st century B.C., and copper fals in 731 A.D. The silver dirhem was in evidence in the 700s, followed by the gold dinar, silver square dirhem, and gold double dinar in the 12th and 13th centuries. The copper double fals was in use in the 1800s and the cupro-nickel francs in the mid-1900s. Decimal coins were used in 1921. The currency today is the dirhem.

Morocco—Type Coinage

DATE	COIN TYPE/VARIETY/METAL	ABP FINE	AVERAGE FINE
□ 1310	1/2 Muzuna, Hasan I, Bronze	$100.00	$225.00
□ 1310	1 Muzuna, Hasan I, Bronze	75.00	160.00
□ 1320–1321	1 Muzuna, Abd Al-Aziz 2nd Coinage, Bronze	1.60	3.00
□ 1330	1 Mizuna, Yusuf: 1st Coinage, Bronze	.75	2.00
□ 1320–1321	2 Muzuna, Abd Al-Aziz 2nd Coinage, Bronze	.80	2.00
□ 1330	2 Mizuna, Yusuf: 1st Coinage, Bronze	.80	2.00
□ 1310	2 1/2 Muzuna, Hasan I, Bronze	60.00	150.00
□ 1310	5 Muzuna, Hasan I, Bronze	30.00	75.00
□ 1320–1322	5 Muzuna, Abd Al-Aziz 2nd Coinage, Bronze	4.50	10.00
□ 1330–1340	5 Mizuna, Yusuf: 1st Coinage, Bronze	.80	2.00
□ 1310	10 Muzuna, Hasan I, Bronze	30.00	75.00
□ 1320–1323	10 Muzuna, Abd Al-Aziz 2nd Coinage, Bronze	.80	2.00
□ 1330–1340	10 Mizuna, Yusuf: 1st Coinage, Bronze	.40	1.00
□ 1974	1 Santim, Monetary Reform, Gold	—	500.00
□ 1974–1975	1 Santim, Monetary Reform, Aluminum	.28	.60
□ 1299–1314	1/2 Durham, Hasan I, Silver	—	2.00
□ 1313–1319	1/2 Durham, Abd Al-Aziz 1st Coinage, Silver	—	2.00
□ 1320–1321	1/20 Rial, Abd Al-Aziz 2nd Coinage, Silver	—	1.75
□ 1974	5 Santimat, Monetary Reform, Gold	—	500.00
□ 1974–1978	5 Santimat, Monetary Reform, Brass	—	.15
□ 1987	5 Santimat, Monetary Reform, Brass	—	.25

DATE	COIN TYPE/VARIETY/METAL	ABP FINE	AVERAGE FINE
□ 1299–1314	1 Durham, Hasan I, Silver	—	3.00
□ 1313–1318	1 Durham, Abd Al-Aziz 1st Coinage, Silver	—	6.00
□ 1320–1321	1/10 Rial, Abd Al-Aziz 2nd Coinage, Silver	—	6.00
□ 1331	1/10 Rial, Yusuf: 1st Coinage, Silver	—	7.00

DATE	COIN TYPE/VARIETY/METAL	ABP FINE	AVERAGE FINE
□ 1974–1978	10 Santimat, Monetary Reform, Brass	—	$.15
□ 1974	10 Santimat, Monetary Reform, Gold	—	600.00
□ 1974	20 Santimat, Monetary Reform, Gold	—	700.00
□ 1974–1978	20 Santimat, Monetary Reform, Brass	—	.25
□ 1299–1314	2½ Durham, Hasan I, Silver	—	5.00
□ 1313–1318	2½ Durham, Abd Al-Aziz 1st Coinage, Silver	—	8.00
□ 1320–1321	¼ Rial, Abd Al-Aziz 2nd Coinage, Silver	—	4.00
□ 1329	¼ Rial, Hafiz, Silver	—	4.00
□ 1331	¼ Rial, Yusuf: 1st Coinage, Silver	—	35.00
□ 1921–1926	25 Centimes, Yusuf: 2nd Coinage, Cupro-Nickel	$ .50	1.25
□ 1299–1314	5 Durham, Hasan I, Silver	—	10.00

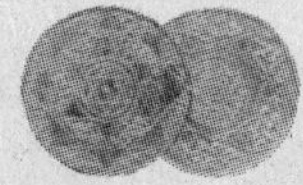

DATE	COIN TYPE/VARIETY/METAL	ABP FINE	AVERAGE FINE
□ 1313–1318	5 Durham, Abd Al-Aziz 1st Coinage, Silver	—	10.00
□ 1320–1323	½ Rial, Abd Al-Aziz 2nd Coinage, Silver	—	18.00
□ 1329	½ Rial, Hafiz, Silver	—	4.00
□ 1331–1336	½ Rial, Yusuf: 1st Coinage, Silver	—	32.00

DATE	COIN TYPE/VARIETY/METAL	ABP FINE	AVERAGE FINE
□ 1921–1924	50 Centimes, Yusuf: 2nd Coinage, Cupro-Nickel	$ .28	$ .60
□ 1945	50 Centimes, Muhammad Bin Yusuf: 2nd Coinage, Aluminum-Bronze	—	.20
□ 1974	50 Santimat, Monetary Reform, Gold	—	700.00
□ 1974–1978	50 Santimat, Monetary Reform, Brass	—	.25
□ 1987	½ Dirham, Monetary Reform, Cupro-Nickel	.40	1.00
□ 1299	10 Durham, Hasan I, Silver	—	18.00

DATE	COIN TYPE/VARIETY/METAL	ABP FINE	AVERAGE FINE
□ 1313	10 Durham, Abd Al-Aziz 1st Coinage, Silver	—	80.00
□ 1320–1321	1 Rial, Abd Al-Aziz 2nd Coinage, Silver	—	20.00
□ 1329	1 Rial, Hafiz, Silver	—	12.00
□ 1331–1336	1 Rial, Yusuf: 1st Coinage, Silver	—	10.00

DATE	COIN TYPE/VARIETY/METAL	ABP FINE	AVERAGE FINE
□ 1921–1924	1 Franc, Yusuf: 2nd Coinage, Cupro-Nickel	.60	1.50
□ 1945	1 Franc, Muhammad Bin Yusuf: 2nd Coinage, Aluminum-Bronze	—	.25
□ 1951	1 Franc, Muhammad Bin Yusuf: 3rd Coinage, Aluminum	—	.12
□ 1960	1 Dirham, Mohammed V: Monetary Reform, Silver	—	1.00
□ 1960	1 Dirham, Mohammed V, Silver	—	1.00
□ 1965–1969	Dirham, Al Hasan II: Monetary Reform, Nickel	.24	.50
□ 1974	Dirham, Monetary Reform, Gold	—	850.00

DATE	COIN TYPE/VARIETY/METAL	ABP FINE	AVERAGE FINE
☐ 1974–1978	Dirham, Monetary Reform, Cupro-Nickel	—	$ .20
☐ 1945	2 Francs, Muhammad Bin Yusuf: 2nd Coinage, Aluminum-Bronze	$ .28	.60
☐ 1951	2 Francs, Muhammad Bin Yusuf: 3rd Coinage, Aluminum	—	.12

DATE	COIN TYPE/VARIETY/METAL	ABP FINE	AVERAGE FINE
☐ 1347–1352	5 Francs, Muhammad Bin Yusuf: 1st Coinage, Silver	—	3.00
☐ 1951	5 Francs, Muhammad Bin Yusuf: 3rd Coinage, Aluminum	—	.12
☐ 1965	5 Dirhams, Al Hasan II: Monetary Reform, Silver	—	5.00
☐ 1975–1987	5 Dirhams, Monetary Reform, Dual Metal	.40	1.00
☐ 1975–1980	5 Dirhams, Monetary Reform, Cupro-Nickel	.40	1.00
☐ 1975	5 Dirhams, Monetary Reform, Silver	—	160.00
☐ 1975	5 Dirhams, Monetary Reform, Gold	—	1200.00

DATE	COIN TYPE/VARIETY/METAL	ABP FINE	AVERAGE FINE
☐ 1347–1352	10 Francs, Muhammad Bin Yusuf: 1st Coinage, Silver	—	3.00
☐ 1366	10 Francs, Muhammad Bin Yusuf: 2nd Coinage, Cupro-Nickel	.16	.40
☐ 1371	10 Francs, Muhammad Bin Yusuf: 3rd Coinage, Aluminum-Bronze	—	.12

DATE	COIN TYPE/VARIETY/METAL	ABP FINE	AVERAGE FINE
□ 1347–1352	20 Francs, Muhammad Bin Yusuf: 1st Coinage, Silver	—	$6.00
□ 1366	20 Francs, Muhammad Bin Yusuf: 2nd Coinage, Cupro-Nickel	—	.25
□ 1371	20 Francs, Muhammad Bin Yusuf: 3rd Coinage, Aluminum-Bronze	—	.12

DATE	COIN TYPE/VARIETY/METAL	ABP FINE	AVERAGE FINE
□ 1371	50 Francs, Muhammad Bin Yusuf: 3rd Coinage, Aluminum-Bronze	$ .12	.30
□ 1975	50 Dirhams, Monetary Reform: 20th Anniversary of Independence, Gold	—	2000.00
□ 1975	50 Dirhams, Monetary Reform: 20th Anniversary of Independence, Silver	—	30.00
□ 1976–1980	50 Dirhams, Monetary Reform: Anniversary of Green March, Gold	—	2000.00
□ 1976–1980	50 Dirhams, Monetary Reform: Anniversary of Green March, Silver	—	30.00
□ 1979	50 Dirhams, Monetary Reform: King Hassan Birthday, Silver	—	30.00
□ 1979	50 Dirhams, Monetary Reform: King Hassan Birthday, Gold	—	1400.00
□ 1979	50 Dirhams, Monetary Reform: Year of the Child, Silver	—	30.00
□ 1979	50 Dirhams, Monetary Reform: Year of the Child, Gold	—	1400.00

DATE	COIN TYPE/VARIETY/METAL	ABP FINE	AVERAGE FINE
□ 1953	100 Francs, Muhammad Bin Yusuf: 3rd Coinage, Silver	—	$3.00
□ 1983	100 Dirhams, 9th Mediterranean Games, Silver	—	40.00
□ 1985	100 Dirhams, Olympic Games, Silver	—	30.00
□ 1985	100 Dirhams, 25th Year of King Hassan, Silver	—	30.00
□ 1986	100 Dirhams, Papal Visit, Silver	—	25.00
□ 1986	100 Dirhams, Anniversary of Green March, Silver	—	50.00
□ 1987	100 Dirhams, Rabat Mint Opening, Silver	—	30.00
□ 1980	150 Dirhams, Hejira Calendar Century, Gold	—	2000.00
□ 1980	150 Dirhams, Hejira Calendar Century, Silver	—	35.00
□ 1981	150 Dirhams, King Hassan's Coronation 20th Anniversary, Gold	—	2000.00
□ 1981	150 Dirhams, King Hassan's Coronation 20th Anniversary, Silver	—	35.00
□ 1953	200 Francs, Muhammad Bin Yusuf: 3rd Coinage, Silver	—	3.00
□ 1987	200 Dirhams, Moroccan American Friendship Treaty, Silver	—	50.00
□ 1989	200 Dirhams, First Francophonie Games, Silver	—	30.00

DATE	COIN TYPE/VARIETY/METAL	ABP FINE	AVERAGE FINE
□ 1956	500 Francs, Mohammed V, Silver	—	10.00
□ 1979–1985	500 Dirhams, King Hassan Birthday, Gold	—	250.00

MOZAMBIQUE

The first coins, crude copper and silver, were used in 1725. The silver onca, a rectangular coin, was in evidence in the 1800s, followed by the silver rupee in the 1860s and the cupro-nickel escudo in the 1930s. Decimal coins appeared in 1935. The currency today is the metical.

Mozambique—Type Coinage

DATE	COIN TYPE/VARIETY/METAL	ABP FINE	AVERAGE FINE
□ 1975	1 Centimo, Popular Republic, Aluminum	$40.00	$100.00
□ 1975	2 Centimos, Popular Republic, Copper-Zinc	30.00	75.00
□ 1975	5 Centimos, Popular Republic, Copper-Zinc	40.00	90.00
□ 1936	10 Centavos, Bronze	.40	1.00
□ 1942	10 Centavos, New Reverse Arms, Bronze	.28	.60
□ 1975	10 Centimos, Popular Republic, Copper-Zinc	40.00	90.00
□ 1936	20 Centavos, Bronze	.40	1.00
□ 1941	20 Centavos, New Reverse Arms, Bronze	.40	1.00

DATE	COIN TYPE/VARIETY/METAL	ABP FINE	AVERAGE FINE
□ 1949–1950	20 Centavos, New Reverse Arms, Bronze	—	$ .30
□ 1975	20 Centimos, Popular Republic, Copper-Zinc	—	.30
□ 1936	50 Centavos, Cupro-Nickel	$ .50	1.25
□ 1945	50 Centavos, New Reverse Arms, Bronze	.28	.60
□ 1950–1951	50 Centavos, New Reverse Arms, Nickel-Bronze	.18	.40

DATE	COIN TYPE/VARIETY/METAL	ABP FINE	AVERAGE FINE
□ 1953–1957	50 Centavos, Decree of January 21, 1952, Bronze	—	.18
□ 1975	50 Centimos, Popular Republic, Copper-Zinc	75.00	180.00
□ 1980–1982	50 Centavos, Monetary Reform: Instrument, Aluminum	—	.20

DATE	COIN TYPE/VARIETY/METAL	ABP FINE	AVERAGE FINE
□ 1936	1 Escudo, Cupro-Nickel	1.25	3.00
□ 1945	1 Escudo, New Reverse Arms, Bronze	.40	1.00
□ 1950–1951	1 Escudo, New Reverse Arms, Nickel-Bronze	.30	.75
□ 1953–1974	1 Escudo, Decree of January 21, 1952, Bronze	—	.25
□ 1975	1 Metical, Popular Republic, Cupro-Nickel	18.00	40.00
□ 1980–1982	1 Metical, Monetary Reform: Female Student, Brass	.18	.40
□ 1986	1 Metical, Monetary Reform: Female Student, Aluminum	—	.30

DATE	COIN TYPE/VARIETY/METAL	ABP FINE	AVERAGE FINE
☐ 1935	2½ Escudos, Silver	—	$6.00
☐ 1938–1951	2½ Escudos, New Reverse Arms, Silver	—	3.00
☐ 1952–1973	2½ Escudos, Decree of January 21, 1952, Cupro-Nickel	$ .18	.35
☐ 1975	2½ Meticais, Popular Republic, Cupro-Nickel	55.00	130.00
☐ 1980–1986	2½ Meticais, Monetary Reform: Harbor Scene, Aluminium	—	30.00
☐ 1935	5 Escudos, Silver	—	2.50
☐ 1938–1949	5 Escudos, New Reverse Arms, Silver	—	2.00
☐ 1960	5 Escudos, Decree of January 21, 1952, Silver	—	.60
☐ 1980–1986	5 Meticais, Monetary Reform: Tractor, Aluminum	.18	.40
☐ 1936	10 Escudos, Silver	—	8.00
☐ 1938	10 Escudos, New Reverse Arms, Silver	—	7.00
☐ 1952–1966	10 Escudos, Decree of January 21, 1952, Silver	—	2.25
☐ 1980–1981	10 Meticais, Monetary Reform: Industrial Skyline, Cupro-Nickel	.28	.60
☐ 1986	10 Meticais, Monetary Reform: Industrial Skyline, Aluminum	.18	.40
☐ 1952–1966	20 Escudos, Decree of January 21, 1952, Silver	—	2.00
☐ 1980–1982	20 Meticais, Monetary Reform: Panzer Tank, Cupro-Nickel	.38	.80
☐ 1986	20 Meticais, Monetary Reform: Panzer Tank, Aluminum	.28	.60
☐ 1983	50 Meticais, Monetary Reform: World Fisheries Conference, Cupro-Nickel	1.60	3.00
☐ 1983	50 Meticais, Monetary Reform: World Fisheries Conference, Gold	—	1500.00
☐ 1983	50 Meticais, Monetary Reform: World Fisheries Conference, Silver	—	35.00
☐ 1986	50 Meticais, Monetary Reform: Woman & Soldier, Aluminum	—	1.00

DATE	COIN TYPE/VARIETY/METAL	ABP FINE	AVERAGE FINE
☐ 1985	250 Meticais, Monetary Reform: 10th Anniversary of Independence, Cupro-Nickel	$4.50	$10.00
☐ 1985	250 Meticais, Monetary Reform: 10th Anniversary of Independence, Silver	—	50.00
☐ 1980	500 Meticais, Monetary Reform: 5th Anniversary of Independence, Silver	—	40.00
☐ 1989	500 Meticais, Monetary Reform: Defense of Nature—Moorish Idol Fish, Silver	—	60.00
☐ 1989	500 Meticais, Monetary Reform: Defense of Nature—Lions, Silver	—	60.00
☐ 1989	500 Meticais, Monetary Reform: Defense of Nature—Giraffes, Silver	—	60.00
☐ 1988	1000 Meticais, Monetary Reform: Papal Visit, Silver	—	50.00
☐ 1985	2000 Meticais, Monetary Reform: 10th Anniversary of Independence, Gold	—	800.00
☐ 1980	5000 Meticais, Monetary Reform: 5th Anniversary of Independence, Gold	—	400.00

NEPAL

The first coins, used in the 6th century A.D., were of silver and copper. Small gold, silver, and copper coins were used in the 12th to 16th centuries. The silver mohur was used in the 17th century, followed by the gold presentation coin in the 1700s, the copper paisas in the 1800s, and the aluminum paisas in the 1900s. Decimal coins were used in 1932. The currency today is the rupee.

Nepal—Type Coinage

DATE	COIN TYPE/VARIETY/METAL	ABP FINE	AVERAGE FINE
□ 1954	5 Paisa, Bronze	$ .30	$ .75
□ 1954	10 Paisa, Hands Praying, Bronze	—	.20
□ 1954	20 Paisa, Bronze	20.00	35.00
□ 1935–1936	20 Paisa, Trident, Rev: Sword, Silver	—	2.00
□ 1940–1948	50 Paisa, Trident, Rev: Sword, Silver	—	3.00
□ 1954	50 Paisa, Head of Tribhubana, Silver	—	.60
□ 1950	Rupee, Trident, Rev: Sword, Silver	—	3.00
□ 1932–1943	Rupee, Trident, Rev: Sword, Silver	—	3.00

NETHERLANDS

The first coins were base-gold tremisses, then silver deniers. A revival of gold coinage occurred in the 14th century. In 1606 a new range of coins was established, including the gold ducat and the silver rijksdaalder. In 1680 gulden pieces were added. In 1830 a decimal system, consisting of 100 cents to the gulden, was established and is still in use today.

Netherlands—Type Coinage

□ 1850–1877	½ Cent, Copper	3.75	8.00

DATE	COIN TYPE/VARIETY/METAL	ABP FINE	AVERAGE FINE
☐ 1878–1901	1/2 Cent, Obv: KONINGRIJK, Bronze	$2.25	$5.00
☐ 1903–1906	1/2 Cent, Obv: KONINKRIJK, Bronze	1.20	3.00
☐ 1909–1940	1/2 Cent, Wilhelmina—3rd Coinage, Bronze	1.20	3.00
☐ 1850–1877	1 Cent, Copper	4.50	10.00

DATE	COIN TYPE/VARIETY/METAL	ABP FINE	AVERAGE FINE
☐ 1878–1901	1 Cent, Obv: KONINGRIJK, Bronze	2.50	6.00
☐ 1901	1 Cent, Obv: KONINKRIJK, Bronze	1.75	4.00
☐ 1902–1907	1 Cent, Obv: KONINKRIJK, Bronze	1.20	3.00
☐ 1913–1941	1 Cent, Wilhelmina—3rd Coinage, Bronze	.60	1.50
☐ 1941–1944	1 Cent, WWII Occupation, Zinc	.80	2.00
☐ 1950–1980	1 Cent, Juliana, Bronze	—	.10

DATE	COIN TYPE/VARIETY/METAL	ABP FINE	AVERAGE FINE
☐ 1877–1898	2 1/2 Cents, Obv: KONINGRIJK, Bronze	2.25	5.00
☐ 1903–1906	2 1/2 Cents, Obv: KONINKRIJK, Bronze	1.20	3.00
☐ 1912–1941	2 1/2 Cents, Wilhelmina—3rd Coinage, Bronze	3.00	7.00
☐ 1941–1942	2 1/2 Cents, WWII Occupation, Zinc	1.20	3.00

DATE	COIN TYPE/VARIETY/METAL	ABP FINE	AVERAGE FINE
☐ 1850–1887	5 Cents, Willem III, Silver	—	$6.00
☐ 1907–1909	5 Cents, Wilhelmina—2nd Coinage, Cupro-Nickel	$2.75	6.00
☐ 1913–1940	5 Cents, Wilhelmina—3rd Coinage, Cupro-Nickel	.80	2.00
☐ 1941–1943	5 Cents, WWII Occupation, Zinc	2.00	4.00
☐ 1950 to Date	5 Cents, Juliana, Bronze	—	.10
☐ 1849–1890	10 Cents, Willem III, Silver	—	15.00
☐ 1892–1897	10 Cents, Wilhelmina—1st Coinage, Obv: Child Head, Rev: Value in Wreath, Silver	—	10.00
☐ 1898–1901	10 Cents, Wilhelmina—2nd Coinage, Obv: Young Head, Silver	—	25.00
☐ 1903	10 Cents, Wilhelmina—2nd Coinage, Obv: Large Head, Silver	—	10.00
☐ 1904–1906	10 Cents, Wilhelmina—2nd Coinage, Obv: Small Head, Silver	—	12.00

DATE	COIN TYPE/VARIETY/METAL	ABP FINE	AVERAGE FINE
☐ 1910–1925	10 Cents, Wilhelmina—3rd Coinage, Obv: Adult Head, Silver	—	4.00
☐ 1926–1945	10 Cents, Wilhelmina—4th Coinage, Obv: Older Head, Silver	—	2.00
☐ 1941–1943	10 Cents, WWII Occupation, Zinc	.40	1.00
☐ 1950 to Date	10 Cents, Juliana, Nickel	—	.10
☐ 1849–1890	25 Cents, Willem III, Silver	—	120.00
☐ 1892–1897	25 Cents, Wilhelmina—1st Coinage, Obv: Child Head, Rev: Value in Wreath, Silver	—	20.00
☐ 1898–1906	25 Cents, Wilhelmina—2nd Coinage, Silver	—	18.00
☐ 1910–1925	25 Cents, Wilhelmina—3rd Coinage, Obv: Adult Head, Silver	—	10.00

DATE	COIN TYPE/VARIETY/METAL	ABP FINE	AVERAGE FINE
□ 1926–1945	25 Cents, Wilhelmina—4th Coinage, Obv: Older Head, Silver	—	$2.00
□ 1950–1980	25 Cents, Juliana, Nickel	—	.18
□ 1980 to Date	25 Cents, Juliana, Aluminum	—	.10
□ 1853–1868	½ Gulden, Willem III, Silver	—	15.00
□ 1898	½ Gulden, Wilhelmina—2nd Coinage, Silver	—	30.00
□ 1904–1909	½ Gulden, Wilhelmina—2nd Coinage, Silver	—	15.00
□ 1910–1919	½ Gulden, Wilhelmina—3rd Coinage, Obv: Adult Head, Silver	—	10.00
□ 1921–1930	½ Gulden, Wilhelmina—4th Coinage, Obv: Older Head, Silver	—	1.75
□ 1849–1975	1 Ducat, Trade Coins, Gold	—	100.00
□ 1851–1866	1 Gulden, Willem III, Silver	—	20.00
□ 1892–1897	1 Gulden, Wilhelmina—1st Coinage, Obv: Child Head, Rev: Value in Wreath, Silver	—	15.00
□ 1898–1901	1 Gulden, Wilhelmina—2nd Coinage, Silver	—	35.00
□ 1904–1909	1 Gulden, Wilhelmina—2nd Coinage, Silver	—	15.00
□ 1910–1917	1 Gulden, Wilhelmina—3rd Coinage, Obv: Adult Head, Silver	—	12.00

DATE	COIN TYPE/VARIETY/METAL	ABP FINE	AVERAGE FINE
□ 1922–1945	1 Gulden, Wilhelmina—4th Coinage, Obv: Older Head, Silver	—	5.00
□ 1954–1967	1 Gulden, Juliana, Silver	—	2.00

DATE	COIN TYPE/VARIETY/METAL	ABP FINE	AVERAGE FINE
☐ 1980 to Date	1 Gulden, Nickel	$ .50	$ .80
☐ 1989	1 Silver Ducat, Silver Wedding Anniversary, Silver	—	15.00
☐ 1854–1967	2 Ducat, Trade Coins, Gold	—	20,000.00
☐ 1849–1874	2½ Gulden, Willem III, Silver	—	20.00
☐ 1898	2½ Gulden, Wilhelmina—2nd Coinage, Silver	—	200.00

DATE	COIN TYPE/VARIETY/METAL	ABP FINE	AVERAGE FINE
☐ 1929–1940	2½ Gulden, Wilhelmina—4th Coinage, Obv: Older Head, Silver	—	10.00
☐ 1959–1966	2½ Gulden, Juliana, Silver	—	5.00
☐ 1969 to Date	2½ Gulden, Juliana, Nickel	—	1.75
☐ 1817–1832	3 Gulden, Willem, Silver	—	300.00

DATE	COIN TYPE/VARIETY/METAL	ABP FINE	AVERAGE FINE
☐ 1851	5 Gulden, Willem III, Gold	—	350.00
☐ 1912	5 Gulden, Wilhelmina—3rd Coinage, Obv: Adult Head, Gold	—	60.00
☐ 1987 to Date	5 Gulden, Willem, Clad	2.00	2.75

DATE	COIN TYPE/VARIETY/METAL	ABP FINE	AVERAGE FINE
☐ 1851	10 Gulden, Willem III, Gold	—	500.00

DATE	COIN TYPE/VARIETY/METAL	ABP FINE	AVERAGE FINE
□ 1875	10 Gulden, Willem III, Rev: Date at Top, Gold	—	$100.00
□ 1876–1889	10 Gulden, Willem III, Rev: Date at Bottom, Gold	—	125.00
□ 1892–1897	10 Gulden, Wilhelmina—1st Coinage, Obv: Child Head, Rev: Value in Wreath, Gold	—	1500.00
□ 1898	10 Gulden, Wilhelmina—2nd Coinage, Gold	—	150.00
□ 1911–1917	10 Gulden, Wilhelmina—3rd Coinage, Obv: Adult Head, Gold	—	100.00
□ 1925–1933	10 Gulden, Wilhelmina—4th Coinage, Obv: Older Head, Gold	—	100.00
□ 1851–1853	20 Gulden, Willem III, Gold	—	750.00
□ 1982	50 Gulden, Dutch American Friendship, Gold	—	2200.00
□ 1982	50 Gulden, Dutch American Friendship, Silver	—	55.00
□ 1984	50 Gulden, 400th Anniversary of Death of William of Orange, Silver	—	30.00
□ 1987	50 Gulden, Golden Wedding of Queen Mother, Silver	—	30.00
□ 1988	50 Gulden, 300th Anniversary of William & Mary, Silver	—	30.00
□ 1990	50 Gulden, 100 Years of Queens, Silver	—	30.00
□ 1991	50 Gulden, Silver Wedding Anniversary, Silver	—	30.00

NEW ZEALAND

Various foreign coins including Spanish-American, French, Indian, and British were in use in the early 19th century. In 1859, the copper halfpenny token was in use, followed by the silver florin in the 1930s. New Zealand's first coinage was issued in 1933 and included silver threepences, sixpences, shillings, florins, and halfcrowns. Decimal coins were used in 1967. The currency today is the dollar.

New Zealand—Type Coinage

DATE	COIN TYPE/VARIETY/METAL	ABP FINE	AVERAGE FINE
☐ 1940–1947	½ Penny, George VI, Bronze	$ .18	$ .40
☐ 1949–1952	½ Penny, King George the Sixth, Bronze	—	.12
☐ 1953–1965	½ Penny, Elizabeth II, Bronze	—	.10

DATE	COIN TYPE/VARIETY/METAL	ABP FINE	AVERAGE FINE
☐ 1940–1947	1 Penny, George VI, Bronze	.18	.30
☐ 1949–1952	1 Penny, King George the Sixth, Bronze	—	.18
☐ 1953–1965	1 Penny, Elizabeth II, Bronze	—	.10

DATE	COIN TYPE/VARIETY/METAL	ABP FINE	AVERAGE FINE
☐ 1967–1988	1 Cent, Decimal Coinage: Silver Fern Leaf, Bronze	—	.10
☐ 1933–1936	3 Pence, George V, Silver	—	.40

DATE	COIN TYPE/VARIETY/METAL	ABP FINE	AVERAGE FINE
☐ 1937–1946	3 Pence, George VI, Silver	—	$ .40
☐ 1947	3 Pence, George VI, Cupro-Nickel	—	.18
☐ 1948–1952	3 Pence, King George the Sixth, Cupro-Nickel	—	.20
☐ 1953–1965	3 Pence, Elizabeth II, Cupro-Nickel	—	.10
☐ 1967–1988	2 Cents, Decimal Coinage: Kowhai Leaves, Bronze	—	.15
☐ 1933–1936	6 Pence, George V, Silver	—	.75
☐ 1937–1946	6 Pence, George VI, Silver	—	.60
☐ 1947	6 Pence, George VI, Cupro-Nickel	$ .28	.60
☐ 1948–1952	6 Pence, King George the Sixth, Cupro-Nickel	.24	.50
☐ 1953–1965	6 Pence, Elizabeth II, Cupro-Nickel	—	.18

DATE	COIN TYPE/VARIETY/METAL	ABP FINE	AVERAGE FINE
□ 1933–1935	1 Shilling, George V, Silver	—	$4.00
□ 1937–1946	1 Shilling, George VI, Silver	—	3.00
□ 1947	1 Shilling, George VI, Cupro-Nickel	$ .40	1.00
□ 1948–1952	1 Shilling, King George the Sixth, Cupro-Nickel	.30	.75
□ 1953–1965	1 Shilling, Elizabeth II, Cupro-Nickel	—	.10

DATE	COIN TYPE/VARIETY/METAL	ABP FINE	AVERAGE FINE
□ 1967 to Date	5 Cents, Decimal Coinage: Tuatara, Cupro-Nickel	—	.10

DATE	COIN TYPE/VARIETY/METAL	ABP FINE	AVERAGE FINE
□ 1933–1936	1 Florin, George V, Silver	—	2.00
□ 1937–1946	1 Florin, George VI, Silver	—	2.00
□ 1947	1 Florin, George VI, Cupro-Nickel	.40	1.00
□ 1948–1951	1 Florin, King George the Sixth, Cupro-Nickel	.40	1.00
□ 1953–1965	1 Florin, Elizabeth II, Cupro-Nickel	—	.15

DATE	COIN TYPE/VARIETY/METAL	ABP FINE	AVERAGE FINE
□ 1967 to Date	Decimal Coinage: Maori Mask, Cupro-Nickel	—	$ .10
□ 1933–1935	½ Crown, George V, Silver	—	4.00
□ 1937–1946	½ Crown, George VI, Silver	—	3.00
□ 1940	½ Crown, George VI: Centennial of British Settlement, Silver	—	4.00
□ 1947	½ Crown, George VI, Cupro-Nickel	$ .40	1.00
□ 1948–1951	½ Crown, King George the Sixth, Cupro-Nickel	.30	.75
□ 1953–1965	½ Crown, Elizabeth II, Cupro-Nickel	.30	.75
□ 1967–1989	20 Cents, Decimal Coinage: Kiwi, Cupro-Nickel	—	.12
□ 1990 to Date	20 Cents, Decimal Coinage: 1990 Anniversary Celebrations, Silver	—	.75
□ 1990 to Date	20 Cents, Decimal Coinage: 1990 Anniversary Celebrations, Cupro-Nickel	.18	.40

DATE	COIN TYPE/VARIETY/METAL	ABP FINE	AVERAGE FINE
☐ 1935	1 Crown, George V: 25th Year of Reign—Treaty of Waitangi, Silver	—	$1000.00
☐ 1949	1 Crown, King George the Sixth: Proposed Royal Visit, Cupro-Nickel	$2.00	4.00
☐ 1953	1 Crown, Elizabeth II, Cupro-Nickel	.80	2.00
☐ 1967–1985	50 Cents, Decimal Coinage: Endeavour, Cupro-Nickel	.18	.40
☐ 1986 to Date	50 Cents, Decimal Coinage: Elizabeth II, Cupro-Nickel	.18	.30
☐ 1967–1976	1 Dollar, Decimalization Commemorative, Lettered Edge, Cupro-Nickel	1.75	3.00
☐ 1969	1 Dollar, Captain Cook—200th Anniversary, Cupro-Nickel	.40	1.00
☐ 1970	1 Dollar, Cook Islands, Cupro-Nickel	5.00	12.00
☐ 1970	1 Dollar, Royal Visit—Mount Cook, Cupro-Nickel	.40	1.00
☐ 1974	1 Dollar, Commonwealth Games, Cupro-Nickel	.40	1.00

DATE	COIN TYPE/VARIETY/METAL	ABP FINE	AVERAGE FINE
□ 1974	1 Dollar, Commonwealth Games, Silver	—	$35.00
□ 1974	1 Dollar, New Zealand Day—Kotuku, Cupro-Nickel	$2.25	5.00
□ 1977	1 Dollar, Waitangi Day—Treaty House, Cupro-Nickel	1.40	3.00
□ 1977	1 Dollar, Waitangi Day—Treaty House, Silver	—	20.00
□ 1978	1 Dollar, Coronation 25th Anniversary—Parliament, Silver	—	15.00
□ 1978	1 Dollar, Coronation 25th Anniversary—Parliament, Cupro-Nickel	.40	1.00
□ 1979	1 Dollar, Cupro-Nickel	.40	1.00
□ 1979	1 Dollar, Silver	—	12.00
□ 1980	1 Dollar, Fantail, Cupro-Nickel	.40	1.00
□ 1980	1 Dollar, Fantail, Silver	—	12.00
□ 1981	1 Dollar, Royal Visit—English Oak, Cupro-Nickel	.40	1.00
□ 1981	1 Dollar, Royal Visit—English Oak, Silver	—	12.00
□ 1982	1 Dollar, Takaha, Silver	—	15.00
□ 1982	1 Dollar, Takaha, Cupro-Nickel	.60	1.50
□ 1983	1 Dollar, 50 Years of Coinage, Silver	—	25.00
□ 1983	1 Dollar, Royal Visit, Cupro-Nickel	1.40	3.00
□ 1983	1 Dollar, Royal Visit, Silver	—	18.00
□ 1983	1 Dollar, 50 Years of Coinage, Cupro-Nickel	.40	1.00
□ 1984	1 Dollar, Chatham Island Black Robin, Cupro-Nickel	1.40	3.00
□ 1984	1 Dollar, Chatham Island Black Robin, Silver	—	18.00
□ 1985	1 Dollar, Black Stilt, Silver	—	20.00
□ 1985	1 Dollar, Black Stilt, Cupro-Nickel	.80	2.00
□ 1986	1 Dollar, Royal Visit, Silver	—	25.00
□ 1986	1 Dollar, Royal Visit, Cupro-Nickel	.80	2.00
□ 1986	1 Dollar, Kakapo, Silver	—	18.00
□ 1986	1 Dollar, Kakapo, Cupro-Nickel	.80	2.00
□ 1987	1 Dollar, National Parks Centennial, Cupro-Nickel	.80	2.00
□ 1987	1 Dollar, National Parks Centennial, Silver	—	18.00
□ 1988	1 Dollar, Yellow-eyed Penguin, Cupro-Nickel	.80	2.00
□ 1988	1 Dollar, Yellow-eyed Penguin, Silver	—	40.00
□ 1989	1 Dollar, XIV Commonwealth Games—Runner, Cupro-Nickel	.80	2.00
□ 1989	1 Dollar, XIV Commonwealth Games—Swimmer, Silver	—	20.00

DATE	COIN TYPE/VARIETY/METAL	ABP FINE	AVERAGE FINE
□ 1989	1 Dollar, XIV Commonwealth Games—Weightlifter, Silver	—	$20.00
□ 1989	1 Dollar, XIV Commonwealth Games—Weightlifter, Cupro-Nickel	$ .80	2.00
□ 1989	1 Dollar, XIV Commonwealth Games—Runner, Silver	—	20.00
□ 1989	1 Dollar, XIV Commonwealth Games—Swimmer, Cupro-Nickel	.80	2.00
□ 1989	1 Dollar, XIV Commonwealth Games—Gymnast, Silver	—	20.00
□ 1989	1 Dollar, XIV Commonwealth Games—Gymnast, Cupro-Nickel	.80	2.00
□ 1990	1 Dollar, Kiwi Bird, Silver	—	12.00
□ 1990	1 Dollar, Anniversary Celebrations, Silver	—	30.00
□ 1990	1 Dollar, Anniversary Celebrations, Cupro-Nickel	.80	2.00
□ 1990	1 Dollar, Kiwi Bird, Aluminum-Bronze	1.40	3.00
□ 1990	2 Dollars, White Heron, Silver	—	18.00

DATE	COIN TYPE/VARIETY/METAL	ABP FINE	AVERAGE FINE
□ 1990	2 Dollars, White Heron, Aluminum-Bronze	1.40	3.00
□ 1990	5 Dollars, ANZAC Memorial, Aluminum-Bronze	2.25	5.00
□ 1991	5 Dollars, Rugby World Cup, Cupro-Nickel	4.75	10.00
□ 1991	5 Dollars, Rugby World Cup, Silver	—	50.00
□ 1992	5 Dollars, 25th Anniversary of Decimalization, Cupro-Nickel	4.75	10.00
□ 1992	5 Dollars, 25th Anniversary of Decimalization, Silver	—	40.00
□ 1990	150 Dollars, Kiwi, Gold	—	400.00

NORWAY

In the 9th century some Anglo-Saxon and Frankish coins were in circulation, but were most likely used as jewelry. Silver pennies were minted in the late 10th century, followed by bracteates and skillings, ducats, and dalers. Anglo-Saxon and German coins were important in the 980s and 990s, but English coins dropped and Danish coins became more important after 1050. The main Norwegian series began around 1047. By the 12th century, the Norwegian penny was a bracteate. The only coins struck in Norway at first were base-silver hvids. Larger silver coins were issued in the 16th century. In 1874 a new decimal system was based on the krone.

Norway—Type Coinage

DATE	COIN TYPE/VARIETY/METAL	ABP FINE	AVERAGE FINE
☐ 1837–1841	1/2 Skilling, Charles XIV, Rev: Lion, Copper	$2.75	$6.00

DATE	COIN TYPE/VARIETY/METAL	ABP FINE	AVERAGE FINE
☐ 1863–1872	1/2 Skilling, Charles XV, Rev: Lion, Copper	2.40	5.00
☐ 1819–1837	1 Skilling, Charles XIV, Rev: Lion, Copper	18.00	30.00
☐ 1867–1872	1 Skilling, Charles XV, Rev: Lion, Copper	1.75	4.00

DATE	COIN TYPE/VARIETY/METAL	ABP FINE	AVERAGE FINE
□ 1876–1902	1 Ore, Oscar II, Rev: Lion, Bronze	$2.25	$5.00
□ 1906–1950	1 Ore, Haakon VII, Monograms, Bronze	.20	.50
□ 1952–1953	1 Ore, Postwar, Obv: Lion, Rev: Monogram	—	.10
□ 1822–1836	2 Skilling, Charles XIV, Rev: Lion, Copper	3.75	8.00
□ 1876–1902	2 Ore, Oscar II, Rev: Lion, Bronze	1.20	3.00

DATE	COIN TYPE/VARIETY/METAL	ABP FINE	AVERAGE FINE
□ 1906–1950	2 Ore, Haakon VII, Monograms, Bronze	.20	.50
□ 1952	2 Ore, Postwar, Obv: Lion, Rev: Monogram, Bronze	—	.10
□ 1870–1872	2 Skilling, Charles XV, Rev: Lion, Copper	1.75	4.00
□ 1868–1872	3 Skilling, Charles XV, Rev: Lion, Silver	—	6.00
□ 1825–1842	4 Skilling, Charles XIV, Rev: Lion, Silver	—	5.00

DATE	COIN TYPE/VARIETY/METAL	ABP FINE	AVERAGE FINE
□ 1875–1902	5 Ore, Oscar II, Rev: Lion, Bronze	1.20	3.00
□ 1907–1950	5 Ore, Haakon VII, Monograms, Bronze	.28	.60
□ 1952–1953	5 Ore, Postwar, Obv: Lion, Rev: Monogram, Bronze	—	.10

DATE	COIN TYPE/VARIETY/METAL	ABP FINE	AVERAGE FINE
□ 1819–1827	8 Skilling, Charles, XIV, Rev: Lion, Silver	—	$18.00
□ 1845–1856	12 Skilling, Oscar I, Rev: Lion, Silver	—	6.00
□ 1861–1872	12 Skilling, Charles XV, Rev: Lion, Silver	—	500.00
□ 1874–1903	10 Ore, Oscar II, Rev: Lion, Silver	—	50.00
□ 1909–1920	10 Ore, Haakon VII, Monograms Around Hole, Silver	—	5.00

DATE	COIN TYPE/VARIETY/METAL	ABP FINE	AVERAGE FINE
□ 1920–1949	10 Ore, Haakon VII, Monograms Around Hole, Cupro-Nickel	—	.10
□ 1951–1953	10 Ore, Postwar, Obv: Lion, Rev: Monogram, Cupro-Nickel	—	.10
□ 1819–1836	24 Skilling, Charles XIV, Rev: Lion, Silver	—	25.00
□ 1845–1855	24 Skilling, Oscar I, Rev: Lion, Silver	—	12.00
□ 1861–1872	24 Skilling, Charles XV, Rev: Lion, Silver	—	—
□ 1876–1904	25 Ore, Oscar II, Rev: Lion, Silver	—	500.00
□ 1909–1919	25 Ore, Haakon VII, Monograms Around Hole, Silver	—	10.00

DATE	COIN TYPE/VARIETY/METAL	ABP FINE	AVERAGE FINE
□ 1920–1950	25 Ore, Haakon VII, Monograms Around Hole, Cupro-Nickel	$ .20	$ .50
□ 1952	25 Ore, Postwar, Obv: Lion, Rev: Monogram, Cupro-Nickel	—	.10
□ 1819–1844	½ Speciedaler, Charles XI, Rev: Lion, Silver	—	75.00
□ 1846–1855	½ Speciedaler, Oscar I, Rev: Lion, Silver	—	60.00

DATE	COIN TYPE/VARIETY/METAL	ABP FINE	AVERAGE FINE
□ 1861–1872	½ Speciedaler, Charles XV, Rev: Lion, Silver	—	250.00
□ 1874–1904	50 Ore, Oscar II, Rev: Lion, Silver	—	20.00
□ 1909–1917	50 Ore, Haakon VII, Monograms Around Hole, Silver	—	3.00

DATE	COIN TYPE/VARIETY/METAL	ABP FINE	AVERAGE FINE
□ 1920–1949	50 Ore, Haakon VII, Monograms Around Hole, Cupro-Nickel	.18	.30
□ 1953	50 Ore, Postwar, Obv: Lion, Rev: Monogram, Cupro-Nickel	—	.25

DATE	COIN TYPE/VARIETY/METAL	ABP FINE	AVERAGE FINE
☐ 1819–1836	1 Speciedaler, Charles XIV, Rev: Lion, Silver	—	$ 75.00
☐ 1846–1857	1 Speciedaler, Oscar I, Rev: Lion, Silver	—	60.00
☐ 1861–1872	1 Speciedaler, Charles XV, Rev: Lion, Silver	—	250.00
☐ 1875–1904	Krone, Oscar II, Rev: Lion, Silver	—	35.00
☐ 1908–1917	Krone, Haakon VII, Monograms Around Hole, Silver	—	15.00

DATE	COIN TYPE/VARIETY/METAL	ABP FINE	AVERAGE FINE
☐ 1925–1950	Krone, Haakon VII, Monograms Around Hole, Cupro-Nickel	$ .20	.50
☐ 1951	Krone, Postwar, Obv: Lion, Rev: Monogram, Cupro-Nickel	—	.25
☐ 1878–1904	2 Kroner, Oscar II, Rev: Lion, Silver	—	50.00
☐ 1906–1907	2 Kroner, Haakon VII, Rev: St. Olaf Standing, Silver	—	15.00
☐ 1909–1917	2 Kroner, Haakon VII, Rev: Lion & Shields, Silver	—	35.00
☐ 1914	2 Kroner, Haakon VII, Centenary of Constitution, Silver	—	8.00
☐ 1873–1902	10 Kroner, Oscar II, Rev: Lion, Gold	—	200.00
☐ 1910	10 Kroner, Haakon VII, Rev: St. Olaf Standing, Gold	—	100.00
☐ 1873–1902	20 Kroner, Oscar II, Rev: Lion, Gold	—	175.00
☐ 1910	20 Kroner, Haakon VII, Rev: St. Olaf Standing, Gold	—	200.00

PAKISTAN

The first coins were used in the 4th century B.C. and were of silver, followed by copper. The gold stater was in evidence in 130, and the silver dirhem in 1028. The silver rupee appeared in 1826. The decimal system was established in 1961. The currency used today is the rupee.

Pakistan—Type Coinage

DATE	COIN TYPE/VARIETY/METAL	ABP FINE	AVERAGE FINE
□ 1961	1 Pice, Bronze	—	$ .10
□ 1961–1965	1 Paisa, Bronze	—	.10
□ 1965–1966	1 Paisa, Nickel-Brass	—	.10
□ 1967–1979	1 Paisa, Aluminum	—	.10
□ 1964–1966	2 Paisa, Bronze	—	.10

DATE	COIN TYPE/VARIETY/METAL	ABP FINE	AVERAGE FINE
☐ 1966–1976	2 Paisa, Aluminum	—	$ .10

DATE	COIN TYPE/VARIETY/METAL	ABP FINE	AVERAGE FINE
☐ 1961–1961	5 Pice, Nickel-Brass	—	.10
☐ 1961–1974	5 Paisa, Nickel-Brass	—	.10
☐ 1974–1988	5 Paisa, Aluminum	—	.10
☐ 1950	1 Pie, Bronze	—	.10
☐ 1961	10 Pice, Cupro-Nickel	—	.10
☐ 1961–1974	10 Paisa, Cupro-Nickel	—	.10
☐ 1974–1990	10 Paisa, Aluminum	—	.10
☐ 1948–1952	1 Pice, Holed, Bronze	—	.10
☐ 1953–1959	1 Pice, Nickel-Brass	—	.10
☐ 1963–1967	25 Paisa, Nickel	—	.10
☐ 1967 to Date	25 Paisa, Cupro-Nickel	—	.10
☐ 1976	50 Paisa, Anniversary of Mohammed Ali Jinnah, Cupro-Nickel	—	.10
☐ 1981	50 Paisa, AH1401—1400th Anniversary of Hegira, Cupro-Nickel	—	.10
☐ 1948–1951	1/2 Anna, Crescent, Cupro-Nickel	—	.10
☐ 1953–1958	1/2 Anna, Nickel-Brass	—	.10
☐ 1963–1969	50 Paisa, Nickel	—	.10
☐ 1969 to Date	50 Paisa, Cupro-Nickel	—	.10
☐ 1948–1949	1 Rupee, Crescent to Right, Nickel	—	.15
☐ 1977	1 Rupee, Islamic Summit Conference, Cupro-Nickel	—	.15
☐ 1977	1 Rupee, Centennial of Birth of Allama Mohammad Iqbai, Cupro-Nickel	—	.15
☐ 1979–1988	1 Rupee, Cupro-Nickel	—	.15
☐ 1981	1 Rupee, World Food Day, Cupro-Nickel	—	.15
☐ 1981	1 Rupee, 1400th Hegira Anniversary, Cupro-Nickel	—	.15
☐ 1948–1952	1 Anna, Crescent to Right, Cupro-Nickel	—	.10
☐ 1950	1 Anna, Crescent to Left, Cupro-Nickel	—	.10
☐ 1953–1958	1 Anna, Cupro-Nickel	—	.10
☐ 1948–1952	2 Annas, Crescent to Right, Cupro-Nickel	—	.15
☐ 1950	2 Annas, Crescent to Left, Cupro-Nickel	—	.10
☐ 1953–1959	2 Annas, Cupro-Nickel	—	.10
☐ 1948–1951	1/4 Rupee, Crescent to Right, Nickel	$.10	.25

DATE	COIN TYPE/VARIETY/METAL	ABP FINE	AVERAGE FINE
□ 1950	1/4 Rupee, Crescent to Left, Nickel	$ .10	$ .25
□ 1948–1951	1/2 Rupee, Crescent to Right, Nickel	.10	.25
□ 1976	100 Rupees, Conservation Series—Pheasant, Silver	—	.30
□ 1976	100 Rupees, Centennial of Birth of Mohammad Ali Jinnah, Silver	—	.30
□ 1977	100 Rupees, Centennial of Birth of Allama Mohammad Iqbai, Silver	—	.35
□ 1977	100 Rupees, Islamic Summit Conference, Silver	—	.25
□ 1976	150 Rupees, Conservation Series—Crocodile, Silver	—	.35
□ 1977	150 Rupees, Centennial of Birth Allama Mohammad Iqbai, Gold	—	110.00
□ 1977	1000 Rupees, Islamic Summit Conference, Gold	—	200.00
□ 1976	3000 Rupees, Conservation Series—Astor Markhor, Gold	—	600.00

PALESTINE

The following group of coins were produced during Great Britain's rule of Palestine (1922–1948). In 1948, when Palestine became the state of Israel, the coinage was changed significantly to the coins that you will find listed under the ISRAEL section of this book.

Palestine-Type Coinage

DATE	COIN TYPE/VARIETY/METAL	ABP FINE	AVERAGE FINE
□ 1927–1948	Mil, Hebrew-English-Arabic Legends, Rev: Olive Sprig, Bronze	KM-1 1927 XF	$2.00
□ 1927–1947	2 Mils, Hebrew-English-Arabic Legends, Rev: Olive Sprig, Bronze	KM-2 1927 VF	2.00
□ 1927–1947	5 Mils, Wreath, Cupro-Nickel	KM3 1927 VF	2.00
□ 1942–1944	5 Mils, Bronze	—	2.00
□ 1927–1947	10 Mils, Wreath, Cupro-Nickel	—	2.00
□ 1942–1943	10 Mils, Bronze	Y4 1942 VF	8.00
□ 1927–1947	20 Mils, Holed Wreath, Cupro-Nickel	—	5.00
□ 1942–1944	20 Mils, Bronze	—	5.00
□ 1927–1942	50 Mils, Olive Sprig, Silver	—	6.00

DATE	COIN TYPE/VARIETY/METAL	ABP FINE	AVERAGE FINE
□ 1927–1942	100 Mils, Olive Sprig, Silver	KM7 1935 XF	$20.00

PHILIPPINES

The first small, gold coins known as piloncitos were used before the 13th century, followed by cast-bronze square-holed coins. Silver dollars were issued in 1827. The silver reales and copper quarto were in use in the 1800s, followed by the silver peso and cupro-nickel piso in the 1900s. The decimal system was established in 1861. Today's currency is the piso.

Philippines—Spanish Colonies Coinage

DATE	COIN TYPE/VARIETY/METAL	ABP FINE	AVERAGE FINE
☐ 1864–1868	10 Centimos, Isabel II, Silver	—	$80.00
☐ 1880–1885	10 Centimos, Alfonso XII, Silver	—	20.00
☐ 1864–1868	20 Centimos, Isabel II, Silver	—	18.00
☐ 1880–1885	20 Centimos, Alfonso XII, Silver	—	15.00
☐ 1865–1868	50 Centimos, Isabel II, Silver	—	300.00
☐ 1880–1885	50 Centimos, Alfonso XII, Silver	—	15.00
☐ 1861–1868	1 Peso, Isabel II, Gold	—	50.00
☐ 1897	1 Peso, Alfonso XIII, Silver	—	30.00
☐ 1861–1868	2 Pesos, Isabel II, Gold	—	75.00
☐ 1861–1868	4 Pesos, Isabel II, Gold	—	150.00
☐ 1880–1885	4 Pesos, Alfonso XII, Gold	—	3000.00

Philippines—U.S. Territorial Coinage

DATE	COIN TYPE/VARIETY/METAL	ABP FINE	AVERAGE FINE
☐ 1903–1908	1/2 Centavo, U.S. Territory, Bronze	$ .28	.60
☐ 1903–1936	Centavo, U.S. Territory, Bronze	.28	.60
☐ 1903–1928	5 Centavos, U.S. Territory, Cupro-Nickel	.40	1.00

DATE	COIN TYPE/VARIETY/METAL	ABP FINE	AVERAGE FINE
☐ 1930–1935	5 Centavos, U.S. Territory, Cupro-Nickel	$ .40	$1.00
☐ 1903–1906	10 Centavos, U.S. Territory, Silver	—	2.00
☐ 1907–1935	10 Centavos, U.S. Territory, Silver	—	2.00
☐ 1903–1906	20 Centavos, U.S. Territory, Silver	—	3.00
☐ 1907–1929	20 Centavos, U.S. Territory, Silver	—	3.00
☐ 1903–1906	50 Centavos, U.S. Territory, Silver	—	4.00
☐ 1907–1921	50 Centavos, U.S. Territory, Silver	—	3.00
☐ 1903–1906	1 Peso, U.S. Territory, Silver	—	8.00

DATE	COIN TYPE/VARIETY/METAL	ABP FINE	AVERAGE FINE
☐ 1907–1912	1 Peso, U.S. Territory, Silver	—	5.00

Philippines—Commonwealth Coinage

DATE	COIN TYPE/VARIETY/METAL	ABP FINE	AVERAGE FINE
□ 1937–1944	1 Centavo, Commonwealth, Bronze	$ .18	$ .30
□ 1937–1941	5 Centavos, Commonwealth, Cupro-Nickel	.40	1.00

DATE	COIN TYPE/VARIETY/METAL	ABP FINE	AVERAGE FINE
□ 1944–1945	5 Centavos, Commonwealth, Copper-Nickel-Zinc	—	.10

DATE	COIN TYPE/VARIETY/METAL	ABP FINE	AVERAGE FINE
□ 1937–1945	10 Centavos, Commonwealth, Silver	—	.60

DATE	COIN TYPE/VARIETY/METAL	ABP FINE	AVERAGE FINE
□ 1937–1945	20 Centavos, Commonwealth, Silver	—	$1.00
□ 1936	50 Centavos, Commonwealth Establishment of Commonwealth—Murphy & Quezon, Silver	—	18.00
□ 1944–1945	50 Centavos, Commonwealth, Silver	—	6.50
□ 1936	1 Peso, Commonwealth, Establishment of Commonwealth—Murphy & Quezon, Silver	—	50.00
□ 1936	1 Peso, Commonwealth, Establishment of Commonwealth—Roosevelt & Quezon, Silver	—	50.00

Philippines—Republic Coinage

DATE	COIN TYPE/VARIETY/METAL	ABP FINE	AVERAGE FINE
□ 1958–1966	1 Centavo, Republic, Central Bank, Bronze	—	.10

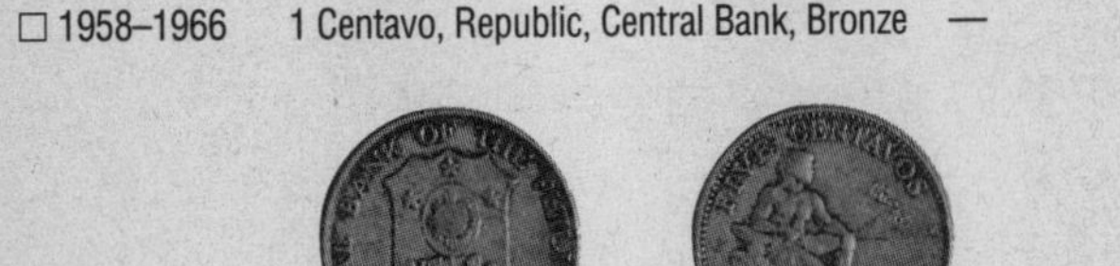

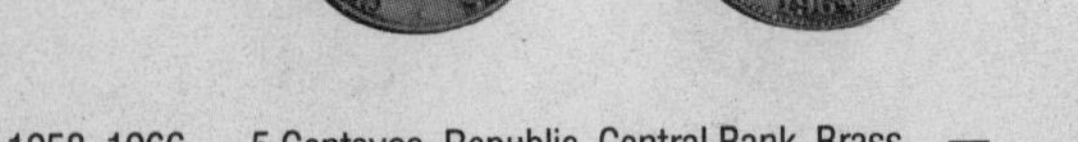

DATE	COIN TYPE/VARIETY/METAL	ABP FINE	AVERAGE FINE
□ 1958–1966	5 Centavos, Republic, Central Bank, Brass	—	.10

DATE	COIN TYPE/VARIETY/METAL	ABP FINE	AVERAGE FINE
☐ 1958–1966	10 Centavos, Republic, Central Bank, Nickel-Brass	—	$.10

DATE	COIN TYPE/VARIETY/METAL	ABP FINE	AVERAGE FINE
☐ 1958–1966	25 Centavos, Republic, Central Bank, Nickel-Brass	—	.10

DATE	COIN TYPE/VARIETY/METAL	ABP FINE	AVERAGE FINE
☐ 1947	50 Centavos, Republic, MacArthur, Silver	—	7.00
☐ 1961	½ Peso, Republic, Birth of Rizal Centennial, Silver	—	4.00
☐ 1958–1964	50 Centavos, Republic, Central Bank, Nickel-Brass	—	.20

DATE	COIN TYPE/VARIETY/METAL	ABP FINE	AVERAGE FINE
□ 1947	1 Peso, Republic, MacArthur, Silver	—	$8.00
□ 1961	1 Peso, Republic, Birth of Rizal Centennial, Silver	—	7.00
□ 1963	1 Peso, Republic, Birth of Bonifacio Centennial, Silver	—	7.00
□ 1964	1 Peso, Republic, Birth of Mabini Centennial, Silver	—	7.00
□ 1967	1 Peso, Republic, Fall of Bataan & Corregidor—25th Anniversary, Silver	—	7.00

Philippines—Current Coinage

□ 1967–1974	1 Sentimo, Aluminum	—	.30
□ 1975–1982	1 Sentimo, Aluminum	—	.30
□ 1983–1990	1 Sentimo, Aluminum	—	.30

□ 1967–1974	5 Sentimos, Brass	—	.20
□ 1975–1982	5 Sentimos, Brass	—	.20
□ 1983–1991	5 Sentimos, Orchid, Aluminum	—	.20

DATE	COIN TYPE/VARIETY/METAL	ABP FINE	AVERAGE FINE
☐ 1967–1982	10 Sentimos, Orchid, Cupro-Nickel	—	$ .20
☐ 1983–1992	10 Sentimos, Aluminum	—	.20

DATE	COIN TYPE/VARIETY/METAL	ABP FINE	AVERAGE FINE
☐ 1975–1982	25 Sentimos, Cupro-Nickel	—	.20
☐ 1983–1992	25 Sentimos, Butterfly, Cupro-Nickel	—	.20

DATE	COIN TYPE/VARIETY/METAL	ABP FINE	AVERAGE FINE
☐ 1967–1975	50 Sentimos, Marcelo del Pilar, Cupro-Nickel	—	.15
☐ 1983–1990	50 Sentimos, Eagle, Cupro-Nickel	—	.15
☐ 1992	50 Sentimos, Eagle, Brass	—	.15
☐ 1969	1 Piso, Birth of Aquinaldo—100th Anniversary, Silver	—	7.00
☐ 1970	1 Piso, Papal Visit, Silver	—	8.00

DATE	COIN TYPE/VARIETY/METAL	ABP FINE	AVERAGE FINE
☐ 1970	1 Piso, Papal Visit, Nickel	$ .40	1.00
☐ 1970	1 Piso, Papal Visit, Gold	—	500.00
☐ 1972–1982	1 Piso, Jose Rizal, Cupro-Nickel	—	.20
☐ 1983–1990	1 Piso, Bull, Cupro-Nickel	—	.10
☐ 1991	1 Piso, Waterfall, Ship, & Flower, Cupro-Nickel	.40	1.00
☐ 1983–1990	2 Piso, Bonifacio, Cupro-Nickel	—	.20

DATE	COIN TYPE/VARIETY/METAL	ABP FINE	AVERAGE FINE
□ 1991	2 Piso, Quirino, Cupro-Nickel	$ .80	$2.00
□ 1991	2 Piso, Bonifacio, Stainless Steel	.40	1.00
□ 1975–1982	5 Piso, Ferdinand Marcos, Nickel	.28	.60
□ 1974	10 Piso, Bank Anniversary—25th, Silver	—	12.00
□ 1975	10 Piso, Aquinaldo, Silver	—	12.00
□ 1976	10 Piso, FAO Issue, Silver	—	15.00
□ 1977	10 Piso, Rice Terraces, Silver	—	20.00
□ 1978	10 Piso, Birth of Quezon—100th Anniversary, Silver	—	18.00
□ 1979	10 Piso, UN Conference, Silver	—	18.00
□ 1980	10 Piso, Birth of MacArthur—100th Anniversary, Silver	—	20.00
□ 1981	10 Piso, World Food Day, Silver	—	18.00
□ 1982	10 Piso, Ferdiand Marcos & Ronald Reagan, Silver	—	60.00
□ 1986	10 Piso, Washington Visit of Aquino, Silver	—	225.00
□ 1975	50 Piso, New Society Anniversary, Silver	—	18.00
□ 1976	50 Piso, International Monetary Fund Meeting, Silver	—	18.00
□ 1977	50 Piso, Mint Inauguration, Silver	—	20.00
□ 1978	50 Piso, Birth of Quezon—100th Anniversary, Silver	—	18.00
□ 1979	50 Piso, Year of the Child, Silver	—	18.00
□ 1981	50 Piso, Papal Visit, Silver	—	35.00
□ 1982	50 Piso, Bataan-Corregidor 40th Anniversary, Silver	—	20.00
□ 1983	100 Piso, National University 75th Anniversary, Silver	—	20.00
□ 1991	150 Piso, Southeast Asian Games, Silver	—	35.00
□ 1987	200 Piso, Wildlife Fund—Buffalo, Silver	—	30.00
□ 1990	200 Piso, Save the Children, Silver	—	50.00
□ 1988	500 Piso, People's Revolution, Silver	—	60.00
□ 1975	1000 Piso, New Society—3rd Anniversary, Silver	—	150.00
□ 1976	1500 Piso, International Monetary Fund, Gold	—	300.00
□ 1977	1500 Piso, New Society—5th Anniversary, Gold	—	300.00
□ 1978	1500 Piso, Mint Inauguration, Gold	—	350.00
□ 1981	1500 Piso, Papal Visit, Gold	—	400.00
□ 1982	1500 Piso, Bataan-Corregidor 40th Anniversary, Gold	—	400.00
□ 1977	2500 Piso, New Society—5th Anniversary, Gold	—	1000.00
□ 1980	2500 Piso, Birth of MacArthur—100th Anniversary, Gold	—	400.00

DATE	COIN TYPE/VARIETY/METAL	ABP FINE	AVERAGE FINE
☐ 1986	2500 Piso, Aquino Washington Visit, Gold	—	$800.00
☐ 1992	10000 Piso, People's Power, Gold	—	1000.00

PITCAIRN ISLANDS

British and New Zealand currency was initially used. The only coins issued in the name of Pitcairn are commemorative pieces, the silver 50 dollar, and the gold 250 dollar produced in 1988.

Pitcairn Islands—Type Coinage

DATE	COIN TYPE/VARIETY/METAL	ABP FINE	AVERAGE FINE
☐ 1988	1 Dollar, Elizabeth II: Drafting of Pitcairn Islands Constitution, Silver	—	$30.00 Proof
☐ 1988	1 Dollar, Elizabeth II: Drafting of Pitcairn Islands Constitution, Cupro-Nickel	$1.50	2.50
☐ 1989	1 Dollar, Elizabeth II: Mutiny on the Bounty, Silver	—	30.00 Proof
☐ 1989	1 Dollar, Elizabeth II: Mutiny on the Bounty, Cupro-Nickel	1.50	2.50
☐ 1990	1 Dollar, Elizabeth II: Burning of the HMAV Bounty, Cupro-Nickel	1.50	2.50
☐ 1990	1 Dollar, Elizabeth II: Burning of the HMAV Bounty, Silver	—	30.00 Proof
☐ 1988	50 Dollars, Elizabeth II: Drafting of Pitcairn Islands Constitution, Silver	—	100.00 Proof
☐ 1989	50 Dollars, Elizabeth II: Mutiny on the Bounty, Silver	—	100.00 Proof
☐ 1990	50 Dollars, Elizabeth II: Burning of the HMAV Bounty, Silver	—	100.00 Proof
☐ 1988	250 Dollars, Elizabeth II: Drafting of Pitcairn Islands Constitution, Gold	—	300.00 Proof
☐ 1989	250 Dollars, Elizabeth II: Mutiny on the Bounty, Gold	—	300.00 Proof

DATE	COIN TYPE/VARIETY/METAL	ABP FINE	AVERAGE FINE
☐ 1990	250 Dollars, Elizabeth II: Burning of the HMAV Bounty, Gold	—	$400.00 Proof

POLAND

The first coins, silver denars, were used in the late 10th century and into the 12th century. Then came the silver bracteate denar and the silver schilling in the 1400s. The silver taler, gold ducat, and copper boratinki followed in the 1500s and 1600s. The copper polsgrosz and the silver kopek were in use in the 1800s. The first decimal coins were used in 1923. The currency today is the zloty.

Poland—Type Coinage

DATE	COIN TYPE/VARIETY/METAL	ABP FINE	AVERAGE FINE
☐ 1918	Fenig, WWI Military, Iron	$ .40	1.00
☐ 1923–1939	1 Grosz, Republic, Bronze	.14	.30
☐ 1923	1 Grosz, Republic, Brass	11.00	20.00
☐ 1939	1 Grosz, WWII Occupation, Holed, Zinc	.28	.60
☐ 1949	1 Grosz, Republic, Aluminum	—	.10

DATE	COIN TYPE/VARIETY/METAL	ABP FINE	AVERAGE FINE
☐ 1923	2 Grosze, Republic, Brass	.18	.40
☐ 1923–1939	2 Grosze, Republic, Bronze	—	.25
☐ 1949	2 Grosze, Republic, Aluminum	—	.10
☐ 1917–1918	5 Fenigow, WWI Military, Iron	.28	.60

DATE	COIN TYPE/VARIETY/METAL	ABP FINE	AVERAGE FINE
☐ 1923	5 Groszy, Republic, Brass	$ .28	$ .60
☐ 1923–1939	5 Groszy, Republic, Bronze	—	.25
☐ 1939	5 Groszy, WWII Occupation, Holed, Zinc	.80	2.00
☐ 1949	5 Groszy, Republic, Bronze	—	.10
☐ 1917	10 Fenigow, WWI Military, Zinc	12.00	30.00
☐ 1917–1918	10 Fenigow, WWI Military, Iron	.28	.60

DATE	COIN TYPE/VARIETY/METAL	ABP FINE	AVERAGE FINE
☐ 1923	10 Groszy, WWII Occupation, Zinc	—	.25
☐ 1923	10 Groszy, Republic, Nickel	—	.25
☐ 1949	10 Groszy, Republic, Cupro-Nickel	.12	.35
☐ 1949	10 Groszy, Republic, Aluminum	—	.25
☐ 1917	20 Fenigow, WWI Military, Zinc	18.00	40.00
☐ 1917–1918	20 Fenigow, WWI Military, Iron	1.40	3.00

DATE	COIN TYPE/VARIETY/METAL	ABP FINE	AVERAGE FINE
☐ 1923	20 Groszy, Republic, Nickel	.18	.40
☐ 1949	20 Groszy, Republic, Cupro-Nickel	.18	.40
☐ 1949	20 Groszy, Republic, Aluminum	—	.10

DATE	COIN TYPE/VARIETY/METAL	ABP FINE	AVERAGE FINE
□ 1923	50 Groszy, Republic, Nickel	$ .20	$ .50
□ 1938	50 Groszy, WWII Occupation, Iron	.60	1.50
□ 1949	50 Groszy, Republic, Cupro-Nickel	.25	.60
□ 1949	50 Groszy, Republic, Aluminum	—	.10
□ 1924–1925	1 Zloty, Republic, Silver	—	2.00
□ 1929	1 Zloty, Republic, Nickel	.25	.60
□ 1949	1 Zloty, Republic, Aluminum	—	.10
□ 1949	1 Zloty, Republic, Cupro-Nickel	.40	1.00
□ 1924–1925	2 Zlote, Republic, Silver	—	8.00
□ 1932–1934	2 Zlote, Republic, Silver	—	2.00
□ 1934–1936	2 Zlote, Republic, Silver	—	3.00
□ 1936	2 Zlote, Republic, Silver	—	4.00
□ 1925	5 Zlotych, Republic, Silver	—	200.00
□ 1928–1932	5 Zlotych, Republic, Silver	—	15.00
□ 1930	5 Zlotych, Republic, Revolt Against Russians Centennial, Silver	—	15.00
□ 1932–1934	5 Zlotych, Republic, Silver	—	5.00
□ 1934	5 Zlotych, Republic, Founding of Rifle Corps 20th Anniversary, Silver	—	5.00
□ 1934–1938	5 Zlotych, Republic, Silver	—	5.00
□ 1936	5 Zlotych, Republic, Silver	—	7.00
□ 1925	10 Zlotych, Republic, Death of Boleslaus I 900th Anniversary, Gold	—	60.00
□ 1932–1933	10 Zlotych, Republic, Silver	—	7.00
□ 1933	10 Zlotych, Republic, 250th Anniversary of Relief of Vienna, Silver	—	12.00
□ 1933	10 Zlotych, Republic, Second Revolt Against Russians 70th Anniversary, Silver	—	12.00
□ 1934	10 Zlotych, Republic, Founding of Rifle Corps 20th Anniversary, Silver	—	8.00

DATE	COIN TYPE/VARIETY/METAL	ABP FINE	AVERAGE FINE
□ 1934–1939	10 Zlotych, Republic, Silver	—	$8.00
□ 1925	20 Zlotych, Republic, Death of Boleslaus I 900th Anniversary, Gold	—	125.00

PORTUGAL

The first coins originated in the 2nd century B.C. In 1128 base-silver dinheiros and mealhas were produced, and later the gold morabitino. A range of coins in gold, silver, and base-silver were produced in the 1300s. In the 15th century most coinage was silver leals, with some base-silver reals branco. In the late 15th century the real became the main unit of coinage. In the 1600s systematic dating began appearing on coins. The first decimal coins were used in 1836. The escudo is the currency used today.

Portugal—Type Coinage

DATE	COIN TYPE/VARIETY/METAL	ABP FINE	AVERAGE FINE
□ 1868–1875	III Reis, Luis I, Copper	$1.40	3.00
□ 1867–1879	5 Reis, Luis I, Copper	3.75	8.00
□ 1882–1886	5 Reis, Luis I, Bronze	.30	.80
□ 1890–1906	5 Reis, Carlos I, Bronze	.20	.50
□ 1910	5 Reis, Emanuel II, Bronze	.18	.30

DATE	COIN TYPE/VARIETY/METAL	ABP FINE	AVERAGE FINE
□ 1867–1877	10 Reis, Luis I, Copper	$ .40	$1.00
□ 1882–1886	10 Reis, Luis I, Bronze	.60	1.50
□ 1891–1892	10 Reis, Carlos I, Bronze	.60	1.50

DATE	COIN TYPE/VARIETY/METAL	ABP FINE	AVERAGE FINE
□ 1867–1874	20 Reis, Luis I, Copper	.60	1.50
□ 1882–1886	20 Reis, Luis I, Bronze	.40	1.00
□ 1891–1892	20 Reis, Carlos I, Bronze	.40	1.00
□ 1862–1889	50 Reis, Luis I, Silver	—	1.50
□ 1893	50 Reis, Carlos I, Silver	—	3.00
□ 1900	50 Reis, Carlos I, Cupro-Nickel	.20	.60
□ 1864–1889	100 Reis, Luis I, Silver	—	3.00
□ 1890–1898	100 Reis, Carlos I, Silver	—	2.00

DATE	COIN TYPE/VARIETY/METAL	ABP FINE	AVERAGE FINE
□ 1900	100 Reis, Carlos I, Cupro-Nickel	.18	.30
□ 1909–1910	100 Reis, Emanuel II, Silver	—	1.50

DATE	COIN TYPE/VARIETY/METAL	ABP FINE	AVERAGE FINE
☐ 1862–1863	200 Reis, Luis I, Silver	—	$4.00
☐ 1865–1888	200 Reis, Luis I, Silver	—	30.00
☐ 1891–1903	200 Reis, Carlos I, Silver	—	2.00
☐ 1898	200 Reis, Carlos I, 400th Anniversary: Voyages of Discovery, Silver	—	3.00
☐ 1909	200 Reis, Emanuel II, Silver	—	2.00

DATE	COIN TYPE/VARIETY/METAL	ABP FINE	AVERAGE FINE
☐ 1863–1889	500 Reis, Luis I, Silver	—	4.00
☐ 1891–1908	500 Reis, Carlos I, Silver	—	4.00
☐ 1898	500 Reis, Carlos I, 400th Anniversary: Voyages of Discovery, Silver	—	6.00
☐ 1908–1909	500 Reis, Emanuel II, Silver	—	4.00
☐ 1910	500 Reis, Commemorative, Marquis de Pombal Silver	—	12.00
☐ 1910	500 Reis, Commemorative, Peninsular War Centennial, Silver	—	7.00

DATE	COIN TYPE/VARIETY/METAL	ABP FINE	AVERAGE FINE
☐ 1898	1000 Reis, Carlos I, 400th Anniversary: Voyages of Discovery, Silver	—	12.00

DATE	COIN TYPE/VARIETY/METAL	ABP FINE	AVERAGE FINE
☐ 1899	1000 Reis, Carlos I, Silver	—	$15.00
☐ 1910	1000 Reis, Commemorative, Peninsular War Centennial, Silver	—	18.00
☐ 1864–1866	2000 Reis, Luis I, Rev: Arms in Wreath, Gold	—	75.00
☐ 1868–1888	2000 Reis, Luis I, Rev: Mantled Arms, Gold	—	100.00
☐ 1862–1863	5000 Reis, Luis I, Rev: Arms in Wreath, Gold	—	175.00
☐ 1867–1889	5000 Reis, Luis I, Rev: Mantled Arms, Gold	—	175.00
☐ 1878–1889	10000 Reis, Luis I, Rev: Mantled Arms, Gold	—	300.00

Portugal—Port-Republic Coinage

DATE	COIN TYPE/VARIETY/METAL	ABP FINE	AVERAGE FINE
☐ 1917–1921	1 Centavo, 2nd Coinage, Bronze	—	.20
☐ 1918	2 Centavos, 1st Coinage, World War I Provisional Issue, Iron	$6.00	15.00
☐ 1918–1921	2 Centavos, 2nd Coinage, Bronze	—	.10
☐ 1917–1919	4 Centavos, 2nd Coinage, Cupro-Nickel	—	.20
☐ 1920–1922	5 Centavos, 2nd Coinage, Bronze	—	.25
☐ 1924–1927	5 Centavos, 3rd Coinage, Bronze	—	.10
☐ 1915	10 Centavos, 1st Coinage, Silver	—	1.50
☐ 1920–1921	10 Centavos, 2nd Coinage, Cupro-Nickel	—	.20
☐ 1924–1940	10 Centavos, 3rd Coinage, Bronze	—	.20
☐ 1942–1969	10 Centavos, 3rd Coinage, Bronze	—	.10
☐ 1969–1979	10 Centavos, 4th Coinage, Aluminum	—	.10
☐ 1913–1916	20 Centavos, 1st Coinage, Silver	—	3.00
☐ 1920–1922	20 Centavos, 2nd Coinage, Cupro-Nickel	.12	.30
☐ 1924–1925	20 Centavos, 3rd Coinage, Bronze	.12	.30
☐ 1942–1969	20 Centavos, 3rd Coinage, Bronze	—	.10
☐ 1969–1974	20 Centavos, 4th Coinage, Aluminum	—	.10
☐ 1912–1916	50 Centavos, 1st Coinage, Silver	—	4.00
☐ 1924–1926	50 Centavos, 3rd Coinage, Aluminum-Bronze	—	.20
☐ 1927–1968	50 Centavos, 3rd Coinage, Nickel-Bronze	—	.10
☐ 1969–1979	50 Centavos, 4th Coinage, Bronze	—	.10
☐ 1910	1 Escudo, 1st Coinage, Birth of Republic—October 5th, 1910, Silver	—	15.00

DATE	COIN TYPE/VARIETY/METAL	ABP FINE	AVERAGE FINE
□ 1915–1916	1 Escudo, 1st Coinage, Silver	—	$10.00
□ 1924–1926	1 Escudo, 3rd Coinage, Aluminum-Bronze	$1.75	5.00
□ 1927–1968	1 Escudo, 3rd Coinage, Nickel-Bronze	—	.20
□ 1969–1980	1 Escudo, 4th Coinage, Bronze	—	.10
□ 1981–1986	1 Escudo, 5th Coinage, Nickel-Brass	—	.10
□ 1986 to Date	1 Escudo, 6th Coinage, Nickel-Brass	—	.10
□ 1932–1951	2½ Escudos, 3rd Coinage, Silver	—	1.00
□ 1963–1986	2½ Escudos, 4th Coinage, Cupro-Nickel	—	.10
□ 1977	2½ Escudos, 4th Coinage, 100th Anniversary—Death of Alexandro Herculano, Cupro-Nickel	—	.10
□ 1983	2½ Escudos, 4th Coinage, FAO Issue, Cupro-Nickel	—	.10
□ 1983	2½ Escudos, 4th Coinage, World Roller Hockey Championship, Cupro-Nickel	—	.10
□ 1986 to Date	2½ Escudos, 6th Coinage, Nickel-Brass	—	.10

DATE	COIN TYPE/VARIETY/METAL	ABP FINE	AVERAGE FINE
□ 1932–1951	5 Escudos, 3rd Coinage, Silver	—	$3.00
□ 1960	5 Escudos, 3rd Coinage, Death of Henry the Navigator—500th Anniversary, Silver	—	2.00
□ 1928	10 Escudos, 3rd Coinage, Battle of Ourique 1139, Silver	—	7.00
□ 1932–1948	10 Escudos, 3rd Coinage, Silver	—	6.00
□ 1954–1955	10 Escudos, 3rd Coinage, Silver	—	3.00
□ 1960	10 Escudos, 3rd Coinage, Death of Henry the Navigator—500th Anniversary, Silver	—	3.00
□ 1971–1974	10 Escudos, 4th Coinage, Cupro-Nickel	—	.25
□ 1986 to Date	10 Escudos, 6th Coinage, Nickel-Brass	—	.20

DATE	COIN TYPE/VARIETY/METAL	ABP FINE	AVERAGE FINE
□ 1953	20 Escudos, 3rd Coinage, 25 Years of Financial Reform, Silver	—	6.00
□ 1960	20 Escudos, 3rd Coinage, Death of Henry the Navigator—500th Anniversary, Silver	—	12.00
□ 1966	20 Escudos, Opening of Salazar Bridge, Nickel-Brass	$ .80	2.00
□ 1986 to Date	20 Escudos, Nickel-Brass	—	.20
□ 1977–1978	25 Escudos, Cupro-Nickel	.20	.50
□ 1977–1978	25 Escudos, 100th Anniversary—Death of Alexandre Herculano, Cupro-Nickel	.25	.60
□ 1979–1986	25 Escudos, International Year of the Child, Cupro-Nickel	.20	.50
□ 1983	25 Escudos, World Roller Hockey Championship, Cupro-Nickel	.25	.60
□ 1983	25 Escudos, FAO Issue, Cupro-Nickel	.25	.60
□ 1984	25 Escudos, Revolution—100th Anniversary, Cupro-Nickel	.20	.50
□ 1984	25 Escudos, International Year of Disabled Persons, Cupro-Nickel	.20	.50
□ 1985	25 Escudos, Anniversary—Battle of Aljubarrotta, Cupro-Nickel	.25	.60
□ 1985	25 Escudos, Anniversary—Battle of Aljubarrotta, Silver	—	18.00

DATE	COIN TYPE/VARIETY/METAL	ABP FINE	AVERAGE FINE
☐ 1986	25 Escudos, Admission to European Common Market, Silver	—	$50.00
☐ 1986	25 Escudos, Admission to European Common Market, Cupro-Nickel	$ .20	.50
☐ 1968	50 Escudos, Anniversary of Birth of Alvares Cabral, Silver	—	7.00
☐ 1969	50 Escudos, 500th Anniversary— Birth of Vasco de Gama, Silver	—	7.00
☐ 1969	50 Escudos, Centennial— Birth of Marshall Carmone, Silver	—	7.00
☐ 1971	50 Escudos, 125th Anniversary— Bank of Portugal, Silver	—	8.00
☐ 1972	50 Escudos, 400th Anniversary— Heroic Epic "O Lusiadas," Silver	—	8.00
☐ 1986 to Date	50 Escudos, Silver	—	2.50
☐ 1974	100 Escudos, 1974 Revolution, Silver	—	6.00
☐ 1984	100 Escudos, International Year of Disabled Persons, Cupro-Nickel	.35	.80
☐ 1985	100 Escudos, 800th Anniversary— Death of King Henriques, Cupro-Nickel	.35	.80
☐ 1985	100 Escudos, 800th Anniversary— Death of King Henriques, Silver	—	30.00
☐ 1985	100 Escudos, 600th Anniversary— Battle of Aljubarrotta, Cupro-Nickel	.35	.80
☐ 1985	100 Escudos, 600th Anniversary— Battle of Aljubarrotta, Silver	—	30.00
☐ 1985	100 Escudos, 50th Anniversary— Death of Fernando Pessoa (Poet), Cupro-Nickel	.35	.80
☐ 1985	100 Escudos, 50th Anniversary— Death of Fernando Pessoa (Poet), Silver	—	30.00
☐ 1986	100 Escudos, World Cup Soccer— Mexico, Silver	—	25.00
☐ 1986	100 Escudos, World Cup Soccer— Mexico, Cupro-Nickel	.35	.80
☐ 1987	100 Escudos, Golden Age of Portuguese Discoveries, Cupro-Nickel	.35	.80
☐ 1987	100 Escudos, Amadeo De Souza Caroso, Cupro-Nickel	.35	.80
☐ 1987	100 Escudos, Golden Age of Portuguese Discoveries, Silver	—	25.00
☐ 1987	100 Escudos, Amadeo De Souza Caroso, Silver	—	25.00
☐ 1987	100 Escudos, Golden Age of Portuguese Discoveries, Gold	—	600.00

DATE	COIN TYPE/VARIETY/METAL	ABP FINE	AVERAGE FINE
☐ 1988	100 Escudos, Golden Age of Portuguese Discoveries, Platinum	—	$1000.00
☐ 1989	100 Escudos, Discovery of Madeira, Palladium	—	700.00
☐ 1989	100 Escudos, Discovery of Madeira, Silver	—	25.00
☐ 1989	100 Escudos, Discovery of Canary Islands, Cupro-Nickel	$1.75	4.00
☐ 1989	100 Escudos, Discovery of Madeira, Gold	—	675.00
☐ 1989	100 Escudos, Discovery of Canary Islands, Gold	—	700.00
☐ 1989 to Date	100 Escudos, Dual Metal	3.75	5.00
☐ 1989	100 Escudos, Discovery of Azores, Gold	—	600.00
☐ 1989	100 Escudos, Discovery of Canary Islands, Silver	—	25.00
☐ 1989	100 Escudos, Discovery of Azores, Silver	—	25.00
☐ 1989	100 Escudos, Discovery of Azores, Cupro-Nickel	1.75	4.00
☐ 1990	100 Escudos, Celestial Navigation, Cupro-Nickel	1.75	4.00
☐ 1990	100 Escudos, Camilo Castelo Branco, Cupro-Nickel	1.75	4.00
☐ 1990	100 Escudos, Celestial Navigation, Gold	—	675.00
☐ 1990	100 Escudos, Celestial Navigation, Silver	—	25.00
☐ 1990	100 Escudos, Camilo Castelo Branco, Silver	—	18.00
☐ 1990	100 Escudos, 350th Anniversary—Portuguese Independence, Cupro-Nickel	1.75	4.00
☐ 1990	100 Escudos, Celestial Navigation, Platinum	—	1750.00
☐ 1990	100 Escudos, 350th Anniversary—Portuguese Independence, Silver	—	18.00
☐ 1991	100 Escudos, Westward Navigation, Gold	—	600.00
☐ 1991	100 Escudos, Westward Navigation, Silver	—	22.00
☐ 1991 to Date	100 Escudos, Dual Metal	2.75	6.00
☐ 1991	100 Escudos, Columbus & Portugal, Gold	—	600.00
☐ 1991	100 Escudos, Columbus & Portugal, Silver	—	22.00
☐ 1991	100 Escudos, Columbus & Portugal, Palladium	—	300.00
☐ 1992	100 Escudos, New World America—Columbus & Ships, Gold	—	600.00
☐ 1992	100 Escudos, Cabrilho—Map, Silver	—	22.00
☐ 1992	100 Escudos, Portugal's Presidency of European Community, Cupro-Nickel	2.75	6.00

DATE	COIN TYPE/VARIETY/METAL	ABP FINE	AVERAGE FINE
☐ 1992	100 Escudos, New World America—Columbus & Ships, Silver	—	$22.00
☐ 1992	100 Escudos, Olympics—Runner, Silver	—	45.00
☐ 1992	100 Escudos, Olympics—Runner, Cupro-Nickel	$2.75	6.00
☐ 1992	100 Escudos, Portugal's Presidency of European Community, Silver	—	28.00
☐ 1992	100 Escudos, Cabrilho—Map, Cupro-Nickel	2.75	6.00
☐ 1992	100 Escudos, New World America—Columbus & Ships, Cupro-Nickel	2.75	6.00
☐ 1992	100 Escudos, Cabrilho—Map, Platinum	—	1750.00
☐ 1992	100 Escudos, Cabrilho—Map, Gold	—	600.00
☐ 1974	250 Escudos, 1974 Revolution, Silver	—	10.00
☐ 1984	250 Escudos, World Fisheries, Cupro-Nickel	1.40	3.00
☐ 1984	250 Escudos, World Fisheries, Silver	—	75.00
☐ 1988	250 Escudos, Seoul Olympics—Runners, Cupro-Nickel	1.40	3.00
☐ 1988	250 Escudos, Seoul Olympics—Runners, Silver	—	34.00
☐ 1989	250 Escudos, 850th Anniversary—Founding of Portugal, Silver	—	28.00
☐ 1989	250 Escudos, 850th Anniversary—Founding of Portugal, Cupro-Nickel	3.50	7.00
☐ 1983	500 Escudos, XVII European Art Exhibition, Silver	—	12.00
☐ 1983	750 Escudos, XVII European Art Exhibition, Silver	—	12.00
☐ 1980	1000 Escudos, 400th Anniversary—Death of Louis de Camoes, Silver	—	20.00
☐ 1983	1000 Escudos, XVII European Art Exhibition, Silver	—	22.00
☐ 1991	1000 Escudos, Ibero—American Series, Silver	—	50.00

RUSSIA

The first coins were used in the 5th century B.C. and were bronze pieces cast in the shape of dolphins, followed by coin-shaped pieces. In the 4th century, coins were produced in gold, silver, and bronze. Gold staters became popular in 100 A.D., followed by the silver denga in the 15th century, and the silver grossus and silver kopek in the 16th century. The first decimal coins were used in 1704. The currency today is the ruble.

Russia—Type Coinage

DATE	COIN TYPE/VARIETY/METAL	ABP FINE	AVERAGE FINE
□ 1855–1867	1/4 Kopek, Alexander II, Copper	$1.40	$3.00
□ 1867–1881	1/4 Kopek, Alexander II, Copper	1.40	3.00
□ 1881–1894	1/4 Kopek, Alexander III, Copper	1.00	2.50
□ 1894–1916	1/4 Kopek, Nikolai II, Copper	.28	.60

DATE	COIN TYPE/VARIETY/METAL	ABP FINE	AVERAGE FINE
□ 1855–1858	1/2 Ruble, Czarist Empire, Silver	—	6.00
□ 1859–1885	1/2 Ruble, Czarist Empire, 2nd Coinage, Silver	—	35.00
□ 1855–1867	1/2 Kopek, Alexander II, Copper	1.40	3.00
□ 1867–1881	1/2 Kopek, Alexander II, Copper	1.00	2.00
□ 1881–1894	1/2 Kopek, Alexander III, Copper	.35	.80
□ 1894–1916	1/2 Kopek, Nikolai II, Copper	.12	.30

DATE	COIN TYPE/VARIETY/METAL	ABP FINE	AVERAGE FINE
□ 1855–1858	1 Ruble, Czarist Empire, Silver	—	$60.00
□ 1859	1 Ruble, Nikolai I, Silver	—	65.00
□ 1859–1885	1 Ruble, Czarist Empire, 2nd Coinage, Silver	—	20.00
□ 1883	1 Ruble, Alexander III, Silver	—	38.00
□ 1886–1894	1 Ruble, Alexander III, Silver	—	22.00
□ 1895–1915	1 Ruble, Nikolai II, Silver	—	15.00
□ 1896	1 Ruble, Coronation Comm, Silver	—	30.00
□ 1898	1 Ruble, Alexander II, Silver	—	150.00
□ 1912	1 Ruble, Alexander III, Silver	—	225.00
□ 1912	1 Ruble, Napoleon Defeat, Silver	—	75.00
□ 1913	1 Ruble, Romanoff Dynasty, Silver	—	15.00
□ 1914	1 Ruble, Battle of Gangut, Silver	—	450.00
□ 1855–1867	1 Kopek, Alexander II, Copper	$ .35	.80

DATE	COIN TYPE/VARIETY/METAL	ABP FINE	AVERAGE FINE
□ 1867–1916	1 Kopek, Czarist Empire, 2nd Coinage, Copper	4.00	8.00
□ 1855–1859	2 Kopek, Czarist Empire, Copper	.35	.80
□ 1859–1867	2 Kopeks, Czarist Empire, 2nd Coinage, Copper	.35	.80

DATE	COIN TYPE/VARIETY/METAL	ABP FINE	AVERAGE FINE
☐ 1867–1916	2 Kopeks, Czarist Empire, 2nd Coinage, Copper	$ .25	$ .60
☐ 1855–1859	3 Kopek, Czarist Empire, Copper	1.40	3.00
☐ 1859–1867	3 Kopeks, Czarist Empire, 2nd Coinage, Copper	.80	2.00

DATE	COIN TYPE/VARIETY/METAL	ABP FINE	AVERAGE FINE
☐ 1867–1916	3 Kopeks, Czarist Empire, 2nd Coinage, Copper	.28	.60
☐ 1869–1885	3 Rubles, Czarist Empire, 2nd Coinage, Gold	—	200.00
☐ 1855–1858	5 Kopek, Czarist Empire, Silver	—	2.00
☐ 1855–1859	5 Kopek, Czarist Empire, Copper	1.75	4.00
☐ 1859–1867	5 Kopeks, Czarist Empire, 2nd Coinage, Copper	1.00	2.50
☐ 1859–1866	5 Kopeks, Czarist Empire, 2nd Coinage, Silver	—	2.00
☐ 1867–1916	5 Kopeks, Czarist Empire, 2nd Coinage, Copper	1.00	2.50
☐ 1867–1915	5 Kopeks, Czarist Empire, 2nd Coinage, Silver	—	2.00
☐ 1855–1858	5 Rubles, Czarist Empire, Gold	—	125.00
☐ 1859–1885	5 Rubles, Czarist Empire, 2nd Coinage, Gold	—	125.00
☐ 1886–1894	5 Rubles, Alexander III, Gold	—	100.00
☐ 1895–1896	5 Rubles, Gold	—	2500.00
☐ 1897–1911	5 Rubles, Reduced Weight Gold, Gold	—	60.00
☐ 1897	7½ Rubles, Reduced Weight Gold, Gold	—	100.00
☐ 1855–1858	10 Kopeks, Czarist Empire, Silver	—	3.00
☐ 1859–1866	10 Kopeks, Czarist Empire, 2nd Coinage, Silver	—	1.00
☐ 1867–1917	10 Kopeks, Czariest Empire, 2nd Coinage, Silver	—	.75
☐ 1886–1894	10 Rubles, Alexander III, Gold	—	275.00
☐ 1895–1897	10 Rubles, Gold	—	2000.00
☐ 1898–1911	10 Rubles, Reduced Weight Gold, Gold	—	110.00
☐ 1859–1866	15 Kopeks, Czarist Empire 2nd Coinage, Silver	—	1.00

DATE	COIN TYPE/VARIETY/METAL	ABP FINE	AVERAGE FINE
☐ 1867–1917	15 Kopeks, Czarist Empire 2nd Coinage, Silver	—	$1.00
☐ 1897–1897	15 Rubles, Reduced Weight Gold, Gold	—	200.00
☐ 1855–1858	20 Kopek, Czarist Empire, Silver	—	3.00
☐ 1859–1866	20 Kopeks, Czarist Empire, 2nd Coinage, Silver	—	2.00
☐ 1867–1917	20 Kopeks, Czarist Empire, 2nd Coinage, Silver	—	1.00

DATE	COIN TYPE/VARIETY/METAL	ABP FINE	AVERAGE FINE
☐ 1855–1858	25 Kopeks, Czarist Empire, Silver	—	3.00
☐ 1859–1885	25 Kopeks, Czarist Empire, 2nd Coinage, Silver	—	18.00
☐ 1886–1894	25 Kopeks, Alexander III, Silver	—	22.00

DATE	COIN TYPE/VARIETY/METAL	ABP FINE	AVERAGE FINE
☐ 1895–1901	25 Kopeks, Nikolai II, Silver	—	6.00
☐ 1876	25 Rubles, Czarist Empire, 2nd Coinage, Gold	—	20,000.00
☐ 1896–1908	25 Rubles, Gold	—	5000.00
☐ 1902	37½ Rubles, Reduced Weight Gold, Gold	—	3500.00

DATE	COIN TYPE/VARIETY/METAL	ABP FINE	AVERAGE FINE
□ 1886–1894	50 Kopeks, Alexander III, Silver	—	$18.00
□ 1895–1914	50 Kopeks, Nikolai II, Silver	—	6.00

Russia—Empire Type Coinage

DATE	COIN TYPE/VARIETY/METAL	ABP FINE	AVERAGE FINE
□ 1803–1810	1 Poluska, Alexander I, 1st Coinage, Copper	$8.00	20.00
□ 1839–1846	Poluska, Nikolai I, 3rd Coinage, Copper	1.40	3.00
□ 1849–1855	Poluska, Nikolai I, 4th Coinage, Copper	2.00	4.00
□ 1855–1861	Poluska, Alexander II, Copper	2.00	4.00
□ 1867–1881	Poluska, Alexander II, 2nd Coinage, Copper	1.40	3.00
□ 1882–1891	Poluska, Alexander III, 2nd Coinage, Copper	1.00	2.00
□ 1894–1916	Poluska, Nikolai II, 2nd Coinage, Copper	.28	.60
□ 1804–1808	1 Denga, Alexander I, 1st Coinage, Copper	28.00	60.00
□ 1810–1825	1 Denga, Alexander I, 2nd Coinage, Copper	2.25	5.00
□ 1827–1830	1 Denga, Nicholas I, 1st Coinage, Copper	1.00	3.00
□ 1839–1848	1 Denga, Nicholas I, 3rd Coinage, Copper	1.00	3.00
□ 1849–1855	1 Denga, Nicholas I, 4th Coinage, Copper	.80	2.00
□ 1855–1861	1 Denga, Alexander II, Copper	2.00	4.00
□ 1855–1861	1 Denga, Alexander II, 1st Coinage, Cooper	.35	.80
□ 1882–1894	1 Denga, Alexander III, Copper	.12	.30
□ 1884–1916	1 Denga, Nikolai II, Copper	.12	.30
□ 1804–1810	1 Kopek, Alexander I, 1st Coinage, Cooper	12.00	30.00
□ 1810–1825	1 Kopek, Alexander I, 2nd Coinage, Cooper	1.00	2.00
□ 1826–1830	1 Kopek, Nicholas I, 1st Coinage, Cooper	1.00	2.00
□ 1830–1839	1 Kopek, Nicholas I, 2nd Coinage, Copper	1.00	2.00
□ 1839–1847	1 Kopek, Nicholas I, 3rd Coinage, Copper	.35	.80
□ 1849–1856	1 Kopek, Nicholas I, 4th Coinage, Copper	.40	1.00
□ 1855–1864	1 Kopek, Alexander II, 1st Coinage, Cooper	.80	1.50
□ 1867–1881	1 Kopek, Alexander II, 2nd Coinage, Cooper	.28	.60
□ 1882–1894	1 Kopek, Alexander III, Copper	.12	.30
□ 1894–1916	1 Kopek, Nicholas II, Copper	.12	.30
□ 1802–1810	2 Kopeks, Alexander I, 1st Coinage, Cooper	10.00	28.00

DATE	COIN TYPE/VARIETY/METAL	ABP FINE	AVERAGE FINE
□ 1810–1825	2 Kopeks, Alexander I, 2nd Coinage, Cooper	$1.00	$2.00
□ 1826–1830	2 Kopeks, Nicholas I, 1st Coinage, Cooper	1.40	3.00
□ 1830–1839	2 Kopeks, Nicholas I, 2nd Coinage, Cooper	2.00	4.00
□ 1839–1848	2 Kopeks, Nicholas I, 3rd Coinage, Cooper	1.00	2.00
□ 1849–1855	2 Kopeks, Nicholas I, 4th Coinage, Cooper	1.40	3.00
□ 1855–1865	2 Kopeks, Alexander II, 1st Coinage, Cooper	.35	.80
□ 1882–1894	2 Kopeks, Alexander III, Copper	.28	.60
□ 1894–1916	2 Kopeks, Nicholas II, Copper	.28	.60
□ 1839–1848	3 Kopeks, Nicholas I, 3rd Coinage, Cooper	2.25	5.00
□ 1849–1855	3 Kopeks, Nicholas I, 4th Coinage, Cooper	1.00	2.00
□ 1855–1865	3 Kopeks, Alexander II, 1st Coinage, Cooper	1.00	2.00
□ 1867–1881	3 Kopeks, Alexander II, 2nd Coinage, Cooper	.35	.80
□ 1882–1894	3 Kopeks, Alexander III, Copper	.35	.80
□ 1894–1916	3 Kopeks, Nicholas II, Copper	.28	.60
□ 1802–1810	5 Kopeks, Alexander I, 1st Coinage, Cooper	5.00	12.00
□ 1810–1825	5 Kopeks, Alexander I, Silver	—	4.00
□ 1826–1835	5 Kopeks, Nicholas I, Silver	—	4.00
□ 1830–1839	5 Kopeks, Nicholas I, 2nd Coinage, Cooper	2.00	4.00
□ 1833–1855	5 Kopeks, Nicholas I, Silver	—	1.50
□ 1849–1855	5 Kopeks, Nicholas I, 4th Coinage, Cooper	2.25	5.00
□ 1855–1881	5 Kopeks, Alexander II, Silver	—	2.00
□ 1855–1866	5 Kopeks, Alexander II, 1st Coinage, Cooper	1.40	3.00
□ 1867–1881	5 Kopeks, Alexander II, 2nd Coinage, Cooper	1.00	2.00
□ 1881–1892	5 Kopeks, Alexander III, Silver	—	6.00
□ 1882–1894	5 Kopeks, Alexander III, Copper	.35	.80
□ 1894–1916	5 Kopeks, Nicholas II, Copper	18.00	40.00
□ 1796–1801	10 Kopeks, Paul I, Silver	—	30.00
□ 1802–1825	10 Kopeks, Alexander I, Silver	—	3.00
□ 1826–1832	10 Kopeks, Nicholas I, Silver	—	3.00
□ 1833–1855	10 Kopeks, Nicholas I, Silver	—	8.00
□ 1855–1881	10 Kopeks, Alexander II, Silver	—	1.50

DATE	COIN TYPE/VARIETY/METAL	ABP FINE	AVERAGE FINE
□ 1881–1892	10 Kopeks, Alexander III, Silver	—	$1.00
□ 1860–1881	15 Kopeks, Alexander II, Silver	—	1.00
□ 1887–1887	15 Kopeks, Alexander III, Silver	—	.80
□ 1810–1825	20 Kopeks, Alexander I, Silver	—	3.00
□ 1833–1855	20 Kopeks, Nicholas I, Silver	—	3.00
□ 1855–1881	20 Kopeks, Alexander II, Silver	—	1.50
□ 1881–1892	20 Kopeks, Alexander III, Silver	—	1.00
□ 1826–1835	25 Kopeks, Nicholas I, Silver	—	6.00
□ 1855–1881	25 Kopeks, Alexander II, Silver	—	10.00
□ 1881–1894	25 Kopeks, Alexander III, Silver	—	25.00
□ 1886–1904	25 Kopeks, Nicholas II, Silver	—	20.00
□ 1881–1892	50 Kopeks, Alexander III, Silver	—	20.00
□ 1896–1904	50 Kopeks, Nicholas II, Silver	—	6.00
□ 1801–1825	1 Ruble, Alexander I, Silver	—	20.00
□ 1826–1832	1 Ruble, Nicholas I, Silver	—	25.00
□ 1833–1855	1 Ruble, Nicholas I, Silver	—	20.00
□ 1855–1881	1 Ruble, Alexander II, Silver	—	22.00
□ 1881–1894	1 Ruble, Alexander III, Silver	—	25.00
□ 1894–1916	1 Ruble, Nicholas II, Silver	—	25.00
□ 1828–1845	3 Rubles, Platinum	—	250.00
□ 1826–1855	5 Rubles, Gold	—	120.00
□ 1829–1845	6 Rubles, Platinum	—	1100.00
□ 1830–1845	12 Rubles, Platinum	—	1750.00

SOUTH AFRICA

The first coins, the silver guilders, were used in 1802. The silver pence, bronze penny, and gold pond were used in the 1800s. The silver florin was used in the 1900s, as were the cupro-nickel shilling, brass cent, and gold krugerrand. The first decimal coins were used in 1961. Today's currency is the rand.

South Africa—Republic Type Coinage

DATE	COIN TYPE/VARIETY/METAL	ABP FINE	AVERAGE FINE
☐ 1892–1898	1 Penny, Paul Kruger, Bronze	$1.75	$4.00
☐ 1892–1897	3 Pence, Paul Kruger, Silver	—	3.00

☐ 1892–1897	6 Pence, Paul Kruger, Silver	—	6.00

☐ 1892–1897	1 Shilling, Paul Kruger, Silver	—	15.00
☐ 1892–1897	2 Shillings, Paul Kruger, Silver	—	7.00

☐ 1892–1897	2½ Shillings, Paul Kruger, Silver	—	10.00
☐ 1892	5 Shillings, Paul Kruger, Silver	—	75.00
☐ 1892–1897	½ Pond, Paul Kruger, Gold	—	100.00
☐ 1892–1900	1 Pond, Paul Kruger, Gold	—	150.00
☐ 1902	1 Pond, Veld, Gold	—	600.00

South Africa—Union Type Coinage

DATE	COIN TYPE/VARIETY/METAL	ABP FINE	AVERAGE FINE
□ 1923–1931	1 Farthing, George V, Legend ZUID-AFRIKA, Bronze	$1.00	$2.00
□ 1931–1936	1 Farthing, George V, Legend SUID-AFRIKA, Bronze	3.25	6.00
□ 1937–1947	1 Farthing, George VI, Legend SUID-AFRIKA, Bronze	.18	.30
□ 1948–1950	1 Farthing, George VI, Obverse Legend GEORGIUS SEXTUS REX, Bronze	.18	.30

DATE	COIN TYPE/VARIETY/METAL	ABP FINE	AVERAGE FINE
□ 1951–1952	1 Farthing, George VI, Reverse Legend SUID-AFRIKA—SOUTH AFRICA, Bronze	—	.20
□ 1953–1960	1 Farthing, Elizabeth II, Reverse Legend SUID-AFRIKA—SOUTH AFRICA, Bronze	—	.20
□ 1923–1931	½ Penny, George V, Legend ZUID-AFRIKA, Bronze	2.75	5.00
□ 1931–1936	½ Penny, George V, Legend SUID-AFRIKA, Bronze	.65	1.75
□ 1937–1947	½ Penny, George VI, Legend SUID-AFRIKA, Bronze	.18	.30
□ 1948–1952	½ Penny, George VI, Legend GEORGIUS SEXTUS REX, Bronze	.18	.30

DATE	COIN TYPE/VARIETY/METAL	ABP FINE	AVERAGE FINE
□ 1953–1960	½ Penny, Elizabeth II, Legend GEORGIUS SEXTUS REX, Bronze	—	.20
□ 1923–1930	1 Penny, George V, Bronze	1.40	3.00

DATE	COIN TYPE/VARIETY/METAL	ABP FINE	AVERAGE FINE
☐ 1931–1936	1 Penny, George V, Legend SUID-AFRIKA, Bronze	$ .65	$1.50
☐ 1937–1947	1 Penny, George VI, Legend SUID-AFRIKA, Bronze	.18	.30
☐ 1948–1950	1 Penny, George VI, Legend GEORGIUS SEXTUS REX, Bronze	.18	.30
☐ 1951–1952	1 Penny, George VI, Legend SUID AFRIKA—SOUTH AFRICA, Bronze	.18	.30
☐ 1953–1960	1 Penny, Elizabeth II, Legend SUID AFRIKA—SOUTH AFRICA, Bronze	—	.20
☐ 1923–1930	3 Pence, George V, Legend ZUID AFRIKA, Silver	—	1.50
☐ 1931–1936	3 Pence, George V, Legend SUID AFRIKA, Silver	—	1.25

DATE	COIN TYPE/VARIETY/METAL	ABP FINE	AVERAGE FINE
☐ 1937–1947	3 Pence, George VI, Legend SUID AFRIKA, Silver	—	.65
☐ 1948–1950	3 Pence, George VI, Legend, GEORGIUS SEXTUS REX, Silver	—	.60
☐ 1953–1960	3 Pence, Elizabeth II, Silver	—	.30
☐ 1923–1930	6 Pence, George V, Legend ZUID AFRIKA, Silver	—	3.00
☐ 1931–1936	6 Pence, George V, Legend SUID AFRIKA, Silver	—	1.50
☐ 1937–1947	6 Pence, George VI, Legend SUID AFRIKA, Silver	—	1.50

DATE	COIN TYPE/VARIETY/METAL	ABP FINE	AVERAGE FINE
□ 1948–1950	6 Pence, George VI, Legend GEORGIUS SEXTUS REX, Silver	—	$1.00
□ 1951–1952	6 Pence, George VI, Legend SUID AFRIKA—SOUTH AFRICA, Silver	—	.60
□ 1953–1960	6 Pence, Elizabeth II, Silver	—	.60
□ 1923–1930	1 Shilling, George V, Legend ZUID AFRIKA, Silver	—	10.00
□ 1931–1936	1 Shilling, George V, Legend SUID AFRIKA, Silver	—	4.00

DATE	COIN TYPE/VARIETY/METAL	ABP FINE	AVERAGE FINE
□ 1937–1947	1 Shilling, George VI, Silver	—	2.00
□ 1948–1952	1 Shilling, George VI, Legend GEORGIUS SEXTUS REX, Silver	—	2.00
□ 1953–1960	1 Shilling, Elizabeth II, Silver	—	1.00
□ 1923–1930	1 Florin, George V, Legend ZUID AFRIKA, Silver	—	6.00
□ 1931–1936	2 Shillings, George V, Legend SUID AFRIKA, Silver	—	5.00
□ 1937–1947	2 Shillings, George VI, Legend SUID AFRIKA, Silver	—	15.00
□ 1948–1950	2 Shillings, George VI, Legend GEORGIUS SEXTUS REX, Silver	—	20.00
□ 1951–1952	2 Shillings, George VI, Legend SUID AFRIKA—SOUTH AFRICA, Silver	—	2.00
□ 1953–1960	2 Shillings, Elizabeth II, Silver	—	1.75
□ 1923–1930	2½ Shillings, George V, Silver	—	6.00
□ 1931–1936	2½ Shillings, George V, Legend SUID AFRIKA, Silver	—	5.00

DATE	COIN TYPE/VARIETY/METAL	ABP FINE	AVERAGE FINE
☐ 1937–1947	2½ Shillings, George VI, Legend SUID AFRIKA, Silver	—	$5.00
☐ 1948–1952	2½ Shillings, George VI, Legend GEORGIUS SEXTUS REX, Silver	—	35.00
☐ 1953–1960	2½ Shillings, Elizabeth I, Silver	—	3.00
☐ 1947	5 Shillings, Royal Visit Co, Silver	—	18.00

DATE	COIN TYPE/VARIETY/METAL	ABP FINE	AVERAGE FINE
☐ 1948–1950	5 Shillings, George VI, Silver	—	15.00
☐ 1951	5 Shillings, George VI, Legend SUID AFRIKA—SOUTH AFRICA, Silver	—	10.00
☐ 1952	5 Shillings, Capetown Comm, Silver	—	10.00
☐ 1953–1959	5 Shillings, Elizabeth II, Silver	—	8.00
☐ 1960	5 Shillings, 50th Anniversa, Silver	—	5.00
☐ 1923–1926	½ Sovereign, George V, Gold	—	75.00
☐ 1952	½ Pound, George VI, Silver	—	75.00
☐ 1953–1960	½ Pound, Elizabeth II, Gold	—	100.00

DATE	COIN TYPE/VARIETY/METAL	ABP FINE	AVERAGE FINE
☐ 1923–1932	1 Sovereign, George V, Gold	—	125.00
☐ 1952	1 Pound, George VI, Gold	—	140.00
☐ 1953–1960	1 Pound, Elizabeth II, Gold	—	150.00

South Africa—Republic Coinage

DATE	COIN TYPE/VARIETY/METAL	ABP FINE	AVERAGE FINE
☐ 1961–1964	1/2 Cent, Brass	—	$ .15
☐ 1970–1976	1/2 Cent, Bronze	—	.10
☐ 1979	1/2 Cent, Bronze	$1.00	2.00
☐ 1982	1/2 Cent, Bronze	1.00	2.00
☐ 1961–1964	1 Cent, Brass	—	.18
☐ 1965–1969	1 Cent, Bronze	—	.10
☐ 1968	1 Cent, Bronze	—	.10
☐ 1970–1989	1 Cent, Bronze	.12	.30
☐ 1976	1 Cent, Bronze	.20	.50
☐ 1979	1 Cent, Bronze	.18	.40
☐ 1982	1 Cent, Bronze	.18	.40
☐ 1990 to Date	1 Cent, Copper Steel	—	.25
☐ 1965–1969	2 Cents, Bronze	—	.12
☐ 1968	2 Cents, Bronze	—	.25
☐ 1970–1990	2 Cents, Bronze	.12	.30

DATE	COIN TYPE/VARIETY/METAL	ABP FINE	AVERAGE FINE
☐ 1961–1964	2 1/2 Cents, Silver	—	1.75
☐ 1961–1964	5 Cents, Silver	—	.60
☐ 1965–1969	5 Cents, Nickel	—	.10
☐ 1968	5 Cents, Nickel	—	.10
☐ 1970–1989	5 Cents, Nickel	—	.10
☐ 1976	5 Cents, Nickel	.18	.40
☐ 1979	5 Cents, Nickel	.18	.40
☐ 1982	5 Cents, Nickel	.18	.40
☐ 1990 to Date	5 Cents, Copper Steel	.15	.35
☐ 1961–1962	10 Cents, Silver	—	1.00

DATE	COIN TYPE/VARIETY/METAL	ABP FINE	AVERAGE FINE
□ 1965–1969	10 Cents, Nickel	—	$ .10
□ 1968	10 Cents, Nickel	$1.40	3.00
□ 1970–1989	10 Cents, Nickel	—	.12
□ 1976	10 Cents, Nickel	—	.50
□ 1979	10 Cents, Nickel	—	.50
□ 1982	10 Cents, Nickel	—	.50
□ 1990 to Date	10 Cents, Brass Steel	—	.50
□ 1961–1964	20 Cents, Silver	—	1.50
□ 1965–1969	20 Cents, Nickel	—	.20
□ 1968	20 Cents, Nickel	1.50	3.50
□ 1970–1990	20 Cents, Nickel	—	.20
□ 1976	20 Cents, Nickel	.40	1.00
□ 1979	20 Cents, Nickel	.40	1.00
□ 1982–1982	20 Cents, Nickel	.40	1.00
□ 1990 to Date	20 Cents, Brass Steel	—	.20

DATE	COIN TYPE/VARIETY/METAL	ABP FINE	AVERAGE FINE
□ 1961–1964	50 Cents, Silver	—	20.00
□ 1965–1969	50 Cents, Nickel	.28	.50
□ 1968	50 Cents, Nickel	.30	.60
□ 1970–1990	50 Cents, Nickel	—	.50
□ 1976	50 Cents, Nickel	—	.80
□ 1979	50 Cents, Nickel	—	.80
□ 1982	50 Cents, Nickel	—	.80
□ 1990 to Date	50 Cents, Brass Steel	2.75	6.00
□ 1961–1983	1 Rand, Gold	—	1.00
□ 1965–1968	1 Rand, Silver	—	6.00

DATE	COIN TYPE/VARIETY/METAL	ABP FINE	AVERAGE FINE
□ 1970–1989	1 Rand, Silver	—	10.00
□ 1977–1990	1 Rand, Nickel	.40	1.00

DATE	COIN TYPE/VARIETY/METAL	ABP FINE	AVERAGE FINE
□ 1961–1983	2 Rands, Gold	—	BV*
□ 1989	2 Rands, Copper-Nickel	$ .90	$2.00

South Africa—Bullion Coinage

□ 1980	1/10 Krugerrand, Gold	—	BV
□ 1980	1/4 Krugerrand, Gold	—	BV
□ 1980	1/2 Krugerrand, Gold	—	BV
□ 1967	Krugerrand, Gold	—	BV

***BV** = These coins are relatively current so their collector value is minimal. Since these coins were minted and sold primarily for their bullion value, their current value is determined by the current "spot" price of the precious metal indicated. For accurate prices, contact your local coin dealer.

SPAIN

The earliest coins from the 4th century B.C. were marked Em. The silver denarius was popular from about 100 B.C. to 45 B.C., with bronze coins and the gold tremissis becoming popular by 600 to 700. Gold coins were popular in the mid-1400s. Decimal coins appeared in 1848, with the peseta being the coin used today.

Spain—Type Coinage

□ 1866–1868	1/2 Centimo, Isabell II, 3rd Decimal Coinage, Bronze	1.40	3.00
□ 1866–1868	1 Centimo, Isabell II, 3rd Decimal Coinage, Bronze	2.75	6.00
□ 1870	1 Centimo, Provisional, Bronze	.28	.60
□ 1906	1 Centimo, Alfonso XIII, 4th Coinage, Bronze	.18	.40
□ 1911–1913	1 Centimo, Alfonso XIII, 5th Coinage, Bronze	.90	2.00
□ 1870	1 Centimos, Provisional, Bronze	.28	.60

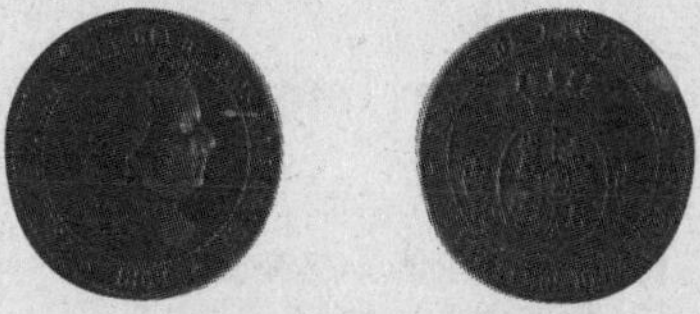

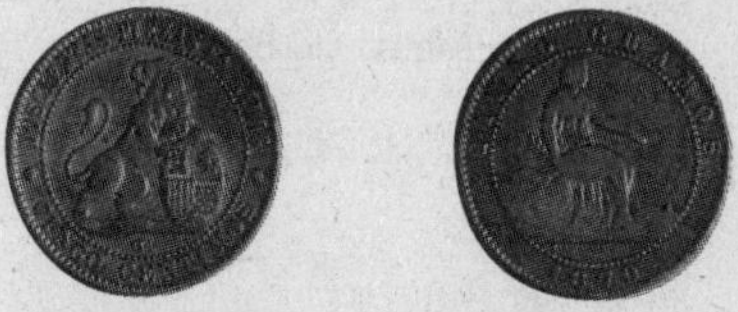

DATE	COIN TYPE/VARIETY/METAL	ABP FINE	AVERAGE FINE
□ 1904–1905	2 Centimos, Alfonso XIII, 4th Coinage, Bronze	$ .18	$ .40
□ 1911–1912	2 Centimos, Alfonso XIII, 5th Coinage, Bronze	.18	.40
□ 1866–1868	2½ Centimos, Isabell II, 3rd Decimal Coinage, Bronze	1.40	3.00
□ 1868	25 Milesimas, Provisional, Battle of Alcolea Bridge, Bronze	30.00	75.00
□ 1854–1864	5 Centimos de Real, Isabell, 2nd Decimal Coinage, Copper	3.50	5.00
□ 1866–1868	5 Centimos, Isabell II, 3rd Decimal Coinage, Bronze	2.75	6.00
□ 1870	5 Centimos, Provisional, Bronze	5.00	10.00
□ 1875	5 Centimos, Carlos VII, Bronze	8.00	20.00
□ 1877–1879	5 Centimos, Alfonso XII, 2nd Coinage, Bronze	.28	.60
□ 1937	5 Centimos, Republic, 2nd Coinage, Iron	.18	.40
□ 1940–1953	5 Centimos, Nationalist Govt, 1st Coinage, Aluminum	—	.10
□ 1854–1864	10 Centimos, Isabell II, 2nd Decimal Coinage, Copper	1.75	3.50
□ 1864–1868	10 Centimos, Isabell II, 3rd Decimal Coinage, Silver	—	8.00

DATE	COIN TYPE/VARIETY/METAL	ABP FINE	AVERAGE FINE
☐ 1870	10 Centimos, Provisional, Bronze	$ .90	$2.00
☐ 1875	10 Centimos, Carlos VII, Bronze	8.00	18.00
☐ 1877–1879	10 Centimos, Alfonso XII, 2nd Coinage, Bronze	.18	.40
☐ 1940–1953	10 Centimos, Nationalist Govt, 1st Coinage, Aluminum	—	.12
☐ 1959	10 Centimos, Kingdom, Aluminum	—	.10
☐ 1865–1868	20 Centimos, Isabell II, 3rd Decimal Coinage, Silver	—	10.00
☐ 1869–1870	20 Centimos, Provisional, Obverse Legend: Espana, Silver	—	12.00
☐ 1949	20 Centimos, Nationalist Govt, 2nd Coinage, Cupro-Nickel	—	.10
☐ 1925	25 Centimos, Alfonso XIII, 6th Coinage, Nickel-Brass	.18	.40
☐ 1927	25 Centimos, Alfonso XIII, 6th Coinage, Cupro-Nickel	.18	.40
☐ 1933	1 Peseta, Republic, 1st Coinage, Silver	—	2.50
☐ 1934	25 Centimos, Republic, 1st Coinage, Nickel-Bronze	—	.25
☐ 1937	25 Centimos, Nationalist Govt, 1st Coinage, Cupro-Nickel	—	.30
☐ 1938	25 Centimos, Republic, 2nd Coinage, Copper	.40	1.00
☐ 1864–1868	40 Centimos, Isabell II, 3rd Decimal Coinage, Silver	—	6.00
☐ 1848–1853	1/2 Real, Isabell II, Copper	—	.40
☐ 1869–1870	50 Centimos, Provisional, Obverse Legend: Espana, Silver	—	15.00
☐ 1880–1885	50 Centimos, Alfonso XII, 3rd Coinage, Silver	—	2.00
☐ 1889–1892	50 Centimos, Alfonso XIII, 1st Coinage, Silver	—	8.00
☐ 1894	50 Centimos, Alfonso XIII, 2nd Coinage, Silver	—	4.00

DATE	COIN TYPE/VARIETY/METAL	ABP FINE	AVERAGE FINE
☐ 1896–1900	50 Centimos, Alfonso XIII, 3rd Coinage, Silver	—	$2.00
☐ 1904	50 Centimos, Alfonso XIII, 4th Coinage, Silver	—	1.00
☐ 1910	50 Centimos, Alfonso XIII, 5th Coinage, Silver	—	1.00
☐ 1926	50 Centimos, Alfonso XIII, 6th Coinage, Silver	—	1.00
☐ 1937	50 Centimos, Republic, 2nd Coinage, Copper	$ .18	.40
☐ 1949–1963	50 Centimos, Kingdom, Cupro-Nickel	—	.10
☐ 1949–1963	50 Centimos, Nationalist Govt, 2nd Coinage, Cupro-Nickel	—	.10
☐ 1966–1975	50 Centimos, Kingdom, Aluminum	—	.10
☐ 1980	50 Centimos, Kingdom, World Cup Soccer Games, Aluminum	—	.10
☐ 1850–1855	1 Real, Isabell II, Arms Without Pillars, Silver	—	4.00
☐ 1857–1864	1 Real, Isabell II, 2nd Decimal Coinage, Silver	—	6.00
☐ 1865–1868	1 Escudo, Isabell II, 3rd Decimal Coinage, Silver	7.00	15.00
☐ 1869–1870	1 Peseta, Provisional, Obverse Legend: Espana, Silver	—	20.00
☐ 1869	1 Peseta, Provisional, Obverse Legend: Gobierno Provisional, Silver	—	4.00
☐ 1876	1 Peseta, Alfonso XII, 2nd Coinage, Silver	—	4.00
☐ 1881–1885	1 Peseta, Alfonso XII, 3rd Coinage, Silver	—	5.00
☐ 1889–1891	1 Peseta, Alfonso XIII, 1st Coinage, Silver	—	20.00
☐ 1893–1894	1 Peseta, Alfonso XIII, 2nd Coinage, Silver	—	12.00
☐ 1896–1902	1 Peseta, Alfonso XIII, 3rd Coinage, Silver	—	3.00
☐ 1903–1905	1 Peseta, Alfonso XIII, 4th Coinage, Silver	—	5.00
☐ 1937	1 Peseta, Republic, 2nd Coinage, Brass	.28	.40
☐ 1944	1 Peseta, Nationalist Govt, 1st Coinage, Aluminum-Bronze	.18	.30
☐ 1947–1975	1 Peseta, Kingdom, Alluminum-Bronze	.18	.30

DATE	COIN TYPE/VARIETY/METAL	ABP FINE	AVERAGE FINE
☐ 1947–1963	1 Peseta, Nationalist Govt, 2nd Coinage, Aluminum-Bronze	—	$ .15

DATE	COIN TYPE/VARIETY/METAL	ABP FINE	AVERAGE FINE
☐ 1980	1 Peseta, Kingdom, World Cup Soccer Games, Aluminum-Bronze	—	.10
☐ 1982 to Date	1 Peseta, Kingdom, Aluminum	—	.10
☐ 1852–1855	1 Reales, Isabell II, Arms Without Pillars, Silver	—	15.00
☐ 1857–1864	2 Reales, Isabell II, 2nd Decimal Coinage, Silver	—	10.00
☐ 1865–1868	2 Escudos, Isabell II, 3rd Decimal Coinage, Silver	—	10.00
☐ 1865	2 Escudos, Isabell II, 3rd Decimal Coinage, Gold	—	20.00
☐ 1869–1870	2 Pesetas, Provisional, Obverse Legend: Espana, Silver	—	10.00
☐ 1879–1884	2 Pesetas, Alfonso XII, 3rd Coinage, Silver	—	4.00
☐ 1889–1892	2 Pesetas, Alfonso XIII, 1st Coinage, Silver	—	4.00
☐ 1893–1894	2 Pesetas, Alfonso XIII, 2nd Coinage, Silver	—	6.00
☐ 1905	2 Pesetas, Alfonso XIII, 4th Coinage, Silver	—	30.00
☐ 1982–1984	2 Pesetas, Kingdom, Aluminum	—	.10
☐ 1953	2½ Pesetas, Kingdom, Aluminum-Bronze	—	.10
☐ 1953	2½ Pesetas, Nationalist, 2nd Coinage, Aluminum-Bronze	—	.10
☐ 1852–1855	4 Reales, Isabell II, Arms Without Pillars, Silver	—	10.00
☐ 1856–1864	4 Reales, Isabell II, 2nd Decimal Coinage, Silver	—	40.00
☐ 1865–1868	4 Escudos, Isabell II, 3rd Decimal Coinage, Gold	—	75.00
☐ 1869–1870	5 Pesetas, Provisional, Obverse Legend: Espana, Silver	—	12.00
☐ 1871	5 Pesetas, Amadeo I, Obverse Legend: Espana, Silver	—	12.00
☐ 1873	5 Pesetas, Republic, Cartagena Mint, Silver	—	15.00

DATE	COIN TYPE/VARIETY/METAL	ABP FINE	AVERAGE FINE
☐ 1875–1876	5 Pesetas, Alfonso XII, 1st Coinage, Silver	—	$12.00
☐ 1877–1882	5 Pesetas, Alfonso XII, 2nd Coinage, Silver	—	15.00
☐ 1882–1885	5 Pesetas, Alfonso XII, 3rd Coinage, Silver	—	12.00
☐ 1888–1892	5 Pesetas, Alfonso XIII, 1st Coinage, Silver	—	12.00
☐ 1892–1894	5 Pesetas, Alfonso XIII, 2nd Coinage, Silver	—	12.00
☐ 1896–1899	5 Pesetas, Alfonso XIII, 3rd Coinage, Silver	—	10.00

DATE	COIN TYPE/VARIETY/METAL	ABP FINE	AVERAGE FINE
☐ 1949	5 Pesetas, Kingdom, Nickel	$ .18	.30
☐ 1949	5 Pesetas, Nationalist Govt, 2nd Coinage, Nickel	.18	.30
☐ 1957–1975	5 Pesetas, Kingdom, Cupro-Nickel	—	.10
☐ 1980	5 Pesetas, Kingdom, World Cup Soccer Games, Cupro-Nickel	—	.10
☐ 1982–1989	5 Pesetas, Kingdom, Cupro-Nickel	—	.10
☐ 1989 to Date	5 Pesetas, Kingdom, Aluminum-Bronze	—	.10
☐ 1851–1856	10 Reales, Isabell II, Arms Flanked by Pillars, Silver	—	30.00
☐ 1857–1864	10 Reales, Isabell II, 2nd Decimal Coinage, Silver	—	75.00
☐ 1865–1868	10 Escudos, Isabell II, 3rd Decimal Coinage, Gold	—	185.00
☐ 1878–1879	10 Pesetas, Alfonso XII, 2nd Coinage, Gold	—	200.00
☐ 1983–1985	10 Pesetas, Kingdom, Cupro-Nickel	—	.10
☐ 1845–1855	20 Reales, Isabell II, Silver	—	40.00
☐ 1850–1855	20 Reales, Isabell II, Arms Flanked by Pillars, Silver	—	40.00

DATE	COIN TYPE/VARIETY/METAL	ABP FINE	AVERAGE FINE
☐ 1856–1864	20 Reales, Isabell II, 2nd Decimal Coinage, Silver	—	$30.00
☐ 1861–1863	20 Reales, Isabell II, 2nd Decimal Coinage, Gold	—	175.00
☐ 1887–1890	20 Pesetas, Alfonso XIII, 1st Coinage, Gold	—	150.00
☐ 1892	20 Pesetas, Alfonso XIII, 2nd Coinage, Gold	—	900.00
☐ 1896–1899	20 Pesetas, Alfonso XIII, 3rd Coinage, Gold	—	125.00
☐ 1904	20 Pesetas, Alfonso XIII, 4th Coinage, Gold	—	—
☐ 1876–1880	25 Pesetas, Alfonso XII, 2nd Coinage, Gold	—	1200.00
☐ 1881–1885	25 Pesetas, Alfonso XII, 3rd Coinage, Gold	—	195.00

DATE	COIN TYPE/VARIETY/METAL	ABP FINE	AVERAGE FINE
☐ 1957–1984	25 Pesetas, Kingdom, Cupro-Nickel	—	.25
☐ 1980	25 Pesetas, Kingdom, World Cup Soccer Games, Cupro-Nickel	—	.25
☐ 1990–1991	25 Pesetas, Kingdom, 1992 Olympics—High Jumper, Nickel-Bronze	—	.25
☐ 1990–1991	25 Pesetas, Kingdom, 1992 Olympics—Discus, Nickel-Bronze	—	.25
☐ 1992	25 Pesetas, Kingdom, Sevilla Tower, Nickel-Bronze	—	.25
☐ 1861–1863	40 Reales, Isabell II, 2nd Decimal Coinage, Gold	—	75.00

DATE	COIN TYPE/VARIETY/METAL	ABP FINE	AVERAGE FINE
□ 1957–1984	50 Pesetas, Kingdom, Cupro-Nickel	$ .28	$.60
□ 1980	50 Pesetas, Kingdom, World Cup Soccer Games, Cupro-Nickel	.28	.60
□ 1990	50 Pesetas, Kingdom, Expo 92—Juan Carlos, Cupro-Nickel	1.40	3.00
□ 1990–1991	50 Pesetas, Kingdom, Expo 92—City View, Cupro-Nickel	1.40	3.00
□ 1851–1855	100 Reales, Isabell II, Gold	—	500.00
□ 1856–1862	100 Reales, Isabell II, 2nd Decimal Coinage, Gold	—	150.00
□ 1897	100 Pesetas, Alfonso XIII, 3rd Coinage, Gold	—	700.00

DATE	COIN TYPE/VARIETY/METAL	ABP FINE	AVERAGE FINE
□ 1966	100 Pesetas, Kingdom, Silver	—	4.00
□ 1975	100 Pesetas, Kingdom, Cupro-Nickel	.40	1.00
□ 1980	100 Pesetas, Kingdom, World Cup Soccer Games, Cupro-Nickel	.40	1.00
□ 1982–1990	100 Pesetas, Kingdom, Aluminum-Bronze	.80	1.50
□ 1989	100 Pesetas, Kingdom, Discovery of America—Mayan Pyramid, Silver	—	5.00
□ 1990	100 Pesetas, Kingdom, Brother Juniper Serra, Silver	—	8.00
□ 1991	100 Pesetas, Kingdom, Celestino Mutis, Silver	—	8.00
□ 1986–1988	200 Pesetas, Kingdom, Celestino Mutis, Cupro-Nickel	1.40	3.00
□ 1987	200 Pesetas, Kingdom, Madrid Numismatic Exposition, Cupro-Nickel	18.00	30.00
□ 1989	200 Pesetas, Kingdom, Discovery of America—Astrolabe, Silver	—	
□ 1990	200 Pesetas, Kingdom, Alonso de Frcilla, Silver	—	12.00
□ 1990	200 Pesetas, Kingdom, Cupro-Nickel	1.75	5.00
□ 1991	200 Pesetas, Kingdom, Las Casas, Silver	—	12.00
□ 1992	200 Pesetas, Kingdom, Madrid—Capitol of European Culture, Silver	—	30.00

DATE	COIN TYPE/VARIETY/METAL	ABP FINE	AVERAGE FINE
□ 1987–1990	500 Pesetas, Kingdom, Wedding Anniversary—Juan Carlos & Sofia, Copper-Aluminum-Nickel	$2.75	$6.00
□ 1989	500 Pesetas, Kingdom, Discovery of America—Juego De Pelota Game, Silver	—	12.00
□ 1990	500 Pesetas, Kingdom, Juan de la Costa, Silver	—	12.00
□ 1991	500 Pesetas, Kingdom, Jorge Juan, Silver	—	14.00
□ 1989	1000 Pesetas, Kingdom, Discovery of America—Capture of Granada, Silver	—	20.00
□ 1990	1000 Pesetas, Kingdom, Magellanes and Elcano, Silver	—	25.00
□ 1991	1000 Pesetas, Kingdom, Simon Bolivar & San Martin, Silver	—	25.00
□ 1989	2000 Pesetas, Kingdom, Discovery of America—Columbus, Silver	—	35.00
□ 1990	2000 Pesetas, Kingdom, 1992 Olympics—Archer, Silver	—	40.00
□ 1990	2000 Pesetas, Kingdom, 1992 Olympics—Basketball Players, Silver	—	40.00
□ 1990	2000 Pesetas, Kingdom, 1992 Olympics—Human Pyramid, Silver	—	40.00
□ 1990	2000 Pesetas, Kingdom, Hidalgo, Morelos and Juarez, Silver	—	40.00
□ 1990	2000 Pesetas, Kingdom, 1992 Olympics, Symbols, Silver	—	45.00
□ 1990	2000 Pesetas, Kingdom, 1992 Olympics, Soccer Player, Silver	—	45.00
□ 1990	2000 Pesetas, Kingdom, 1992 Olympics, Pelotal Player, Silver	—	40.00
□ 1990	2000 Pesetas, Kingdom, 1992 Olympics, Greek Runner, Silver	—	45.00
□ 1990	2000 Pesetas, Kingdom, 1992 Olympics, Ancient Boat, Silver	—	40.00

DATE	COIN TYPE/VARIETY/METAL	ABP FINE	AVERAGE FINE
□ 1991	2000 Pesetas, Kingdom, Ibero American Series, Silver	—	$50.00
□ 1991	2000 Pesetas, Kingdom, Olympics—Medieval Rider, Silver	—	50.00
□ 1991	2000 Pesetas, Kingdom, Olympics—Torch & Flag, Silver	—	50.00
□ 1991	2000 Pesetas, Kingdom, Olympics—Tennis Player, Silver	—	45.00
□ 1991	2000 Pesetas, Kingdom, Olympics—Bowling, Silver	—	45.00
□ 1991	2000 Pesetas, Kingdom, Federman, Quesada and Benalcazar, Silver	—	40.00
□ 1992	2000 Pesetas, Kingdom, Olympics—Chariot Racing, Silver	—	45.00
□ 1992	2000 Pesetas, Kingdom, Olympics—Sprinters, Silver	—	45.00
□ 1992	2000 Pesetas, Kingdom, Olympics—Tug of War, Silver	—	45.00
□ 1992	2000 Pesetas, Kingdom, Olympics—Wheelchair Basketball, Silver	—	45.00
□ 1989	5000 Pesetas, Kingdom, Discovery of America—Compass Face, Gold	—	120.00
□ 1989	5000 Pesetas, Kingdom, Discovery of America—Santa Maria, Silver	—	120.00
□ 1990	5000 Pesetas, Kingdom, Philip V, Gold	—	130.00
□ 1990	5000 Pesetas, Kingdom, Cortes, Montezuma, and Marina, Silver	—	125.00
□ 1991	5000 Pesetas, Kingdom, Pizarro & Atahualpa, Silver	—	130.00
□ 1991	5000 Pesetas, Kingdom, Fernando VI, Gold	—	135.00
□ 1989	10000 Pesetas, Kingdom, Discovery of America—Sphere, Gold	—	195.00
□ 1990	10000 Pesetas, Kingdom, Quauchtemoc, Gold	—	210.00
□ 1990	10000 Pesetas, Kingdom, Olympics—Field Hockey, Gold	—	200.00
□ 1990	10000 Pesetas, Kingdom, Olympics—Gymnast, Gold	—	195.00
□ 1991	10000 Pesetas, Kingdom, Regional Autonomy, Silver	—	210.00
□ 1991	10000 Pesetas, Kingdom, Discoverers & Liberators, Silver	—	220.00
□ 1991	10000 Pesetas, Kingdom, Tupac Amaru II, Gold	—	210.00
□ 1991	10000 Pesetas, Kingdom, Spanish Royal Family, Silver	—	195.00

DATE	COIN TYPE/VARIETY/METAL	ABP FINE	AVERAGE FINE
☐ 1991	10000 Pesetas, Kingdom, Olympics—Karate, Gold	—	$220.00
☐ 1991	10000 Pesetas, Kingdom, Olympics—Baseball, Gold	—	215.00
☐ 1989	20000 Pesetas, Kingdom, Discovery of America—Pinzon Brother, Gold	—	375.00
☐ 1990	20000 Pesetas, Kingdom, Tupac Amaru I, Gold		
☐ 1990	20000 Pesetas, Kingdom, Huascar, Gold	—	400.00
☐ 1990	20000 Pesetas, Kingdom, Olympics—Cathedral Tower, Gold	—	425.00
☐ 1990	20000 Pesetas, Kingdom, Olympics—Dome Building, Gold	—	400.00
☐ 1990	20000 Pesetas, Kingdom, Olympics—Ruins, Gold	—	420.00
☐ 1990	20000 Pesetas, Kingdom, Olympics—Montjuic Stadium, Gold	—	450.00
☐ 1989	40000 Pesetas, Kingdom, Discovery of America—Sea Monster Attacking Ship, Gold	—	700.00
☐ 1990	40000 Pesetas, Kingdom, Juan Carlos, Gold	—	750.00
☐ 1991	40000 Pesetas, Kingdom, Imperial Double Eagle, Gold	—	700.00
☐ 1989	80000 Pesetas, Kingdom, Discovery of America—Ferdinand & Isabella, Gold	—	1275.00
☐ 1990	80000 Pesetas, Kingdom, Carlos V, Gold	—	1400.00
☐ 1990	80000 Pesetas, Kingdom, Olympics—Discus, Gold	—	1350.00
☐ 1990	80000 Pesetas, Kingdom, Olympics—Prince Carlos on Horseback, Gold	—	1400.00
☐ 1991	80000 Pesetas, Kindgom, Olympics—Women Tossing Man, Gold	—	1200.00
☐ 1991	80000 Pesetas, Kingdom, Carlos III, Gold	—	1350.00
☐ 1992	80000 Pesetas, Olympics—Children Playing, Gold	—	1250.00

SWITZERLAND

The first coins were Celtic issues of gold staters and fractions. The Swiss series began in the 3rd century B.C., and silver coins were issued in the 1st century B.C. In the 6th and 7th centuries, gold tremisses were produced, then silver deniers. In the 13th century, bracteate pfennigs were made. Gold coins were produced in the 1400s. The decimal system was developed in 1798. The currency in use today is the Swiss franc.

Switzerland—Type Coinage

DATE	COIN TYPE/VARIETY/METAL	ABP FINE	AVERAGE FINE
☐ 1922–1954	5 Francs, William Tell, Rev: Shield, Silver	—	$16.00
☐ 1936	5 Francs, Commemorative, Armament Fund, Silver	—	20.00
☐ 1939	5 Francs, Commemorative, Zurich Exposition, Silver	—	85.00
☐ 1939	5 Francs, Commemorative, Laupen, Silver	—	600.00
☐ 1941	5 Francs, Commemorative, Confederation 650th Anniversary, Silver	—	60.00
☐ 1944	5 Francs, Commemorative, Battle of St. Jakob 500th Anniversary, Silver	—	40.00

DATE	COIN TYPE/VARIETY/METAL	ABP FINE	AVERAGE FINE
□ 1948	5 Francs, Commemorative, Swiss Confederation Centenary, Silver	—	$12.00
□ 1911–1922	10 Francs Peasant Girl, Rev: Shield, Gold	—	75.00
□ 1901–1935	20 Francs Peasant Girl, Rev: Shield, Gold	—	75.00

Switzerland—Shooting Festival Coinage

DATE	COIN TYPE/VARIETY/METAL	ABP FINE	AVERAGE FINE
□ 1855	5 Francs, Shooting Festival Solothurn, Silver	—	1500.00
□ 1857	5 Francs, Shooting Festival Berne, Silver	—	375.00
□ 1859	5 Francs, Shooting Festival Zurich, Silver	—	210.00
□ 1861	5 Francs, Shooting Festival Nidwalden, Silver	—	210.00
□ 1863	5 Francs, Shooting Festival La Chaux-de-Fonds, Silver	—	210.00
□ 1865	5 Francs, Shooting Festival Schaffhausen, Silver	—	120.00

DATE	COIN TYPE/VARIETY/METAL	ABP FINE	AVERAGE FINE
□ 1867	5 Francs, Shooting Festival Schwyz, Silver	—	150.00
□ 1869	5 Francs, Shooting Festival Zug, Silver	—	150.00
□ 1872	5 Francs, Shooting Festival Zurich, Silver	—	110.00
□ 1874	5 Francs, Shooting Festival St. Gallen, Silver	—	95.00
□ 1876	5 Francs, Shooting Festival Lausanne, Silver	—	80.00
□ 1879	5 Francs, Shooting Festival Basle, Silver	—	60.00
□ 1881	5 Francs, Shooting Festival Fribourg, Silver	—	60.00
□ 1883	5 Francs, Shooting Festival Lugano, Silver	—	60.00
□ 1885	5 Francs, Shooting Festival Berne, Silver	—	60.00

Switzerland—Heletian Confederation Coinage

DATE	COIN TYPE/VARIETY/METAL	ABP FINE	AVERAGE FINE
□ 1879–1954	5 Centimes, Helvetia Head. Rev: Wreath & Shield, Cupro-Nickel	$ .50	$1.00

DATE	COIN TYPE/VARIETY/METAL	ABP FINE	AVERAGE FINE
□ 1879–1954	10 Centimes, Helvetia Head. Rev: Wreath & Shield, Cupro-Nickel	.25	.50

DATE	COIN TYPE/VARIETY/METAL	ABP FINE	AVERAGE FINE
□ 1881–1954	20 Centimes, Helvetia Head. Rev: Wreath & Shield, Cupro-Nickel	.20	.40
□ 1850–1851	½ Franc, Helvetia, Silver	5.00	12.00

DATE	COIN TYPE/VARIETY/METAL	ABP FINE	AVERAGE FINE
☐ 1875–1953	½ Franc, Helvetia Standing. Rev: Wreath. Silver	—	$10.00
☐ 1850–1861	Franc, Helvetia, Silver	—	5.00

DATE	COIN TYPE/VARIETY/METAL	ABP FINE	AVERAGE FINE
☐ 1875–1945	Franc, Helvetia Standing. Rev: Wreath, Silver	—	4.00
☐ 1850–1863	2 Francs, Helvetia, Silver	—	4.50

DATE	COIN TYPE/VARIETY/METAL	ABP FINE	AVERAGE FINE
☐ 1874–1948	2 Francs, Helvetia Standing. Rev: Wreath, Silver	—	4.00
☐ 1850–1874	5 Francs, Helvetia, Silver	—	4.00
☐ 1888–1916	5 Francs, Helvetia Head. Rev: Wreath & Shield, Silver	—	4.00

SYRIA

The first coins were used in the 5th century B.C. and were Greek issues of silver coinage. The silver tetradrachm was in evidence in 200 B.C., followed by bronze coins in 200 A.D. The copper fals was used in the 600s, followed by the copper dinar, silver dirhem, and silver coins and dirhems in the 12th to 16th centuries. The nickel-brass, cupro-nickel, and aluminum-bronze piastre was used in the 1900s. Decimal coins were used in 1921. The currency today is the pound.

Syria—UAR

DATE	COIN TYPE/VARIETY/METAL	ABP FINE	AVERAGE FINE
□ 1962–1973	2½ Piastres, Aluminum-Bronze	—	$ .60
□ 1962–1965	5 Piastres, Aluminum-Bronze	—	.30

DATE	COIN TYPE/VARIETY/METAL	ABP FINE	AVERAGE FINE
□ 1971–1979	5 Piastres, FAO Issue, Aluminum-Bronze	—	$ .30
□ 1962–1974	10 Piastres, Aluminum-Bronze	—	.15
□ 1976–1979	10 Piastres, FAO Issue, Aluminum-Bronze	—	.15
□ 1968–1974	25 Piastres, Nickel	—	.15
□ 1976	25 Piastres, FAO Issue, Nickel	—	.15
□ 1979	25 Piastres, Cupro-Nickel	—	.15
□ 1968–1976	50 Piastres, Nickel	—	.15
□ 1979	50 Piastres, Cupro-Nickel	—	.10
□ 1968–1978	1 Pound, Nickel	—	.25
□ 1979	1 Pound, Cupro-Nickel	—	.25
□ 1991	1 Pound, Stainless Steel	—	.25

Syria—Syria Republic

DATE	COIN TYPE/VARIETY/METAL	ABP FINE	AVERAGE FINE
□ 1960	2½ Piastres, Aluminum-Bronze	—	.05
□ 1960	5 Piastres, Aluminum-Bronze	—	.05
□ 1960	10 Piastres, Aluminum-Bronze	—	.05
□ 1958	25 Piastres, Silver	—	1.00
□ 1958	50 Piastres, Silver	—	2.00
□ 1959	50 Piastres, Anniversary of Founding of United Arab Republic, Silver	—	2.25

TURKEY

The first coins were used in the late 7th century B.C. and were made of electrum, an alloy of gold and silver. Pure gold and silver coins were produced in 500 B.C. Bronze and copper coins followed through several different periods in Turkey. The decimal system was set up in 1844. A new coinage was initiated in 1934. The currency today is the lira.

Turkey—Type Coinage

DATE	COIN TYPE/VARIETY/METAL	ABP FINE	AVERAGE FINE
☐ 1918–1919	2 Kurus, Mohammed VI, 1st Coinage, Silver	—	$120.00
☐ 1923–1924	100 Para, Republic, Aluminum-Bronze	$ .40	1.00
☐ 1926	100 Para, Republic, Aluminum-Bronze	.40	1.00
☐ 1918–1919	5 Kurus, Mohammed VI, 1st Coinage, Silver	—	.75
☐ 1923–1924	5 Kurus, Republic, Aluminum-Bronze	.40	1.00
☐ 1926	5 Kurus, Republic, Aluminum-Bronze	.90	2.00
☐ 1918–1919	10 Kurus, Mohammed VI, 1st Coinage, Silver	—	150.00
☐ 1923–1924	10 Kurus, Republic, Aluminum-Bronze	1.00	2.00
☐ 1926	10 Kurus, Republic, Aluminum-Bronze	.90	2.00
☐ 1918–1919	20 Kurus, Mohammed VI, 1st Coinage, Silver	—	35.00
☐ 1918–1919	25 Kurus, Mohammed VI, 1st Coinage, Gold	—	40.00
☐ 1924	25 Kurus, Republic, Nickel	1.40	3.00
☐ 1926–1928	25 Kurus, Republic, Nickel	.90	2.00
☐ 1927–1928	25 Kurus, Republic, Monnaies de Luxe, Gold	—	60.00
☐ 1918–1922	50 Kurus, Mohammed VI, 1st Coinage, Gold	—	120.00
☐ 1926–1928	50 Kurus, Republic, Gold	—	75.00
☐ 1927–1928	50 Kurus, Republic, Monnaies de Luxe, Gold	—	85.00
☐ 1918–1919	100 Kurus, Mohammed VI, 1st Coinage, Gold	—	120.00
☐ 1926–1929	100 Kurus, Republic, Gold	—	120.00
☐ 1927–1928	100 Kurus, Republic, Monnaies de Luxe, Gold	—	150.00
☐ 1918	250 Kurus, Mohammed VI, 1st Coinage, Gold	—	2000.00
☐ 1926–1928	250 Kurus, Republic, Gold	—	275.00
☐ 1927–1928	250 Kurus, Republic, Monnaies de Luxe, Gold	—	265.00
☐ 1918–1920	500 Kurus, Mohammed VI, 1st Coinage, Gold	—	1000.00
☐ 1926–1929	500 Kurus, Republic, Gold	—	550.00
☐ 1927–1928	500 Kurus, Republic, Monnaies de Luxe, Gold	—	550.00

Turkey—Western Date Coinage

DATE	COIN TYPE/VARIETY/METAL	ABP FINE	AVERAGE FINE
□ 1940–1942	10 Para, Aluminum-Bronze	$ .12	$ .30
□ 1948	½ Kurus, Brass	200.00	350.00

DATE	COIN TYPE/VARIETY/METAL	ABP FINE	AVERAGE FINE
□ 1935–1937	1 Kurus, President Ataturk, Cupro-Nickel	.12	.50
□ 1938–1944	1 Kurus, President Inonu, Cupro-Nickel	.12	.50
□ 1947–1951	1 Kurus, Brass	—	.50
□ 1948–1951	2½ Kurus, Brass	.12	.30

DATE	COIN TYPE/VARIETY/METAL	ABP FINE	AVERAGE FINE
□ 1935–1943	5 Kurus, President Ataturk, Cupro-Nickel	.18	.40
□ 1949–1957	5 Kurus, Brass	.50	1.00

DATE	COIN TYPE/VARIETY/METAL	ABP FINE	AVERAGE FINE
□ 1935–1940	10 Kurus, President Ataturk, Cupro-Nickel	.50	1.00
□ 1949–1956	10 Kurus, Brass	—	.10

DATE	COIN TYPE/VARIETY/METAL	ABP FINE	AVERAGE FINE
☐ 1935–1937	25 Kurus, President Ataturk, Silver	—	$120.00
☐ 1943	25 Kurus, President Ataturk, Gold	—	95.00
☐ 1943–1949	25 Kurus, President Inonu, Gold	—	75.00
☐ 1944–1946	25 Kurus Nickel-Brass	$ .28	.60
☐ 1948–1956	25 Kurus, Brass	—	.10
☐ 1935–1937	50 Kurus, President Ataturk, Silver	—	4.00
☐ 1943–1951	50 Kurus, President Inonu, Gold	—	100.00
☐ 1943	50 Kurus, President Ataturk, Gold	—	120.00
☐ 1947–1948	50 Kurus, Silver	—	100.00
☐ 1934	100 Kurus, President Ataturk, Silver	—	5.00
☐ 1937–1939	1 Lira, President Ataturk, Silver	—	6.00
☐ 1940–1941	1 Lira, President Inonu, Silver	—	6.00
☐ 1947–1948	1 Lira, Silver	—	2.00
☐ 1943–1949	100 Kurus, President Inonu, Gold	—	160.00
☐ 1943–1980	100 Kurus, President Ataturk, Gold	—	120.00
☐ 1943–1980	250 Kurus, President Ataturk, Gold	—	265.00
☐ 1943–1947	250 Kurus, President Inonu, Gold	—	275.00
☐ 1943	500 Kurus, President Ataturk, Gold	—	550.00
☐ 1943–1948	500 Kurus, President Inonu, Gold	—	550.00

UNITED KINGDOM

Britain's first coins in the 1st century B.C. were potin pieces, a combination of tin and bronze, generally called staters. In 55–54 B.C. gold coins were being struck, followed by silver and bronze. In the late 6th century the gold thrymasas or shillings were reduced and replaced by silver pennies, or sceattas. By the 1200s, halfpennies, farthings, and groats were produced, and in 1344 the florin, then the noble. The pound, angel, and sovereign existed in the 1500s, then the farthing and guinea in the 1600s. In 1971, the system of pounds, shillings, and pence was abandoned for the decimal system.

THE MODERN ROYAL MINT

Courtesy of the Royal Mint

Today the Royal Mint has become both a business and a Government Department. Since 1975 it has operated as a Government Trading Fund, giving it a degree of commercial freedom but at the same time requiring that income should not only balance expenditure but that there should be an additional return on the capital employed. The Deputy Master, who remains a civil servant like the 1000 or so other members of the staff, presides over a board of directors and acts as chief executive. After ten years under the new system, cumulative sales have exceeded £600 million and the Mint has operated profitably in each of the ten years, achieving an average return on capital which compares favourably with the private sector.

Acting under contract with the Treasury, the Mint continues to be responsible for the production and issue of the United Kingdom coinage. In recent years it has had to cope with the introduction of two new coins, the 20 pence and the pound; the 1/2 penny, on the other hand, has been demonetised and withdrawn, and the Mint is constantly exploring with the help of outside experts the ways in which the coinage might develop in the future. Commemorative coins have become rather more frequent, with particularly successful crown pieces being issued in 1977 for the Queen's Silver Jubilee and in 1981 for the wedding of HRH The Prince of Wales. In 1986 a special two-pound piece was issued for the Commonwealth Games, the first time that a sporting occasion had been commemorated on the United Kingdom coinage. All new designs continue to be submitted to the Royal Mint Advisory Committee which, under the Presidency of HRH The Prince Philip since 1952, now normally meets at Buckingham Palace.

The striking of overseas coins has remained a large and successful feature of Mint output, reflecting a deservedly high reputation for quality and delivery in a business which has become more and more competitive. In most years well over half of total production is exported and in the financial year 1984/85, for instance, the Mint struck coins for no fewer than 67 countries, ranging from Ascension Island to Zambia. Sales staff based in the London office make regular trips overseas, and the Mint cooperates in a consortium with two private mints in Birmingham and the Currency Division of the De La

Rue Company to ensure that as many orders as possible are won for the United Kingdom. As part of its service to overseas customers, the Mint also operates with De La Rue a joint company, Royal Mint Services Limited, to provide advice and technical assistance to foreign mints. Results have been such that since the Mint moved to Llantrisant it has twice won the Queen's Award for Export Achievement, first in 1973 and then again in 1977.

An increasingly important aspect of Mint activity has been the sale of proof and uncirculated coins to collectors. Following the outstanding success of the sets of the last £sd coins of 1970 and of the first decimal coins of 1971, proof sets of United Kingdom coins have been struck every year. An expanding range of proof and uncirculated United Kingdom and overseas coins, in gold and silver as well as base metal, is now available by direct mail order from Llantrisant. The regular issue of colourful bulletins and brochures has been a new departure and the Mint has become a frequent exhibitor at shows and conventions, particularly in North America, which has proved a highly receptive market for collectors' coins.

More traditional activities, such as the making of medals and seals, have continued. As at Tower Hill, the production of medals still calls for the hand skills of craftsmen such as silversmiths, but like the rest of the Mint the Medal Department is not immune from pressure. In 1982, for instance, it responded with speed and success to the urgent requirement for medals to be awarded to those taking part in the campaign in the South Atlantic. As well as the normal range of military and civilian decorations, it produces a large variety of prize and commemorative medals for learned societies and private companies. Overseas orders are also received and the Medal Department accordingly makes a contribution to the Mint's export trade.

The modern Royal Mint at Llantrisant houses some of the most advanced coining machinery in the world and it has a larger capacity than any other mint in Western Europe. It is a mint in which the microprocessor and computer are increasingly prominent, yet at the same time there remains a vital role for the inherited skills and craftsmanship which have been built up during an unbroken history of more than 100 years. Clearly it is more than the thread of history which links the present Royal Mint to its Anglo-Saxon predecessor.

MINTING PROCESSES AT LLANTRISANT

The first stage in the coining process is the melting of the constituent metals, usually copper, nickel, zinc or tin, in the appropriate proportions for the alloy required. At Tower Hill this was essentially a small-scale affair, with the molten metal being poured into vertical moulds, but the new mint has a continuous casting unit in operation twenty-four hours a day. By this system, virgin metals and process scrap are melted in primary electric furnaces and, when examination of a sample by X-ray fluorescence spectrometry has confirmed that the alloy is correct, the molten metal is transferred to holding furnaces. From the holding furnace it is drawn horizontally and continuously in the form of a strip about 200 millimetres wide and 15 millimetres thick, with cutting equipment built into the casting line dividing the strip into manageable 10 metre lengths weighing some 200 kilograms each.

A tandem rolling mill begins the process of reducing the metal to coin thickness. If, as with nickel-brass, intermediate annealing or softening is necessary, the strip is passed slowly through a furnace at a temperature of about 650°C. During the rolling process, for ease of handling, five of the cast lengths are welded together to create a large coil weighing about one tonne. A finishing mill then completes the task, its rolls reversible so that the coil of strip can pass backwards and forwards until it is reduced to the thickness required. From the finished coils blank discs are punched out in large presses at rates of up to 14,000 blanks a minute and collected in drums. The scrap metal, known for centuries as scissel, is passed back to the furnace for re-melting.

The drums of blanks are then transferred from the Melting, Rolling and Blanking Unit to the Annealing and Pickling Block. Here they are fed from large hoppers into gas-fired annealing furnaces where they are softened by being heated to high temperature, 850°C in the case of cupro-nickel and 750°C for bronze. After cooling they are passed to automatic pickling barrels where stains are removed by a solution of sulphuric acid and, after a final washing in tartaric acid, they are rinsed in water and dried by hot air. Most blanks then go to the marking machines, where they are rolled under pressure down a narrow groove to force the metal inwards in order to thicken the edge of the blank. This then makes it easier to give the coin a raised rim to protect it from wear and to enable coins to be stacked in piles.

The final process is the stamping on the blanks of the obverse and reverse designs and, when required, the milling on the edge. These operations are carried out simultaneously in a coining press, into which the blanks are fed by hopper. With most presses the blank is automatically placed on top of the lower die and is held in position by a restraining collar, which will be plain or milled depending on the type of edge required. The upper die is then squeezed down onto the blank with a force of up to 100 or more tonnes, so that the blank receives the impression of both dies while at the same time the metal is forced outwards to take up the shape and pattern of the collar. The rate of striking depends on factors such as the size and design of the coins but with the sophisticated engineering of modern presses 400 coins can often be struck in a minute. A new generation of presses is likely to be faster still, achieving rates of up to 700 coins a minute.

After striking, the coins are automatically ejected from the press and fall into a container for inspection. A statistical sampling technique is used to ensure a regorous quality control and after passing inspection the coins are counted into bags and checkweighed, the first task on which a robot has been used in the Mint. The bags are then conveyed to a secure area to await despatch, either overseas or by the road to cash centres in the United Kingdom. Samples of all United Kingdom coins except bronze are taken for submission to the Trial of the Pyx which continues, as it has done for more than seven centuries, to provide an independent check on the accuracy of the coins struck by the Royal Mint.

A separate proof coin section is responsible for the special coins which are struck for sale to collectors. Since the seventeenth century proof coins have represented the perfection of the minter's art, and it is the combination of traditional skills and modern technology which has enabled Royal Mint proofs to reach their current level of excellence. The dies are given a matt finish and then a craftsman, using diamond paste, carefully polishes parts of the surface to produce a pleasing contrast between the frosted features of the design and the mirror background of the field. The blanks, too, are specially polished, either by burnishing or buffing, before being struck in a dust-free atmosphere.

Proofs are struck one at a time on a coining press and receive more than one blow from the dies to ensure that every detail of the designs is faithfully reproduced. The dies are kept clean and are replaced immediately they show any sign of deterioration. After striking, each coin is carefully removed from the press to prevent damage and once it has satisfied trained inspectors it soon finds its way into the attractive packaging which is a feature of these special issues from the Mint.

DIE-MAKING AT LLANTRISANT

Modern die-making has been transformed by the introduction of the reducing machine. The traditional method whereby engravers cut a matrix or punch by hand, a painstaking process which might easily take three or four weeks, has now been largely superseded by the machine, which produces a master punch in relief from an electrotype copy of an artist's plaster model. The first of these machines to be used in the Mint was acquired by Benedetto Pistrucci in 1819 and a second was officially ordered for William Wyon in 1824; but it was probably not until the turn of the century, when machines were purchased from Janvier of Paris, that the Mint began to make full use of the reducing machine.

The plaster model, prepared either by a private artist or by a member of the Mint's small but highly skilled Engraving Department, is usually between six and ten inches in diameter.

Stages in die-making; the artist at work on his sketch; the preparation of a plaster model; the growing of the electrotype; and an engraver perfecting the steel matrix.

A silicon rubber mould is taken from the model and after one day's curing to make it pliable and flexible the mould is made electrically conductive to enable it to be plated with nickel. After about two hours it is transferred to a copper plating bath, where it is left for three days to allow a sufficiently thick deposit of copper to back up the nickel on the mould. It is this nickel-faced copper electrotype which is then mounted on the reducing machine.

The machine is essentially a three-dimensional pantograph, so simple in its operation that the Mint craftsmen are still happiest with the old Janvier machines which were transferred from Tower Hill. The details of the electrotype, set firmly in wax and revolving slowly at one end of the machine, are scanned by a tracer at the free end of a rigid bar. The movements of the tracer as it follows the contours of the electrotype are communicated by the bar in reduced amplitude to a rotating cutter at the other end. The cutter, as it moves in and out, accordingly reproduces the details of the design at coin scale onto a block of steel to form a master punch with features in relief as on a coin. A first, or rough, cut takes a day, to be followed by a second cut which takes another day.

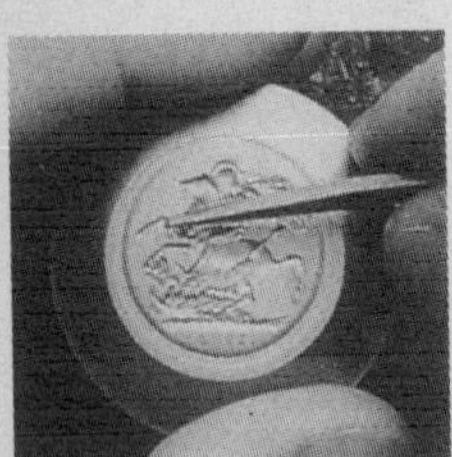

Above, left. An engraver ensures that there are no flaws or blemishes on the matrix.

Above, right. One of the Janvier reducing machines at work.

Minute blemishes and flaws are removed from the reduction punch by hand. It is then hardened so that it can be placed in a hydraulic press and its design transferred under pressure to a piece of soft steel. On this new tool, called a matrix, the design is incuse and it is at this stage that the engraver is able to add by hand the beads, the figures of the date or any other feature not included on the original model. Once work on the matrix has been completed, it is hardened and then placed in a hydraulic press to produce the working punch. This, like the reduction punch, is in relief, and after turning and shaping it is returned to the engravers for final adjustment and cleaning. It is from this punch that working dies, all absolutely identical, are made for the coining presses.

To protect their surface and prolong their life the dies are chrome plated. Even so the life of an individual die remains a little unpredictable, though most now comfortably exceed 200,000 coins.

United Kingdom—Type Coinage

DATE	COIN TYPE/VARIETY/METAL	ABP FINE	AVERAGE FINE
□ 1839–1856	½ Farthing, Victoria, Young Portrait, Copper	$1.50	$3.50
□ 1838–1860	1 Farthing, Victoria, Young Portrait, Copper	1.25	3.00
□ 1860–1895	1 Farthing, Victoria, Young Portrait, Bronze	.90	2.00
□ 1895–1901	1 Farthing, Victoria, Aged Portrait, Bronze	.15	.40
□ 1902–1910	1 Farthing, Edward VII, Bronze	.30	1.25
□ 1911–1936	1 Farthing, George V, Bronze	—	.20

DATE	COIN TYPE/VARIETY/METAL	ABP FINE	AVERAGE FINE
□ 1937–1948	1 Farthing, George VI, Bronze	—	$ .12
□ 1949–1952	1 Farthing, George VI, 2nd Coinage, Bronze	—	.11
□ 1953	1 Farthing, Elizabeth II, Bronze	—	.12
□ 1954–1956	1 Farthing, Elizabeth II, 2nd Coinage, Bronze	—	.11
□ 1838–1859	½ Penny, Victoria, Young Portrait, Copper	$ .75	1.50

DATE	COIN TYPE/VARIETY/METAL	ABP FINE	AVERAGE FINE
□ 1860–1894	½ Penny, Victoria, Young Portrait, Bronze	.65	1.50
□ 1895–1901	½ Penny, Victoria, Aged Portrait, Bronze	.35	.70
□ 1902–1910	½ Penny, Edward VII, Bronze	.50	1.00
□ 1911–1927	½ Penny, George V, Bronze	.30	.70
□ 1928–1936	½ Penny, George V, Bronze	—	.30
□ 1937–1948	½ Penny, George VI, Bronze	—	.20
□ 1949–1952	½ Penny, George VI, 2nd Coinage, Bronze	—	.15
□ 1953	½ Penny, Elizabeth II, Bronze	—	.15
□ 1954–1967	½ Penny, Elizabeth II, 2nd Coinage, Bronze	—	.10
□ 1902–1910	1 Penny, Edward VII, Bronze	.25	.80

DATE	COIN TYPE/VARIETY/METAL	ABP FINE	AVERAGE FINE
□ 1911–1927	1 Penny, George V, Bronze	.25	.70

DATE	COIN TYPE/VARIETY/METAL	ABP FINE	AVERAGE FINE
☐ 1928–1936	1 Penny, George V, Bronze	—	$ .24
☐ 1937–1948	1 Penny, George VI, Bronze	—	.12
☐ 1949–1951	1 Penny, George VI, 2nd Coinage, Bronze	—	.12
☐ 1953	1 Penny, Elizabeth II, Bronze	—	.25
☐ 1954–1970	1 Penny, Elizabeth II, 2nd Coinage, Bronze	—	.10
☐ 1841–1860	1 Penny, Victoria, Young Portrait, Copper	$1.75	4.00
☐ 1860–1894	1 Penny, Victoria, Young Portrait, Bronze	1.75	4.00
☐ 1895–1901	1 Penny, Victoria, Aged Portrait, Bronze	1.40	3.00
☐ 1838–1887	3 Pence, Victoria, Young Portrait, Silver	—	4.00
☐ 1887–1893	3 Pence, Victoria, Golden Jubilee, Silver	—	2.00
☐ 1893–1901	3 Pence, Victoria, Aged Portrait, Silver	—	1.00

DATE	COIN TYPE/VARIETY/METAL	ABP FINE	AVERAGE FINE
☐ 1902–1910	3 Pence, Edward VII, Silver	—	2.50
☐ 1911–1926	3 Pence, George V, Silver	—	1.50
☐ 1927–1936	3 Pence, George V, Silver	—	20.00 Proof
☐ 1937–1944	3 Pence, George VI, Silver	—	2.00
☐ 1949–1952	3 Pence, George VI, 2nd Coinage, Nickel-Brass	—	.25
☐ 1953	3 Pence, Elizabeth II, Nickel-Brass	—	.20
☐ 1954–1970	3 Pence, Elizabeth II, 2nd Coinage, Nickel-Brass	—	.10

DATE	COIN TYPE/VARIETY/METAL	ABP FINE	AVERAGE FINE
☐ 1838–1862	4 Pence, Victoria, Young Portrait, Silver	—	8.00
☐ 1838–1887	6 Pence, Victoria, Young Portrait, Silver	—	4.50
☐ 1887	6 Pence, Victoria, Golden Jubilee, Silver	—	2.00

DATE	COIN TYPE/VARIETY/METAL	ABP FINE	AVERAGE FINE
□ 1887–1893	6 Pence, Victoria, Golden Jubilee, Silver	—	$2.50
□ 1893–1901	6 Pence, Victoria, Aged Portrait, Silver	—	1.75
□ 1902–1910	6 Pence, Edward VII, Silver	—	3.50
□ 1911–1927	6 Pence, George V, Silver	—	1.25
□ 1927–1936	6 Pence, George V, Silver	—	1.00
□ 1937–1946	6 Pence, George VI, Silver	—	.20
□ 1947–1948	6 Pence, George VI, Cupro-Nickel	—	.15
□ 1949–1952	6 Pence, George VI, 2nd Coinage, Cupro-Nickel	—	.15
□ 1953	6 Pence, Elizabeth II, Cupro-Nickel	—	.10

DATE	COIN TYPE/VARIETY/METAL	ABP FINE	AVERAGE FINE
□ 1954–1970	6 Pence, Elizabeth II, 2nd Coinage, Cupro-Nickel	—	.10
□ 1838–1887	Shilling, Victoria, Young Portrait, Silver	—	3.50

DATE	COIN TYPE/VARIETY/METAL	ABP FINE	AVERAGE FINE
□ 1887–1892	Shilling, Victoria, Golden Jubilee, Silver	—	3.00
□ 1893–1901	Shilling, Victoria, Aged Portrait, Silver	—	2.50
□ 1902–1910	Shilling, Edward VII, Silver	—	3.50
□ 1911–1927	Shilling, George V, Silver	—	3.00
□ 1927–1936	Shilling, George V, Silver	—	1.25

DATE	COIN TYPE/VARIETY/METAL	ABP FINE	AVERAGE FINE
☐ 1937–1946	Shilling, George VI, Silver	—	$ .10
☐ 1947–1948	Shilling, George VI, Cupro-Nickel	—	.10
☐ 1949–1951	Shilling, George VI, 2nd Coinage, Cupro-Nickel	—	.10
☐ 1953	1 Shilling, Elizabeth II, Cupro-Nickel	$ .50	1.25
☐ 1954–1970	1 Shilling, Elizabeth II, 2nd Coinage, Cupro-Nickel	—	.10
☐ 1849	1 Florin, Victoria, Gothic, Silver	—	10.00
☐ 1851–1887	1 Florin, Victoria, Gothic, Silver	—	6.50
☐ 1887–1892	1 Florin, Victoria, Golden Jubilee, Silver	—	4.00

DATE	COIN TYPE/VARIETY/METAL	ABP FINE	AVERAGE FINE
☐ 1893–1901	1 Florin, Victoria, Aged Portrait, Silver	—	10.00
☐ 1902–1910	1 Florin, Edward VII, Silver	—	9.00
☐ 1911–1926	1 Florin, George V, Silver	—	2.50
☐ 1927–1936	1 Florin, George V, Silver	—	1.50
☐ 1937–1946	2 Shillings, George VI, Silver	—	1.00
☐ 1947–1948	2 Shilling, George VI, Cupro-Nickel	—	.25
☐ 1949–1951	2 Shillings, George VI, 2nd Coinage, Cupro-Nickel	—	.25
☐ 1953	2 Shillings, Elizabeth II, Cupro-Nickel	—	.25
☐ 1954–1970	2 Shillings, Elizabeth II, 2nd Coinage, Cupro-Nickel	—	.15
☐ 1839–1887	½ Crown, Victoria, Young Portrait, Silver	—	9.50
☐ 1887–1892	½ Crown, Victoria, Golden Jubilee, Silver	—	8.00

DATE	COIN TYPE/VARIETY/METAL	ABP FINE	AVERAGE FINE
☐ 1893–1901	½ Crown, Victoria, Aged Portrait, Silver	—	8.50
☐ 1902–1910	½ Crown, Edward VII, Silver	—	10.00
☐ 1911–1927	½ Crown, George V, Silver	—	3.75
☐ 1927–1936	½ Crown, George V, Silver	—	3.00

DATE	COIN TYPE/VARIETY/METAL	ABP FINE	AVERAGE FINE
□ 1937–1946	½ Crown, George VI, Silver	—	$1.50
□ 1947–1948	½ Crown, George VI, Cupro-Nickel	—	.20
□ 1949–1952	½ Crown, George VI, 2nd Coinage, Cupro-Nickel	$ .10	.40
□ 1953	½ Crown, Elizabeth II, Cupro-Nickel	.25	.60
□ 1954–1970	½ Crown, Elizabeth II, 2nd Coinage, Cupro-Nickel	—	.35
□ 1887–1890	2 Florins, Victoria, Golden Jubilee, Silver	—	9.00

DATE	COIN TYPE/VARIETY/METAL	ABP FINE	AVERAGE FINE
□ 1935	1 Crown, George V, Silver Jubilee, Silver	—	10.50
□ 1839–1847	1 Crown, Victoria, Young Portrait, Silver	—	20.00
□ 1847–1853	1 Crown, Victoria, Gothic, Silver	—	2500.00 Proof
□ 1887–1892	1 Crown, Victoria, Golden Jubilee, Silver	—	15.00
□ 1893–1901	1 Crown, Victoria, Aged Portrait, Silver	—	16.00
□ 1902	1 Crown, Edward VII, Silver	—	22.00
□ 1927–1936	1 Crown, George V, Silver	—	50.00
□ 1937	1 Crown, George VI, Silver	—	7.50
□ 1951	5 Shillings, George VI, 2nd Coinage, Cupro-Nickel	40.00.	100.00
□ 1953	5 Shillings, Elizabeth II, Cupro-Nickel	.40	1.00
□ 1838–1885	½ Sovereign, Victoria, Young Portrait, Gold	—	70.00
□ 1887–1893	½ Sovereign, Victoria, Golden Jubilee, Gold	—	62.00
□ 1893–1901	½ Sovereign, Victoria, Aged Portrait, Gold	—	55.00
□ 1902–1910	½ Sovereign, Edward VII, Gold	—	50.00
□ 1911–1915	½ Sovereign, George V, Gold	—	55.00
□ 1937	½ Sovereign, George VI, Gold	—	200.00 Proof
□ 1838–1874	1 Sovereign, Victoria, Young Portrait, Gold	—	125.00
□ 1871–1885	1 Sovereign, Victoria, Young Portrait, Gold	—	125.00
□ 1887–1892	1 Sovereign, Victoria, Golden Jubilee, Gold	—	125.00
□ 1893–1901	1 Sovereign, Victoria, Aged Portrait, Gold	—	125.00
□ 1902–1910	1 Sovereign, Edward VII, Gold	—	125.00
□ 1911–1925	1 Sovereign, George V, Gold	—	125.00
□ 1937	1 Sovereign, George VI, Gold	—	500.00 Proof
□ 1957–1968	1 Sovereign, Elizabeth II, 2nd Coinage, Gold	—	100.00

DATE	COIN TYPE/VARIETY/METAL	ABP FINE	AVERAGE FINE
☐ 1887	2 Pounds, Victoria, Golden Jubilee, Gold	—	$210.00
☐ 1893	2 Pounds, Victoria, Aged Portrait, Gold	—	210.00
☐ 1902	2 Pounds, Edward VII, Gold	—	210.00
☐ 1911	2 Pounds, George V, Gold	—	1000.00 Proof
☐ 1937	2 Pounds, George VI, Gold	—	800.00
☐ 1887	5 Pounds, Victoria, Golden Jubilee, Gold	—	650.00
☐ 1893	5 Pounds, Victoria, Aged Portrait, Gold	—	650.00
☐ 1902	5 Pounds, Edward VII, Gold	—	650.00
☐ 1911	5 Pounds, George V, Gold	—	2000.00 Proof
☐ 1937	5 Pounds, George VI, Gold	—	1000.00

United Kingdom—Decimal and Bullion Coinage

☐ 1971–1981	½ New Penny, Elizabeth II, Bronze	—	.25
☐ 1981–1984	½ Penny, Elizabeth II, Bronze	—	.25

☐ 1971–1981	1 New Penny, Elizabeth II, Bronze	—	.25
☐ 1981–1992	1 Penny, Elizabeth II, Bronze	—	.25

☐ 1993 to Date	1 Penny, Elizabeth II, Copper-plated Steel	—	.25

DATE	COIN TYPE/VARIETY/METAL	ABP FINE	AVERAGE FINE
□ 1971–1981	2 New Pence, Elizabeth II, Bronze	$ .75	$ 1.50
□ 1982–1984	2 Pence, Elizabeth II, Bronze	—	.05

DATE	COIN TYPE/VARIETY/METAL	ABP FINE	AVERAGE FINE
□ 1993 to Date	2 Pence, Elizabeth II, Copper-plated Steel	—	.05

DATE	COIN TYPE/VARIETY/METAL	ABP FINE	AVERAGE FINE
□ 1968–1981	5 New Pence, Elizabeth II, Cupro-Nickel	—	.10
□ 1990 to Date	5 Pence, Elizabeth II, Smaller Planchet, Cupro-Nickel	—	.25
□ 1982–1990	5 Pence, Elizabeth II, Cupro-Nickel	—	.10
□ 1990	5 Pence, Elizabeth II, Silver	—	.10

DATE	COIN TYPE/VARIETY/METAL	ABP FINE	AVERAGE FINE
☐ 1968–1981	10 New Pence, Elizabeth II, Cupro-Nickel	$1.00	$2.10
☐ 1982–1992	10 Pence, Elizabeth II, Cupro-Nickel	—	.15
☐ 1990–1993	10 Pence, Elizabeth II, Smaller Planchet, Cupro-Nickel	—	.10
☐ 1990	10 Pence, Elizabeth II, Smaller Planchet, Silver	—	.10
☐ 1992 to Date	10 Pence, Elizabeth II, Silver	—	.10

DATE	COIN TYPE/VARIETY/METAL	ABP FINE	AVERAGE FINE
☐ 1982 to Date	20 Pence, Elizabeth II, Cupro-Nickel	—	.25
☐ 1972	25 New Pence, Elizabeth II, Royal Silver Wedding Anniversary, Silver	—	20.00 Proof
☐ 1972	25 New Pence, Elizabeth II, Royal Silver Wedding Anniversary, Cupro-Nickel	.50	1.25
☐ 1977	25 New Pence, Elizabeth II, Silver Jubilee, Cupro-Nickel	1.00	.40

DATE	COIN TYPE/VARIETY/METAL	ABP FINE	AVERAGE FINE
☐ 1977	25 New Pence, Elizabeth II, Silver Jubilee, Silver	—	15.00 Proof
☐ 1980	25 New Pence, Elizabeth II, Queen Mother—80th Birthday, Cupro-Nickel	.20	.50
☐ 1980	25 New Pence, Elizabeth II, Queen Mother—80th Birthday, Silver	—	.30
☐ 1981	1 Crown, Elizabeth II, Wedding of Prince Charles & Lady Diana, Silver	—	.30
☐ 1981	1 Crown, Elizabeth II, Wedding of Prince Charles & Lady Diana, Cupro-Nickel	.50	1.00
☐ 1981	50 New Pence, Elizabeth II, Cupro-Nickel	.25	.75
☐ 1982 to Date	50 Pence, Elizabeth II, Cupro-Nickel	.25	.80

DATE	COIN TYPE/VARIETY/METAL	ABP FINE	AVERAGE FINE
☐ 1973	50 Pence, Elizabeth II, European Economic Community Entry, Cupro-Nickel	$ .20	$1.00
☐ 1992	50 Pence, Elizabeth II, European Council of Ministers—British Presidency, Cupro-Nickel	.40	1.50
☐ 1992	50 Pence, Elizabeth II, European Council of Ministers—British Presidency, Silver	—	30.00 Proof
☐ 1992	50 Pence, Elizabeth II, European Council of Ministers—British Presidency, Gold	—	500.00 Proof
☐ 1983	1 Pound, Elizabeth II, Silver	—	40.00 Proof

DATE	COIN TYPE/VARIETY/METAL	ABP FINE	AVERAGE FINE
☐ 1983	1 Pound, Elizabeth II, Nickel-Brass	.75	1.50
☐ 1984	1 Pound, Elizabeth II, Scottish Thistle, Silver	—	70.00
☐ 1984	1 Pound, Elizabeth II, Scottish Thistle, Nickel-Brass	.80	1.50
☐ 1985	1 Pound, Elizabeth II, Welsh Leek, Nickel-Brass	.80	1.50
☐ 1985	1 Pound, Elizabeth II, Welsh Leek, Silver	—	70.00
☐ 1985	1 Pound, Elizabeth II, Blooming Flax, Silver	—	60.00 Proof
☐ 1986	1 Pound, Elizabeth II, Blooming Flax, Nickel-Brass	.75	1.50
☐ 1987	1 Pound, Elizabeth II, Oak Tree, Nickel-Brass	.75	1.50
☐ 1987	1 Pound, Elizabeth II, Oak Tree, Silver	—	30.00
☐ 1988	1 Pound, Elizabeth II, Silver	—	30.00
☐ 1988	1 Pound, Elizabeth II, Copper-Zinc-Nickel	.80	1.50
☐ 1989	1 Pound, Elizabeth II, Scottish Flora, Silver	—	30.00
☐ 1989	1 Pound, Elizabeth II, Scottish Flora, Nickel-Brass	.80	1.50
☐ 1990	1 Pound, Elizabeth II, Welsh Leek, Nickel-Brass	.80	1.50

DATE	COIN TYPE/VARIETY/METAL	ABP FINE	AVERAGE FINE
□ 1990	1 Pound, Elizabeth II, Welsh Leek, Silver	—	$30.00
□ 1993	1 Pound, Elizabeth II, Scottish Flora, Nickel-Brass	$ .80	1.50
□ 1993	1 Pound, Elizabeth II, Scottish Flora, Silver	—	30.00 Proof
□ 1986	2 Pounds, Elizabeth II, Commonwealth Games, Silver	—	20.00 Proof
□ 1986	2 Pounds, Elizabeth II, Commonwealth Games, Gold	—	180.00 Proof
□ 1986	2 Pounds, Elizabeth II, Commonwealth Games, Nickel-Brass	1.50	2.50
□ 1989	2 Pounds, Elizabeth II, Bill of Rights Tercentenary, Nickel-Brass	1.00	2.50
□ 1989	2 Pounds, Elizabeth II, Bill of Rights Tercentenary, Silver	—	21.00
□ 1989	2 Pounds, Elizabeth II, Claim of Right Tercentenary, Silver	—	21.00
□ 1989	2 Pounds, Elizabeth II, Claim of Right Tercentenary, Nickel-Brass	1.00	2.50
□ 1990	5 Pounds, Elizabeth II, Queen Mother—90th Birthday, Silver	—	25.00
□ 1990	5 Pounds, Elizabeth II, Queen Mother—90th Birthday, Gold	—	500.00
□ 1990	5 Pounds, Elizabeth II, Queen Mother—90th Birthday, Cupro-Nickel	1.50	4.00
□ 1993	5 Pounds, Elizabeth II, Reign—40th Anniversary, Cupro-Nickel	2.00	4.00
□ 1987–1989	10 Pounds, Gold	—	50.00 Proof
□ 1990 to Date	10 Pounds, Gold-Silver	—	50.00 Proof
□ 1987–1989	25 Pounds, Gold	—	110.00 Proof
□ 1990 to Date	25 Pounds, Gold-Silver	—	225.00 Proof
□ 1987–1989	50 Pounds, Gold	—	210.00 Proof
□ 1990 to Date	50 Pounds, Gold-Silver	—	450.00 Proof
□ 1987–1989	100 Pounds, Gold	—	450.00 Proof
□ 1990 to Date	100 Pounds, Gold-Silver	—	850.00 Proof

USSR

USSR—Type Coinage

DATE	COIN TYPE/VARIETY/METAL	ABP FINE	AVERAGE FINE
□ 1921–1922	1 Ruble, 1st Coinage, Legend: PCOCP, Silver	—	$6.00
□ 1924–1925	1 Kopek, 2nd Coinage, Legend: CCCP, Bronze	$1.00	2.00

DATE	COIN TYPE/VARIETY/METAL	ABP FINE	AVERAGE FINE
□ 1924	1 Ruble, 2nd Coinage, Legend: CCCP, Silver	—	16.00
□ 1925–1928	1/2 Kopek, 2nd Coinage, Legend: CCCP, Bronze	2.75	4.00
□ 1926–1935	1 Kopek, 3rd Coinage, Legend: CCCP, Aluminum-Bronze	.28	.60
□ 1935–1936	1 Kopek, 4th Coinage, Legend: CCCP, Aluminum-Bronze	.28	.60
□ 1937–1946	1 Kopek, 5th Coinage, Legend: CCCP, Aluminum-Bronze	.18	.40
□ 1948–1956	1 Kopek, 6th Coinage, Legend: CCCP, Aluminum-Bronze	.28	.60
□ 1957	1 Kopek, 7th Coinage, Legend: CCCP, Aluminum-Bronze	.40	1.00

DATE	COIN TYPE/VARIETY/METAL	ABP FINE	AVERAGE FINE
☐ 1961 to Date	1 Kopek, 8th Coinage, Legend: CCCP, Brass	—	$ .10
☐ 1924–1925	2 Kopeks, 2nd Coinage, Legend: CCCP, Bronze	$2.75	4.00
☐ 1926–1935	2 Kopeks, 3rd Coinage, Legend: CCCP, Aluminum-Bronze	.18	.30
☐ 1935–1936	2 Kopeks, 4th Coinage, Legend: CCCP, Aluminum-Bronze	.28	.40
☐ 1937–1946	2 Kopeks, 5th Coinage, Legend: CCCP, Aluminum-Bronze	.18	.30
☐ 1948–1956	2 Kopeks, 6th Coinage, Legend: CCCP, Aluminum-Bronze	.28	.40
☐ 1957	2 Kopeks, 7th Coinage, Legend: CCCP, Aluminum-Bronze	.20	.50
☐ 1961 to Date	2 Kopeks, 8th Coinage, Legend: CCCP, Brass	—	.10
☐ 1924	3 Kopeks, 2nd Coinage, Legend: CCCP, Bronze	2.75	4.00
☐ 1926–1935	3 Kopeks, 3rd Coinage, Legend: CCCP, Aluminum-Bronze	.18	.30
☐ 1935–1936	3 Kopeks, 4th Coinage, Legend: CCCP, Aluminum-Bronze	.28	.40
☐ 1937–1946	3 Kopeks, 5th Coinage, Legend: CCCP, Aluminum-Bronze	.18	.30
☐ 1948–1956	3 Kopeks, 6th Coinage, Legend: CCCP, Aluminum-Bronze	.18	.30

DATE	COIN TYPE/VARIETY/METAL	ABP FINE	AVERAGE FINE
□ 1957	3 Kopeks, 7th Coinage, Legend: CCCP, Aluminum-Bronze	$ .28	$ .60

DATE	COIN TYPE/VARIETY/METAL	ABP FINE	AVERAGE FINE
□ 1961 to Date	3 Kopeks, 8th Coinage, Legend: CCCP, Brass	—	.10
□ 1924	5 Kopeks, 2nd Coinage, Legend: CCCP, Bronze	2.75	6.00
□ 1926–1935	5 Kopeks, 3rd Coinage, Legend: CCCP, Aluminum-Bronze	.28	.60
□ 1935–1936	5 Kopeks, 4th Coinage, Legend: CCCP, Aluminum-Bronze	1.40	3.00
□ 1937–1946	5 Kopeks, 5th Coinage, Legend: CCCP, Aluminum-Bronze	.18	.30
□ 1948–1956	5 Kopeks, 6th Coinage, Legend: CCCP, Aluminum-Bronze	.18	.30
□ 1957	5 Kopeks, 7th Coinage, Legend: CCCP, Aluminum-Bronze	.50	1.20

DATE	COIN TYPE/VARIETY/METAL	ABP FINE	AVERAGE FINE
□ 1961 to Date	5 Kopeks, 8th Coinage, Legend: CCCP, Aluminum-Bronze	—	.10
□ 1921–1923	10 Kopeks, 1st Coinage, Legend: PCOCP, Silver	—	1.50
□ 1923–1923	1 Chervonetz, 1st Coinage Legend: PCOCP, Gold	—	150.00
□ 1924–1931	10 Kopeks, 2nd Coinage, Legend: CCCP, Silver	—	.60
□ 1931–1934	10 Kopeks, 3rd Coinage, Legend: CCCP, Cupro-Nickel	.12	.30

DATE	COIN TYPE/VARIETY/METAL	ABP FINE	AVERAGE FINE
☐ 1935–1936	10 Kopeks, 4th Coinage, Legend: CCCP, Cupro-Nickel	$ .18	$ .40
☐ 1937–1946	10 Kopeks, 5th Coinage, Legend: CCCP, Cupro-Nickel	.12	.30
☐ 1948–1956	10 Kopeks, 6th Coinage, Legend: CCCP, Cupro-Nickel	.12	.30
☐ 1957	10 Kopeks, 7th Coinage, Legend: CCCP, Cupro-Nickel	.12	.30

DATE	COIN TYPE/VARIETY/METAL	ABP FINE	AVERAGE FINE
☐ 1961 to Date	10 Kopeks, 8th Coinage, Legend: CCCP, Cupro-Nickel-Zinc	—	.10
☐ 1975–1980	1 Chervonetz, 1st Coinage Legend: PCOCP, Gold	—	100.00
☐ 1921–1923	15 Kopeks, 1st Coinage, Legend: PCOCP, Silver	—	3.00
☐ 1924–1931	15 Kopeks, 2nd Coinage, Legend: CCCP, Silver	—	1.50
☐ 1931–1934	15 Kopeks, 3rd Coinage, Legend: CCCP, Cupro-Nickel	.28	.60
☐ 1935–1936	15 Kopeks, 4th Coinage, Legend: CCCP, Cupro-Nickel	.20	.50
☐ 1937–1946	15 Kopeks, 5th Coinage, Legend: CCCP, Cupro-Nickel	.18	.40
☐ 1948–1956	15 Kopeks, 6th Coinage, Legend: CCCP, Cupro-Nickel	.18	.40

DATE	COIN TYPE/VARIETY/METAL	ABP FINE	AVERAGE FINE
☐ 1957	15 Kopeks, 7th Coinage, Legend: CCCP, Cupro-Nickel	.18	.40

DATE	COIN TYPE/VARIETY/METAL	ABP FINE	AVERAGE FINE
□ 1921–1923	20 Kopeks, 1st Coinage, Legend: PCOCP, Silver	—	$3.00
□ 1924–1927	20 Kopek, 2nd Coinage, Legend: CCCP, Silver	—	1.50
□ 1924–1931	20 Kopeks, 2nd Coinage, Legend: CCCP, Silver	—	2.00
□ 1931–1934	20 Kopeks, 3rd Coinage, Legend: CCCP, Cupro-Nickel	$ .28	.60

DATE	COIN TYPE/VARIETY/METAL	ABP FINE	AVERAGE FINE
□ 1935–1936	20 Kopeks, 4th Coinage, Legend: CCCP, Cupro-Nickel	.28	.60
□ 1937–1946	20 Kopeks, 5th Coinage, Legend: CCCP, Cupro-Nickel	.20	.50
□ 1948–1956	20 Kopeks, 6th Coinage, Legend: CCCP, Cupro-Nickel	.20	.50
□ 1957	20 Kopeks, 7th Coinage, Legend: CCCP, Cupro-Nickel	.20	.50
□ 1961 to Date	20 Kopeks, 8th Coinage, Legend: CCCP, Cupro-Nickel-Zinc	—	.20
□ 1921–1922	50 Kopeks, 1st Coinage, Legend: PCOCP, Silver	—	6.00
□ 1961–1980	50 Kopeks, 8th Coinage, Legend: CCCP, Cupro-Nickel-Zinc	—	.25
□ 1961–1980	Rouble, 8th Coinage, Legend: CCCP, Cupro-Nickel-Zinc	.20	.50

VATICAN CITY

The Kingdom of Italy took over the last remaining part of the Papal States in 1870, and the Papacy ceased issuing coinage until 1929. The centesimi and 1 and 2 lire were base metal. The 5 and 10 lire were silver until 1947, when they were changed to aluminum. The gold 100 lire was changed to stainless steel in 1959. Decimal coins were first used in 1929. The currency today is the lira.

Vatican City—Trade Coinage

DATE	COIN TYPE/VARIETY/METAL	ABP FINE	AVERAGE FINE
☐ 1929–1938	5 Centesimi, Pius XI, Bronze	$ .90	$2.00
☐ 1933	5 Centesimi, Pius XI, Jubilee, Bronze	1.00	3.50
☐ 1939–1941	5 Centesimi, Pius XII, Bronze	.90	2.00
☐ 1942–1946	5 Centesimi, Pius XII, Aluminum-Bronze	6.00	10.00

DATE	COIN TYPE/VARIETY/METAL	ABP FINE	AVERAGE FINE
☐ 1929–1938	10 Centesimi, Pius XI, Bronze	.60	1.50
☐ 1933	10 Centesimi, Pius XI, Jubilee, Bronze	.60	1.50
☐ 1939–1941	10 Centesimi, Pius XII, Bronze	.75	1.75
☐ 1942–1946	10 Centesimi, Pius XII, Aluminum-Bronze	4.50	10.00

DATE	COIN TYPE/VARIETY/METAL	ABP FINE	AVERAGE FINE
□ 1929–1937	20 Centesimi, Pius XI, Nickel	$ .60	$1.50
□ 1933	20 Centesimi, Pius XI, Jubilee, Nickel	1.25	3.00
□ 1939	20 Centesimi, Pius XII, Nickel	.50	1.25
□ 1940–1941	20 Centesimi, Pius XII, Stainless Steel	.50	1.25
□ 1942–1946	20 Centesimi, Pius XII, Stainless Steel	4.50	10.00

DATE	COIN TYPE/VARIETY/METAL	ABP FINE	AVERAGE FINE
□ 1929–1937	50 Centesimi, Pius XI, Nickel	1.25	3.00
□ 1933	50 Centesimi, Pius XI, Jubilee, Nickel	.80	2.00
□ 1939	50 Centesimi, Pius XII, Nickel	.60	1.50
□ 1940–1941	50 Centesimi, Pius XII, Stainless Steel	.60	1.50
□ 1942–1946	50 Centesimi, Pius XII, Stainless Steel	6.00	10.00
□ 1929–1937	1 Lira, Pius XI, Nickel	.60	1.50
□ 1933	1 Lira, Pius XI, Jubilee, Nickel	1.25	3.00
□ 1939	1 Lira, Pius XII, Nickel	.80	2.00
□ 1940–1941	1 Lira, Pius XII, Stainless Steel	.60	1.50

DATE	COIN TYPE/VARIETY/METAL	ABP FINE	AVERAGE FINE
□ 1942–1946	1 Lira, Pius XII, Stainless Steel	6.00	10.00
□ 1947–1949	1 Lira, Pius XII, Aluminum	.50	1.25
□ 1950	1 Lira, Pius XII, Holy Year—MCML, Aluminum	.30	.60

DATE	COIN TYPE/VARIETY/METAL	ABP FINE	AVERAGE FINE
☐ 1951–1958	1 Lira, Pius XII, Aluminum	$ .40	$1.00
☐ 1959–1962	1 Lira, John XXIII, Aluminum	.40	1.00
☐ 1962	1 Lira, John XXIII, Ecumenical Council, Aluminum	—	.50
☐ 1929–1937	2 Lire, Pius XI, Nickel	.60	1.50
☐ 1933	2 Lire, Pius XI, Jubilee, Nickel	.60	1.50
☐ 1939	2 Lire, Pius XII, Nickel	.40	1.00

DATE	COIN TYPE/VARIETY/METAL	ABP FINE	AVERAGE FINE
☐ 1940–1941	2 Lire, Pius XII, Stainless Steel	—	.50
☐ 1942–1946	2 Lire, Pius XII, Stainless Steel	6.00	10.00
☐ 1947–1949	2 Lire, Pius XII, Aluminum	.40	1.00
☐ 1950	2 Lire, Pius XII, Holy Year—MCML, Aluminum	.30	.80
☐ 1951–1958	2 Lire, Pius XII, Aluminum	—	.15
☐ 1959–1962	2 Lire, John XXIII, Aluminum	.30	.80
☐ 1962	2 Lire, John XXIII, Ecumenical Council, Aluminum	.30	.80
☐ 1929–1937	5 Lire, Pius XI, Silver	—	3.00
☐ 1933	5 Lire, Pius XI, Jubilee, Silver	—	3.00
☐ 1939	5 Lire, Sede Vacante, Jubilee, Silver	—	4.00

DATE	COIN TYPE/VARIETY/METAL	ABP FINE	AVERAGE FINE
☐ 1939–1941	5 Lire, Pius XII, Silver	—	2.00
☐ 1942–1946	5 Lire, Pius XII, Silver	—	12.00
☐ 1947–1949	5 Lire, Pius XII, Aluminum	.40	1.00
☐ 1950	5 Lire, Pius XII, Holy Year—MCML, Aluminum	.40	1.00
☐ 1951–1958	5 Lire, Pius XII, Aluminum	—	.10
☐ 1959–1962	5 Lire, John XXIII, Aluminum	.40	1.00

DATE	COIN TYPE/VARIETY/METAL	ABP FINE	AVERAGE FINE
☐ 1962	5 Lire, John XXIII, Ecumenical Council, Aluminum	—	$ .25
☐ 1929–1937	10 Lire, Pius XI, Silver	—	5.00
☐ 1933	10 Lire, Pius XI, Jubilee, Silver	—	6.00
☐ 1939	10 Lire, Sede Vacante, Jubilee, Silver	—	4.00
☐ 1939–1941	10 Lire, Pius XII, Silver	—	7.00
☐ 1942–1946	10 Lire, Pius XII, Silver	—	25.00
☐ 1947–1949	10 Lire, Pius XII, Aluminum	$ .80	2.00
☐ 1950	10 Lire, Pius XII, Holy Year—MCML, Aluminum	.60	1.50

DATE	COIN TYPE/VARIETY/METAL	ABP FINE	AVERAGE FINE
☐ 1951–1958	10 Lire, Pius XII, Aluminum	.10	.40
☐ 1959–1962	10 Lire, John XXIII, Aluminum	.60	1.50
☐ 1962	10 Lire, John XXIII, Ecumenical Council, Aluminum	.25	.75
☐ 1957–1958	20 Lire, Pius XII, Aluminum-Bronze	.25	.50
☐ 1959–1962	20 Lire, John XXIII, Aluminum-Bronze	.25	.50
☐ 1962	20 Lire, John XXIII, Ecumenical Council, Aluminum-Bronze	.25	.60
☐ 1955–1958	50 Lire, Pius XII, Stainless Steel	.30	.80
☐ 1959–1962	50 Lire, John XXIII, Stainless Steel	.30	.80
☐ 1929–1937	100 Lire, Pius XI, Gold	—	100.00
☐ 1933	100 Lire, Pius XI, Jubilee, Gold	—	100.00
☐ 1939–1941	100 Lire, Pius XII, Gold	—	120.00

DATE	COIN TYPE/VARIETY/METAL	ABP FINE	AVERAGE FINE
☐ 1942–1949	100 Lire, Pius XII, Gold	—	150.00
☐ 1950	100 Lire, Pius XII, Holy Year—MCML, Gold	—	100.00

DATE	COIN TYPE/VARIETY/METAL	ABP FINE	AVERAGE FINE
☐ 1951–1958	100 Lire, Pius XII, Gold	—	$180.00
☐ 1955–1958	100 Lire, Pius XII, Stainless Steel	—	.30
☐ 1959–1962	100 Lire, John XXIII, Stainless Steel	$ .25	.60
☐ 1959	100 Lire, John XXIII, Gold	—	400.00
☐ 1962	100 Lire, John XXIII, Ecumenical Council, Stainless Steel	—	.35
☐ 1958	500 Lire, Sede Vacante, Silver	—	3.00

DATE	COIN TYPE/VARIETY/METAL	ABP FINE	AVERAGE FINE
☐ 1958	500 Lire, Pius XII, Silver	—	3.00
☐ 1959–1962	500 Lire, John XXIII, Silver	—	3.00
☐ 1962	500 Lire, John XXIII, Ecumenical Council, Silver	—	4.00
☐ 1963	500 Lire, Sede Vacante, Silver	—	3.00

VENEZUELA

The first coins were used in 1802 and were mostly Spanish coins. Between 1808 and 1813, coins were issued in Maracaibo. In 1817, the copper real was issued, followed by the centavo, bolivares, and copper-clad steel centimos. The first decimal coins were used in 1843. The currency today is the bolivar.

Venezuela—Type Coinage

DATE	COIN TYPE/VARIETY/METAL	ABP FINE	AVERAGE FINE
□ 1843–1852	1/4 Centavo, Liberty Head, Copper	$4.50	$10.00

DATE	COIN TYPE/VARIETY/METAL	ABP FINE	AVERAGE FINE
□ 1843–1852	1/2 Centavo, Liberty Head, Copper	1.75	4.00

DATE	COIN TYPE/VARIETY/METAL	ABP FINE	AVERAGE FINE
□ 1843–1863	1 Centavo, Liberty Head, Copper	1.40	3.00
□ 1858	1 Real, Liberty Head, Silver	—	65.00
□ 1858	2 Reales, Liberty Head, Silver	—	45.00

DATE	COIN TYPE/VARIETY/METAL	ABP FINE	AVERAGE FINE
□ 1858	5 Reales, Liberty Head, Silver	—	200.00

VIETNAM

The first coins were used in 970 and were cast, round, bronze coins with a square hole. Zinc coins were used in the 19th century, as were the silver ounce bar coin and the silver dollar. The first decimal coins were used circa 1830. The currency today is the dong.

Vietnam—Type Coinage

DATE	COIN TYPE/VARIETY/METAL	ABP FINE	AVERAGE FINE
☐ 1958	1 Xu, Aluminum	$ .40	$1.00
☐ 1958	2 Xu, Aluminum	.40	1.00
☐ 1958	5 Xu, Aluminum	.60	1.50
☐ 1953	10 Su, Aluminum	.12	.30
☐ 1945	20 Xu, Aluminum	.28	60.00
☐ 1953	20 Su, Aluminum	.18	.40
☐ 1946	5 Hao, Aluminum	15.00	35.00
☐ 1953	50 Su, Aluminum	.90	2.00
☐ 1960	50 Su, Aluminum	.12	.30
☐ 1963	50 Xu, Cupro-Nickel	—	.25

DATE	COIN TYPE/VARIETY/METAL	ABP FINE	AVERAGE FINE
☐ 1946	1 Dong, Aluminum	30.00	65.00
☐ 1960	1 Dong, Cupro-Nickel	—	.20
☐ 1946	2 Dong, Bronze	10.00	25.00